Henry Cockton

Sylvester Sound, the Somnambulist

Henry Cockton

Sylvester Sound, the Somnambulist

ISBN/EAN: 9783743323544

Manufactured in Europe, USA, Canada, Australia, Japa

Cover: Foto ©ninafisch / pixelio.de

Manufactured and distributed by brebook publishing software (www.brebook.com)

Henry Cockton

Sylvester Sound, the Somnambulist

PREFACE.

SOMNAMBULISM has been in all ages known. Aristotle says, "There are individuals who rise in their sleep and walk about, seeing as clearly as those that are awake." Diogenes Laertius states that Theon, the philosopher, was a somnambulist. Galen slept whilst on a road, and pursued his journey, until he was awakened by tripping on a stone. Felix Pater fell asleep while playing on the lute, and was startled only by the fall of the instrument;* while the present age teems with instances of the most astounding character.

Dr. Dyce, of Aberdeen, describes the case of "a girl, in which this affection began with fits of somnolency, which came upon her suddenly during the day, and from which she could at first be roused by shaking or by being taken into the open air. During these attacks she was in the habit of talking of things that seemed to pass before her like a dream, and was not at the time sensible of anything that was said to her. On one occasion she repeated the entire of the baptismal service of the Church of England, and concluded with an extemporary prayer. In her subsequent paroxysms she began to understand what was said to her, and to answer with a considerable degree of consistency, though these replies were in a certain measure influenced by her hallucination. She also became capable of following her usual employment during the paroxysm. At one time she would lay out the table for breakfast, and repeatedly dressed herself and the children, her eyes remaining shut the whole time. The remarkable circumstance was now discovered that,

* Curiosities of Medical Experience.

during the paroxysm, she had a distinct recollection of what had taken place in former attacks, though she had not the slightest recollection of it during the intervals. She was taken to church during the paroxysm, and attended the service with apparent devotion, and at one time was so affected by the sermon that she actually shed tears; yet in the interval she had no recollection whatever of the circumstance, but in the following paroxysm she gave a most distinct account of it, and actually repeated the passage of the sermon that had so much affected her. This sort of somnambulism, relating distinctly to two periods, has been called, perhaps erroneously, a *state of double consciousness.*"

"A girl aged seven years," says Dr. Abercrombie, "an orphan of the lowest rank, residing in the house of a farmer, by whom she was employed in tending cattle, was accustomed to sleep in an apartment separated by a very thin partition from one which was frequently occupied by an itinerant fiddler. This person was a musician of very considerable skill, and often spent a part of the night in performing pieces of a refined description; but his performance was not taken notice of by the child, except as a disagreeable noise. After a residence of six months in this family she fell into bad health, and was removed to the house of a benevolent lady, where, on her recovery after a protracted illness, she was employed as a servant. Some years after she came to reside with this lady, the most beautiful music was often heard in the house during the night, which excited no small interest and wonder in the family; and many a waking hour was spent in endeavours to discover the invisible minstrel. At length the sound was traced to the sleeping-room of the girl, who was found fast asleep, but uttering from her lips a sound exactly resembling the sweetest tones of a small violin. On further observation it was found that, after being about two hours in bed, she became restless, and began to mutter to herself; she then uttered sounds precisely resembling the tuning of a violin, and at length, after some prelude, dashed off into an elaborate piece of music, which she performed in a clear and accurate manner, and with a sound exactly resembling the most delicate modulation of the instrument, and then began exactly where she had stopped in the most correct manner. These paroxysms occurred at regular intervals, varying from one to fourteen and even twenty nights; and they were generally followed by a degree of fever and pain over various parts of the body.

"After a year or two, her music was not confined to the imitation of the violin, but was often exchanged for that of a piano, of a very old description, which she was accustomed to hear in the house in which she now lived, and then she would begin to sing, imitating exactly the voices of several ladies of the family.

"In another year from this time she began to talk a great deal in her sleep, in which she fancied herself instructing a young companion. She often descanted with the utmost fluency and correctness on a variety of subjects, both political and religious, the men of the day, the historical parts of Scripture, public characters, and particularly of the character of the members of the family and their visitors. In these discussions she showed the most wonderful discrimination, often combined with sarcasm, and astonishing powers of mimicry. Her language through the whole was fluent and correct, and her illustrations often forcible and even eloquent. She was fond of illustrating her subjects by what she called *a fable*, and in these her imagery was both appropriate and correct. The justice and truth of her remarks on all subjects excited the utmost astonishment in those who were acquainted with her limited means of acquiring information.

"She had been known to conjugate correctly Latin verbs, which she had probably heard in the school-room of the family, and she was once heard to speak several sentences very correctly in French, at the same time stating that she had heard them from a foreign gentleman whom she had met accidentally in a shop. Being questioned on this subject when awake, she remembered having seen the gentleman, but could not repeat a word of what he had said.

"During her paroxysms it was almost impossible to awake her, and when her eyelids were raised, and a candle brought near the eye, the pupil seemed insensible to the light. For several years she was, during the paroxysm, entirely unconscious of the presence of other persons; but about the age of sixteen she began to observe those who were in the apartment, and she could tell correctly their number, though the utmost care was taken to have the room darkened. She now also became capable of answering questions that were put to her, and of noticing remarks made in her presence, and, with regard to both, she showed astonishing acuteness. Her observations indeed were often of such a nature, and corresponded so accurately with character and events, that, by the country people, she was believed to be endowed with supernatural power.

"During the whole period of this remarkable affection, which seems to have gone on for at least ten or eleven years, she was, when awake, a dull, awkward girl, very slow in receiving any kind of instruction, though much care was bestowed upon her; and in point of intellect she was much inferior to the other servants of the family. In particular, she showed no kind of turn for music. She did not appear to have any recollection of what passed in her sleep; but during her nocturnal ramblings, she was more than once heard to lament her infirmity of speaking in her sleep, adding how fortunate it was she did not sleep among the other servants, as they teased her enough about it as it was."

Dr. Macnish, in "The Philosophy of Sleep," has moreover given us the following cases:—"A female servant, in the town of Chelmsford, surprised the family, at four o'clock one morning, by walking down a flight of stairs in her sleep and rapping at the bedroom door of her master, who inquired what she wanted; when, in her usual tone of voice, she requested some cotton, saying that she had torn her gown, but hoped that her mistress would forgive her; at the same time bursting into tears. Her fellow-servant, with whom she had been conversing some time, observed her get out of bed, and quickly followed her, but not before she had related the pitiful story. She then returned to her room, and a light having been procured, she was found groping to find her cotton-box. Another person went to her, when, perceiving a difference in the voice, she called out, 'That is a different voice; that is my mistress,' which was not the case—thus clearly showing that she *did not see* the object before her, although her eyes were *wide open*. Upon inquiry as to what was the matter, she only said that she wanted some cotton, but that her fellow-servant had been to her master and mistress, making a fuss about it. It was now thought prudent that she should be allowed to remain quiet for some short time, and she was persuaded to lie down with her fellow-servant until the usual hour of rising, thinking that she might then awake in her accustomed manner. This failing in effect, her mistress went up to her room, and rather angrily desired her to get up, and go to her work, as it was now six o'clock: this she refused, telling her mistress that if she did not please her, she might look out for another servant, at the same time saying that she would not rise up at two o'clock (pointing to the window) to injure her health for any one. For the sake of a joke, she was told to pack up her things, and start off immediately, but to this she made no reply. She rebuked her fellow-servant for not remaining longer in bed, and shortly after this she became quiet. She was afterwards shaken violently, and awoke. She then rose, and seeing the cotton-box disturbed, demanded to know why it had been meddled with, not knowing that she alone was the cause of it. In the course of the day, several questions were put to her in order to try her recollection, but the real fact, of her walking, was not made known to her; and she is still quite unconscious of what has transpired.

"The next case is of a different description, and exhibits a dormant state of the sense of hearing, while sight appears throughout to have been in active operation.

"A young man named Johns, who works at Cardrew, near Redruth, being asleep in the sump-house of that mine, was observed by two boys to rise and walk to the door, against which he leaned; shortly after quitting that position, he walked to the engine-shaft, and safely descended to the depth of twenty fathoms, where he was found by his comrades soon after, with his back resting on the ladder. They called to him to apprise him of the perilous situation in which he was, but he did not hear them, and they were obliged to shake him roughly till he awoke, when he appeared totally at a loss to account for his being so situated.

"The stories related of sleep-walkers are, indeed, of so extraordinary a kind, that they would almost seem fictitious, were they not supported by the most incontrovertible evidence. To walk on the house-top, to scale precipices, and descend to the bottom of frightful ravines, are common exploits with the somnambulist; and he performs them with a facility far beyond the power of any man who is completely awake.

"Somnambulism, as well as lunacy, sometimes bestows supernatural strength upon the individual. Mr. Dubrie, a musician in Bath, affords an instance of this kind. One Sunday, while awake, he attempted in vain to force open the window of his bedroom, which chanced to be nailed down; but having got up in his sleep, he repeated the attempt successfully, and threw himself out, by which he unfortunately broke his leg.

"Sleep-walking is sometimes periodical. Martinet describes the case of a watchmaker's apprentice who had an attack of it every fortnight. In this state, though insensible to all external impressions, he would perform his work with his usual accuracy, and was always astonished, on awaking, at the progress he had made. The paroxysm began with a sense of heat in the epigastrium extending to the head, followed by confusion of ideas and complete insensibility, the eyes remaining open with a fixed and vacant stare. This case, which undoubtedly originated in some diseased state of the brain, terminated in epilepsy. Dr. Gall relates that he saw at Berlin a young man, sixteen years of age, who had, from time to time, very extraordinary fits. He moved about unconsciously in bed, and had no perception of anything that was done to him; at last he would jump out of bed, and walk with rapid steps about the room, his eyes being fixed and open. Several obstacles which were placed by Dr. Gall in his way, he either removed or cautiously avoided. He then threw himself suddenly again upon the bed, moved about for some time, and finished by jumping up awake, not a little surprised at the number of curious people about him.

"The facility with which somnambulists are awakened from the paroxysms differs extremely in different cases. One man is aroused by being gently touched or called upon, by a flash of light, by stumbling in his peregrinations, or by setting his foot in water. Another remains so heavily asleep that it is necessary to shout loudly, to shake him with violence, and make use of other excitations equally powerful. In this condition, when the sense of vision chances to be dormant, it is curious to look at his eyes. Sometimes they are shut; at other times wide open; and when the latter is the case, they are observed to be fixed and inexpressive, 'without speculation' or energy, while the pupil is contracted, as in the case of perfect sleep.

"It is not always safe to arouse a sleep-walker; and many

cases of the fatal effects thence arising have been detailed by authors. Nor is it at all unlikely that a person, even of strong nerves, might be violently agitated by awaking in a situation so different from that in which he lay down. Among other examples, that of a young lady, who was addicted to this affection, may be mentioned. Knowing her failing, her friends made a point of locking the door, and securing the window of her chamber in such a manner that she could not possibly get out. One night, these precautions were unfortunately overlooked, and, in a paroxysm of somnambulism, she walked into the garden behind the house. While there, she was recognised by some of the family, who were warned by the noise she made on opening the door, and they followed and awoke her; but such was the effect produced upon her nervous system, that she almost instantly expired."

Having adduced these cases, in order to justify the introduction of the scenes described in the following—not too profoundly written pages—I have only to beg of those who read the work as a whole, to bear in mind that it originally appeared in monthly parts.

H. C.

CONTENTS.

CHAPTER		PAGE
I.	THE INTRODUCTION	15
II.	INTRODUCES AUNT ELEANOR, THE PASTOR, AND HIS PEACHES	16
III.	IN WHICH THE FIRST ALARM IS CREATED	28
IV.	THE CHURCHYARD	39
V.	THE MYSTERY	53
VI.	THE GHOST HUNT	57
VII.	THE PICKLED SMALLS	65
VIII.	ROSALIE	77
IX.	THE GUARDIANS OF THE NIGHT	88
X.	THE GUARDIANS DISCOVERED	99
XI.	THE "SPIRIT" APPEARS TO THE PASTOR AND JONES	107
XII.	THE FEARFUL CONJECTURE	123
XIII.	THE EGGS AND EXOTICS	131
XIV.	THE DEPARTURE FROM THE VILLAGE	140
XV.	SYLVESTER'S FIRST NIGHT IN LONDON	160
XVI.	TOM AND HIS WOBAD	173
XVII.	JULIA	182
XVIII.	THE MAN-TRAP	198
XIX.	THE DELICATE DISCLOSURE	215
XX.	THE BELLS	224
XXI.	THE PROPOSAL	236
XXII.	TOM APPEARS TO GIVE EVIDENCE IN A CASE	244
XXIII.	THE LOVERS' RETURN	267
XXIV.	LOVE	283
XXV.	THE MAIDEN SPEECH IN PARLIAMENT	296

CHAPTER		PAGE
XXVI.	THE ACCUSATION	303
XXVII.	THE MEETING	309
XXVIII.	PIER-GLASS PRACTICE	326
XXIX.	SYLVESTER REVISITS COTHERSTONE GRANGE	338
XXX.	THE SUSPICION	353
XXXI.	THE VILLAGE FAIR	373
XXXII.	SYLVESTER IS RECALLED TO TOWN	397
XXXIII.	THE PROOF	404
XXXIV.	THE LAST REQUEST	417
XXXV.	THE TRIAL	424
XXXVI.	SYLVESTER'S NEW PROTECTOR	442
XXXVII.	THE MYSTERY SOLVED	468
XXXVIII.	THE RECONCILIATION	488
XXXIX.	THE CONCLUSION	500

SYLVESTER SOUND

THE SOMNAMBULIST.

CHAPTER I.

THE INTRODUCTION.

AMONG the ancient historians a practice prevailed which may be described thus: Whenever they wrote the lives of men, they explained, *in limine,* who those men were. This is in all their works manifest. They may have been right: they may have been wrong: it is not proposed to dive to any very great depth with the view of discovering the absolute necessity for the pursuit of this course; it is sufficient for the world to know that they held such explanation to be essential to the perfect knowledge of the very men whose characters they portrayed, and as the practice is extremely convenient, it may not, even in this age, be deemed incorrect—however admirable originality may in itself be—to follow their example by explaining at once who Sylvester Sound the Somnambulist was.

Assuming then the correctness of the course prescribed to be admitted, it now becomes proper to state that Sylvester Sound was the only son of Horatio Sound, M.D.; that the doctor's lady departed this life very soon after Sylvester's birth; that the doctor himself survived her several years; that a circumstance—of which the particulars will be dealt upon anon—not only caused the loss of his practice, but eventually broke his heart; and that, up to the period of his death, Sylvester—for a reason which the doctor himself never explained—was educated by him and lived constantly with him.

CHAPTER II.

INTRODUCES AUNT ELEANOR, THE PASTOR, AND HIS PEACHES.

Having—it is to be hoped satisfactorily—explained who Sylvester was, it will now be quite right to proceed.

And it will, in the first place, be necessary to state that Sylvester, at the period of the death of Dr. Sound, was in the seventeenth year of his age.

He was tall and slightly made, and while his features were finely formed, his jet black hair, which hung in ringlets over his shoulders, contrasted strongly with his countenance, which was pale in the extreme, and of which the expression was that of repose. There was, indeed, the spirit of mischief lurking in his eye, but while he was awake that spirit was asleep: it developed itself only in his dreams. It was then that it prompted him to perpetrate all sorts of wild and extraordinary tricks: it was then that it converted him from a calm, graceful, amiable youth, into a perfect little devil.

This, to a certain extent, was known to the doctor: hence it was that he was kept so constantly at home; but it was not known to any other creature in existence: it was not known even to Sylvester himself; he was perfectly unconscious of being a somnambulist: he had not even the most remote suspicion of the fact; nor had he, when awake, the slightest recollection of the dreams upon which he had acted. During sleep, indeed, his recollection of their nature was most perfect—he would, for example, frequently commence a letter one night and finish it the next—but when awake, his memory, as far as those dreams were concerned, was in oblivion.

Anxiously had the doctor watched him night after night. He had even allowed him to go from his chamber; but although he closely followed, he never checked him. He felt perfectly sure that the means which he had adopted in his own case—he having been himself a somnambulist—would eventually cure his son; and certainly, in the case of Sylvester, a cure might by those means have been effected, but just as a change became perceptible, the doctor unhappily died.

During the week which elapsed between the death of Dr.

Sound and his funeral, Sylvester remained in the house; but the day following that on which the ceremony was performed, his Aunt Eleanor—a maiden lady of exemplary character—took him to her cottage at Cotherstone Grange—about fifteen miles from the residence of her late brother—conceiving that an immediate change of scene might be highly beneficial to his health, as he was then more than usually languid.

On their way to the Grange, Sylvester was silent, and as of course Aunt Eleanor ascribed this silence to the grief which sprang from the loss they had sustained, she felt it to be her duty as a Christian to offer him all the consolation at her command. And she did so; but without much apparent effect. She, moreover, with the view of diverting his thoughts, pointed out, as they proceeded, every object which she held to be in the slightest degree remarkable; but nothing could cheer him—nothing could rouse him from the reverie in which he indulged, until they approached the parsonage-house, which stood within three hundred yards of the cottage. Of this place Sylvester took especial notice; and it was an exceedingly beautiful little place, in the centre of a most delightful garden, and surrounded by a wall, which appeared to be studded with nectarines and peaches. He even—albeit languidly—expressed his admiration of the fine appearance of this delicious fruit; but it was soon lost to view, and he was silent again.

Now, much has been written and said of old maids. They have been spoken of in terms of the deepest contempt; painters have represented them with crabbed aspects, scraggy necks, yellow complexions, busts particularly bony, and fingers long, fleshless, and cold; while writers have described them as being skinny, toothless, arrogant, malicious, and wretched; but if the libellous painters and writers in question mean to contend that these are the prevailing characteristics of old maids in the aggregate, it will be at once perfectly clear that they never have studied the real flesh and blood. Theirs are merely conventional old maids! Henceforth let these libellers paint and write from Nature! *Let* them do justice to those who compose that honourable—albeit peculiar—species of humanity, who have studied the respective characters of their suitors too deeply to be ensnared —who have met with none but those whose views were selfish, and whose affections were impure—who have not allowed their judgment to be blinded by passion — who have imagined man's love to be ethereal, but have not found it so—who have never had the wish to make, in a worldly sense, a *good* match, and who have had sufficient sense to escape the miseries of a bad one! It is, of course, admitted that a *few* of these honourable old maids—for even their contemptuous sobriquet is associated with honour!—may be bony and not very mild; but the idea of making unamiable skeletons of them *all* is monstrous! sufficiently monstrous to inspire indignation. Aunt Eleanor was an old maid, and she was no skeleton; nor was she malicious, nor toothless, nor wretched. On the contrary, her figure approached *embonpoint ;* her teeth were white and sound, and her skin was soft and clear: she had, perhaps, a finer—a more animated—bust than any other lady in the country! She was, moreover, just, benevolent, amiable, and pure, while her heart was full of tranquil joy; for she was in spirit wedded to her God.

Nor was there in this lovely cottage of hers the slightest thing indicative of the residence of an old maid. Everything indeed was neat and elegant; everything was arranged with the most exquisite taste; but there was no minute primness perceptible: nor must it be imagined for a moment that if the whole of her highly-prized china and glass had been swept from the sideboard and broken to atoms, she would have shed a single tear. No: nothing but love and sympathy could wring a tear from *her*.

For twenty years she had lived in that cottage, and although her pecuniary means were comparatively large, her establishment was small, inasmuch as it consisted only of a cook, a housemaid, and a gardener, who officiated also as groom. By her uniform kindness she had completely won the hearts of these domestics; they were strongly, deeply attached to her; and hence, when they flew to the gate as the chaise drew up, they welcomed her home indeed.

Knowing the time exactly at which her mistress would return, the cook had prepared a delicious dinner, which, as soon as Aunt Eleanor had changed her dress, was served up with characteristic elegance.

And Sylvester, albeit calm and silent, did justice to the viands prepared; and Aunt Eleanor, in order to cheer him, insisted upon his taking two glasses of wine! but finding after dinner that he still felt languid, she, conceiving that the excitement of the preceding day, and the journey that morning, had exhausted his spirits, prevailed upon him to retire to his chamber, and enjoined the servants not to disturb him.

To his chamber accordingly Sylvester repaired, and having partially undressed himself, reposed on the bed and went to sleep. He had not, however, slept ten minutes, when he began to dream of the nectarines and peaches he had seen on the wall of the parsonage garden, and being inspired to action by the dinner he had eaten, and the wine—the two glasses of wine—he had drank, he re-dressed himself, and left the cottage unperceived.

As he quietly walked towards the garden of the parsonage, none could have supposed that he was then fast asleep! His eyes were open, and he looked—not vacantly, nor with an intense stare, but precisely as if he had been awake—at every object he passed. And thus he reached the garden wall, which he mounted with alacrity and ease, and having cleared from a very convenient spot the broken bottles, which the reverend gentleman had most humanely caused to be stuck upon the wall—in reality with the view of phlebotomising trespassers, but nominally in order to keep off the cats—he sat down and freely partook of the peaches, which really were very fine indeed. And he enjoyed them much, and ate no inconsiderable quantity of them, for they were in his judgment delicious. But just as he had eaten to satiety, the reverend gentleman, to whom the fruit legally belonged, espied him, and, having recovered from the shock which this proceeding—which he held to be one of the most barefaced audacity—induced, rushed into the garden with all the velocity his shortness of breath, and portliness of person would permit, exclaiming, "Jones! Jones!" in tones of indignation—for he really was very indignant at the time—and in an instant Jones, the gardener, appeared.

"Jones," he continued, pointing fiercely to Sylvester, "*that's* how the peaches go. That's the way."

Jones looked at Sylvester utterly astounded. Was it—could it be—possible? And that, too, before his very eyes. He was about to spring upon him with all the ferocity of a tiger; but Sylvester, having eaten all the peaches he *could* eat, at that moment dropped from the wall, and disappeared.

"He's off!" cried the pastor. "Follow him, Jones! but don't say a word: he is clearly respectable. See where he goes, Jones, and then let me know."

Jones rushed to the gate and followed Sylvester's footsteps; and when he saw him actually enter the cottage, he returned to the pastor and made the fact known.

But then—what was to be done? Aunt Eleanor was a lady for whom the reverend gentleman entertained the highest respect! The question with him therefore was, whether he ought to wound her feelings by complaining of that which had occurred, or to take no further notice of the matter. He was soon, however, prompted to answer this question by the thought of his peaches. He could not in silence endure the loss of them. They were the finest in the county!—nay, in his judgment, Europe could not produce peaches at all comparable with them. He therefore resolved to proceed to the cottage, and to the cottage he did proceed, followed by the gentle Jones, who absolutely swelled with indignation.

As they passed through the gate, Aunt Eleanor, who saw them, and who held the reverend gentleman in very high esteem, rang the bell for the servant to open the door, and then received him with all her characteristic cordiality and grace, while the highly indignant Jones remained swelling at the door.

"My dear madam," said the pastor, as soon as he had recovered the power to speak, for the occurrence had induced a dreadful state of excitement, which his sharp walk to the cottage had by no means subdued—"My dear madam, I regret—I exceedingly regret—that I should have to call on business of a nature so unpleasant; but you have, I believe, a young gentleman here?"

"My nephew!" replied Aunt Eleanor. "I brought him with me this morning, and a sweet little fellow he is!"

"I am sorry," returned the reverend gentleman, "I am indeed very sorry to be compelled to say that he is unhappily addicted to practices which I will not exactly designate audacious"——

"Sir!"

"But which are, in my judgment, highly improper."

"You amaze me!" exclaimed Aunt Eleanor; and really the amazement she expressed was very striking. "My nephew addicted to practices which you deem highly improper! Why, he is one of the mildest and most inoffensive little fellows that ever breathed! He would not hurt a worm!"

"It may be true that he would not hurt a worm; but I know him to be very fond of peaches."

"That is very possible; and I submit very natural. But may I be permitted to know what you mean?"

"Why, it is, my dear madam, with the greatest reluctance that I make a complaint of this nature to you: but I think that it may be highly beneficial to him, for we know that if our vices in youth be unchecked they grow with our growth and strengthen with our strength."

"Dear me!" cried Aunt Eleanor; "why, what on earth can have occurred?"

"Sitting in my study, ten minutes ago, I perceived through the window a youth upon the wall, freely helping himself to my peaches. Well, as I, of course, disapproved of this proceeding—for, had he asked me for the peaches he should have had them with pleasure—I went out, and calling Jones, my gardener, desired him to expostulate with the youth; but the moment he appeared the youth dropped from the wall, and Jones, who followed him, informs me that he saw him enter here."

"Impossible!" exclaimed Aunt Eleanor. "My nephew is the only youth I have about the premises!"

"What is the age of your nephew, may I ask?"

"About seventeen."

"Has he black hair, flowing freely over his shoulders?"

"He has."

"I am sorry then to say, my dear madam, that he is the youth who purloined my peaches."

"But really!—my dear *sir!*—oh! it cannot *be!* The dear boy has been in bed and asleep for the last hour."

"Is he asleep now?" inquired the reverend gentleman.

Aunt Eleanor rang the bell, and when the servant appeared, she desired her to go into Sylvester's room, and to ascertain whether he really was asleep or not.

"This is strange," said Aunt Eleanor; "very strange indeed!" And the pastor echoed this observation, by saying that it *was* strange, very strange, indeed.

"Well, Mary?" said Aunt Eleanor, when the servant reappeared.

"Master Sylvester sleeps like a top, ma'am," promptly replied Mary.

"I thought so!" observed Aunt Eleanor. "I knew that he would. The poor dear boy was exhausted."

"Well, this is very extraordinary!" said the reverend gentleman, who couldn't tell at all what to make of it. "Really, I should very much indeed like to see him."

"For your satisfaction, he shall be at once awakened."

"Oh, dear me, no! There is not the least necessity for that."

"Then will you do me the favour to walk up and see him?"

"Why, if you particularly wish me to do so," replied the reverend gentleman, "I will." And he rose from his seat, and Aunt Eleanor rose, too; and Mary, who couldn't conceive what it meant, led the way up to Sylvester's room.

"Poor boy!" said Aunt Eleanor. "There he is, and there he has been for the last hour."

That he was there then, appeared to the reverend gentleman to be abundantly clear; but that there he had been for the last hour, was, in his calm judgment, apocryphal—very. He could *not* believe it. Why—it was the very face—the very hair! It was moreover plain, that he was then sleeping soundly: the pastor had no doubt at all about that; but, as he wished very much indeed to see him awake, he dropped his stick—very accidentally, of course—and thus produced a noise which had the effect desired.

"My dearest boy!" said Aunt Eleanor. "Oh, I am sorry that we have disturbed you."

Sylvester sat up in bed and rubbed his eyes, and then looked at the reverend gentleman, precisely as if he wished to know who he was and what he wanted.

"Lie down, dear, again," said Aunt Eleanor soothingly. "You must be fatigued, dear: you look very weary still."

The reverend gentleman shook his head, and that, too, with so much significance, that any close observer might at once have perceived that Sylvester was, in his view, very artful. Aunt Eleanor, however, did not observe this; she felt that the "mistake" had been sufficiently seen, and therefore left the chamber, followed by her reverend friend.

"Well!" said that gentleman, on his return to the parlour, "really! Upon my word he bears a very striking resemblance to the youth whom I saw upon my garden wall."

"Indeed! Well, that is strange," returned Aunt Eleanor; "I know of no youth at all like him."

"There must be one in the vicinity whom he very *much* resembles."

"How very extraordinary! Why, whom *can* it be?"

"Indeed, I know not," returned the reverend gentleman; "there appears to be some little mystery about it, which probably time will solve. I have only to say that I am sorry the affair happened, and beg to apologise for the trouble I have given."

At this moment Sylvester entered the room in the same dress as that in which he appeared upon the wall, and no sooner had he entered, than the pastor—who now, of course, felt quite convinced of his being the delinquent—said, "Well, young gentleman, did you *enjoy* those peaches?"

Sylvester looked at him earnestly for a moment, and then observed calmly, "What peaches do you allude to? I do not *know* that I have tasted a peach this season!"

The reverend gentleman hereupon regarded him with an expression of horror. He felt it to be awful in the extreme, and shuddered at the thought that a falsehood so flagrant should proceed from the lips of a sinner so young. Recovering himself, however, from the shock thus produced, he, with an aspect of severity, said, "Pray, sir, have you ever heard or read of Ananias?"

"I have, sir. But why put that question to me?"

"Because you have said distinctly that you have not, to your knowledge, tasted a peach this season; whereas, within the last half-hour, I saw you upon my garden wall eating *my* peaches to absolute satiety."

"Let me assure you, sir," returned Sylvester firmly, "that you are mistaken. I feel that I am utterly incapable of such bad conduct."

The calmness, the firmness, the apparent truthfulness with which this assurance was given had a manifest tendency to shake the reverend gentleman's conviction. And yet—*was* it possible that he could be mistaken? There stood the very youth; or, if he were not the very youth, how strong was the resemblance! He had preached the fallibility of the flesh; he felt that he himself was not, in a general sense, infallible: but then, in this *particular*,—and yet the very presence, the very look, the very tones of the youth who stood before him, were indicative of innocence. He had never before felt so perfectly puzzled; still he did say, eventually, "*Well*, my dear madam, I suppose that I *must* be mistaken—but really!—perhaps, however, you will allow me to call in my gardener?"

"Oh, my dear sir," said Aunt Eleanor, "do so at once, by all means." And Jones was accordingly summoned.

"Do you know this young gentleman, Jones?" said the pastor.

"Know him, sir!" replied Jones, utterly astonished at the question being asked; "I should know him from a million."

"But are you *sure*, Jones, that this is the identical youth whom we saw on the wall just now?"

"Sure!" echoed Jones, who really felt the idea of his *not* being sure to be perfectly ridiculous, "of course, sir, I am sure."

"Man!" said Aunt Eleanor, "adhere to the truth."

"Oh! that's true enough, ma'am. I'd swear it."

"Swear it!"

"I know him by the cut of his clothes."

"Although, Jones, that is strong collateral evidence," observed the reverend gentleman, profoundly, "I do not hold it to be conclusive. There may be other garments of the same description. *I* look at the countenance. Man may copy the works of man, but Nature never copies herself. Among the myriads of human beings in existence there are not even two individuals to be found with features precisely alike, albeit there may be, as in this case, a striking resemblance. Nor is this amazing peculiarity confined exclusively to the human species. The flocks that range the verdant fields, the beasts which prowl in the frightful jungle, the fish that inhabit the boundless sea, and the birds which float in the balmy air, nay, even the very vermin which tunnel the earth, have all the same wonderful individuality. Still, as one sheep may be mistaken for another by those who know not the peculiar expression of that sheep, so may one youth be mistaken for another, as we have, in this case, perhaps sufficiently proved."

All that Jones understood of this he appreciated, but half of that which reached his understanding was not much. He had no notion at all, however, of giving the thing up in this way, and therefore he said, with much point, "But does the young genelman himself mean to say it ain't him?"

"I mean to say," returned Sylvester calmly, "that I have been fast asleep for the last hour."

"Well, send I may live!" exclaimed Jones.

"Hush, hush!" cried the reverend gentleman.

"Well, but in all creepings *up!*" resumed Jones. "Here, take me afore a justice. I'll oath it it's him afore any judge or jury in nature. But," he added, turning to Sylvester, "do you mean to look me in the face, and tell *me* that it *warnt* you as was upon our wall a pegging away at them peaches there?—only say?"

"I hope, my dear aunt," observed Sylvester, with unaffected mildness, "that you do not believe I could have been guilty of such an act?"

"No, my dear—certainly not."

"Sir," added Sylvester, addressing the reverend gentleman, "I should be utterly ashamed of myself even if I felt that I could."

The pastor, notwithstanding the resemblance was still in his judgment amazing, was now inspired by Sylvester's tranquil bearing, with the conviction that he must be mistaken, and tried to inoculate Jones with the same conviction; but Jones would not have it. He knew what he knew!—he knew that the youth who stood before him, and the youth who was on the wall, were one and the same youth; and said so; and stuck to it firmly—indeed so firmly, that the reverend gentleman at length desired him to leave the room.

Now it happened that Judkins, Aunt Eleanor's gardener—who, conceiving that Jones had come there with a view to supplant him, had kept an exceedingly sharp look-out—was at hand; and it also happened that Judkins had a great contempt for Jones, seeing that Jones, at the last horticultural meeting of the county, had gained the first prize for carrots; while Jones had as great a contempt for Judkins, seeing that Judkins had gained the first prize for onions, whereas Jones *knew* that his onions were superior to those which Judkins had produced, while in Judkins's judgment, his carrots were finer than any which Jones had the *nous* to raise. Their hatred of each other was therefore rooted; and, as Judkins had heard the substance of all that had been said about the peaches, he taunted Jones severely on his being desired to leave the room; and as Jones most vehemently retorted and maintained still that Sylvester *was* the youth by whom his master's peaches had been stolen, Judkins said something very severe about Jones's carrots, and invited him to the meadow, with the view of deciding whether Sylvester was the youth in question or not. At this Jones was nothing daunted: he accepted the challenge; and when Judkins had called a mutual friend from the road, for the purpose of seeing fair play, they repaired to the meadows with bosoms fraught with disgust.

There have always been, even from the most remote period of which history takes cognisance, advocates for that grand social scheme which comprehends trial by battle. Some have chosen clubs for these trials, some axes, some daggers, some spears, while others have preferred rifles, pistols, and swords; but a far more civilised mode of deciding thus the merits of a case in dispute is, unquestionably, that which was in this particular instance adopted by Judkins and Jones.

Certainly, the practice of doing battle with the fist was the first step to civilisation. When men began to substitute the weapons with which Nature had provided them for battle-axes, tomahawks, and knives, society made a most important stride towards perfection. As civilisation progresses, men will substitute the use of the tongue for that of the fist; when that has been sufficiently practised, the use of the brow will supersede that of the tongue; and when we shall have reached the perfection of civilisation, men will merely treat with contempt those whom they know to be unworthy of respect. At the period of Judkins's and Jones's battle, civilisation had made but that one important stride; and as they were not behind the age in which they lived, they—repudiating pistols, knives, and swords—repaired to the meadow and stripped.

It was a lovely day! [It is of course highly essential to the progress of this history that these most remarkable observations should be made.] The sun shone—as the sun *will* sometimes shine—brilliantly, and while it shone, all nature, with the exception of Jones and Judkins, looked gay. The sheep in the distance were nibbling the turnips; the stubble was studded with crows; the leaves on the trees around looked green; and the larks were merrily singing in the air! This was precisely the extraordinary state of things when Judkins and Jones assumed the attitude of defiance, and looked at each other with a species of ferocity perhaps altogether unexampled. As pugilists, however, they were not scientific. They were, moreover, bulky and very short-winded, and therefore exceedingly slow; nor was there any particular time kept. No: at the end of each round, that is to say, when they retreated from each other with the view of "taking breath," they sat upon the grass, sometimes for three minutes, sometimes for five. Time to them was a matter of no importance—they had not been in the habit of hurrying themselves, and they had not the least intention to hurry themselves then. Nor was their friend in any sort of haste; he was remarkably patient and remarkably impartial—indeed, so impartial, that when, at the expiration of twenty minutes, Judkins, who had neither received nor given any blow of importance, wanted some beer, he declared that he wouldn't fetch it unless he had a like commission from Jones. For this commission, however, he had not to wait long, and when he started for the beer, it was with this understanding, that there was to be an absolute cessation of hostilities until he returned. The truce thus established neither of the combatants had the least desire to violate; it was, therefore, on both sides, honourably observed; but during the absence of their mutual friend reflection came, and their indignation cooled; and hence, on the return of that friend, Judkins said to Jones, "Now, you know I'm not afraid of you—quite the contrary—*but* as I shouldn't like to have a black eye, and as the parson, I know, wouldn't like to see you with your front teeth knocked out" (Judkins thought that this was about the strongest way to put it), "if you like, we'll establish no hitting in the face."

"Where are we to hit, then?" said Jones, who was tired of it—quite!—it was very hard work. "If we are not to hit in the face, where are we to hit?"

"I'll tell you," interposed their mutual friend, "hit each other in the hand, and then drink and make it up. If you don't do this, I'll spill the beer."

This settled the matter at once. Judkins thought of Jones's carrots, and Jones thought of Judkins's onion prize; but as it was perfectly clear to them both that they couldn't get on without beer, they, with a laudable show of reluctance, allowed their friend to join their hands, and thus preserved their honour intact, inasmuch as their bright reputation for courage remained untarnished, albeit the real point at issue was undecided still.

During the progress of this memorable battle, Aunt Eleanor prevailed upon the reverend gentleman to remain and take tea, and as Sylvester soon became a favourite with the pastor, he, in the course of the evening, proposed a ride round the adjoining park. Sylvester of course consented at once; and when the pastor's horse had been sent for, and Aunt Eleanor's pony had been saddled, they started, and after riding until the moon rose, the reverend gentleman saw him safely home, and bade him adieu for the night.

CHAPTER III.

IN WHICH THE FIRST ALARM IS CREATED.

How soft and serene is the harvest moon! How calm, how beautiful, how bright! When all around is tranquil and clear, and the nightingale sings in her sweetest strain, how touching the tones of endearment sound! Who would not kiss? Who could not love? Then Night discards her sombre veil, and, mounting her white one studded with brilliants, celebrates that lovely morn when she became the bride of Day.

Now these few important remarks have been suggested by two most extraordinary facts, namely, that on the night that Sylvester slept at the cottage, the harvest moon was at the full, and that about twelve o'clock that very night, Aunt Eleanor's cook heard a noise. She and Mary—they slept together—had been in bed nearly two hours; but cook was twenty years Mary's senior, and, being afflicted with pains in the joints, was far more wakeful than Mary, who invariably buried herself in the clothes, and slept away profoundly.

And the difference between the various species of sleep is amazing: some will sleep quietly, others very noisily; some very lightly, others very heavily; some very sweetly, others very wildly; some very languidly, others very soundly. But without going into any deeply philosophical treatise on sleep, it will be, perhaps, sufficient here to state, that a bedfellow's snore is a most unique nuisance, and that anything equal to Mary's snore in the annals of snoring could never be found.

"Mary!" whispered cook, when she first heard the noise; "Mary! Did you hear that? Mary!—*Are* you dead?"

That the question "Are you dead?" was supererogatory, is a fact which must, it is submitted, be to every highly intellectual person apparent; inasmuch as in the first place a question implies the expectation of an answer, and in the next it is perfectly well known to the intelligent that dead individuals never snore. This affords another sad and unequivocal proof of the lamentable want of education. Had this cook been conversant with the classics, she never could have asked such a question; but as she knew nothing at all about them—and moreover didn't want to know—she not only put this question to Mary, but announced it as being her unbought opinion that the girl really was dead—she slept so soundly and snored so well.

"Mary!" continued cook, as the noise increased; "Mary!" Here she shook and pinched her angrily. "The girl *must* be dead. Mary! Mary!"

"It isn't six yet!" yawned Mary.

"Six!—listen!—hush!—do you hear?"

"What's the matter?" said Mary.

"Hark!"

"Oh, it's the cat."

"It's no cat, Mary. Hark! There it is again!"

At this awful moment they both very distinctly heard footsteps—and every step seemed to press upon their hearts.

"Oh!" exclaimed Mary, "what is to become of us!"

"Hush!" cried cook: "hush! hush!"

The footsteps approached; they came gradually nearer, and still more near; and cook and Mary hugged each other closely, with a view to mutual protection. At length the footsteps reached the door, and cook's heart sank within her.

"D-d-d-on't be frightened, Mary!" she exclaimed; "d-d-d-on't be frightened! Oh! if we should both be ruined!"

"Shall we scream?" said Mary.

"Hark!" cried cook, as the footsteps receded; "hark, they are going downstairs; do you hear them?"

"I d-d-d-do!" replied Mary. "Oh, how d-d-dreadful!"

The sound of the footsteps grew more and more faint, until they were heard in the passage below, when the noise increased. The very chairs seemed to move. Then bolts were withdrawn, and at length a door closed, when all was still as death again.

"They're gone!" said cook, who, while intensely listening to these dreadful sounds, had perspired with so much freedom, that the sheets were quite wet. "Thank Heaven, they are gone."

"Are you sure of it?" cried Mary, trembling frightfully: "quite sure?"

"Quite," replied the cook; "I heard the door close."

No sooner had Mary been assured of this fact, than she uttered a series of the most fearful screams that ever proceeded from a human throat. "Murder!" she continued, in tones the most piercing. "Murder! Thieves! Fire! Mur-*der!*"

"Mary! Mary!" exclaimed cook: "hark!"

The bell rang with violence. Their mistress had been alarmed. But then what was to be done?

"Answer the bell, Mary," said cook; "go and answer the bell."

"*Me* answer the bell!" cried Mary. "*Me!* I couldn't *do* it; no, not if you'd give me the world. Why, they may be in missis's room; who knows, they may be a-murdering of her now. Oh, isn't it horrid!"

The bell still violently rang, but neither cook nor Mary could stir. To protect their mistress they would at any other time have done much, but then—with their imagination teeming with murder—they could *not* answer that bell.

They now heard footsteps again in the passage; and at the very next moment, to their utter horror, they heard a loud knocking at their door—they would, if they could, have sunk into the earth. They were speechless with terror—they ceased to breathe, and felt that all was lost.

From this frightful state of suspense, they were soon relieved, for their mistress having opened her chamber door to ascertain what had caused those dreadful screams, was immediately answered by Judkins. They knew his voice, and could have blessed him. Harsh as it was, celestial music could not then, in their ears, have sounded more sweetly.

"Why, what on earth *can* be the matter?" inquired Aunt Eleanor. "What can it be?"

"I don't know, ma'am, I'm sure," replied Judkins; "there's suffin wrong, somewhere: somebody shruck dreadful."

"The shrieking *was* dreadful indeed; it must have been Mary."

"I've knocked at the door, but they seem dead asleep."

"*Oh*, Judkins!" cried cook. "Oh, wait but a moment—oh, we're not asleep!" and she put on her petticoat hastily, while Mary threw hers round her shoulders, and then struck a light. O ma'am," continued cook, as she opened the door, "there's been thieves in the house—a whole gang of 'em! Oh, we're so frightened! I really thought that murdered we all should have been."

"You've been dreaming," said Judkins; "that's my notion. There's been no thieves here. Was that you that shruck?"

"Oh no, that was Mary. She knows as well as me, there was five or six of 'em at least!"

"*That* there was," said Mary; "and murdered we *must* have been, if I hadn't screamed."

"It's my belief you dreamt it," said Judkins. "I didn't hear any noise."

"Nor did I," interposed Aunt Eleanor. "But let us go down, and see if the things are disturbed."

Downstairs they accordingly went;—Judkins boldly leading the way with a candle and a poker; but it was at a glance plain that no thieves had been there. The rooms were precisely as they had left them; there was not a thing out of its place. The china was safe; the plate was secure; the front door was fast—in short, everything appeared so exactly as it should be, that Aunt Eleanor freely subscribed to the opinion that the whole affair had originated in a dream.

"There, go to bed again, you silly people," she observed; "go to bed, and don't sleep on your backs. I am glad that that dear boy has not been disturbed. There, go to bed, both of you, and, for Heaven's sake, let us have no more screaming."

"Well, but I'm sure, ma'am," said Mary. "Oh! if I didn't"——

"There, don't say another word about it—good-night."

As they separated, cook looked at Judkins with great significance, and Judkins—who didn't at all approve of having his rest broken thus — looked with equal significance at her; but he passed her in silence: nor did she even bid him good-night. On returning to her room, however, she said, in strict confidence to Mary, "Now I'll tell you what it is, you know it's all perfect nonsense about our dreaming—that's of course stuff: I know I heard footsteps, and so did you, and so there can be no mistake about that. Now I'll tell you what, Mary, between you and me, it's my belief, that the footsteps we heard were those of no other man in the world than Judkins! I am sure of it, Mary; and I'm not often wrong. Now, what right had he there, I ask? What was he *doing?* Depend upon it, Mary, he was after no good!"

Certainly Judkins, who slept over the kitchen, and who had a private staircase to his room, had no right, unless summoned, to be in any other part of the premises at midnight; and, as he was the very person who had suggested that they had been dreaming, it unquestionably did in cook's judgment seem strange; but just as she was about to take a somewhat more comprehensive view of the private character of Judkins, she went to the window, and through it beheld a white figure mounted upon a white horse, leaping the hedges, and dashing through the meadows as if he had been following the hounds in full cry.

"Mary! Heaven preserve us!" she exclaimed. "What is this?"

Mary rushed to the window, and in an instant cried—"Oh! it's a ghost."

"Nonsense!—ghosts don't ride on horseback!"

"Oh! but they do though, sometimes."

"It's no ghost, I tell you; that there is a thief, and that thief is your sweetheart, the miller."

"I tell you it is not, then!" cried Mary indignantly. "He a thief, indeed! Well, I'm sure."

"I *know* him by the way in which he rides, and I never did think he was better than he should be. Depend upon it, Mary, he's been in the house, and when we frightened him away, he's stole the horse out of the stable, for I'll take my oath that's Snorter—look."

Away the white figure flew over the fields, and then made a circuit, and then crossed the road, when, as the moon shone full upon him, and he could with the utmost distinctness be seen, they made up their minds at once to point him out to Judkins, and with that view went to his door and knocked.

"*Who's* there?" cried Judkins, somewhat startled, for he had just got into his second sleep.

"Me!" replied cook; "it's only me, Judkins!"

"Well, what do you want?"

"I was right after all. *Do* come to the door."

"Not a bit of it!—not if I know it. Go to bed, and don't bother."

"I tell you there's a thief about the premises."

"I know there's a fool about the premises."

"I've seen him," returned cook. "He's just stolen Snorter."

"I wish *you* were a Snorter, with all my soul," said Judkins, on getting out of bed. "Well," he continued, while putting on his smalls, "*this* is a very pretty game, I think. There's certainly nothing like a change, and such a change as this is, I *must* say, a treat. Now then," he added, on opening the door, "what fresh maggot's this you've got into your head?"

"It's no maggot, Judkins," said cook; "it's a fact. Look through the window, and there you'll see Snorter a galloping off with a man on his back."

Judkins went to the window and looked, but as *he* could see nothing at all of the kind, he said pointedly, "What do you mean? Are you taken so often?"

"I don't care," said cook, when, on looking herself, she found that the figure had vanished. "I know there was some man on Snorter. Am I not to believe my own eyes? Mary saw it as well!"

"Oh, you saw it, *too*," said Judkins, "did you? Well, what was it like?"

"It was for all the world like a ghost?" replied Mary.

"It *was* a ghost," said Judkins ironically, "and nothing but a ghost. What sort of a swell was he, Mary?"

"He was dressed all in white?" replied Mary. "There was not a bit of black at all about him."

"Then of course he was a ghost. He must have been a ghost. And didn't he spit fire, Mary?—and didn't his horse breathe blue flame?—and didn't his eyeballs roll about?—and wasn't he in a white cloud?"

C

"I'll tell you what it is," said cook, "I don't care a bit about what you say; I know what I know, and I'll tell you again, I saw a man riding away upon Snorter. Do you go down to the stable and look; if you find Snorter there, then I've done. Just put on your coat and go down."

"Why, what do you take me for?" said Judkins. "Who do you think you're a playing upon. You call this a frolic, I s'pose? You've begun a nice game, I know; but you don't play it out upon me. Go to bed, and let's have no more of your nonsense. If you come here again I'll call missis; she'll very soon put you to rights. You take me, I s'pose, for a fool, don't you? Be off!"

Cook, perceiving that Judkins was highly indignant, muttered something severe, and retired; and when she had had a few warm words with Mary, who felt extremely wroth at its being supposed that the miller was not all her fancy had painted, they both went to sleep, and slept well.

But Judkins for a long time could *not* go to sleep, his indignation at the thought of being considered a fool was so excessive. And, of all ideas of an unpleasing character, there is probably not one so galling to a man as that of his being considered a fool. He may think like a fool, he may speak like a fool, he may be conscious of having acted in a very foolish manner, he may even, confidentially, call himself a fool; but no man thinks that he is a fool in the abstract, nor can any man bear to be thought a fool. And this is a wise provision of Nature. A *wise* provision of Nature! Well, it is an absurd conventional term, inasmuch as *all* Nature's provisions are wise; and, therefore, perhaps, it had better be put thus: it is one of the provisions of Nature, and its admirable character is manifest in this, that if fools knew they *were* fools, their value in their own estimation would be small, and all fools would be consequently wretched; while the fact of its coming to their knowledge that they are by others supposed to be fools, prompts them to endeavour at least to act thenceforth wisely.

This, *primâ facie*, may appear to be very severe upon Judkins; but it is in reality not so, seeing that he was no fool, and that no one ever supposed him to be anything like a fool. He was kept awake so long by the idea of its being *imagined* that he was a fool. But when he had sufficiently reflected upon the matter—that is, when he had proved himself to himself, beyond all dispute on the part of himself, to be *no* fool—he went to sleep and slept until six in the morning.

Being, however, anxious to prove to the cook that he would have been a fool had he allowed himself to act on her suggestion, he no sooner rose than he went to the stable, which he found, to all appearance, externally, just as he had left it. The door was locked; the key was still in the secret place above the door, and the way in which it turned when applied to the lock, convinced him fully that the lock had not been forced. But the moment he entered he saw at a single glance that something was wrong. There stood the pony, and there stood Snorter; but Snorter was saddled, and not only saddled, but literally covered with steaming foam!

Judkins stood for a moment looking at the animal with an expression of amazement the most intense, and having thus viewed him from head to tail, he asked himself the following questions:—First, Where could the horse have been? Secondly, Who could have taken him out? Thirdly, What, under the circumstances, was he to do? The two first questions he couldn't at all answer; he knew only this, that the horse had been out, and that he who had taken him out was no stranger; he therefore passed them to be considered anon, conceiving that the question which demanded his immediate consideration was the third—what, under the circumstances, was he to do?

Should he go in and explain how matters stood in the stable? Would it be wise to do so? He thought not. When he had dwelt upon the triumphant position in which cook would be thereby placed, he *could* not think that the pursuit of such a course would be at all indicative of wisdom. Well, then, should he set to work and clean the horse at once, and say nothing whatever about it? This question was the germ of deep thought. It was, however, perfectly clear that Snorter in any case must be rubbed down, and, as Judkins felt that while rubbing him down he should have sufficient time to arrive at some decision, he pulled off his jacket and went to work at once.

Now, while he was thus intently engaged, and hissing away like an angry serpent, cook glided past the stable door. She had come out expressly with the view of breaking loose in the event of Snorter having been stolen; it was her immovably fixed determination to open in that event her whole mind to Judkins, and, therefore, it is not irrational to suppose that, had matters stood as she expected they would stand, and as indeed she really wished them to stand, she would have walked into him warmly; but as she saw the horse in reality there, and therefore felt that she must have been mistaken in so far as the identity of the animal was concerned, she deemed it prudent to hold her peace, and silently worked her way back.

During the performance of this extraordinary feat, Mary, while assisting her mistress to dress, explained minutely to her all that had occurred, enlarging, of course, upon every point, and swelling each into all possible importance.

At first, Aunt Eleanor appeared to regard the whole affair as an excellent jest, and she really did enjoy the relation of the circumstances highly; but when Mary, with great force and natural feeling, stated that the miller was suspected of having taken the horse from the stable, her mistress, knowing the attachment which existed between him and Mary, felt herself bound to inquire into the matter, with the view of either clearing his character if innocent, or, in the event of his being guilty, of breaking off the match.

She accordingly, on descending to the breakfast-room, at once summoned Judkins and cook, and as cook was the first to attend that summons, she at once told her tale, and made one deep mystery of it. Judkins, however, was not long after her, and as he had decided upon sacrificing all private feeling upon the altar of duty, he came prepared to state the whole case.

"Judkins," said Aunt Eleanor, as he entered, "how does the horse look this morning?"

"Why, he's pretty well, considering, ma'am," replied Judkins.

"Pretty well, *considering*,—considering what?"

"Why, ma'am, considering that in all his born days he never had such a sweating as, somehow or other, he has had since I locked him up last night."

"Oh, then," said cook, who felt greatly relieved, and who turned upon Judkins—and he fully expected it—as if she had made up her mind to have at him, "it *wasn't* Snorter; it *couldn't* be Snorter. I was having a *game* with you, was I! It was one of my maggots! You'll call missis, won't you! It was only a frolic of mine! You are right, and I'm wrong, of course! Now I'll tell you what it is"——

"Presently, cook," interposed Aunt Eleanor; "have patience. We will hear you presently. What do you mean by the *sweating*, Judkins?"

"Why, ma'am, when I went into the stable this morning, I found the horse saddled, and in a muck of sweat. Whoever could have got him out *I* can't *think!* It must have been some one who knows the premises, for the door was locked, and the key was in its right place, over the door."

"Of course," exclaimed cook; "and the miller knew well where to find it."

"Cook," said Aunt Eleanor, "how do you know that?"

"Why, ma'am, he's always after Mary, and of course she tells him all she knows."

"I know, cook, that you are jealous," said Aunt Eleanor; "but in order that the young man may have an opportunity of vindicating his character, I will send for him at once. You know him, Judkins? Go, and without mentioning a syllable to him on the subject, tell him that I shall be glad to speak to him for a moment."

Judkins, casting a look of contempt at cook, then left the room, and, as Sylvester immediately afterwards came in to breakfast, the whole affair was fully explained to him by his aunt, who expressed herself highly delighted at the fact of his not having been disturbed.

And Sylvester, who looked very languid, and felt very sore, expressed his amazement at the circumstances related, and the interest which that relation excited was, in reality, deep in the extreme.

"What could have been the man's object?" said he; "he had clearly no intention to steal the horse, seeing that he brought him back, and locked the stable door. It appears to me to be so unaccountable! I can't understand it at all!"

"It is strange—very strange!" said Aunt Eleanor. "But come, my dear, let us have breakfast. Cook," she added, "send in that tongue."

Cook left the room, and repaired to the pantry; but the state of things there was so startling, that she almost immediately returned, exclaiming, "Now, ma'am, I *know* there's been thieves in the house! No tongue, no pastry, no sausage-rolls: not a single bit of any blessed thing can I find! *Everything's* gone! There must have been half-a-dozen of them at least!"

"Well, this," said Aunt Eleanor, "is indeed extraordinary!"

"And what gormandisers, too, they must have been!' resumed cook. "There was half a tongue, four sausage-rolls, six apple-puffs, three or four tarts, three jam-tarts, you know, ma'am—I know there were three—in short, they've eaten every individual thing!"

"This is very mysterious!" observed Aunt Eleanor calmly; "we shall probably understand it better by-and-by. You must now do the best you can, my dear, with ham and eggs!"

"Do not have anything cooked for me," said Sylvester; "indeed, I've no appetite at all."

Nor had he! The ham and eggs were ordered by his aunt notwithstanding; but, when they were brought, he could not touch either. Nor could he in any way account for this. He usually ate a good breakfast; but he really then felt himself full to repletion. Aunt Eleanor herself became very much alarmed. What on earth could be the cause of it? She couldn't imagine. She felt quite *sure* that he was sickening for something, and was just turning over in her mind the expediency of sending at once for her physician, when Judkins returned from the mill.

On entering the room he was eagerly followed by Mary and cook, who were both extremely anxious to hear the result; and, when it was announced that the miller had started the preceding day to attend a distant market, and would not return until the morrow, Mary's expression of joy contrasted strongly with that of disappointment, which instantly marked the fat features of cook, who sufficiently proved that there are feelings of jealousy which do *not* spring from pure love. For example, she didn't love the miller: still she thought that, instead of proposing to Mary, he should have proposed to her. She, with characteristic candour, admitted it to be true that she was a *trifle* older—say twenty years or *so*—but then she was, in her judgment, a much finer woman! A far more experienced—a larger-boned person! She *could* not imagine how any man, having his eyes about him, could prefer such a skit of a thing as Mary to her. But so it was. Cook felt it to be so acutely, and hence she did hope that it would have been proved that the miller had taken Snorter out of the stable; but as it was then to all abundantly clear that he could not by any possibility have been the man, the question which naturally suggested itself was—

"Whom *could* it have been?" That was the question! And an interesting question it was.

CHAPTER IV.

THE CHURCHYARD.

As the world has ever been governed by mysteries—by mysteries amazed—by mysteries amused—by mysteries excited, subdued, and kept in awe—he, who could be, by his hopes of immortality, prompted to grapple with, to open, and to spread completely out the philosophy of mystery, would be, beyond all dispute, hailed by the mysterious as a great benefactor to his species. It wouldn't, however, do here: there isn't room for it: and even if there were, such a profound interference with the progress of this history wouldn't be exactly correct; but that a mystery is an affair which doth exercise over the human mind an immense amount of influence is manifest in this, that upon the mysterious piece of business in question, Aunt Eleanor during the whole morning dwelt.

She *couldn't* make it out; and in the fact of its being apparently impossible to be made out, consists the chief beauty of a mystery: she sent for her reverend friend, but *he* could throw no light at all upon the subject; feeling, however, bound to do something, he very benevolently proffered his advice.

"With respect," said he, "to the horse affair, I have nothing whatever to say, being utterly unable to conjecture with justice either how it occurred, or who could have been the man, but, as far as the pastry matter is concerned, I *have* a few words of advice to offer. The same thing occurred to me some years ago, when I kept an academy near Chat Moss. I was constantly losing my pastry. Night after night it went with all the regularity imaginable. I couldn't tell how, but it went. I used even to lock the pantry-door and keep the key in my chamber: still it continued to go. Well, at length resolved to discover, if possible, the cause of all this, I one evening introduced a little gentle jalap, and patiently waited the result, which was this, that in the morning there was not a single youth in the establishment perfectly free from qualms! I then at once saw how the matter stood, of course; and although I took no apparent notice of the circumstance, my pastry was thenceforward safe. They wouldn't eat it, even when placed before them. I couldn't persuade them to touch it. I therefore advise you, my dear madam, strongly to adopt the same course. It is certain to cure them. I know—I have proved it to be a specific!"

Aunt Eleanor smiled: she moreover blushed; and, in order to hide that blush, she went to the sideboard, and having got out a decanter of sherry, placed it before him, with a glass and some cake. The very sight of the wine— of which he was fond—made the reverend gentleman eloquent; but the moment he had tasted it down went the glass, and he made one of the most extraordinary faces ever beheld; he screwed up his nose, and compressed his lips, and while drawing the corners right down to his chin, looked precisely as if he had been taking something filthy.

"Good gracious!" exclaimed Aunt Eleanor, laughing—for really the pastor's face was irresistibly droll—"what on earth is the matter?"

The reverend gentleman shuddered and grunted, and shook his head, and pointed to the glass on the table, with the view of intimating his strong disapprobation of the wine.

"Do you not like the flavour of it?"

"No-o-o-o!" replied the reverend gentleman, shuddering, with even more violence than before. "It's phy-z-z-zic!"

"Dear me," said Aunt Eleanor; "why, it came out of the very same bin as the last."

The reverend gentleman did not care much about what particular *bin* it came out of, all he cared about was its peculiar flavour—which flavour really was, in his judgment, bad.

"Some trick has been played with that wine," he observed, as soon as he was able to unscrew his mouth; "depend upon it, some trick has been played."

"Impossible, my dear sir!" exclaimed Aunt Eleanor, rising for a glass, with the view of tasting it herself. "Why, what!" she added, on putting her lips to it; "what in the name of goodness can it be?"

"Filthy, isn't it?" observed the pastor.

"Filthy!" exclaimed Aunt Eleanor, and burst at once into a merry peal of laughter. "Excuse me," she added, as soon as she could; "pray excuse me; I know that I am very, very rude, but you really do make such a *funny* face!"

Well, that, in the reverend gentleman's view, was rich. He would, at that particular moment, have felt great pleasure in being informed what man, possessing anything like a palate, could swallow, as he had swallowed, half a glass or more of that stuff, without making up a face, which might be denominated fairly funny.

"Well," said Aunt Eleanor, who had been highly amused, and who then rang the bell, "we must rectify this."

"You will never be able to rectify that," said the reverend gentleman; "that's past all rectification."

Aunt Eleanor—albeit not much in the habit of laughing —laughed heartily again; and when Mary appeared, she gave her the key of the cellar, with the most tranquil face she could assume, and directed her to bring up a bottle of sherry.

The pastor looked at Mary with an expression which seemed to indicate that he strongly suspected that she had been at that decanter. Mary, however, took no notice of this; she received her instructions and then left the room.

"It's really very unfortunate," said Aunt Eleanor, "that you should have tasted the very first glass out of that particular bottle."

"My dear madam," returned the pastor, "depend upon this, that I have not had the first glass."

"It was decanted yesterday; it has not since been touched."

"To your knowledge it may not have been; but it strikes me forcibly that some one has been at it, substituting vinegar, or something of that sort, for three or four glasses of the wine."

"Oh! I should say," rejoined Aunt Eleanor, "that there was something in the bottle before the wine was put in."

The reverend gentleman, however, still adhered strictly to his original opinion, which the wine in the fresh bottle tended to confirm. That was something like wine! and he said so; he, moreover, drank half a pint of it in order to take the taste of the other out of his mouth, and when this had been effectually accomplished, he briefly adverted to his gentle specific, and then, with many expressions of high consideration, took his leave.

Sylvester during the whole of this time was sleeping soundly on the sofa. He had been prevailed upon by his aunt to lie down immediately after he had made that apology for a breakfast; and as, when he rose, which was not until just before dinner, he ate heartily again, all his fond aunt's apprehensions vanished.

He still, however, looked very languid and pale; and, in order to raise his spirits, she related what had occurred to her reverend friend, and then dwelt more at large upon the mysteries which characterised the preceding night; and after having indulged in a variety of conjectures, of which the majority were very ingenious, she ordered the chaise, took him out for a drive, and then made every effort that affection could suggest to amuse and to cheer him in the evening.

About nine o'clock, however, feeling very much fatigued, he retired to rest. Aunt Eleanor in general went to bed at ten, and so did the servants usually; but on this particular occasion cook and Mary—peace between them and Judkins not having been proclaimed—sat alone till past eleven, over a bright kitchen fire, conversing on the subject of recent events, and relating a variety of ghost-stories to each other in justification of their respective views. These stories, which are always of a deeply interesting character, made them shudder; and as some of them were indeed awful, they were inspired with so much dread that they both felt extremely unwilling to move. They had, moreover, been so intent upon these tales of the imagination, that the candle burned down to the socket unperceived; for while cook, who retained the poker in her hand, kept on stirring the fire continually, Mary's eyes were fixed upon the brightest of the coals, in which she detected with much ingenuity the outlines of divers extraordinary faces.

At length the wick, deserted by that pure flame which had enveloped it so long, and by which it had been so uninterruptedly warmed, sighed forth its dying breath. Cook smelt this, it reached her nostrils first, and, as experience had taught her to know in an instant what it was, she turned, on the impulse of the moment, with the view of consigning it at once to the fire. She had scarcely, however, *touched* the candlestick which contained it, when her blood chilled with horror, for she heard distinctly footsteps approaching. Mary heard those footsteps too, but they had not time to glance at each other before the kitchen door absolutely opened, and they beheld a tall figure enveloped in a sheet. They tried to scream, but could not; terror had struck them dumb. They had risen from their seats, but stood utterly appalled.

The figure, apparently unconscious of their presence, now glided gradually through the kitchen, and turning into the passage which led to the pantry, disappeared. But, although they could not see it then, neither could speak, for they plainly heard it still.

Anon the figure again appeared, and their blood grew apparently colder than before; and while their strained eyeballs seemed ready to burst, they stood as if to that particular spot they had been absolutely rivetted. Still the apparition seemed not to perceive them; it glided without turning its head back to the door at which it had entered, and when it had closed it with the utmost care, they saw the appalling spectre no more.

Now, although they were still half-dead with fright, and continued to tremble with unexampled violence, the very instant the figure had vanished, and all had become quite silent again, they simultaneously uttered a series of screams of the loudest and most piercing character.

Sleeping, as he did, immediately over the kitchen, Judkins heard these frightful screams, and conceiving from their nature that they did in reality mean something, he leaped out of bed and rushed into the passage; but as, by the light of the moon, he perceived, indistinctly, the figure approaching, he rushed back again without any loss of time, and having locked his door in the twinkling of an eye, buried himself beneath the bedclothes in a state of indescribable terror.

The short space of time which the whole of this occupied was indeed amazing. He had never displayed so much alacrity before—he had never in his life made so much haste. Under any other conceivable circumstances he must have been utterly astonished at himself!—he stopped for nothing, he was wonderfully active; no one who knew him could for a moment have imagined that he had so much activity in him.

The screaming, however, continued still; and at length

Aunt Eleanor, throwing a cloak around her, descended with her night-lamp to ascertain the cause. She experienced no difficulty, of course, in discovering from what particular part of the house those screams proceeded; she knew at once that they came from the kitchen, and hence to the kitchen she quickly repaired; but the moment she lifted the latch of the door cook and Mary sank upon their knees and convulsively buried their faces in their hands.

"Why, what, in the name of goodness," said Aunt Eleanor, "can be the meaning of all this? Cook! Mary! Mary! Answer me instantly—what does it mean?"

Cook, who at first imagined that the figure had returned, now summoned sufficient courage to raise her head; and the first words she uttered were, "The gho-o-o-ost!"

"The what?" cried Aunt Eleanor.

"Oh, ma'am!" said Mary; "oh, my good gracious me! Oh, we've been frightened to death, ma'am. A ghost has been here, ma'am! a real ghost! Oh!"

"Nonsense, Mary; how can you be so simple!"

"We saw it come in, ma'am," interposed cook; "and we saw it go out. Oh, it was horrid!"

"Tut, tut! what on earth can be the matter with you both?"

"We saw it, ma'am; indeed we did. We both of us saw it, ma'am, with our own eyes!"

"You saw it in imagination merely. But how is it that you are not in bed before this? Why, it's half-past eleven o'clock! Have you both been asleep?"

"No, ma'am," replied the cook; "Mary and me have been talking."

"I perceive; I perceive it all clearly; you have been talking about ghosts. Now, tell me the truth: is it not so?"

"We *had* been talking about what we'd heard, ma'am; but as to this, I never saw anything plainer in my life."

"Ridiculous, cook. I am surprised that a person of *your* years should not know better. What's that?" she exclaimed, on hearing a noise above, produced apparently by the falling of some heavy weight. "Ring the gardener's bell. There is something going on which I don't understand. Ring the bell."

"Ye-e-es, ma'am," said Mary, who, having been filled with fresh alarm by the noise above, was afraid to move even to the rope. "I am so frightened!"

Aunt Eleanor however rang the bell, but no answer was returned. She rang it again with additional violence; and again! and again! still no answer. She couldn't, of course, pretend to account for it. She thought it very strange; and as the world at large may *also* think it strange, it will be, perhaps, as well at once to explain the real cause.

It has been already stated that it was not long before Judkins got into bed again. Nor was it. He got in anyhow. Nor did he care how!—he wasn't particular. His object was to get into bed, and he got in. But, being extremely anxious to conceal himself effectually, he darted beneath the clothes, which were all on one side, and there lay for a time motionless upon the very brink of the bedstead. Of this fact, however, he was perfectly unconscious, and therefore, when he did attempt to turn, he fell heavily upon the floor. That the ghost had induced this, he at that awful moment had not the slightest doubt. But he was into bed again in an instant, and there—of course utterly heedless of the bell—he remained in perfect silence, until his mistress, tired of ringing, came up to his bedroom door and knocked.

Judkins started! The knock alone seemed to convulse his whole frame. "Oh," he exclaimed; "what *have* I done? what have I done? what have I done?"

"Judkins!" said his mistress; but as she had caught cold, her voice was not sufficiently clear to be recognised; "Judkins!"

"Leave me," he continued, "for Heaven's sake, leave me! I know I'm a miserable sinner, but leave me! Go somewhere else; you've mistaken the room—indeed you have; you have, I assure you!"

When Mary and cook, who had followed their mistress closely, for then they would not have lost sight of her for the world, heard these awful words uttered, they felt quite convinced that whatever *mistake* the ghost might have made, he was then in the room with Judkins. They were sure of it!—perfectly sure; and conceiving that their mistress must have inspired the same conviction, they implored her, in trembling whispers, to retire. But no: her mind was firm! She was resolved to know, if possible, the cause of this delusion, and therefore knocked loudly again at the door.

"Oh, pray go away," said Judkins bitterly, "pray do!"

"Judkins!" exclaimed Aunt Eleanor; "Judkins! 'tis I—your mistress!"

"You, ma'am! Oh, thank Heaven! is it you?"

"Yes, 'tis I. What *is* the matter? Dress yourself instantly, and open the door."

Judkins, who felt of course greatly relieved, threw off the bedclothes, and slipped on his smalls; but when, pale and trembling, he opened the door, his countenance bore still an expression of terror.

"What *is* this, Judkins?" demanded Aunt Eleanor; "what *can* be the meaning of it all?"

"Oh," replied Judkins, who felt very ill, "the house is haunted: I know it is. I've seen," he added, in a harsh, unearthly whisper, "I've seen a horrid ghost."

"Where?" said Aunt Eleanor; "I really have no patience with you. Where did you see it?"

"There!" replied Judkins, still in a whisper, pointing to the passage with startling effect; "there!"

"Are you all *mad?*" exclaimed Aunt Eleanor, perceiving that they all looked towards the passage, as if apprehensive of the "ghost's" reappearance; "or is it all done to alarm me? There is," she added, with an expression of intensity, "there is something, I fear, beneath the surface of this. If you have any bad design—if you are actuated by any unhallowed notions—*if* you have conspired together with the view of accomplishing any wicked object—pray, before you retire to rest, that Heaven may turn your hearts!"

With all the eloquence of which they were capable, they implored her to believe that they were attached to her sincerely; that they had been, and would continue to be, faithful to the last; and that the proceedings of that awful night were ascribable, justly, to no wicked motive, no base conspiracy, no bad design.

"I will speak to you all," she observed, "in the morning; but if—I say *if*—you have conspired together with any wicked object in view, may Heaven forgive you. Good-night."

She then returned to her chamber and locked the door, leaving them greatly distressed at the idea of its being supposed that they had entered into any such conspiracy. They very soon, however, reverted to the ghost, when Judkins exclaimed, with all the fervour at his command, "If I *didn't* see it, why I didn't; *but* if I didn't, I'm dumb!"

"We saw it, too," said cook.

"You did?"

"It came into the kitchen."

"*Didn't* it look horrid?"

"Oh, hideous! Did you see its face?"

"The figure was *quite* enough for me. I think I see it now!"

"*Where?*" cried Mary. "Oh, don't frighten us. Where?"

"No, no; I mean that I shall never forget it! But let us go to bed; missis is angry—I know she's angry; I never saw her angry before; but I'm sure she's no cause. One may be wrong—two may be wrong; but we can't all be wrong. We all of us saw it. Nothing can get over that. But good-night: good-night."

Cook and Mary then retired, and when, with hearts still full of fear, they had got into bed, Mary went to sleep with this expression on her lips, "I'm sure I shall not get a *wink* to-night."

Now, while these scenes were being enacted at the cottage, dreadful excitement prevailed near the church, and as it is essential to the due appreciation of the cause of this excitement, that the whole of the particulars should be known, it will be correct to state those particulars here, with the names of the persons excited.

It happened, then, that on that very evening a party of influential men had assembled at a house, of which the sign was "The Crumpet and Crown." This party consisted of Messrs. Blinkum, Pokey, Bobber, Snorkins, and Quocks, who were joined by another highly influential person, named Obadiah Drant, who was really an immense politician! who could tell what the Emperor of China thought, and what were the strictly private feelings of the Czar! who had the faculty of going over much more ground in the space of five minutes than the Wandering Jew ever did in five years! and whose intimate associates appeared to be persons whom he called Billy Pitt, Harry Brougham, Johnny Russell, Charley Fox, and Bobby Peel!

It may moreover be remarked—for it is remarkable—that in England we very seldom meet with a church without perceiving a public-house at hand. Sometimes it is opposite, sometimes next door, and sometimes even in the very churchyard. But whatever the relative positions may be, they are almost invariably found to be within a few yards of each other, as if every inhabitant, like every representative of *Cato*, were expected to exclaim, " My bane and antidote are both before me ! " Some, indeed, may ascribe this remarkable association to the spirits, and some may attribute it solely to the beer ; to some it may suggest the idea of those bosom friends—brandy and bitters—while others may imagine that the common announcement of " Good entertainment for man and beast," refers to the two establishments : but whatever may be the meaning of this association, it is perfectly certain that the Crumpet and Crown was within twenty yards of the church—that the party assembled at the Crumpet and Crown had to go through that very churchyard—and that although the house was usually closed at ten, the argument in which they were engaged was not finished at eleven. They had still one little point to settle ; a point which they felt it to be their duty to settle before they parted, it being neither more nor less than " How the country could be saved from a sanguinary revolution ! " Mr. Blinkum contended, that unless a law were passed to protect the British butcher, an universal slaughter would be inevitable. Mr. Bobber thought that a poll-tax might avert it. Mr. Pokey begged to say, and to have it understood, that it could be averted only by an equitable adjustment; and while Mr. Snorkins declared it to be his unbought opinion that it was to be done by an alteration in the iron trade alone, Mr. Quocks maintained that it could be done only by an immediate and unconditional repeal of the Corn Laws. Eventually, however, Mr. Obadiah Drant recapitulated the various arguments adduced, and having summed up with all his characteristic perspicuity, delivered his judgment to the effect that— *Nothing* could save this mighty nation from one chaotic mass of unextinguishable flames !

The point in question having thus been decided to the entire satisfaction of all concerned, the party broke up ; and all, with the exception of Obadiah, who *would* have a glass at the bar, left the house, and proceeded homewards through the churchyard.

The churchyard ! To the contemplative, how awful is a churchyard at midnight, when a solemn stillness pervades the scene over which, for a time, Death reigns triumphant ! Who, without inspiring feelings of awe, can, at such a time, reflect, that beneath the surface of that solemn scene, hearts that have throbbed with love, sympathy, and joy, and those from which sprang only baseness and crime, together perish?—that the marrowless bones of the noble and the base, the virtuous and the vicious, the intellectual and the animal, the lofty and the lowly, the generous and the selfish, the philanthropist and the misanthrope, lie levelled; some fleshless, some crumbled into dust, some crumbling fast, and some cased in corruption still; but all levelled, or distinguished only by the vanity of the living; while Death, upon the loftiest tomb, sits grinning at the distinction, conscious that they *are* all levelled, and that thus they will remain till the last trump shall sound, when his power will cease for ever?

Perhaps no one. But to those who had just left the Crumpet and Crown this scene was not awful at all. These reflections then did not occur to them—they didn't reflect upon anything of the sort. They were all elated, thoughtless, careless, fearless: that is, they feared nothing, seeing nothing to fear: they were joyous, merry, happy, generous, friendly, and affectionate. But when they had got half-way across the churchyard, Pokey, who was somewhat in advance of the rest, started back with a look of horror, and with frightful effect exclaimed, "What's that?"

"What's what?—what do you mean?" demanded Snorkins.

"Look there!" returned Pokey, with vehemence, pointing to a tall, white figure, which appeared to be contemplating the tombs.

And they did look there: and on the instant terror seized them. Two ran back to the Crumpet and Crown, and the rate at which they ran surpassed everything on record in the annals of running; but the rest didn't run, because they couldn't. They stood as if struck with paralysis; they were as pale as any spectre could hope to be; and while their hearts ceased to perform their natural functions, and their quivering lips were livid with fear, their knees smote each other with a species of violence altogether unexampled. Well, what was to be done? There it was, a real, regular ghost! There was no mistake about it; there *couldn't* exist two opinions on the subject; but what was to be done? Should they run?—they couldn't. Should they call out?—they couldn't. Well, were they to stop there and watch till it vanished? They didn't at all like to do so, but

D

what else could they do? Nothing. There they remained, and while they were there, in a state of speechless terror, Obadiah Drant, being a valiant man, on hearing the facts of the case stated by Bobber and Quocks, who had run back so bravely to the Crumpet and Crown, seized a carving-knife which lay near a huge round of beef, and while flourishing it boldly declared, with that vehemence for which he was distinguished, that as he cared no more for a ghost than he did for Bobby Peel, he'd go at once and "settle the swell!" which really was a very irreverent expression, and therefore extremely incorrect. But seeing such valour displayed, Legge, the landlord, who had never seen a ghost, but who had a great desire to see one, did offer to accompany Obadiah Drant, and despite the remonstrances of Mrs. Legge, actually quitted the house with him, leaving Bobber and Quocks to fill Mrs. Legge's mind with all sorts of horrors.

Legge, however, on reaching the churchyard, perceived that Obadiah somewhat relaxed, and on mentioning this with all the delicacy of which he was capable, Obadiah pronounced this opinion :—That as spectres were "not sensible to feeling as to sight," it would not be at all a fair match. Still, with an assumption of valour which was, in reality, a stranger to his heart, he went on; but he had no sooner reached the spot on which his friends stood, and beheld the white figure distinctly before him, than the carving-knife dropped, and he fell upon his knees, which would not then allow him to stand.

But Legge, who assumed nothing, was comparatively calm. He saw the figure, and believed it to be a spirit, and therefore his heart did not beat with its wonted regularity; still, compared with the rest, he was tranquil and firm. He even proposed to approach the "spirit," and to ascertain, if possible, why it had appeared; but not one would accompany him—not one could accompany him—and having at home a wife and five children, he didn't think it would be exactly prudent for him to go alone.

"But come, come," said he, "we have nothing to fear. We have murdered no one, robbed no one, injured no one—why should we fear? It will not harm us. It may have something to communicate—some secret perhaps, which, until it has been revealed, will not allow it to rest. Let us go."

At this moment the figure—which, during the whole of the time, had been moving slowly from tomb to tomb—came towards them; but as it advanced they simultaneously receded, and continued to recede, looking constantly behind them, until they reached the gate, which they had no sooner passed than, making themselves up for one grand effort, they darted towards the Crumpet and Crown with all the energy at their command.

The figure, notwithstanding this, continued to advance. It seemed to be in no haste whatever—it took its own time; and having passed the gate, appeared to have made up its mind to look in at the Crumpet and Crown. But the moment they perceived this apparent inclination on the part of the "spectre," they closed the door, locked it, shot both the bolts, and then rushed to the window in a state of breathless anxiety. They were not, however, kept here in that state long: they had in fact scarcely reached the window, when they saw it pass slowly and solemnly by, without appearing even to notice the house—which was a comfort to them all; they breathed again, and were again courageous—indeed, so courageous, that when they felt perfectly sure that it was gone, they went to the door again in order to watch it. But it was not gone, although it was going, which was in their judgment the next best thing. They therefore did watch it —nay, they even followed it—at a most respectful distance, it is true—still they followed it, and continued to follow it, for nearly twenty yards, when it vanished—they couldn't tell how; but it vanished—and that, too, into Aunt Eleanor's cottage! One thought he saw it walk through the brick wall; another conceived that it flew through the window; a third felt convinced that it opened the door; a fourth imagined that it darted through the panels; but on the one grand point they were all agreed—they all saw it enter the cottage.

And *didn't* they pity Aunt Eleanor? Yes; even from their souls they pitied her; but — they returned to the Crumpet and Crown.

"Well!" said Mr. Pokey, "I never see such a job in *my* life! And didn't it smell!"

"I smelt nothing," observed the landlord.

"What! not brimstone?"

"No; not a bit of it."

"I can't say as I smelt brimstone," interposed Mr. Bobber; "it seemed like the burning of charcoal, to me."

"Charcoal!" exclaimed Mr. Blinkum; "it was just for all the world like burnt bones. You get the leg-bone of a bullock, and burn it, and see if it won't smell—oh, offal! and it stands to reason that if the bones of a bullock smell, the bones of a man also will smell likewise."

"But *has* a spirit bones?" demanded Mr. Bobber.

"Why, if it hadn't, you fool, how could it hold together? A spirit is a skeleton—it must be a skeleton, because spirits have no flesh."

"What do you call it a spirit for?" inquired Mr. Quocks.

"Why, what do you call it?"

"A ghost, to be sure."

"A ghost!" said Mr. Pokey; "I call it a vision!"

"Nonsense!" exclaimed Mr. Snorkins; "it's a apparition—that's what it is—and I'll bet you glasses round of it—come."

Hereupon Mr. Legge interposed an observation to the effect that half the difference between ghosts, spirits, visions, and apparitions wasn't much; but Obadiah, to whom nothing could be unknown, and who was consequently conversant with every species of spectre, contended stoutly that the difference between them was as great as the difference between those familiar friends of his, Billy Pitt, Harry Brougham, Johnny Russell, and Bobby Peel. He, moreover, learnedly enlarged upon this; and, having adduced innumerable analogous cases, concluded by observing, with a view of proving the distinction beyond all doubt, that the appearance of Billy Pitt would be a spirit—that of Harry Brougham a vision—that of Bobby Peel an apparition—and that of Johnny Russell a ghost.

Meanwhile, the agitation of Mrs. Legge was excessive. Nothing could surpass it! nothing ever equalled it! Certain she was that she never should be able to get through the night. The state of her nerves was altogether frightful! Twenty times during the discussion had she begged of them to leave, but in vain: they could not be prevailed upon to move—they were perfectly deaf to her entreaties, so long as she continued to supply their demands; but when she at length announced her firm determination that they shouldn't have another drop in her house that night, if she knew it, they made up their minds to go round by the road, shook Legge by the hand, and departed.

CHAPTER V.

THE MYSTERY.

There is, perhaps, nothing connected with our nature more easily excited than suspicion. However much disposed we may be to confide in the honour and sincerity of those around us, we cannot extinguish that feeling of suspicion that appears to be inherent in our hearts. It may be latent—it may even for years be dormant—but it is to be aroused by a single word, and when it is aroused it frequently develops itself with so much malignity, that prudence, pride, love, honour, justice, and reason fall before it. Some imagine that there is so much deception beneath the surface of society, suspicion is absolutely essential to security—and it certainly is not safe to be too confiding—but it really does seem most ungenerous to suspect, in a world in which there is such an immense amount of superficial honesty. There is, however, something very pleasing in suspicion after all; for it involves the hope that that which we suspect will be realised. If even it be prejudicial to ourselves, what a comfort there is in an opportunity of paying a compliment to our own acuteness! —what self-satisfaction is derived from the exclamation, "I knew, of course, how it would be!—I suspected it all along! —and I have not been deceived!" We do not like to be deceived—nay, we cannot, in this respect, bear to be deceived!

It is questionable—ay, very questionable—whether any one is, or ever was, entirely free from the feeling of suspicion; but then it is not to be said that all who possess that feeling are suspicious! No: Aunt Eleanor was not, in the common acceptation of the term, suspicious. She wished to believe that all around her were honest, just, virtuous, and pure; she had as much faith in their integrity as any one could have, but as she could not in any way account for that which had occurred, she felt convinced that there must be something wrong, and that conviction haunted her throughout the night.

In the morning, however, being anxious, as usual, to act with the utmost discretion, she resolved on not recurring to the subject before the servants until she had consulted her reverend friend, and, in pursuance of this resolution, she wrote a note to that gentleman, requesting the favour of a call, but, before she had despatched that note, he came, ostensibly with the view of reminding her, that that was the very day on which the village would have a certain periodical visit.

Now in this visit much mystery was involved, and as it forms a subject which must of necessity be resorted to anon, it will be perhaps as well to explain now that a gentleman named Howard, his daughter Henriette, and a lady, whose assumed name was Greville, had for some years honoured the village with their presence, for one hour, on the first of April and the first of October, for a purpose which no one connected with that village had ever been able to learn. It may also be stated that Henriette was an elegant girl, gentle, amiable, and accomplished. She had been educated with the utmost care, under the surveillance of her father, whose every earthly hope seemed fixed upon her: she was the pride of his heart—his idol; most fondly—most dearly did he love her; but often, while gazing upon her in silence, would he burst into tears. Henriette constantly marvelled at this. To her it was indeed mysterious. She could not ascertain—nay, she could not even conceive, the cause. True, he was almost invariably sad; he was seldom, indeed, seen to smile; and when he did smile, his features in an instant assumed an expression of sadness again: but why he should be unable to look at her intently without shedding tears, she was utterly at a loss to imagine. That there was something heavy at his heart was abundantly clear; but she sought to know the cause of his sorrow in vain. They moreover lived in the most perfect seclusion. They saw no society. She never went out in the morning without him; while he invariably passed his evenings with her at home. She was all the world to him; he appeared to live only for her; and, as she had no companion save him and her governess, whose lips on the subject had been effectually sealed, she continued to live enveloped in a mystery, without even the prospect of its ever being solved. That, however, which appeared to her to be most strange, was the fact of her going, twice a year, with her father, to meet this lady, whom she never on any other occasion saw; and with whom she was permitted to remain but one hour. This did appear to her to be strange indeed. She had been instructed by her father to address her as Mrs. Greville; but he himself never saw her. Henriette invariably entered the room alone, and the moment she entered, Mrs. Greville would eagerly receive her in her arms, and while indulging in a passionate flood of tears, would kiss her, and bless her, and press her to her heart with the most intense affection. In person, Mrs. Greville was above the middle height: her features were regular and handsome, and, while her manners were extremely elegant, her figure was commanding; but she always appeared to be overwhelmed with grief, although the presence of Henriette seemed to inspire her with the most ecstatic joy. Often would Henriette inquire anxiously why she did not visit them—why they met there—why at those particular times, and so on; but Mrs. Greville, while the tears were gushing forth, would only answer that she was forbidden to explain—that she was indeed happy, most happy, to see her—that she loved her—dearly, passionately loved her—and that it was for her own happiness that she knew no more.

But even this was unknown in the village. It was not known even to the landlady of the inn, which was wisely ordered—wisely, because, had it been known to her, of course her curiosity would have been seriously diminished, and without curiosity, how could such ladies live and thrive?

Perhaps, however, Aunt Eleanor took more interest in the matter than any other person in the village. She knew not exactly why she should feel so much interest in an affair of this nature, but she nevertheless did; and hence, on being reminded that that was the day on which the parties in question met, she thought less of the mystery of the preceding night. She did, however, eventually allude to it, and that, too, in a most feeling strain, and the result was, that her reverend friend shook his head, and advised her to wait patiently, and to watch with diligence, albeit he knew no more what she was to watch for, than she knew what to suspect, or what design it was against which she ought to guard.

In the meantime, the village was in a state of commotion. The apparition of course had been variously described; and the gossips had so ingeniously improved upon each description, that it soon became a monster—twelve feet high. In the height of a ghost, a few feet, more or less, is a matter of very slight importance; but when to its height they had added their conceptions of its breadth, depth, and general deportment, the picture was truly appalling.

The gentlemen who had absolutely seen it, of course met early at the Crumpet and Crown. There was but one absent, and that was Mr. Pokey, before the door of whose residence chaff had been laid. It was the custom at that period, and in that part of the country, to strew chaff before the door of every gentleman who physically corrected his wife, chaff being held to be indicative of a threshing; but in this particular instance, it was strewn in consequence of the lady having corrected her husband, Mrs. Pokey being extremely indignant at the fact of Mr. Pokey having kept out so horribly late. The story of the ghost failed to tranquillise her spirit. She wouldn't believe it—which was very wrong, because Pokey declared that it was true upon his honour—she knew better—she wouldn't have it—hence she thrashed him, and hence she would not in the morning suffer him to stir from his board, for Mr. Pokey was a tailor of great celebrity in the village, and, withal, a perfect master of his needle.

But the absence of Mr. Pokey, although under the circumstances deeply regretted, was not allowed to operate as a check upon the vivid imagination of his friends. They entered into the matter with infinite spirit, and made the most that could be made of every important point.

But the cause of this mysterious appearance!—not one could divine the cause. That a murder had been committed by some one, was, by the majority, held to be clear; but who was the murderer—who was the most likely man in the village to commit such a crime? Who looked most like a murderer? They really couldn't say. They remembered that about five-and-twenty years before, a gentleman, who resided opposite, mysteriously disappeared with the amount of a whole quarter's poors'-rate. He might have been murdered. Who could tell? It was possible! It was moreover held to be possible by all, save one, and that one was Obadiah Drant, who expressed his conviction that that which they had seen was the spirit of a miser, who had then been dead about fifteen years, and in whose house only sixty guineas had been found, when every one supposed him to be worth as many thousands. He had not the slightest doubt of its being the spirit of that miser, which couldn't rest, because it didn't like the idea of leaving so much money undiscovered behind him. But this opinion was not subscribed to by the rest. Indeed, there was only one point upon which all were agreed, and that point was, that the spirit might, perchance, reappear that night. This every man present believed to be highly probable, and the consequence was, that they unanimously resolved to reassemble at night with the view of watching its manœuvres.

CHAPTER VI.

THE GHOST HUNT.

IN a village like Cotherstone, of which the inhabitants were tradesmen with plenty of time on their hands, labourers trained to thoughtless toil, and persons who, having retired from trade, were anxiously waiting to die, such an occurrence as that of the appearance of a ghost could not fail to create a sensation. Nor did it. Nor was the sensation thus created either slight or ephemeral; it was deep, very deep, and therefore lasting. There was not one in the village upon whom the ghost had not made a powerful impression. Even the exemplary wife of Mr. Pokey—who, during the whole of the morning, had been engaged upon a series of nice calculations, of which the result was, that as Pokey since his marriage had taken nearly five thousand ounces of snuff, and upwards of twenty-five thousand quarts of beer (beer enough to deluge the village, and snuff sufficient to fill up his grave), they would, had he saved the money thus squandered, have had more than five hundred pounds then to play with—even she, repudiating incredulity, became so excessively interested in the spirit that she actually allowed Mr. Pokey in the evening to go up again to the Crumpet and Crown.

And oh! what a theatre of excitement it was. Not only the party of the previous evening, but almost every man in the village was present; but although Mr. Pokey came late, and was, moreover, hailed on his arrival with significance, they, being unwilling to wound his private feelings, did not then allude to the chaff.

Obadiah, of course, was there, and he was as usual very dictatorial and deep; but he had one grand object to achieve—he had to justify his conduct on the preceding night. He admitted that that conduct was not indicative of bravery—he freely admitted that it was not exactly characterised by that peculiar boldness for which he was ardently anxious to become distinguished. "But," said he, with much point, "you must view this affair in all its fructifying ramifications. Place before me anything tangible—anything with which I can grapple, my boys—and then see how I'll act."

"But you didn't even speak to it," said Legge.

"Speak to it!" returned Obadiah. "Why, what's the good of speaking to a spirit?—what's the good of arguing with a ghost?—what principle, either moral, religious, social, political, or municipal, can you drive into the head of an apparition? Place brains before me—give me fructifying intelligence—give me Harry Brougham, or even Bobby Peel, my boys—and then you'd see how I'd go in; but the idea of speaking to a spectre—pooh! what's the good?"

By this ingenious species of ratiocination—this word is employed here in compliment to him, for ratiocination and fructification were the two stock weapons which he on all occasions used to defeat his opponents, and without which he couldn't well argue a point—he endeavoured to justify himself. But he didn't succeed. His friends attributed his silence in the churchyard to fear—they would not hear of its being ascribable to anything else; and when he found that he could not then shake this conviction, he, in order to subdue them for the time being, promised to show them that night what he *would* say, and how he would act in the event of the spirit's reappearance.

This grand point having been thus far settled, he reverted to politics, in which he knew, of course, that he was perfectly at home, and in possession of the ability to beat them hollow.

Of all highly influential men, there is not one more capable of commanding the attention of those who form the circle of which he is the centre, than a village politician. Nor would it be correct if there were, for what a patriot he is!—what a pure philanthropist!—nay, what a deeply indignant man! How profound is his political wisdom!—and how boldly he denounces the conduct of the party to whom he is, on principle, opposed! What rogues—what reckless, rampant rogues

—does he prove them to be! To his knowledge, what intrigues are they connected with—what flagrant follies are they guilty of—what *dead* robberies do they commit! In his view, with what tenacity do they stick to the property of the people!—how they batten on corruption!—how they live on pure plunder!—how richly they deserve to be hanged! With what fiery indignation does he declare them to be wretches!—how rotten, how venal, how utterly contemptible does he labour to make them all appear, when, to get a coat to make, or a boot to mend, he would take off his hat to the first he met. Precisely such a patriot was Obadiah Drant. But although he would denounce the aristocracy at night, and bow to them with all humility in the morning, it merely proved the force of example—he would boldly philippicise people of property, and bend low to get the smallest share; but as men envy only the possessors of that which they have not, this was merely the effect of education. He would, moreover, loudly declaim against rank, state, and splendour, and yet—

> "lick absurd pomp,
> And crook the pregnant hinges of the knee,
> That thrift might follow fawning;"

but that was a natural matter of business. He was a patriot, notwithstanding a tyrant and a slave, and was highly respected by those whom he met at the sign of the Crumpet and Crown.

But on this particular night he was singularly eloquent. He indeed surpassed himself. He explained what the Ministers ought to have done, and what he would have done had he been at the helm; he showed them how easily and how equitably *he* would have swept off the National Debt—how he would have settled the Currency question—how confidence and credit proved the nation's curse—how France should have been made directly tributary to England—how Russian ambition should have been levelled with the dust—how we should have countenanced American repudiation—and how a British colony *should* have been made of the Celestial Empire at once.

And thus he amused and amazed them all, until the hour had arrived at which the spirit was expected to reappear; when, summoning all the courage they had, they repaired to the quiet churchyard.

The night was clear. The moon was bright, and seemed to smile at the scene below; and while the stars merrily winked at each other, as if they enjoyed it too, the small white clouds in a playful spirit assumed shapes bearing the semblance of ghosts, and flew before the moon in the perfect conviction that she would at once cast their shadows to earth. But in this they were mistaken. The moon would do nothing at all of the sort. The light was not her own; it was but borrowed: and, therefore, she didn't feel justified in lending it for any such purpose to these little scamps.

Accordingly, no shadow appeared; and the party became quite bold. They even went right round the church! which was daring. They kept all together, it is true—not one of them would move without the rest—still they went completely round, and seemed to dare that or any other spectre to appear!—nay, on finding that nothing of the kind became visible, some began to treat the affair with contempt, and felt inclined to laugh, when Pokey, who had kept a remarkably sharp look-out, exclaimed—

"There!—there you are!—that's it!—there it is!"

And there it was!—a narrow tomb, surmounted by an urn about the size of a very thick head.

Being, however, utterly unconscious of this, and having their minds on the instant wrought up to a state fit to receive any frightful impression, they looked with terror at the object before them, and felt as if their time was come.

But then it didn't move!—this they held to be extraordinary: nor did it seem as if it intended to move:—which they thought more extraordinary still. That it was a ghost, no doubt existed; but the fact of its being a fixture beat them.

At length Click, the farrier, who was not a coward, proposed that they should approach it *en masse*, and this proposition was seconded by Legge; but as it was almost unanimously negatived, Click and Legge made up their minds to go together, and went, leaving their valiant friends trembling behind them. Long, however, before they had reached the object in view, they saw distinctly what it was; and Legge, on the impulse of the moment, was about to call out to them, but Click checked him promptly.

"Hold your tongue, Legge!" said he. "Now we'll have a game."

And he led him to the tomb and groaned deeply, and then led him back to his friends, who felt ill!

"Obadiah Drant," said Click, on his return, in the most solemn tone he could assume, "it wishes to speak with Obadiah Drant."

"With me?" cried Obadiah. "You don't mean with me?"

"With you!" returned Click, in an awful growl.

"No, no, no, no, I shan't go! not a bit of it! What does it want? I shan't go!"

"You MUST," growled Click, who instantly locked his arms in those of Obadiah, and carried him, *dos-à-dos*, towards the tomb.

But on the way, oh! how sharp were the strictly private feelings of this great man! He felt his heart sink deeper and deeper still at every step, and as the cold sweat bedewed his highly intellectual brow, he was half dead with "fructifying" fright. He did not even try to evade the iron grasp of Click, for Nature had taught him, in his early youth, the inutility of attempting that which he knew to be impossible: he rode on, a martyr to this eternal principle, and riding as he did—with his back towards the horrible object he was approaching—he gave himself up for lost.

"Behold!" exclaimed Click, on reaching the spot. "Behold!" and having uttered this awful exclamation, he turned sharply round, and presented the face of his terror-stricken load to the tomb.

Obadiah—who felt very faint—looked at the urn with an expression of despair, but, his eyes being veiled with a film of horror, he couldn't at first see what it was. Gradually, however, that film disappeared, and as it vanished, the changes which his countenance underwent were of the most extraordinary character perhaps ever beheld: but, even when he had become completely conscious of what it was—when he had touched the urn, and found that it was stone, and therefore knew that it was no ghost—although he felt a little better, his features expressed infelicity still.

"Mr. Click, sir," said he, between a sigh and a groan, "I'll never forgive you; I'll never forgive you."

Click, as he released him, laughed loudly, and continued to laugh; and as Legge had, in the interim, explained all to his friends, they approached the spot, and laughed loudly too. They were highly amused: they enjoyed it much: they were all, indeed, in most excellent spirits: but Obadiah was indignantly dumb. He viewed the contortions of Mr. Click and his disciples with disgust. As they pealed forth their merriment, and held their sides, and irreverently trampled upon the graves around to subdue the pain which the laughter created, he scowled at them all with refined disdain, and, contemning their practices, left them.

"This is your ghost, then, is it?" cried Click, when the laughter had somewhat subsided. "This is your fiery-eyed phantom, after all, then?"

"No," replied Legge, "we have been deceived by this, it is true; but this is not that which we saw last night. That was a spirit—a real spirit, if ever a spirit appeared upon earth."

"I don't believe it," retorted the incredulous Click; "nothing can make me believe it."

"But I saw it, I tell you! I saw it walk — I'm not exactly blind! I saw it pass my house, and go straight to the cottage."

"Let's go to the cottage now, then," interposed Pokey. "As it isn't here, I dare say we shall see it there. Let's go to the cottage."

"Ay—let's go!" exclaimed several of his friends; "let's all go together."

"You may go if you like," said Click, "but you don't catch *me* ghost-hunting again. I'll have no more of it. *I* shall go in and smoke a pipe, and so I tell you."

"Well, go—what's the odds?" cried Pokey, who had become extremely *valiant.* "I'll be bound to say we shall find our way without you. Come along, my Britons. Here we goes. Let them as is afeared stop behind, that's all."

They then boldly left the churchyard, led on by the courageous Pokey, and as they passed the Crumpet and Crown, Click and Legge turned in, but the rest went on to the cottage.

Here all was still. Not a sound was heard. The lights were out, and the blinds were down. But as they stood before the gate they fancied they saw the curtains move.

"It's in there, now," said Pokey to Quocks; "depend upon it, it's in there, now."

"I cert'ney see something," said Quocks. And the friends around him saw something; but what that something was, they wouldn't undertake to say, although, at any other time, they would have sworn, and safely too, that it was really a white curtain, and nothing else. But then fancy converted that curtain into all sorts of shapes, and as ghosts are white by prescription, it so far resembled a ghost, while the difficulty experienced in conceiving a head, was, under the circumstances, small.

"Do you see it?" "Yes: what?" "There it is, you fool!" "Oh!" "There's the head." "That the head?" "To be sure." "Where's the tail?" "What tail?" "What *tail*?" "Oh!" "Ah!" "No doubt."

This is a very fair epitome of the sentiments expressed, when Aunt Eleanor, hearing a most extraordinary buzz about the premises, slipped out of bed with the view of ascertaining whence it proceeded; but the moment she drew the white curtain aside, and appeared in her night-dress before them, the effect was electric! Her appearance alone inspired them with terror! But when she proceeded to open the window, for the purpose of asking them what it all meant, even as affrighted sheep follow their leader, so did they follow the valiant Pokey, who did instantaneously take to his heels.

In vain she called on them to stop. They didn't like to do it. "What do you want, my good people?" she cried. "What on earth *do* you all want?"

They heard her; but, conceiving the voice to be that of some fiend, they went right on; nor did they stop until they arrived at the Crumpet and Crown.

"Have you seen it?" cried Legge, as they rushed in wildly.

"Yes!" replied Pokey, panting for breath. "At the cottage—it's there!"

"I don't believe a word of it," said Click; "it's all stuff."

"Well, go and look for yourself," cried Pokey; "that's all. There it is at the window!"

"Is it there now?"

"If it isn't I'll forfeit a couple of gallons."

"Good," said Click. "Legge and I will go at once. You had better come with us."

"I!" exclaimed Pokey.

"To be satisfied, of course!"

"Well, we don't want to go very near?"

"Oh no; just come with us." And Pokey did go with them; but long before they had reached the gate, he stopped, and cried, pointing to the window—"There—there! There it is! Don't you see it?"

They looked, and certainly did see something: they saw something move: they, moreover, heard a voice: and the voice did proceed from that window.

"Let us go a little nearer," said Click, who at that moment didn't feel exactly the thing; his heart didn't beat with its accustomed regularity; it thumped and stopped, and blundered about, as if it didn't care whether it worked or not; but as he wasn't inspired with absolute fear, they went a little nearer, and as they approached, Aunt Eleanor, who knew Legge well by his arms, which he at all times swung in a most extraordinary fashion, cried out—"Is that you, Mr. Legge?"

"Yes, ma'am," replied Legge promptly, for he knew the voice in an instant. "Is there anything amiss, ma'am?"

"What, in the name of goodness, did those persons want here just now?"

"They thought they saw a ghost, ma'am."

"Ridiculous! I really have no patience with such folly."

"I know," observed Pokey, "that something appeared, and at that very window, too."

"'Twas I, you simple man," said Aunt Eleanor. "You saw me appear at the window. I'm ashamed of you. Tell them from me, Mr. Legge, that if they come here again, I'll have them all taken up: they shall all be punished: I will not submit to be thus annoyed. Good-night."

She then retired from the window, and they, being quite satisfied, returned to their friends; the whole of whom felt exceedingly mortified on learning, not only that they had been thus deceived, but that they had been the cause of annoyance to a lady, who had been so kind to the poor around, and to whom the whole village had reason to be grateful.

They, notwithstanding, had Pokey's two gallons in; and Click, in order to heal the deep wounds he had inflicted upon the feelings of Obadiah, ordered two gallons more, but Obadiah again and again declared he'd never forgive him: nor when the party at midnight broke up had a reconciliation between those two gentlemen been effected.

CHAPTER VII.

THE PICKLED SMALLS.

Upon those who live in the midst of excitement, who not only feel the world's buffets themselves, but see the world buffeting all around them—whose lives are one perpetual struggle—whose career is a series of ups and downs—who are constantly compelled to be on the *qui vive*—who, from morning till night, and from year to year, are engaged in overcoming those barriers by which their progress in life is impeded—who, either to amass wealth, or to gain a mere subsistence, have their minds continually on the stretch— who are surrounded by difficulties springing, not only from honourable competition, but from trickery, malignity, and envy—who are thwarted at every step—who are opposed at every point, and have to dodge through the world, which is to them one huge labyrinth, out of which they scarcely know how to get with honour—troubles of an unimportant caste make but little impression, for they really have not time to think much about them; but they, whose lives are passed in an almost perpetual calm—who live but to live—who have a competence which secures to them comfort—who have nothing but tranquillity around them—nothing to prepare for in this world but the next—whose course is clear, whose career is smooth—who experience neither ups nor downs—who live on, and on, in the spirit of peace, hoping for peace hereafter—who know but little of life, or its vicissitudes—who have nothing to oppose their progress—no difficulties to surmount, no barriers to break down, no competition to encounter, no struggling, no straining, no manœuvring—they magnify every cause of vexation by dwelling upon it, brooding over it, and making it the germ of a thousand conceptions, as if anxious to ascertain what monstrous fruit it can thus be imagined to bear.

The impression, however, is not intended to be conveyed that the difficulties which beset Aunt Eleanor at this period were small: the object proposed is merely to show that, however great they might be, they were perfectly sure to be magnified, seeing that she had never had but one important trouble, and that, with this exception—the nature of which will be hereafter explained—her whole life had been characterised by an almost uninterrupted flow of tranquillity. But, even if this had not been shown, it would scarcely have been deemed, under the circumstances, extraordinary, that these occurrences — for which she could not in any way account—should have seriously interfered with her spirit's peace.

But these annoyances were not all she had been doomed to endure. In the morning, when Mary went to assist her to dress, she went, fraught with another mysterious cause of vexation.

"Oh, ma'am!" she exclaimed, "there's been such goings on! Oh! I never did see, ma'am! The things is all turned topsy-turvy. The picturs, cheers, everything. Oh! it is horrid."

"What is it you mean, Mary?"

"Oh, ma'am! only jist come downstairs, ma'am; that's all."

"But what do you mean?"

"There's been thieves in the house, ma'am! But do come and see. Jist slip on your things, ma'am, and only jist look at the horrid upset."

Aunt Eleanor did slip on her things, and on reaching the door of her favourite parlour, beheld a scene of unexampled confusion. Everything had been displaced. The tables had been turned upside down, and the chairs piled ingeniously upon them: the pictures had been taken from the walls and placed round the room upon the carpet: the vases, the lambs, dogs, lions, and tigers, had been removed from the mantel-piece to the couch: the china and glass had been taken from the sideboard, and arranged fantastically upon the piano, while, in order to compromise the matter with the sideboard, the hearth-rug, coal-scuttle, fire-irons, and fender had been in due form placed upon it; but nothing had been broken— nothing even injured!

Aunt Eleanor gazed for a few moments upon this most extraordinary state of things in silence; but having at length observed calmly that it demanded minute investigation, she locked the door, and taking the key with her, returned to her chamber to dress.

Here she tranquilly turned the thing over in her mind, and having viewed it in connection with the ghost-hunting party, she resolved on sending for her reverend friend, with the view of placing the matter before him.

In pursuance of this resolution, she, on descending to the breakfast-room, opened her desk and proceeded to write a note to the reverend gentleman: but she had scarcely commenced it, when Mary appeared, and having informed her that neither bread, butter, eggs, nor ham could be found, inquired not only what *was* to become of them, but what was to be done?

"Can you not find enough for breakfast?"

"Lor' bless you, ma'am, they haven't left a mite!"

Aunt Eleanor pressed her lips closely together, and finished the note; and, while folding it, said—

"Light the taper, Mary; and then desire Judkins to come here."

"Judkins, ma'am, can't get up yet," replied Mary.

"Why not! Is he ill?"

"No, ma'am, he isn't *ill*."

"Why, then, can he not get up?"

"Because, ma'am, they've taken away all his things."

"Good gracious! What next shall I hear! Well, put on your bonnet, and take this note, and bring in with you what we require for breakfast."

The note being sealed, Mary left the room, and Sylvester soon after entered the room; and when his aunt, as usual, had kissed him, and expressed her fond hope that he was well, she proceeded to explain to him what had occurred, and thereby to fill him with utter amazement.

"My dear aunt," said he, "what can it all mean?"

"Heaven only knows! I cannot even conjecture. But just come with me, dear, and look at the things. There," she added, on opening the parlour door, "did you ever see a room in such a state of confusion?"

Sylvester looked, and really felt, quite astonished.

"You see," she continued, "there's not a single thing in its place."

"But what *could* have been their object?" said Sylvester.

"The things are disarranged, it is true, but they appear to have disturbed them with great consideration. I cannot conceive what their motive could have been."

"Nor can I; unless, indeed, it were merely to annoy me."

"I should say that had that been their object they would

never have removed them with so much care. The things have not been thrown together, you perceive; it has been a work of time. Look at this china and glass; there is some little taste, you perceive, displayed in the arrangement."

"I do not admire the taste displayed, but they certainly have been most carefully handled. But that, my dear, which annoys me more than all, is the fact of my being unable to imagine, not only who did it, but how it was done. I should say myself that thieves have not been in the house. I miss nothing here. The only things which have disappeared, with the exception of the bread, butter, eggs, and ham, are the clothes of poor Judkins."

"Are they gone? Well, that is strange."

"And especially as there are many things much more portable and infinitely more valuable here: that timepiece, for instance, is worth thirty pounds. However, not a thing shall be touched until Mr. Rouse comes. I'll have the whole matter investigated fully."

She then returned to the breakfast-room, and Sylvester went up to Judkins, whom he found still in bed, for he hadn't a thing to put on.

"Why, how is this, Judkins?" said Sylvester, as he entered; "I hear that you have lost all your clothes."

"Every rag—every individual rag," replied Judkins; "I haven't a mite of anything to put on. I shouldn't have cared if they'd only just left me a pair of breeches; but, blarm 'em, to take away the lot was ondecent."

"Didn't you hear them at all?"

"I only wish for their sakes I had, I'd ha' cooked the goose of one or two of 'em, I'll warrant. It's worse than highway robbery, ten times over. I'd ha' forgiven 'em if they'd stopped me on the road, but to crawl in and steal a man's clothes clandestinely when he's asleep is the warmintest proceeding I ever heered tell on."

"Well, how do you mean to manage? Shall I run to the tailor for you?"

"No, I thank you, sir. Mary's just gone to the parson's gardener to ask *him* to lend me a pair of breeches and a waistcoat; but I don't know whether he will or not, I'm sure."

"My trousers, I suppose, will not fit you?"

"Lor' bless you, I should split 'em all to ribbons; I couldn't get my arms in. Blister 'em; all I wonder at is they didn't take off my shirt. They *have* got my stockings. Shouldn't I like to catch 'em. If ever I do come across 'em, I wish 'em success."

Mary now came to the door with a bundle, for Jones, having heard the whole matter explained, had opened his heart and sent the clothes; and when Sylvester had handed them over to Judkins, he left him to rejoin his aunt.

While at breakfast they, of course, spoke of nothing, thought of nothing, but the confusion so mysteriously created; but the more they endeavoured to guess the cause, the more deeply involved they became. They had scarcely, however, finished their repast, when the reverend gentleman arrived; and when, with a look which denoted concern, he had greeted them with all his characteristic cordiality, Aunt Eleanor eloquently laid the case before him, connecting it ingeniously with the ghost-hunting party who appeared before her cottage the preceding night—and then asked him what he thought of the matter as it stood, and what course he imagined she ought to pursue.

Now the Reverend Mr. Rouse was a man of the world—that is to say, a man of the world in which he lived—a man possessing a most profound knowledge of the sphere in which he moved; he was a man of observation, as well as a man of reflection, and while his perceptive faculties were strong, he was conversant with, although unable to discover the etymology of, certain idioms which were constantly used by those around him. He knew, for example, what was meant by "a spree;" he moreover knew perfectly the meaning of "a lark;" he knew not whence they were derived, it is true—albeit he strongly inclined to the belief that they had one and the same Greek root—but being thus cognisant of their modern definition, he, after a pause, during which he reflected deeply, said, with all the solemnity which the nature and importance of the words demanded, "Will you do me the favour to send for Legge?"

"Certainly, my dear sir," replied Aunt Eleanor, who turned and rang the bell on the instant. "Mary," she added, when the servant appeared, "as Judkins is busy, run and ask Mr. Legge to step over."

"Tell him I desire that he will come immediately," added the pastor, with all that humility by which the order to which he belonged was at that particular period distinguished; and when Mary had left, he in silence proceeded to rehearse that highly important part which it was his intention to perform.

Legge, who was a man of business, and who, by virtue of attending to that business, was doing very well at the Crumpet and Crown, received Mary with his customary custom-winning smile; but when she had delivered not only her mistress's message, but that which the reverend gentleman had sent, his features assumed an expression of thought, and he said, as he passed his hand over his chin, "I wonder now what's in the wind?"

"You'll hear all about it," returned Mary promptly; "but do make haste, for they're anxious, I know."

Mrs. Legge then spoke to Mary, and asked her how she found herself, and pressed her to have a glass of wine, and got her into the bar, and then *made* her have one; and during Legge's progress to the cottage, got out of her all she knew, and more.

The reverend gentleman having decided upon a course, of which the pursuit he thought would have a somewhat stunning effect, assumed a position of great importance as Legge entered the room, and addressed him in tones indicative of that authority with which he felt doubly invested.

"Mr. Legge," said he, with an expression of severity, "I am sorry, Mr. Legge, that I have so much cause to complain of your keeping a disorderly house."

"A disorderly house, sir?" cried Legge.

"Yes, sir," retorted the reverend gentleman; "a disorderly house—for disorderly every house must be, if it be not conducted with propriety and decorum."

"I beg pardon, sir; but really, I never heard before that I kept a disorderly house."

"I say, sir, that it is a disorderly house, and I warn you that, as a disorderly house, it shall be indicted, if the scenes —the disgraceful scenes which are to be witnessed there—be not discontinued."

"What scenes? What disgraceful scenes?" demanded Legge, who, conscious of the propriety of his own conduct, and the consequent fair reputation of his house, began to feel indignant. "What scenes are to be witnessed there?"

"Scenes, sir, of riot and debauchery; scenes"——

"I deny it."

"Silence, sir; how dare you interrupt me?"

"Dare! I'm a plain, blunt man, sir, and will *not* be silent when I hear myself falsely denounced. I am not a clergyman: I do not preach humility and practise tyranny: I am the mere keeper of a public-house; I was not always in that position, but even as I am, I defy the world to prove that my conduct has not been straightforward and just. I am also the father of a family, and my children, you *know*, I have endeavoured to rear in the principles of virtue, morality, and religion. You know this: you know that I would neither set them a bad example myself, nor suffer a bad example to be set them by others; and am I then, by you, sir, to be told, not only that I keep a disreputable house, but "——

"I did not say a disreputable house."

"You said a *disorderly* house."

"I did; but not in your sense, disorderly. All I meant to say was, that occasional scenes of disorder occurred."

"Why, of course they do. Where is there a house of that description in which scenes of disorder do *not* occur occasionally? But is it, therefore, to be called a disorderly house?—a house to be indicted?"

"You keep bad hours, sir; you cannot deny that!"

"Occasionally we are compelled to be rather late, but in general we close between ten and eleven."

"The house, sir, was not closed at twelve last night."

"I am aware of it; but that was under extraordinary circumstances."

"It is to that point we would come," interposed Aunt Eleanor, who, although she had been silent, didn't at all like her reverend friend's mode of proceeding. "We wish to speak of that solely, Mr. Legge. You had a party last night, and that party, or a number of those persons who composed that party, appeared before the gate of my cottage at midnight. We wish, Mr. Legge, to know the motives of those persons; that is the point at which we are anxious to arrive."

"Exactly," added the reverend gentleman; "that *is* the point. Now, sir, what were their motives?"

"I know but of one," replied Legge.

"Ay, that is the ghost story: that we have heard. But do you not know that their principal object, sir, was to annoy this lady?"

"No, sir; on the contrary, I know that it was not. There is not a man amongst them, sir, by whom she is not respected. She is too kind—too good, sir, to be annoyed wantonly by them."

"Then, do you mean to say, Mr. Legge, that you don't know that some of those persons burglariously entered this cottage last night?"

"Entered this cottage?"

"Ay, sir! That is the question. Do you, or do you not, know that fact?"

"Most certainly I do not. Nor do I believe it to be a fact. Why, sir, there isn't one of them, who—leaving inclination out of the question entirely—would, under the circumstances, have *dared*, sir, to enter the cottage!"

"Very well. You are entitled to the full benefit of this opinion; but I'll now just trouble you to look at the state of this room."

The reverend gentleman then rose, and, accompanied by Sylvester and his aunt, proceeded to the parlour, duly followed by Legge, who, as he entered, looked around the room utterly astonished.

"You have, indeed, been annoyed, ma'am," at length he observed, "and I'm very sorry for it; but I'm sure—quite sure—that this was not done by either of those men."

"These things," said the reverend gentleman, "could not have been removed without hands."

"Nor could they have been removed in haste," rejoined Legge. "Were the doors broken open, ma'am?"

"No! all seemed secure in the morning! How ever they got in, I can't imagine."

"Do you think, ma'am, it's likely that any one got in?"

"What else am I to think, Mr. Legge?"

"I ought not perhaps to offer any suggestion."

"Oh, I do hope that you will, for the affair is now so involved in mystery, that if you could throw any light upon the subject I should feel indeed grateful."

"Well, ma'am, of course I don't know that I can; but you have a gardener, and that gardener sleeps in the house. Now, I should be very sorry, even to throw out a hint that would tend to injure any man breathing, but as I know what servants are, and what quarrels—petty quarrels—they have occasionally among themselves, I would suggest that it is possible—just possible—that the gardener, during the night, thus carefully displaced these things—not with any wicked object in view—but merely for the purpose of annoying the maids."

"A very proper suggestion," observed the reverend gentleman, who, finding that stilts wouldn't do, came down. "Very proper, indeed. It is possible: nay, highly probable."

"But," observed Sylvester, "Judkins has lost all his clothes!"

"Have you lost anything of value, ma'am?—anything out of this room?" inquired Legge.

"Not a single thing! Oh! by-the-bye," she added, "where's the silver tankard?"

They looked round the room—it was not to be seen, nor could they see the salver upon which it had stood. Presently, however, the reverend gentleman, perceiving something under the couch, removed it, and there found, not only the tankard and salver, but the bread, butter, ham, and a bundle of clothes, which were instantly known to belong to Judkins!

This altered at once the complexion of things. It was then quite clear to them all that this confusion had been created with no felonious intention; and as it was plain that no entrance had been forced, Aunt Eleanor, as well as her reverend friend, felt convinced, that with the motive assigned by Legge, the things had been thus disturbed by Judkins.

Legge, however, now had a doubt on the subject, and gave Judkins the benefit of that doubt without delay. "I do not," said he, "think it was the gardener now."

"Oh!" cried the pastor, "the case is clear against him. Look at his clothes. How came they here?"

"The very fact," returned Legge, "of their being here, tends to convince me that he is not, after all, the man. I think that if he had done it, he would not have left his clothes—for I do not believe that he has sufficient art to leave them in order that all suspicion might be removed, on the ground that no man, in his senses, would thus convict himself. If he left them at all, he could only have left them for the purpose of having it said, 'Oh, it couldn't have been him: he would never have been such a fool!' and I do not think that he is artful enough for that."

"There's no telling," observed the reverend gentleman.

"Really, the world has got to such a pitch that there's no such thing as knowing the human heart at all."

"But," said Aunt Eleanor, "if it were *not* Judkins, who on earth could it have been?"

"I can't imagine," returned Legge; "still I would not too hastily condemn him. All I can say is, that this was not done by any one of the party at my house last night."

"I believe it," said Aunt Eleanor; "firmly believe it."

"And so do I now," observed the reverend gentleman. "I did at first think that they had done it by way of a frolic, which, in the house of a lady, would have been of course disgraceful. However, as it is, I recall those observations which I made with respect to your house, but I do hope that you will in future keep good hours."

Aunt Eleanor now got out the wine, and requested Legge to help himself, which he, as a matter of course, did; but just as he had filled his glass, Mary came into the room exclaiming—"We've found the eggs, ma'am; but oh! in such a place!"

"Where did you find them?" demanded her mistress.

"In the pickle-tub, ma'am."

"In the pickle-tub?"

"Yes, ma'am; as cook was fishing for a tongue, what should she find but the eggs tied up in an old pair of Judkins's"——

Here she stopped and blushed, and Aunt Eleanor blushed too, and the reverend gentleman turned to smile, but Legge, who had just got his mouth full of sherry, didn't know at all how to get rid of it. He blew out his cheeks, and grunted, and strained, while his face became crimson, and every vein visible seemed in a fit state to burst, until, at length, he made a desperate effort to gulp it, but, as a portion of it went "the wrong way," that portion found out its mistake, and returned, and by virtue of returning thus, caused him to spirt and to cough with unparalleled violence. This was annoying, but he really couldn't help it. Aunt Eleanor knew that he couldn't, and therefore, in order to relieve him from embarrassment, appeared to be unconscious of the circumstance entirely, and, turning to Mary, said to her—"Has cook been quarrelling with Judkins?"

"No, ma'am: they've had a few words, but not about anything particular!"

"Very good," said her mistress; "you can now leave the

room. It is," she added, when Mary had left, "it is, I apprehend, as you suggested, Mr. Legge. These people, no doubt, have been quarrelling, and their object has been to annoy each other. This, however, must be ascertained. But have another glass of wine, Mr. Legge."

Legge was almost afraid, but he took another glass, and managed to drink it with proper effect, and, when Aunt Eleanor had thanked him for his attention, and the reverend gentleman had playfully entreated him to let him know immediately the "ghost" reappeared, he bowed, and left them to contemplate the case as it stood, and to devise the means of gaining the knowledge desired.

Now, while he was thus engaged at the cottage, Mrs. Legge —having ascertained from Mary the substance of all that had occurred, with the simple exception of the eggs being found in that peculiar envelope—had, as a natural matter of course, been retailing the circumstances to all who came, among whom were Mr. Pokey, Mr. Obadiah Drant, Mr. Click, Mr. Quocks, and Mr. Bobber. When, therefore, Legge returned, their anxiety to learn the minutiæ of that of which they had heard but the outline, was intense. They crowded round him, and urged him to begin at the beginning, and pressed him to drink, that he might open more freely; but Legge having whispered to his wife, assumed an expression of mortification, and sat down in silence.

"Why, what is the matter? What's wrong?" inquired Pokey. But Legge returned no answer.

"If there's anything fructifying in your mind, unpleasant," said Obadiah, "out with it, my boy, like a Briton!"

"Who," demanded Legge, with feigned ferocity, "who broke into the Grange Cottage last night?"

"I didn't," said Pokey, "so that's enough for me."

"They who did," said Obadiah, "ought to be served as they used to serve them in Nova Scotia, in the time of Julius Cæsar, and Peter the Great!"

"But was it broken into?" said Click.

"She sent for me, as you have heard, and there were the things! I never in my life witnessed such a scene of confusion. The parson was there, and he told me at once that he should indict me for keeping a disorderly house!"

"The parson! pooh!" exclaimed Obadiah. "Don't they draw nine-and-twenty millions of money, annually, every year, from the vitals of the people ? What do they want more ? Look at the ecclesiastical swindle exposed by Joey Hume ! Could Bobby Peel defend it ? Look, again, at Charley Buller's motion, that was backed by Tommy Duncombe ! Do you mean to tell me "——

" But," interrupted Click, "*was* the cottage broken into last night ? "

" Why, that's involved in mystery," replied Legge ; " no locks appear to have been broken, but, as Mr. Rouse said "——

" Who cares for Teddy Rouse ? " cried Obadiah ; " who cares for the cloth to which Teddy Rouse belongs ? They are what I call the locusts of liberty ! "

" As he said," continued Legge, " the things couldn't have been thus disturbed without hands. And now Pokey will have to prove that *he* didn't disturb them."

" I ! " exclaimed Pokey. " Why do they pitch upon me ? "

" Mrs. Sound saw you near the premises. That's strong circumstantial evidence. You were there twice, which makes the case stronger. The bottom of it is, you're in a mess ! "

" But I'll take my oath "——

" That you'll not be suffered to do. Mind you, *I* don't say that you are the man that broke in, you will recollect that. *I* shall give no evidence against you ; but it strikes me you'd better prepare for your defence."

" I remember," observed Obadiah, "I remember that, during the French Revolution "——

" Blister the French Revolution ! " cried Pokey, who began to feel very much alarmed. " What's the French Revolution to this ? But are you serious, Mr. Legge ? Really, now, are you serious ? "

" Serious ! It isn't a thing to joke about, *I* can tell you. You'd better leave the place till the matter blows over."

" *I* can't leave the place. How can I leave ? I've no less than four pair of breeches in hand ! "

In an instant Legge, unable to control himself, sent forth a loud peal of laughter, and as Click, Bobber, Quocks, and Obadiah perceived that he had only been frightening Pokey, they, to some extent, joined him ; but when he had explained the real cause of his mirth—when he had told them of the eggs being found in the pickle-tub, tied up in Judkins's smalls— they opened their shoulders, and set up a roar which might have been heard at the cottage. Nor was this ebullition of merriment transitory. Peal after peal did they send forth in raptures, now holding their ribs in, and calling out with pain, and then bursting forth again with fresh vigour, until two or three of them became so exhausted that, had not the chairs been established in a row, they really must have rolled on the ground.

"Was the eggs smashed?" cried Pokey, in the midst of this scene. And again they broke loose, though in agony. "I've heered of pickled injuns," he added, and this was the signal for another loud roar, "but pickled breeches," he continued, "pick—pickled"—— Being utterly unable to finish this sentence, he threw himself down on the mat, and panted.

As the thunder succeeds the lightning's flash, so did a roar on this occasion succeed every sentence that was uttered, whether witty or not; but as men cannot even laugh for ever, they at length became sufficiently worn out to sit down in a state of comparative tranquillity.

Legge then explained to them what he had suggested, and they then saw, with perfect distinctness, that a quarrel between Judkins and cook had been the origin of it all. They, moreover, thought it a very fair match; but confessed that cook then had, decidedly, the best of it, seeing that Judkins had done nothing equal to her *assumed* feat of pickling the smalls.

CHAPTER VIII.

ROSALIE.

THE pagans had a little swell whom they called the god of laughter. His name was Comus; and he was fat, as a perfectly natural matter of course. He didn't do much—they who laugh much, very seldom do—but, notwithstanding, in his day he was popular among the pagans. Very good. Now, there are, of course, various species of laughter. There's the natural laugh, the hysterical laugh, the hypocritical laugh, and the laugh of the idiot; but the natural laugh is the only laugh which springs absolutely from pleasure. Comus had a natural laugh, and he was, therefore, fat. Why, what an immense field does this open for the philanthropist to contemplate! Cæsar—who wasn't a fool—didn't like Cassius, because he was lean. If this and that be put together, to what will they amount! Momus—not Comus, but Momus—censured Vulcan for making a man without a window in his breast, that his ill designs and treacheries might be seen, which was all very well; but what necessity, even in that poetic age, would there have been for this window, had a social and political Fatometer obtained? And how infinitely more valuable would it be now—how society would be simplified by virtue of its introduction! Fat is the natural fruit of laughter: natural laughter springs from pleasure: pleasure is derived from happiness: happiness from goodness, and goodness comprehends all the virtues. That is one side of the question: now look at the other. Who ever saw a really laughter-loving man thin? No one. And why? Because laughter opens the shoulders—expands the chest—strengthens and increases the size of the lungs, and thus generates fat. Leanness, then, denotes the absence of laughter; the absence of laughter, the absence of pleasure; the absence of pleasure, the absence of happiness; the absence of happiness, the absence of goodness; and the absence of goodness, the absence of all the virtues. Who—had they been contemporaries—who would not have trusted Daniel Lambert—a man of one-doesn't-know-how-many stone—in preference to Monsieur—what was his name—the Living Skeleton? Let a Fatometer be established, that the amiable fat ones may be caressed, and the treacherous lean ones avoided! Let a standard of fat be fixed; and, as the crafty and designing can never hope to reach it, society will be all the purer.

Now, it is the peculiar province of an author to be cognisant of the most secret thoughts, not only of his heroes and heroines, but of every person whom he introduces to the world. Hence it is that he is held responsible for those introductions—and very properly too; but it would not be fair to attach to him this responsibility were his liberty restrained. For example—he is allowed to follow a lady into her very chamber, and to contemplate her most private thoughts, even while she is there, which would be, under any other circumstances, highly incorrect. The lady herself wouldn't allow it; and, even if she had no great objection, by society it would not, it *could* not, be sanctioned. These remarks are held to be necessary as a sort of an apology, or rather as a species of justification, seeing that it has now to be stated that Aunt Eleanor, immediately after Legge had left the cottage, excused herself to her reverend friend, and went direct to her chamber to have a hearty laugh. And she did laugh heartily, and, therefore, very naturally. She loved to laugh, and hence was fat—that is to say, she had reached that standard which ought, for ladies thus circumstanced, to be universally set up. It is no sufficient argument against the establishment of this standard that they who love to laugh are not at all times happy. The *acmé* of pleasure, for instance, consists in being entirely free from pain; but where are we to find the *acmé* of pleasure, seeing that pleasure and pain are twins? Even Aunt Eleanor, who loved to laugh as well as any lady in the county, was not without troubles, albeit they were few; and even while she was laughing in her chamber, she thought of that mystery which had not yet been solved. Feeling, however, then, that she had something like a clue to its solution, her mind was more tranquil, and when she had become, in her judgment, sufficiently composed, she returned to the reverend gentleman, who suggested that they should at once ascertain the cause beyond doubt; and the immediate consequence of this suggestion was that Judkins was duly summoned.

"Judkins," she observed, with the most perfect composure, "the questions which I am now about to put to you I hope you will answer with truth."

"Cert'ney, ma'am—cert'ney."

"In the first place, then, I have to ask how you account for that extraordinary confusion in the parlour?"

"It's my opinion, ma'am, that the place is bewitched, that's my opinion."

"Judkins, what time did you go to bed last night?"

"About half-past ten, ma'am."

"And what time did you rise?"

"About nine, ma'am. I couldn't get up before, because of my clothes."

"Were you in the room the whole of the time?"

"Yes, ma'am."

"You didn't once leave it, from half-past ten last night until nine o'clock this morning?"

"No, ma'am."

"Are you quite sure of that?"

"Quite."

"Judkins, if I discover that you are not telling me the truth, I will immediately discharge you; but if, repudiating falsehood, you confess to me now that those things in the parlour were disturbed by you "——

"By me, ma'am!" cried Judkins, in a state of astonishment; "*I* disturb the things, ma'am?"

"I have reason to suspect that they *were* disturbed by you."

"Why, I wasn't out of bed, ma'am, the whole livelong night! Besides, why should I disturb them?"

"To annoy cook and Mary. You are not on the most friendly terms, I believe, with either."

"Oh, I don't know, ma'am; I never interfere with 'em. Mary's well enough, but cook's a cook, and you know what cooks is—they're *all* alike. But if they was the very last words I had to speak, ma'am, I'd say I didn't touch them things."

"Judkins, I am at present bound to believe you; but if I find that you have been telling me a falsehood, I will on the instant discharge you!"

"You'll never find that, ma'am, I know; but I suppose, ma'am, that cook's been saying something against me?"

"No, not a word; nor have I at present spoken a word to her on the subject. But desire her to come to me now. The matter must not be allowed to rest here."

Judkins then left the room, and both his mistress and the reverend gentleman felt that he was innocent; while Sylvester, who had been watching the proceedings in silence, declared his *conviction* that Judkins was not the man, and pointed out the utter improbability of his having disturbed the things with the view of annoying cook, seeing that it was not cook's province to replace them. Aunt Eleanor, however, having commenced the investigation, felt bound to proceed, and awaited with composure the appearance of cook, who, on entering the room, felt somewhat flurried.

"Cook," said her mistress, "have you and Judkins been quarrelling?"

"No, ma'am."

"There have been no words between you of an unpleasant nature?"

"Nothing that can be called words, ma'am; only, so sure as I ask him for taters, or turnups, or carrots, or inguns, or salary, or anything in respect of that, so sure he won't bring 'em till the very lastest minute, though I ask him over and over and over and over again. There was only the other day—now, ma'am, only jist to show you "——

"I do not wish," said Aunt Eleanor, "to hear any tales, cook, of that description."

"No, ma'am, I know; but then it puts me in a orkard predicament, as I told him, no longer ago than yesterday. 'Judkins,' says I, 'you know,' says I, 'it isn't my place,' says I, 'to go,' says I, 'pottering about in that garden; and I'm sure,' says I, 'that if missis,' says I, 'was to know it'"——

"All I asked was, whether he and you had been quarrelling—whether, in short, you desired to annoy him?"

"Annoy him, ma'am!—*I* want to annoy him? Then he's been a telling you, ma'am, I want to annoy him, ma'am, has he?"

"No, cook; but answer my question plainly: have you had any *wish* to annoy him?"

"Not I, ma'am!—no, ma'am!"

"Then how do you account for the fact of his clothes being found where they were?"

"*I*, ma'am, account? What, then, has he been a saying that I put 'em there?"

"He has been saying nothing of the sort, cook. I asked you how you accounted for the circumstance?"

"Account for it, ma'am? I can only say it's my belief the house is wholly haunted! If it isn't, ma'am, it's very strange to me! As I said to Mary this blessed morning, 'Mary,' says I"——

"But, cook," said Aunt Eleanor, promptly checking this natural flow of eloquence, "for what purpose did you happen to go to the pickle-tub this morning?"

"I went, ma'am, 'cause, as the ham was gone, I thought I'd bile a tongue. But does he have the imperance to think, ma'am, that I put his clothes there? Where was his clothes, ma'am? In course, in his bedroom! And does he mean to have the howdaciousness to insinivate"——

"He has insinuated nothing of the kind. But by whom do you imagine they *were* put there?"

"I haven't, ma'am, so much as a idea."

"Then, cook, I'm to understand that you can throw no light whatever on the subject?"

"Not the leastest in the world, ma'am!"

F

"Very well; then I have nothing more to say to you at present."

Cook then, although with manifest reluctance, retired; and as she was instantly acquitted of all participation, the mystery resumed its original character. Neither Sylvester, his aunt, nor their reverend friend, could imagine another clue. Even the power to conjecture seemed lost. Neither could suggest—neither could conceive—the slightest means whereby that mystery might be solved.

"We must still," said the reverend gentleman at length, "we must still have patience. Time alone can bring this strange matter to light: and that it will be brought to light, I have not the slightest doubt. We must, therefore, my dear madam, still have patience."

Patience! What an admirable attribute is patience! How sweet are its influences—how softening its effects! In the hour of affliction, how beautiful, how calm, how serene, how sublime is patience! Behold the afflicted, racked with pain, from which Death alone can relieve them. By what are they sustained but by that sweet patience which springs from faith and hope! Patience, ever lovely, shows loveliest then. But who ever met with passive patience co-existing with active suspense? We may endure affliction the most poignant with patience—but we cannot with patience endure suspense. The knowledge of the worst that can befall us may be borne with patience—but patience will hold no communion with our ignorance of that which we are ardently anxious to know. Aunt Eleanor, for example, had she known that the smalls had been put into the pickle-tub by cook, and that Judkins had upset the things in the parlour —nay, had she even known that Mr. Pokey and his companions, or any other gentleman and *his* companions, had actually entered the cottage—she would have endured that knowledge with patience; but as she was utterly ignorant of everything connected with the origin of these mysterious proceedings—as she neither knew what had induced them, nor had the power even to guess the cause to which alone they could have been fairly ascribed—patience was altogether out of the question. Hers was essentially a state of suspense, with which patience had nothing whatever to do.

Still it was, notwithstanding this, all very well for her reverend friend to recommend it: it was, in fact, his province to do so; for having studied deeply the Book of Job, he held patience to be one of the sublimest virtues. It is true—quite true—that he hadn't much himself. But then look at his position. He had to read two sermons every week of his life, and *his* sermons cost him a guinea per dozen! Such a man could not rationally be expected to have patience. Nor, indeed, have men, in general, much. The women are the great cards for patience. Hence it is that they are so frequently termed ducks; seeing that, as ducks, when they are hatching, sit upon their eggs a whole month, they are the legitimate emblems of patience. But men are not ducks.

It must not, however, be imagined, that because Aunt Eleanor was in a state of suspense then, she was not in general a patient person. She was; but *being* then in a state of suspense, she could not have been expected to be patient. She panted to know the cause of these strange proceedings— and people never pant with patience—and although the reverend gentleman had advised her to be patient, she continued to pant anxiously throughout the day; but at night she was as far from the achievement of her object, as she would have been had that object never been proposed.

About half-past ten—being weary of the day—she retired to her chamber, and sat alternately listening and reading until twelve; when, everything both in and around the cottage being still as death, she prayed and went to bed, in the full assurance of protection.

It has been said that there is no virtue in prayer, seeing that He, to whom we pray, knows our thoughts before we attempt to give them utterance; but who, having fervently prayed, has not felt his spirit etherealised, his mind more at ease, his heart lighter, inspired as he then must be with the conviction that, "putting his whole trust and confidence in Him," he has been in communion with his God? "Ask, and ye shall have!" involves a point of faith which teems with the most holy influences; and piety can no more exist without prayer, than prayer can be effective without piety.

Of course it is not necessary to pursue this subject here: the only object of its introduction is, to show how natural it was for Aunt Eleanor, having fervently prayed, to feel assured of protection, and feeling thus assured, to go to sleep.

Sylvester at that time had been asleep nearly two hours, but having in a most enchanting dream fallen desperately in love with a Dryade, he dressed himself with care, and, on leaving the cottage, proceeded by appointment to the arbour.

But the Dryade was not there! He looked anxiously round; but no! What could be the cause of it? That she *would* keep her appointment he felt convinced, and therefore sat down to await her coming; but he had no sooner taken his seat than the scene in an instant changed, and he beheld in imagination a beautiful dell, in the centre of which he sat, upon a couch composed of moss and the still living leaves of wild roses. For a time his eyes were dazzled by this lovely scene, and he saw but indistinctly the objects around him; but anon he could clearly distinguish them all, and he turned with breathless wonder to contemplate their incomparable brightness and beauty. The dell was thickly studded with the sweetest and richest flowers with which the face of Nature teems; fruit of every conceivable species hung in clusters around, and while the herbs lent their fragrance to perfume the air, the mingled odours were delicious in the extreme. Above his head there were myriads of golden-winged butterflies joyously basking in the glorious sun; and as the beautiful birds, whose plumage, reflecting every ray of light, shone with surpassing lustre, were floating around him and skimming the clear miniature lake, of which the surface was like polished silver, and carolling with all the wild sweetness of their nature: it was, altogether, the loveliest scene of which his fancy could boast the creation.

He had not, however, contemplated this scene long, when the warbling of the birds simultaneously ceased, and he heard in the distance, one—as he imagined—burst forth in rich strains of seraphic joy. The effect was ravishing. He listened with feelings of the purest rapture, and with feelings of rapture the birds listened too. How sweet, how enchanting were those liquid notes! How soft, how delightful, how full of wild beauty! What bird, what celestial bird, could it be? The music ceased: and on the instant a sylph imperceptibly approached, and, with balmy breath, softly whispered "Rosalie," and kissed him. That kiss was electric. The blood ran thrilling through his veins, and he felt, with delight, transported. Rosalie! That was the name of her in whom his whole soul was centred. Rosalie! He turned: and she had vanished. But he heard again those ravishing strains, and was thus re-inspired with hope. But again they ceased; and again he *turned;* and Rosalie stood before him. Oh, with what ecstasy did he behold her. What joy, what delight, what rapture he felt as he gazed on her peerless beauty! And she was a most beautiful blonde! Her eyes, which shone like brilliant stars, were orbs of fascination; her cheeks bloomed like the downy peaches; nature's nectar bedewed her lips; and while her rich auburn hair flowed in wild ringlets luxuriantly over her shoulders, her lovely form was enveloped in a veil wrought by zephyrs and silkworms combined.

"Rosalie, sweet Rosalie!" said Sylvester, at length, in the softest and most endearing accents of love, and extended his arms to embrace her; but just as he fondly hoped to clasp her to his heart, a bird of Paradise brought her a beautiful rose, which she placed in his bosom, smiled sweetly, and fled.

"Rosalie, my love," he cried, "let me embrace thee."

Rosalie smiled again and glided round the dell, and then stood on the margin of the lake—her only mirror—and adjusted her ringlets, and sang again, even more sweetly than before; and, while singing, entered a bower, and reclined upon a couch; when, in an instant, the birds flew to the sides of the dell, and having each plucked a leaf from the rose, lily, eglantine, or brier, flew to the couch on which their goddess was reclining, and having strewn the leaves over her beautiful form, commenced warbling their song of repose.

"Rosalie!" again cried Sylvester sweetly. "Dear Rosalie, come to my arms."

Rosalie smiled; but pointing to the couch on which he had been sitting, apparently wished him to sit there again.

Sylvester, however, with that impetuosity which usually mars our loftiest designs, felt resolved to approach the sacred bower, but no sooner, in pursuance of this resolution, did he advance, than myriads of birds flew in a mass to intercept him. He tried to force a passage, but they opposed him still, and when, eventually, they retired, he found himself standing upon the very margin of the lake. For a moment he stood gazing intently at the bower, and the beautiful Rosalie covered with leaves. The lake, then, alone was between them, and feeling still resolved to approach, he was about to plunge in; but again the birds flew in a dense mass towards him, and on being absolutely forced back to the couch, in an instant the whole scene vanished before him, and he found himself sitting in darkness and alone in Aunt Eleanor's arbour again.

Here for some time he remained sighing "Rosalie!—sweet Rosalie!—Rosalie!—my love!" But as darkness still reigned, and the nymph did not appear, he at length returned in sadness and in silence to the cottage, and having passed the outer door, which he omitted to close, proceeded to his chamber, undressed, and went to bed.

Now, as Sylvester made not the slightest noise, he disturbed neither his aunt, nor any one of the servants; they slept soundly and well, and thus continued to sleep for several hours after his return; but in the morning, when cook came down, she, on finding the outer door open, was struck at once with horror, and without giving even a glance, with the view of ascertaining how matters really stood, rushed upstairs again, shrieking "Thieves! thieves! thieves!"

Out rushed Judkins with a gash across his throat—for at the moment the first shriek was uttered he was endeavouring to improve the characteristic respectability of his appearance by shaving—and out rushed Mary, with her hair dishevelled; but their mistress on coming to the door, without leaving her room, demanded to know what was the matter.

"Oh! ma'am," replied cook, "it's a mercy, ma'am, we haven't all been murdered. The door's as wide open as ever it can stick."

"What, the outer door?"

"Yes, ma'am."

"Good gracious!—what *can* all this mean? Why, I saw the door fastened myself. Have any of the things been taken away?"

"I don't know, I'm sure, ma'am. Go, Judkins, and look."

Judkins did go, and found all secure, and then returned to report progress; but while engaged in making that report, Aunt Eleanor, perceiving the sanguinary state of his throat, exclaimed—"Judkins! why, what on earth have you been doing?"

"I was only a shaving, ma'am, when cook shruck."

"For goodness' sake, go and stop the blood immediately. Do not," she added, addressing the cook, "do not suffer a thing to be touched till I come down."

She then closed her door and proceeded to dress; and

Judkins returned to his room, where he found, on consulting his glass, that although he never even contemplated suicide, he looked as if he had not only meant to commit, but had, in reality, committed the act. He had before no idea of having made such an incision. The blood was actually streaming down his neck—it looked frightful—it moreover created the absolute necessity for a clean shirt. Now Judkins, who was a tidy man, had a strong aversion to whiskers; he had also an aversion to the practice of allowing the hair to grow under the chin: he therefore shaved all off, from his temples to his collar-bone, and being endowed with a broad face and neck, he not only had an extensive field of stubble to go over, but as he was not, as a shaver, expert, and as his razors were never in very fine order, he scratched and grinned during the pleasing operation, while the stubble contested the ground, inch by inch, and thus amused himself for more than half an hour every morning of his existence.

On this occasion the entertainment was nearly at an end —he was in the last act, taking the final and triumphant upper scrape—when he heard the first shriek, which so paralysed his frame, that the razor walked in instead of keeping on the surface. No material injury, however, had been inflicted; he bled, it is true, very freely—which, he being a man of full habit, was not at all marvellous—but when he had got his best hat from the box, and had filled up the gash with a handful of nap, he was all right again, and got down just in time to assist his mistress in taking a general survey.

But *there* was nothing wrong—nothing lost—nothing out of its place; everything was found precisely as they had left it, with the single exception of the outer door, and how that had been opened none could tell. It had a lock, two bolts, a bar, and a chain, and as there was not a single mark on the outside to indicate violence, it was perfectly clear that it had not been forced. The only question, therefore, was— how could any one have got *inside* to open it? But this was a question which could not be answered.

CHAPTER IX.

THE GUARDIANS OF THE NIGHT.

A PARSONAGE-HOUSE in an isolated village, is, of all earthly places, the best adapted to the process of deadening a man's wits. If he have no occupation, save that which is strictly enjoined by the church—no hobby but his garden—no society but that of the fat-headed squires around him—his case is indeed desperate. A clergyman thus situated is morally buried. He must be lofty; he must be grave; he must pull a long face; he must look severe; he must walk with excessive circumspection; he must associate with none but those in whose hearts their horses have a much warmer place than their wives, and of whom it may be recorded that, if taken from their horses, not only while animated, but when they become dogs'-meat, the full half of that which they know isn't much. No clashing of intellect does a pastor in that position experience—no new lights look in upon *him;* his mind becomes dim for lack of polish; his imagination soars but to sink; his faculties are weakened by the absence of that exercise which alone can impart to them strength; and he gradually and imperceptibly descends to the recognised level of the sphere in which he moves, severely and securely cloaked up in the arrogant vanity of ignorance.

But this is the rule: Aunt Eleanor's reverend friend was the exception—inasmuch as he actually conceived the means by which the cause of her perplexities *might* be discovered. He conceived an idea, which is very remarkable, that if he sat up at the cottage one night he should know all about it. His mind hadn't struck such a light for a long time. He held it to be brilliant. And so it was: so brilliant that it dazzled him at first; but when he had become somewhat reconciled to its brilliancy, he went to the cottage to show the light there.

He at that time had not the slightest knowledge of the fact that the door of the cottage had been found open that very morning; but, when Aunt Eleanor had duly informed him of the circumstance—although he could not help expressing his amazement—he felt highly pleased, seeing that, as it was clear to him that the parties were determined to carry on their game every night, he, without the necessity for sacrificing more than a single night's rest, should be perfectly certain to catch them.

"The fact is," said he, "this must be put a stop to. It cannot be tolerated. It must not be suffered to continue."

"But how, my dear sir?" cried Aunt Eleanor. "How can I prevent its continuance?"

"You cannot," he replied, "but I can; and I *will* do so, if the scheme which I have conceived meet your approbation."

"My dear sir, whatever you suggest shall be immediately acted upon; gratefully will I adopt any suggestion which may be calculated to relieve me from this painful state of suspense."

"Then allow me, this night, to sit here," said her reverend friend; "here, in this room: take no notice of the arrangement; retire as usual, send the servants to bed, and then leave the rest to me."

"But, my dear sir; oh, but I cannot think for a moment of allowing *you* to sit up."

"Why *not*, my dear madam; why *not*?"

"Oh, it would be so extremely inconsiderate of me to tax your kindness to such an extent."

"My dear madam, *you* do not tax my kindness—if kindness it may be called—the suggestion is mine, not yours."

"Of course I feel extremely grateful; but you do not think of sitting up alone."

"Let me sit up with you, Mr. Rouse," said Sylvester; "*we* shall catch them: and when we do, they ought to be punished severely."

"But have you," said Aunt Eleanor, "have you, my dear, sufficient strength to sit up?"

"Oh, quite," replied Sylvester; "sitting up is nothing."

"But it will not be well for you to do so," said the reverend gentleman. "The primary object is to make everything appear as if no preparation for a discovery had been made."

"Well, it need not *appear*," returned Sylvester; "I can go into my bedroom, and then come down softly again; and then you and I can have a game of chess to keep us awake. I should enjoy it. It will be so very dull for you to sit here alone. *Do* let me sit up with you?"

"I fear," said the reverend gentleman, "that it will tend to defeat the object in view."

"Then let Judkins sit up," said Aunt Eleanor; "he can be in the little room adjoining."

"My dear madam, the character of Judkins is still in—*if* I may so term it—the purgatory of suspicion: it has to be either vindicated clearly or condemned. Against his sitting up with me, I therefore protest."

"But I *cannot* consent to your sitting up alone."

"Well, then—let me see. Oh! suppose, then, I bring Jones, my gardener, with me. He's a very sleepy fellow, it's true, but I'll manage to keep him awake."

"Very well, my dear sir; by all means let him come. I do not care who it is, so long as you have some one with you."

"Then that is decided: Jones comes with me. What time do you usually retire to rest?"

"About ten, or half-past."

"Then at ten o'clock, precisely, we'll be here. When those shutters are closed and the curtains are drawn no light can be seen, I believe?"

"Not a ray."

"Then at ten, my dear madam, expect us. It will of course be necessary for *you* to let us in."

"Of course. I will be at the window at that hour precisely."

The reverend gentleman then took his leave, and Aunt Eleanor congratulated herself on the prospect of the mystery being cleared up. She, at the same time, resolved on having an excellent supper on the table, with wine, whisky, brandy, and books, that there might be no lack of food, either of an animal or an intellectual character; and having, in pursuance of this wise resolution, arranged all her plans, she felt as if a weight had been removed from her heart, and became quite joyous and gay.

Oh, how easily are we elevated—how easily depressed—and when analysed, what puppets we appear, not always the puppets of others, but frequently our own—acting by virtue of the very strings which we pull—the creatures of the very circumstances of which we are the creators—but at all times puppets. It is strange that the human mind—which is often so powerful in its resistance to oppression, so strict in its adherence to principle, so firm in its pursuit of all that is noble, just, virtuous, and true, should be swayed by mere trifles: yet, while possessing all the elements of strength, so it is. A single word may cause our spirits either to rise or to sink: a mere thought of our own may either plunge us into despair, or place us upon the very apex of hope. A cork at sea is more constant than we are; the under-currents may swell and roll, but it still retains its position on the surface; whereas, as we are the sport of every wave—the slightest ripple may upset us. No matter how strong the mind may be, the loftiest, the mightiest, may be wrought upon by trifles. Men scale a mountain, and stumble over a brick.

We are not, it is true, all equally sanguine; but when we are depressed, how soon *may* we be elated, and how frequently *are* we, by virtue of viewing the veriest bubbles which Hope can blow. At such a time that which is nothing *per se*, may be made to amount to a great deal *per saltum*.

In the suggestion of Aunt Eleanor's reverend friend, there was, however, something in reality. The course proposed was, perhaps, the only one at all calculated to lead to the achievement of the object in view. But Aunt Eleanor, instead of waiting for that achievement, viewed the object as being already achieved, in so far as that, after that night, she should be no more annoyed. It was therefore that she felt as if a weight had been removed from her heart, and became joyous. Nor was the pleasure derived therefrom transient. She was joyous throughout the day, and at night, when the village clock struck ten, she went to the window with a smile.

The reverend gentleman was punctual—that is to say, as punctual as reverend gentlemen are in general; he was ten minutes behind—ten minutes being always allowed to the cloth; and when he appeared at the gate, with the gentle Jones, Sylvester quietly opened the door.

Jones had been instructed to make no noise. He therefore made none. As he entered, he walked on the tips of his toes: not elegantly—no, by no means—but carefully, and ground his teeth to indicate the interest he felt in the due preservation of silence.

"My dear sir," whispered Aunt Eleanor, as her reverend friend took her hand, "I really felt so grateful"——

"Not a word, my dear madam, not a word," he replied. "We entered, I believe, unobserved?"

"I think so; I saw no one near."

"Are the servants in bed?"

"They will not go until I retire."

"Very good. Then retire, my dear madam, and leave all to me. I'll lock the door after you, in order that, if it be tried, it may appear that you locked it. I shall catch them, never fear. I only want to know who they are; I only want to see them; there isn't a man in the village whom I shouldn't be able to recognise at a glance."

"Be sure," said Aunt Eleanor, "that you do not expose yourself to danger. I am almost ashamed to leave you; but do make yourself quite at home. You will find some hot water in the kettle, and—let me see—yes, this is cold. Do make a good supper. The sugar and the lemons are on the sideboard, with the nutmegs, and "——

"Really, my dear madam, all this was unnecessary; but as it shows your consideration, I appreciate it."

"Well, but do make yourself, now, as comfortable as possible."

"I will do so."

"You had better let me sit up with you now,' said Sylvester."

"No, my dear fellow, no; that might spoil all. Good-night; good-night. God bless you; good-night!"

Aunt Eleanor and Sylvester then withdrew, and their reverend friend, having locked the door, sat down to contemplate the supper before him, while Jones, in the corner, stood scratching his head, with great constitutional freedom.

It was a very nice supper—very nice indeed—cold, but delicious; unique, but enough. The reverend gentleman eyed it with pleasure; he then eyed the brandy, wine, whisky, and rum; he, moreover, looked at the books—very good; they were very good books; but—*very* good.

"Jones," said he, "you and I are fixed here for the night. Now, sir, repudiating all considerations having reference to station, I invite you to sup with me this evening."

"When you've done, sir, if you please," said Jones.

"Nothing of the sort, sir! Sit down now, and I'll show you how gentlemen enjoy themselves. Under the British constitution, sir, there is no station to which you may not be called. It is highly proper, therefore, that you, and every man, should be cognisant of gentlemanly conduct. Cincinnatus, sir, followed the plough; therefore, sit down at once, like a gentleman!"

Jones didn't understand much of this, but as that which he did understand appeared to him to be very good and much to the point, he did sit down, although with evident reluctance.

"Now, sir," continued the reverend gentleman, who had resolved on enjoying the society of Jones, "consider yourself, for the time being, my equal. You are my friend, and I am yours. We are now gentlemen. What have you there, Mr. Jones?"

"What, that?"

"Yes, that!"

"That's a fowl, sir!"

"A fowl, *sir!* Did I not say that we were on an equality? No gentleman ever says *sir*, but to his servant. Do me the favour to send me a wing."

Jones had never waited at table. He, therefore, didn't know how a fowl was usually dissected. He, notwithstanding, took up a knife and fork, and although his hands trembled with violence, he, by virtue of diligent sawing and digging, got off the wing at last, and with it half the back-bone and part of the ribs.

"Very good," said the reverend gentleman; "*very* good. What can I have the pleasure of helping you to? Allow me to recommend this pigeon-pie."

"If you please. Thank you! I'll take it," said Jones.

Take it! Well! The reverend gentleman sent him the pie, and as Jones thought he couldn't go *very* far wrong, he walked into it bodily, and ate from the dish.

"A glass of wine, Mr. Jones?" said the reverend gentleman.

"Yes, sir," replied Jones; and, having turned over the mustard-pot, poured out a bumper, and handed it politely to his reverend friend.

"Pass the bottle, Mr. Jones," said the reverend gentleman. "That is your glass. I shall be happy to take wine with you."

"Thank you, sir—good health!" said Jones.

"My love to you," said the reverend gentleman.

Jones then proceeded to scrape up the mustard, which certainly didn't look tidy on the cloth; and when he had succeeded in spreading it about, he, not knowing what else on earth to do with the spoon, carefully wiped it on his apron.

"Shall I send you a glass of ale?" said the reverend gentleman, whose gravity was imperturbable, while the face of Jones was fired with confusion.

"Thank you," replied Jones, who made another mess on the cloth, for in his haste to put down his knife and fork to reply, he, having his elbows quite square at the time, upset a decanter of sherry.

The reverend gentleman took no apparent notice of this circumstance: he handed him the glass of ale gracefully; but Jones felt *very* uncomfortable. He didn't enjoy himself at all. He couldn't keep his eyes off his reverend friend. His very anxiety to do nothing wrong, rendered him so nervous, that he could do nothing right.

"How do you get on, Mr. Jones?" said the reverend gentleman, who saw that he didn't and couldn't get on.

"Capital," replied Jones; "the pigeons is nice."

This was said on speculation. The pigeons he had not even tasted. He could do nothing with them. He turned them over and over, and did once try to cut one of them fairly in half, but as his knife slipped, and the gravy flew, he gave the thing up as a bitter bad job. True, he broke in the crust, and fished up a piece of steak, but he dared not again attempt to get a bit of pigeon. He wanted that pie in his tool-house alone—the pigeons would not have got over him there.

"Another glass of wine?" said the reverend gentleman.

Down went the knife and fork again on the instant, for *every* time the reverend gentleman spoke, Jones appeared as if struck with paralysis.

"Good health," said he, having filled his glass.

"My love to you," again said the reverend gentleman.

"Beg pardon: my love to you," echoed Jones, who felt bound to follow whatever suit might be led. But, oh! how sincerely did he wish it all over. "If this here's the way," thought he, "gentlemen enjoys 'emselves, blest if I a'nt pleased I wasn't a gentleman."

"This is very fair wine," said his reverend companion.

"Yes," returned Jones, "this is very fair wine."

"There's some *body* in it."

"Yes, there's some *body* in it," but whether that body were dead or alive, Jones didn't know, nor did he care.

"Have another glass of ale," said the reverend gentleman, when Jones had recommenced operations on the pie, and Jones again left his work and passed the glass; but these startling interruptions were very distressing—indeed, so distressing, that Jones, having drank the glass of ale, which he felt bound to do the very moment he had received it, put his knife and fork together and gave the thing up.

"But you haven't finished," said his reverend friend.

"Done capital well," replied Jones. "Not a mite more, I thank you."

"Well, you have made but a very poor supper."

"I ain't the leastest hungry in life," returned Jones.

"Well, then, let us have the cheese."

Jones rose, and having cleared a sufficient space on the tray, went to the sideboard and brought the cheese; and when the reverend gentleman had sent him a slice, he put it into his mouth with a great degree of comfort.

"A small piece more!" said his reverend friend.

Jones held his plate, and *had* a small piece more. It might have weighed a quarter of a pound; but as he felt that while eating bread and cheese he couldn't make any very great mistake, quantity was not at all an object. He ate it; and then had another small piece, and ate that, and enjoyed it pretty well; and could have eaten a small piece more, but wouldn't.

"Now, then, suppose we have a clearance, Mr. Jones," said the reverend gentleman blandly. "As you are, I believe, the younger man, I'll leave the job to you."

Jones then put all the plates and dishes upon the tray, and cleverly removed it to the sideboard; and when he had placed the various bottles upon the table, the reverend gentleman invited him again to a chair.

"Are you fond of punch, Mr. Jones?" he inquired.

"Yes, I'm very fond of punch. I never tasted none; but I know I'm very fond of it, 'oos everybody as I ever knowed says it's nice."

"Then we'll have some," rejoined the reverend gentleman; "we'll have some, my friend; and I shall be able to say with safety, Mr. Jones, that you never tasted anything like it in your life."

Of punch the reverend gentleman was a great connoisseur. He never drank any but that which he made himself; and, as a maker, he was prepared to back himself against any man in Europe. Such being the case, there were, as a matter of course, great preparations. The lemons were cut in a singular style, the water was measured, the liquors were measured, the sugar was measured, and the jugs were placed in a very peculiar position on the hob, where they remained closely covered with napkins, until Jones thought his reverend friend had forgotten they were there. But this was a mistake altogether. When the time prescribed had duly expired, the reverend gentleman drew off the napkins, and taking a jug in each hand, poured the beverage from jug to jug, backwards and forwards, for a quarter of an hour, during the whole of which time Jones's mouth was wide open. The jugs were then placed on the hob again, and there they remained another quarter of an hour, when they were again taken off, and again filled and emptied, until the reverend gentleman filled a glass, and having three times sipped it, smacked his lips.

"That's the way, my friend, to make punch!" he exclaimed. "Now, Mr. Jones, try that."

Jones accepted a glass, and having drank it, boldly pronounced it to be nice. He liked it much; he admired its flavour, and thought that it was almost worth while being a gentleman, since gentlemen drank such rare stuff as that.

"What do you think of it?" inquired his reverend friend. "Will it do?"

"Capital!" replied Jones. "Out and *out!* But I didn't know what it was till it was gone."

"Then take another glass, Mr. Jones."

And Jones took another glass; but his reverend friend helped himself to the sixth before he asked him to have a third. He then said—

"Now, my friend, have one more—*one* more, Mr. Jones. Beware of the besetting sin of drunkenness."

"You never see me tocksicated yet, sir, I believe."

"Never, Mr. Jones! But a drunkard is not to be trusted. What do you think of my sermons on the subject, Mr. Jones?"

"Capital good! But them hard words puzzles us more than a bit."

"Hard words, Mr. Jones, hit hard; and to hit a man hard is to make a man feel. Certainly; *veritatis simplex oratio est;* but "——

"What say?"

"*Veritatis simplex oratio est.*"

"Them's the dodges as does us."

"Hark! What noise is that? Listen!"

"They're only coming out of the Crumpet," said Jones.

"That's a late house, my friend. People go there to drink till they are drunk, and a drunkard has no command over himself. He cannot even keep his own counsel. *Quod est in corde sobrii est in ore ebrii.* Therefore never get intoxicated, Jones, my friend; never get intoxicated."

"No, sir."

"Never. The practice is bad. It's a bad practice, Jones, a very bad practice. Intoxication—— What's o'clock? Past twelve. Mr. Jones, can I trust you?"

"Trust me, sir?"

"I think I can. Now, Mr. Jones, look here. By this timepiece it's now ten minutes past twelve. Very well. Now I've got a great deal on my mind, and I want to turn it over. I'll therefore just stretch myself here on this couch, and if I *should* drop off, when it's one o'clock call me. You are *sure* that I can trust you?"

"There's no fear of that, sir."

"You'll not go to sleep?"

"Not if it isn't one o'clock for a month."

"Very good. But recollect, if you should go to sleep, I'll discharge you."

"Oh, there's no fear of that," returned Jones. "I'll keep awake if I live."

The reverend gentleman then reclined upon the couch, and in less than five minutes he snored so loudly that Jones felt justified in looking into the jugs, but he found nothing there, they were perfectly empty; and as they were empty, he mixed himself a glass of stiff brandy-and-water.

But brandy-and-water. Brandy-and-water after punch, and *such* punch—pooh! what was brandy-and-water? There had been a time, and that time was not very remote, when he held brandy-and-water to be drink fit for—gods he didn't know anything about, but he thought it fit for actual noblemen—they being the next best things he could think of. But then after punch he didn't relish brandy-and-water. He drank it, it is true—that may be recorded—but he couldn't persuade his palate to relish it! and, as such was the case, "why," thought he, "why shouldn't I try to make a little?" He couldn't see why he should not. He had seen his friend make it, and that friend was then fast asleep. He, of course, felt justified in doing so, and commenced—at the wrong end, it is true—but he commenced. He measured out the whisky, and then measured out the brandy, and then measured out the rum, and then peeled one of the lemons,

G

and then cut it in half, and then squeezed it very properly into the jug, and then put in about the same quantity of sugar as that which his reverend friend had put in; and then—altogether forgetting the water—he covered the jug with a napkin, and placed it upon the hob. Very well! But while it was there, how was he to amuse himself? He thought of the pigeon-pie: and a great thought it was. That pie had been a source of much annoyance, and therefore he resolved on having sat.—sat. being in those days the short for satisfaction—he *would* have sat., and he had it. He took the pigeons up without reference to knife or fork, and pulled them limb from limb! A lot of *pigeons* get over him! Well, it was rich as far as it went; but the idea then appeared to be very ridiculous. And so in reality it was. They didn't get over him then. He cleared the dish—completely cleared it—and having done so, turned with an expression of triumph to see how his punch got on. Well, it smelt very nice. He sipped a little—it was very good; but as it seemed rather strong, he thought a *little* water would do it no harm. He therefore put in a little water, and then, following the example of his reverend friend, poured it from jug to jug, till his arms ached. "Now," said he privately, "master and me is the only two gentlemen in this here village as knows how to make this here punch;" and having delivered himself to this effect, and with the most entire self-satisfaction, he began to enjoy the fruit of his labours; and, having drank several glasses, pronounced it to be better—infinitely better, and nicer and stronger—than that which his reverend friend had made.

But then, how was he to keep himself awake? He couldn't read, he had never been taught to read; but he *had* been taught the game of push-halfpenny. He therefore got three halfpence, and a small piece of chalk out of his pocket, and having drawn five regular bars upon the table—his right hand played with his left.

This, however, didn't last very long. It was not at all an interesting game. There was not much excitement about it. Whether the right hand won or the left hand won was a matter of very slight importance. He therefore turned with the view of conceiving some new delight; but during the process of conception he suddenly fell into the arms of Somnus, when Morpheus, who is generally on the *qui vive*, tickled his fancy with the flavour of punch.

CHAPTER X.

THE GUARDIANS DISCOVERED.

Whenever mortals have inspired a passion for spirits, that passion has always been the germ of infelicity. However strongly it may have been developed, or however ardently reciprocated, discomfiture has invariably been the result. Mortals never yet made matches with spirits. Of their having loved them fondly, we have heard; but in the annals of spirits there is nothing like an absolute match of the kind on record. Nor is this to be lamented. Spirits may indeed do for mortals to love, but they certainly will not do for mortals to marry. They couldn't guide, they couldn't govern, they couldn't hold them. Of all flighty wives they would be the most flighty. They might dance very well, they might sing very well, they might look very well, and be very enchanting, but they would be found to be fit to love only in imagination. It is true that in all cases there is much imagination in love: two-thirds of it is generally composed of imagination; but when love is all imagination, they by whom it is cherished are much to be pitied.

Sylvester's love for Rosalie was all imagination. But then he loved only when asleep. At no other time did it in the slightest degree disturb him: albeit, so strong was its influence then, that, prompted by a vivid recollection of his imaginary interview the preceding night, he rose immediately after Jones had commenced a fine nasal duet with his reverend friend, and proceeded—without at all disturbing those guardians—to the arbour, invoking Rosalie in the most touching tones of endearment.

Here, after having sighed deeply for a time, he beheld the scene suddenly change as before, and found himself seated in the centre of the dell upon the same couch of moss and wild roses. But Rosalie! Where was Rosalie? She was not there!

He looked anxiously round. The flowers were drooping; the birds were silent; the lake had lost its former lustre, and even the butterflies were still.

Something had occurred! Everything around him seemed stricken with grief! What could be the meaning of it? What could be the cause? Was Rosalie dead?

Presently he heard a slight fluttering among the birds; the butterflies came out, although cautiously; the lake reflected a gleam of light, and the flowers raised slowly their beautiful heads.

Sylvester turned, and saw Rosalie approaching. But her steps were lingering and languid. Her head was bowed down, and her countenance was sad, but her *ensemble* still was lovely.

As she entered the dell, he rose to meet her, and the birds sang in concert a melancholy strain, which she answered, and made them more melancholy still.

"Rosalie!" said Sylvester. "Rosalie!"

Rosalie started at the sound of his voice, and having looked at him, blushed and became herself again. Again the butterflies in myriads came forth: again the lake shone like crystal; again the birds sang in their sweetest strain, and again the flowers bloomed and waved, inspired with joy by her beautiful smile.

"Rosalie!" continued Sylvester, "sweet Rosalie!"

Rosalie silently glided to the couch, and having taken her seat at one end, with a smile pointed to the other, upon which in an instant Sylvester sat, and as they looked at each other with expressions of love, birds of Paradise playfully floated between them.

"Sweet youth!" she exclaimed, in a voice which on his ear fell like celestial music; but her countenance changed; she again became sad; the birds ceased to sing, and the flowers ceased to bloom, and the butterflies fell as if dead.

Why, what could be the cause of this? Was she not well?—or had he been too presumptuous?

"Rosalie!" he exclaimed, after a pause, during which they sighed in unison; "Rosalie!—why are you thus? I love you, Rosalie!—sweetest! I love you!"

Rosalie again sighed, and bowed her head in sadness.

"Rosalie!—Rosalie! why are you sad? Tell me, my sweet one? Tell me."

"My beautiful boy!" she exclaimed, and as she spoke, her soft eyes swam in liquid love. "Oh! that I were mortal!"

"Mortal!" echoed Sylvester—"are you not mortal?"

"Alas!" she replied, "I am but a spirit!"

"Then, lovely spirit, let me dwell with you here?"

"It cannot be until you are also a spirit. Then will the purest joy be ours."

"But now, sweet Rosalie!—let me dwell here with you now!"

"It is, alas! impossible. But even while this mortal barrier exists I shall ever be near you; I will watch over, guard, and protect you. When you are sad, I shall be also sad; when you are happy, I shall be happy too."

"But, Rosalie!—dear Rosalie!—my love!—I cannot leave thee!"

Rosalie smiled; and by that smile he felt so inspired, that he rose to embrace her; but in an instant the butterflies flew in a mass before him, and, by shaking the downy feathers from their wings into his eyes, compelled him for a moment to close them!—when they were reopened, all had vanished, and he found himself sitting again in the arbour.

Having dwelt for a time on the beautiful scene from which he had thus been shut out, he with a heavy heart languidly returned to the cottage, and omitting again to close the outer door, proceeded at once to his chamber.

During the whole of this time the reverend gentleman and Jones were keeping up with spirit their nasal duet. By the effect of this, however, no ear could have been charmed. They were both very powerful snorers, but the harmony produced was not perfect. Few, indeed, could have made more noise: few could have kept the thing up with more zeal; but as Jones alternately touched C and F, while the note on which the reverend gentleman dwelt was a very flat D, the combination cannot be said to have been harmonious. The only marvel is, that they didn't wake each other. It is, however, perfectly certain that they didn't, and that they slept and snored without the slightest interruption until cook came down at half-past six, and found the door open as before. Nor would they have been disturbed even then, had not cook been inspired with indignation, and instead of rushing upstairs again, closed the door with so much violence that it shook the whole house.

This did disturb them both, and when the reverend gentleman had succeeded in recollecting where he was, he called out angrily for Jones, who trembled for the consequences of his conduct.

"You have been asleep, sir!" exclaimed his reverend friend.

"Ony jist dropped off, sir—scarce three winks, sir," stammered out Jones.

"Where's the light, sir? The fire out too! Do you *think* that you are fit to be trusted, sir? Hark!" he added, as cook, who had heard them, rushed from the door to tell Judkins that thieves were even then in the house. "Do you hear that?"

"Ye-e-e-es, sir."

"There they are!—Now we shall catch them. Be firm! be firm. Jones! Jones! how came you to let the lamp out? I'll never forgive you, sir! *Where* is the door?"

"Can't find it, sir! Don't know the go of the room! Oh, here"—— he added, sweeping the bottles off the table, for as the shutters were closed, and the curtains were drawn, not a ray of light was visible.

"What on earth are you about, sir?"

"Beg pardon, sir! thought it was the door!" replied Jones, who at that moment swept off one of the jugs.

"You'll break all the things in the room!" exclaimed the reverend gentleman, who, having given forcible expression to this sentiment, groped his way to the sideboard, and knocked down half-a-dozen glasses just as Jones had succeeded in tumbling over the fender, and bringing down the kettle in his fall.

"What are you at now?" cried the reverend gentleman.

"Fender, sir," replied Jones, whose intellectual faculties were then so scattered, and who had become so excessively nervous, that he took his seat at once upon the rug, conceiving that to be the place in which he was likely to do the smallest amount of mischief.

"Tut!—bless my life!—where is this door?"

"Can't think," replied Jones, still retaining his seat; "it's somewheres about, I know."

"Where are you now, Jones?"

"Here, sir."

"Near the fireplace?"

"Yes, sir."

"Then keep to the left till we meet."

Jones had made up his mind not to move from the rug, but on being thus commanded to go to the left, he went to the left on his hands and knees, and the consequence was that, when they met, the reverend gentleman fell fairly over him.

"Bless my life and soul, Jones, what are you about? Are you crazy?"

"Beg pardon, sir," replied Jones, assisting him to rise. "Didn't dream you was so nigh."

"But what in the name of goodness were you doing down there?"

"Thought I shouldn't come in contact with nothing, sir. Thought I shouldn't break no more things. Broke enough already as it is, I'm afeard. Oh, here's the door, sir, here it is, this is it."

"That's right," said the reverend gentleman. "Now, Jones, be firm. But, bless my heart, let me see. I locked the door! Tut! What could I have done with the key?"

"Pocket, p'raps, sir."

"No;—let me—oh, I recollect: I left it on the table. Remain here, now, don't stir an inch from the door."

"Not a ha'porth, sir: not if I know it," said Jones; and his reverend friend approached the table and anxiously felt for the key; and while he was thus engaged, Judkins, cook, and Mary came into the hall, and having stationed themselves at the door, listened with very great intensity.

"They're here, sir," said Jones. "They're ony jist outside, I hear 'em now plain."

"Hush!" said the reverend gentleman. "If they hear us talking they'll be off."

Jones, at the time, felt that that was the best thing they could do. Shivering as he was with cold, and that too in total darkness, he was not then in a state fit to lament such a circumstance. But it did not occur. The people outside were not disposed to be off. On the contrary, the very moment that Judkins became convinced of the fact of there being persons then in the room, he proceeded to make arrangements in order to secure them.

"Do you run to Legge," said he to Mary, in a whisper, "and tell him to come over with a couple of men. We'll fix 'em now safe? And do you run up to missis, cook, and tell her all about it, and ask her what's best to be done. *I'll* keep guard here! They shall not pass *me!*"

Away flew Mary to the Crumpet and Crown, and the moment Legge had ascertained what had been discovered, he rushed, without looking for assistance, to the cottage, in a state of mind bordering on enthusiasm, before cook had had time to explain to her mistress what she really meant.

"Do you mean to say you've got 'em?" said Legge, as he entered.

"They're now in that room," replied Judkins, "safe."

"*We'll* have 'em out!—*we'll* soon see who they are. Why, they've locked themselves in," he added, on trying the door.

"Who's there?" demanded the reverend gentleman.

"It's of no use, young fellows!" said Legge. "So you may as well open the door at once."

"Why," said the reverend gentleman to Jones, on hearing these words indistinctly, "that's Legge's voice. Has *he* turned housebreaker? I know you, John Legge, sir," he added aloud. "I know you, and you shall be punished."

"Do you hear?" cried Legge, who heard some one speaking, although he knew nothing about what was said. "Are you going to open the door now, or are we to burst it open?"

"Bless my life and soul!" cried the reverend gentleman, "where on earth *is* this key?"

At this moment Legge placed his foot near the lock, and as the door flew open without much effort, he seized the reverend gentleman roughly by the collar, while Judkins grasped Jones by the throat.

"So we've caught you at last," cried Legge, "have we? Come to the light, and let's have a look at you!"

"What do you *mean?*" cried the reverend gentleman. "Give me an account of this ruffianly conduct, sir. What do you *mean?*"

Legge, regardless of these expressions of insulted dignity, dragged him to the light; but the moment he recognised the reverend gentleman, he relaxed his hold, and said, "There is some mistake here."

"Some mistake, sir!" cried the reverend gentleman indignantly. "I demand to know the meaning of this outrage. What right have you here?"

"I was sent for, and we thought, on hearing voices in the room, that we had caught those fellows who had been up to their tricks."

"Well, but—bless my life and soul, it's broad daylight! Why, what is it o'clock?"

"Nearly seven."

"Nearly seven! Jones, I'll never forgive you! Don't you *think* that you ought to be ashamed of your conduct?"

Jones didn't say whether he did or not. He, in fact, made no reply. Judkins had grasped his throat so firmly that, on being released, he was anxious, before he attempted to speak, to ascertain well if his swallow were right.

"There *has* been some mistake, I perceive," resumed the reverend gentleman, addressing Legge, with comparative calmness. "The fact is, I have been waiting here all night, with the view of catching those persons. But," he added, as Aunt Eleanor made her appearance, "all will now be explained."

Aunt Eleanor—who, on hearing of the discovery, at once suspected the cause, and had hurried on her things, in order to save the private feelings of her reverend friend from outrage—no sooner saw him standing in the hall, pale and shivering with cold, than she grasped his icy hand and said, "My dear sir! I fear that you omitted to keep the fire up. Mary, run and light one immediately in the breakfast-room, there's a good girl, be quick. Mr. Legge, I feel obliged by your attention. My servants were not aware that Mr. Rouse had been kind enough to offer to sit up with the view of discovering those persons by whom I have been annoyed; but, believe me, I appreciate your prompt desire to serve me, and feel much indebted to your kindness."

"I hope you'll not mention it, ma'am," replied Legge. "I only wish they had been discovered. They were here again in the course of the night, I understand, ma'am!"

"Here—what this last night?" inquired the reverend gentleman.

"Oh, yes, sir!" interposed Judkins. "The door was wide open again this morning."

"Jones! Jones!" exclaimed the reverend gentleman, shaking his head at him very severely; "Jones, this day month, sir, you quit my service."

Jones felt that he deserved this, and therefore said nothing; nor, indeed, did Aunt Eleanor then, although she made up her mind to restore him to favour; but turning to Legge, she observed—in order to save the reverend gentleman from ridicule —"As I feel that you see the necessity for putting an end to these annoyances, Mr. Legge, I am sure you will think with me that the occurrences of this morning should go no further."

"You may rest assured that *I* will not open my lips on the subject to any living soul."

"You see, if it be known that preparations for a discovery are made, those tiresome people will be on their guard; and although my object is prevention, not punishment, they may for a time cease their annoyances and then recommence them."

"I understand, ma'am," replied Legge. "Not a word shall escape me. I'd give five pounds out of my own pocket, ma'am, to know who they are, because I cannot imagine what they can *mean!* And now, sir," he added, addressing the reverend gentleman, "I have to apologise."

"No, not a word—not a word, Mr. Legge. You acted very properly—very."

"But I'm sorry that I handled you so roughly."

"Your conduct, Mr. Legge, was extremely correct; nothing could have been more correct—nothing. I'll therefore not hear a word in the shape of an apology—not a single word."

Legge then respectfully bowed to them both and left the cottage; and Jones, who felt very uncomfortable, tried to leave too, but Aunt Eleanor perceiving his object, said, "I wish to have a word with *you,* Jones, before you go. Cook," she added, "bring me a jug of warm ale. You can go now, Judkins, and attend to your horses. My dear sir, now do go into the breakfast-room and warm yourself; your hands are like ice. How could you think of letting the fire out?"

"Really, I am ashamed," said the reverend gentleman.

"I ought to be ashamed," interrupted Aunt Eleanor, "of having taxed your kindness to such an extent! But go to the fire, there's a good creature. We'll talk about this by-and-by; Jones and I have a word or two to say to each other; we shall soon have settled our little business. Excuse me five minutes; I shall very soon join you."

The reverend gentleman then repaired to the breakfast-room, and cook soon appeared with a jug of warm ale, which she handed to her mistress, who dispatched her at once to prepare as soon as possible a "very nice breakfast."

"Now," said Aunt Eleanor, turning to Jones, who had been marvelling what was about to transpire, "drink up this ale, it will warm you; and when you have finished it, come and assist me."

Jones looked and bowed, and felt grateful. And he took the jug, and emptied it, and wasn't long about it, for although cold without he was parched within, and the ale was nice and smooth.

While he was thus enjoying himself—and it really was to him then a source of great enjoyment—Aunt Eleanor opened the parlour shutters, and having looked round, smiled as he entered the room.

"I'm mortal sorry, ma'am," said he, "that these things is broke. It were all done a searching for the door."

"Never mind," said Aunt Eleanor; "pick up the pieces."

Pick up the pieces! Well! Certainly Jones did think this cool; but he went to work at once, and did pick up the pieces, and put them as he picked them up into his apron, and while *he* was thus employed, Aunt Eleanor was engaged in readjusting the things on the sideboard.

Having very soon succeeded in making the room look tidy again, the amiable creature—who was anxious, for her reverend friend's sake, that the servants should know as little about the matter as possible—went for a basket, and having put into it all that remained of the previous night's supper, requested Jones to leave it at the cottage of Widow Wix.

"And now," she observed, "you must manage to make your peace with your master."

"I will if I can, ma'am," said Jones. "I know 'twas my fault, and I'm very sorry for it; but if *you* would put in a good word for me"——

"Well, we'll see what can be done," she replied, and placing half-a-crown in his hand, started him off.

CHAPTER XL

THE "SPIRIT" APPEARS TO THE PASTOR AND JONES.

THERE are few things more galling to a sensitive man than the fact of his having been found in a ridiculous position; but while no one could have felt more acutely than Aunt Eleanor's reverend friend that the position in which he had that morning been found *was* ridiculous, none could have endeavoured more earnestly than Aunt Eleanor herself to induce him to repudiate that feeling, as one which ought not to be entertained.

"Now, say no more about it," she at length observed, after having heard impatiently a vast deal of eloquence, for the reverend gentleman, on this point, became extremely eloquent, as soon as he had ceased to shiver—"the whole affair resolves itself to this: Feeling fatigued you went to sleep; and who can wonder at it? while Jones, poor fellow, followed your example: no one can marvel at *that!*"

"But he solemnly promised that he would not go to sleep. 'Jones,' said I, 'can I, till one o'clock, trust you?' 'Sir,' he replied, I remember his words, 'I'll not go to sleep if it isn't one o'clock for a month. I'll keep awake if I live!'"

"And he intended to do so, no doubt, poor man. You *must* therefore forgive him. But now, *is* it not strange—is it not mysterious—that that door of mine should thus be opened, night after night, as it is, and for no other purpose than that of annoying me?"

"It is indeed mysterious," replied the reverend gentleman. "But *I'll* solve the mystery—I'll find it out. Having entered into the matter so far, I'll go on with it. Practices of this character, my dear madam, must and *shall* be put a stop to! They are perfectly monstrous. They must not—in a civilised country like ours—they *must* not be suffered to continue; and so firmly resolved am I to get to the bottom of this mystery, that if you will not allow me to occupy your parlour this night, I'll conceal myself in the shrubbery, and watch there!"

"My dear sir," cried Aunt Eleanor, "oh! for Heaven's sake, do not dream of it for a moment!"

"Nothing can alter my firm determination in this matter. I'm resolved to find it out, and I will find it out; and unless you afford me an asylum in your parlour, into the shrubbery this very night I go."

"Oh, but I cannot think of consenting to your sacrificing your rest for me in this way."

"Well, my dear madam, you know my determination: I watch this night in the shrubbery. If you close the gates against me, I'll get over the wall."

"Close the gates against you! My dear sir, neither the gates nor the doors shall be closed against you. But let me prevail upon you to abandon this project—or at least to defer it for a time."

"And in the interim suffer you to be constantly annoyed.

No, my dear madam, it must be done at once. I feel that I am now *bound* to make this discovery. I'll find them out. I am not a man to be easily thwarted: I am not a man to be turned from my purpose by any trifling failure. I ought to be, and I am, ashamed of having failed to make the discovery last night; but this night shall settle it."

"Well, if you are determined, I cannot do less than express my gratitude; but I do still think that it had better be deferred. Consider to-night you will require *much* rest."

"Not at all! I'll manage that: I'll go to bed to-day, and thus prepare myself for night. But no supper!—do not prepare any supper—it is to that I ascribe our failure last night. Had it not been for the supper, *Jones* would not have gone to sleep; these fellows, you know, while there's anything to eat, *will* gormandise, and gormandise, until they have no more animation about them than prize pigs. Therefore prepare no supper. I'll bring something with me to keep us awake."

"Then you mean to allow Jones to sit up with you again?"

"Why, I think that it will be, under the circumstances, as well."

"Much better. But, poor fellow, you'll let him have some rest."

"I'll send him to bed the moment I get home. I'll manage it; and we shall catch them. My dear madam, be assured of this—we shall catch them."

Sylvester now entered the room, and when he had heard the substance of all that occurred, he begged to be allowed to sit up that night with the reverend gentleman and Jones. This, however, was strongly objected to both by his aunt and her reverend friend, on the ground of his apparent physical indisposition; and when they had all made a hearty breakfast, it was finally arranged that the reverend gentleman was to come again that night at ten, that Jones was to accompany him, and that nothing in the shape of supper was to be on this occasion prepared.

This having been decided to the entire satisfaction of all concerned, the reverend gentleman left; and Aunt Eleanor conceiving that the feelings of Judkins might be wounded in consequence of Jones having been elected to sit up the previous night with her reverend friend instead of him, rang the bell and desired his attendance.

"Judkins," she observed, as he entered the room, "although perhaps I ought not to suppose that you are simple enough to imagine that, as Jones sat up with his master last night, I had not sufficient confidence in *you*,—I wish you to understand that that arrangement was made in consequence of Mr. Rouse having preferred, and very naturally, the attendance of his own servant to that of mine."

"Yes, ma'am, I understand; oh! yes," said Judkins, "but if he'd had me with him, things 'ud ha' been different."

"Very likely."

"Why, I've seen that Jones, ma'am—it isn't my place, p'raps, to speak not of no man—but I've seen him go to sleep with the bread in his mouth—I've seen him drop off in the middle of the day!—he's the sleepiest fellow as is. *He* sit up with a gentleman all night! The idear is rotten! He couldn't keep awake by any accident. I'd catch you, ma'am, a dormouse in the winter that would beat him."

"My object," said Aunt Eleanor, "is neither to canvass the character of Jones, nor to dwell upon his eccentricities, but merely to explain to you that want of confidence, on my part, was not the cause of your not being chosen to sit up, and to impress upon you the necessity for keeping whatever arrangements we either have made or may make, with a view to the discovery of these persons, a secret."

"I understand, ma'am. Depend upon me, I shall not say a word to a soul."

"Very good. That is all I require."

Judkins then withdrew, and Aunt Eleanor conceived that she had done all that was necessary to secure silence on the subject; but in this she was mistaken.

Villages appear to contain no secrets. If any be suffered to exist at all, they must find it a difficult matter to live. They must not even breathe but in silence; if they do, they must instantly die. Everybody knows everybody; everybody talks about everybody; everybody's business is everybody's business, and every one is fair gone for the whole. And herein lie the humanities of a village. They must know something—hence they seek to know each other: they must talk about something—hence they talk about each other: they must laugh at something—hence they laugh at each other: they must denounce something, and they hence denounce each other. This may be called "petty;" but then a village is a petty world, containing petty people, whose general intelligence is therein confined.

It might have been thought that Aunt Eleanor *had*, as she imagined, done sufficient to insure secrecy in this matter; but although Legge was silent, and Judkins was silent, and Jones and the reverend gentleman were silent, Mrs. Legge, when she found that she was able to get nothing having reference to it out of Legge himself, sent for Mary, who at once told her all.

Having thus obtained the important information sought, Mrs. Legge told Obadiah Drant, and the moment *he* heard of it, of course the secret died. It was then indeed no longer a secret: for glorying as he always did in everything bearing even the semblance of an opportunity of having what he termed "a regular fructifying cut" at those above him, he went round the village, called on all his associates, and developed his fine inventive faculties strongly. He had received that morning a large order for a quarter of a hundred of bricks, but that of course he could not attend to.

"I say," said he, on reaching Pokey's residence, "I say, my boy! have you heard the news?"

"No!" replied Pokey. "What news?"

"What! haven't you heard about old Teddy Rouse?"

"No! what about *him*?"

"Such a game, my boy!—such a glorious game! Pinned like a cockchafer!—regularly pinned! I'll be bound to say there hasn't been a man so pinned since the time of the French Revolution."

"But how," cried Pokey, "how was he pinned? What was it all *about*?"

"Why, you know Mrs. Sound has been much annoyed lately by ghosts, you know, and all sorts of things. Well, this blessed morning, you know, when she came down, who should she find in her parlour but old Teddy Rouse in his shirt!"

"What! the parson?"

"The parson! Well, in she went, and flew at him, and out she pulled him, and pommelled and scratched him, and shook him, and worried him, until Ted called out for mercy so loud you might have heard him all over the village."

"What! do you mean to say"——

"Yes! Well! when she had him down flat on his back,

with her fingers on his throat, and her knees upon his chest, she sent her maid over for Legge, and when Legge came, she offered to stand a pound if he'd give Ted an out-and-out welting. Legge was a fool not to do it."

"But do you mean to say"——

"Do you think *I* wouldn't have done it? If I had had half a chance, do you think I wouldn't have welted him?"

"Well, but *do* you mean to say now this was the parson?"

"Teddy Rouse, I tell you!—old Teddy Rouse! Did you ever hear of such a game?"

"And do you mean to say, then, that he was the ghost after all?"

"Why, to be sure he was."

"*The* animal!"

"*Wouldn't* we have served him out that night if we had known it! I'll just tell you what I'd have done! I'd have caught him by the scruff of his blessed neck, and when you and Snorkins had fixed his legs, I'd have dragged him to the horse-pond and given him a cooler."

"Well, but I say, what did they do with him?"

"Do with him! Why, like a parcel of fools, they let him go. I only wish I had been there! He wouldn't have been let off so easy, I'll warrant. But isn't it sickening now, when you come to look at it? Isn't it disgusting that we should be compelled to support these vampires? *These* are the locusts that prey upon our vitals?—these are the vultures that finger elevenpence-halfpenny out of every shilling the poor man earns! The fact is, Pokey, between you and me, we *must* have a rattling revolution. It must be a rattler, come when it may. Bobby Peel ought to blush for upholding this downright system of dead robbery. As Johnny Russell told him to his teeth the other night, 'I'll tell you what it is,' said Johnny, 'if you don't knock this fructifying swindle in the head, you may look out for pepper!' And he'll have it! It was just the case in Constantinople, under Peter the Great; it was just the case in China, when the Turkish ambassadors signed the Magna Charta; it was just the case during the Peninsular war, when William the Conqueror upset the lot, and sent Russia off with a flea in her ear; it has been the case, mind you, all over the world, and, mark my words, it will be the case here. Are *we* to be plundered of our substance to support a mob of locusts like old Teddy

Rouse ? Are we to be ground to the earth, and taxed to the tune here of eighteen hundred millions a year, that such men as Ted Rouse may grow fat? Not a bit of it! No, my boy, we shall have a rattler! But I must be off. It's quite clear that Ted has put his foot in it this time. I thought it wouldn't be long before he was caught on the hip. Well, God bless you—I'll work him! I'll stick to him, my boy! But I say, only think, though, of Ted in his shirt! Ha! ha! ha! It's the capitalest go that ever occurred. Ha! ha! ha! Well, ta-ta! Ha! ha! I shall see you to-night. Poor Teddy Rouse. Ha! ha! ha!"

Thus he left Pokey, and thus he went round, fructifying as he proceeded so freely, that the thing assumed a shape of vast local importance; and although Obadiah was pretty well known, he established his falsehoods on the basis of truth with so much ingenuity, that all his associates felt quite convinced that "Ted" had been actually playing the ghost.

Of this the reverend gentleman was, however, unconscious. He went to bed at twelve, and Jones went to bed too, and when they rose about nine in the evening, they had a slight repast, and at ten o'clock precisely repaired to the cottage.

Here Aunt Eleanor received them as before, and when she had indulged in many expressions of gratitude, and Sylvester had reiterated his wish to be allowed to sit up with them, in vain, the reverend gentleman gave them his blessing, and he and his companion were left for the night.

But that friendship which existed the night before had vanished. They were no longer friends. Jones stood near the door with a basket in his hands, while the reverend gentleman sat by the fire.

To say that Jones much admired this arrangement were to say that which is not exactly correct. He did not much admire it. Nor could he conceive how long he should have to stand there. There was, moreover, no show of anything to eat—that in his view looked ominous; still he did fondly imagine that the basket which he held in his hand contained something substantial and nice, of which he might by-and-by perhaps come in for a share. This, therefore, did not distress him much. But when he looked at his position as a servant, standing as he was in the presence of a master who, being indignant, might not, perhaps, even permit him to sit, he did—not presuming to take a seat without permission—think

H

his case hard. It was, however, in his view, perfectly clear that he couldn't continue to stand there all night. He knew that he must drop some time or other, and that was, as far as it went, a comfort. He had not been accustomed to stand long in one position; still, being resolved to keep up as long as possible, he had recourse to a variety of manœuvres. Sometimes his whole weight was on his right leg, and sometimes it rested on his left: sometimes he planted one shoulder against the wall, and sometimes he planted the other; and thus, by virtue of moving about, twisting his hips, and vexing his spine, he managed to stand there for more than an hour.

At length, when he fancied that "drop he must," the reverend gentleman turned round, and said—

"Now, sir, bring me that basket."

This was a great relief to Jones. As he took the basket forward, in the full conviction of there being something therein delicious, he felt reinspired with hope; but when the reverend gentleman, on receiving it, said coldly—"That will do!" he returned to his corner to contemplate the scene in a state of mind bordering on despair.

But even under these adverse circumstances Jones could not curb his imagination. It dived into the basket, and there conceived a couple of ducks, a pigeon-pie, some bread and cheese, and the materials for punch. This he thought was not bad. Nor as a vision was it. It sustained him for a time, and when at length the reverend gentleman drew forth a bottle, he felt that that vision was about to be realised. One bottle only, however, was produced, and that was a peculiarly-shaped bottle. Jones had never seen such a bottle before. It wouldn't stand. But that it contained something nice he felt fully convinced.

"Now, sir, hand me one of those tumblers," said the reverend gentleman. "The largest."

Jones with alacrity obeyed, and when the reverend gentleman had twisted off the wire, and cut the string which secured the cork, that cork flew out with a report so loud, that it caused Jones to stagger as if he had been shot.

"Hark!" cried the reverend gentleman, who at that moment fancied he heard a noise; but after having listened and found all still, he turned and drank that which to Jones appeared to be boiling gin-and-water.

"Now, sir," he continued, feeling sure that the noise which he had heard was made by Jones on being started, "what have you to say in explanation of your conduct last night?"

Jones had nothing to say in explanation. He couldn't see what explanation was required. The case appeared to him to be clear as it stood—he went to sleep. That was all he knew about it, and all he could explain, and as he felt that that explanation was unnecessary, he was silent.

"Do you not think, sir," resumed the reverend gentleman, "that such conduct, after all my kindness, was disgraceful?"

"I'm very sorry for it, sir," replied Jones humbly. "It shan't occur again, it shan't indeed, sir: I hope you'll look over it."

"I gave you notice, sir, this morning, to quit my service in a month. Now, whether that notice be ratified or withdrawn, depends upon your conduct this night."

Jones bowed, and was about to return to his corner, when the reverend gentleman said, "Bring another glass,"—and when the glass had been brought, and he had drawn another bottle from the basket, he added, taking the wire off and cutting the string—"Now, sir, hold the tumbler, and then drink this off." Bang went the cork from the bottle to the ceiling, and out rushed the beverage, which Jones thought hot; so hot indeed that he blew it with great caution before he put it to his lips; while it hissed and boiled, and flew into his eyes, as if every bubble had some spite to spit. He soon, however, found that it was cold, and drank it off, and then gasped for breath and shuddered. He didn't at all like it. It wasn't at all nice. There was nothing in the flavour to recommend it. It was hard and sour, and cold—very cold.

"Did you never take soda-water before?" inquired the reverend gentleman, who saw him shuddering convulsively.

"Never, sir."

"Do you not like it?"

"Why, sir—dessay it's very good."

"It will keep you awake, Jones."

"Shouldn't be surprised, sir."

The reverend gentleman then emptied the basket, and Jones, to his horror, perceived—instead of a couple of ducks and the pigeon-pie—nothing but twelve of these bottles.

"Well," thought he, "here's a pretty basin o' soup. But

he can't mean to say we're agoing for to live upon this here swill *all* the blessed night."

"You can sit down, Jones," said the reverend gentleman.

Sit down! Yes!—that of course was all very well; but Jones was not thinking of that point then. He was turning over, opening, and fairly spreading out the *idea* of two men keeping up all night with nothing to sustain them but this cold stuff.

"What gets over me," said he privately to himself, "is that master prefers this to punch. Dessay it's dear: bound it's dear, although *I* wouldn't give so much as a penny for a pondfull on it, *but* that a gentleman like him, as can have punch whenever he likes, should prefer this here *to* it, is rum. But gentlemen certainly is queer swells. Wonder if they ever gets tipsy upon it. Dessay they do, though, or else they wouldn't drink it."

There was, however, one point upon which Jones reflected very deeply, and that point was this: How could cold water boil? He had seen the soda-water effervesce, he had tasted it during its effervescence, and found it cold! the question with him therefore was, "How as that water was cold could it boil?"

That was indeed a puzzler for Jones. But he stuck to it! —oh! he stuck to it, and brought to bear upon it, too, all the knowledge he had. He could make nothing of it, but he wouldn't give it up! The question still was, How could cold water boil?

Now, while he was thus most intently engaged, and the reverend gentleman was reading a romance called "The Bravo of Blood, or the Sanguinary Smile," there was a scene of excitement at the Crumpet and Crown, which was never, perhaps, in that or any other village, equalled.

Mrs. Legge had fainted. She was not a weak woman, but she had fainted. She had been standing at the door, and as the clock struck twelve she rushed into the parlour and fainted. Vinegar was of course at hand, and vinegar was applied; and when she had been restored to something bearing the semblance of consciousness, she called for the Bible.

"The Bible!" she exclaimed. "My dear! get the Bible."

Legge shifted her head from his arm to that of Pokey, and hastened upstairs for the Bible, and on his return Mrs. Legge cried anxiously, "Turn to Revelations, my dear—Revelations."

Legge did turn to Revelations, and then said, "Phœbe! *What* do you mean?"

"Here," she replied, as he gave her the Bible, and turning at once to the sixth chapter, read,—" And I looked, and behold a pale horse: and his name that sat on him was Death."

"Death!" she exclaimed. "I have seen him. He passed on a pale horse just now."

"What! another of Teddy Rouse's tricks!" cried Obadiah.

"You are a fool," said Legge; and then turning to his wife, added, "Which way, my girl?—which way did it go?"

"Towards the church," she replied. "But oh! do not leave me!"

"But for a moment: I'll not be gone long, my girl."

"No!" she exclaimed, clinging to him. "You must not go—you shall not go. If we are to die to-night, let us die together."

"*I'll* have a go in," exclaimed Obadiah. "Come along, Pokey, come along, Quocks, come along, Bobber, my boy, *we'll* see what he's made of!" And Obadiah, followed by Pokey, Quocks, and Bobber, rushed valiantly out of the Crumpet and Crown.

But the horse and his rider were gone. Obadiah looked anxiously up and down the road, but could see nothing of them. Feeling, however, that a display of valour then was essential to the maintenance of his reputation, he boldly cried out—

"Now, let's go up the road, my boys! Death and his pale horse be bothered!"

"Bravo!" cried Pokey. "Ay, let's go up the road!" And they went up the road seeing nothing to fear.

Having passed the church, however, Pokey suddenly cried "Hark!" and the blood of Obadiah Drant chilled on the instant. "Listen!" he added. "It's coming this way!" They did listen, and heard distinctly something approaching. There were three roads before them; but down which of the three it was coming they couldn't tell. Presently, however —having strained their eyes in those three directions—they saw what at first appeared to them to be a tall white pillar gliding slowly down the hill to their left.

"Here it comes," cried Obadiah, clinging closely to Quocks. "What—what can it be?"

"Don't be frightened," said Quocks—"do-o-on't be alarmed!"

It now came sufficiently near for them to distinguish the outline of a horse bearing a figure which looked like that of a giant!

Terror seized them on the instant. They could not move! The figure came nearer and still more near, and, with uplifted hands and eyes darting from their sockets, they saw it slowly and solemnly pass.

Both the horse and his rider were white—quite white—and both seemed enveloped in a cloud. White smoke appeared to issue from the nostrils of the horse, while the rider wore a long flowing robe, which to them looked like a vast winding-sheet. They thought of the passage in Revelations and trembled. It must be—it could but be—Death! He had, in their view, come to swallow up all, seeing that all whom he visits are doomed.

As the figure disappeared each resumed his former attitude, and when it was completely lost to view they breathed again, but were still filled with horror.

"Let us go," said Obadiah. "Come, let us return. Such sights as this are dreadful. We are but men, and as man is but man, these scenes are too horrid for man to bear. Let us go; come, now let us go."

They had not, however, proceeded far—locked in each other's arms, with a view to mutual security—when they again beheld "Death," rushing furiously towards them.

"Preserve us!" cried Obadiah, darting into the hedge, closely followed by his companions. "Preserve us, or we are lost!"

But before "Death" had reached them, he urged his fiery steed to the right and sprang over the hedge, and then flew across the fields, over bank, ditch, and hurdle, until he was lost to view again.

They then returned quickly to the Crumpet and Crown; but before they could speak of the horrors they had seen they each had a large glass of brandy.

But even then they were not so communicative as might have been expected. They were thoughtful—very thoughtful. They looked at each other and shook their heads with great significance; but when they had explained briefly that they had seen that which Mrs. Legge saw, namely, "Death on a pale horse," they were silent; and thus they remained until half-past one, when Pokey, who had his reasons for making a move, suggested the propriety of parting—a suggestion upon which they almost immediately acted, and thoughtfully repaired to their respective homes.

During the progress of these extraordinary proceedings, Jones, who felt that he was victimised, had swallowed on compulsion four bottles of that beverage which he abhorred, and sat dwelling on the problem he had proposed having reference to cold boiling water, while the reverend gentleman was reading the romance.

Up to half-past two they had not been disturbed. They had heard no noise—with the exception of that which reached the reverend gentleman's ears while opening the first bottle of soda-water—and as all around them then continued silent as the grave, they began to think that nothing at all calculated to call forth the courage they had in them would occur.

About three o'clock, however, while the reverend gentleman was absorbed in a soul-stirring chapter of the romance, he imagined that he heard the outer gate close, and started.

"What's that?" exclaimed Jones.

"Hush! hush!" cried the reverend gentleman. "Listen!"

They did listen, and distinctly heard footsteps on the path.

"Shall I go to the window?" said Jones.

"No! no!" cried the reverend gentleman. "Let us hear how they attempt to get in. Keep your seat and be silent. Now, hark!"

At that moment they saw the handle of the door move.

"Who's there?" cried the reverend gentleman in a whisper which startled both Jones and himself.

No answer was returned, but again the handle moved, and then the door opened gradually, and then a tall figure, enveloped in a sheet, slowly entered the room.

"Angels of light protect us!" exclaimed the reverend gentleman, while Jones, who appeared to be at once deprived of life, dropped in an instant upon the rug and hid his face.

Of these proceedings the figure took no notice. It walked slowly to the sideboard, and having looked for a moment, shook its head, as if to indicate that there was nothing at all there that it wanted, and then turned and left the room as it had entered.

The feelings experienced by the reverend gentleman then

were awful. He sank back in his chair, and for the first time felt that no one knows what he would do until placed in the position to do that which he conceives he should do. His heart had never before quailed, but it then sank within him. He seemed fixed to the spot—completely spell-bound. Nor was it until some time after the figure, which he conceived to be a spirit, had disappeared, that he summoned sufficient courage to speak to Jones, who had given himself altogether up for lost.

"Jones," said he, at length, in a scarcely audible whisper, which made the poor fellow start convulsively, conceiving that the spirit himself had called him—"Jones: rise and put your trust in Him, who can and will protect us."

Jones, with an aspect of horror, looked up, and in trembling accents cried, "O-o-o-o-o! is it you?"

"It is," replied the reverend gentleman. "Arise."

Jones did arise, and having rolled his eyes fearfully round the room, with the view of being *sure* that it was gone, sank into his chair exhausted.

Horror had chilled them both, and having nothing but soda-water within them, they were both still cold, and continued to tremble.

"Jones," said the reverend gentleman, after a pause, "reach the brandy; it is there, on the sideboard."

"Oh, sir," replied Jones, "I *dare* not."

The reverend gentleman nerved himself; and turning his eyes in every direction, walked with comparative firmness to the sideboard, and returned to his chair with the decanter and a glass, which he filled with all the steadiness at his command, and then at once drank it off.

"Now, Jones," said he, when the glass had been refilled, "take this." And Jones, whose teeth at the time violently chattered, did take it, and swallowing the contents at one gulp, was very thankful.

They now began to feel somewhat better; and although the improvement as yet was but slight, they were able to look round the room—timidly, it is true—but without that wildness of vision by which their looks had just before been characterised.

"Pray, sir, give me a little more brandy," said Jones.

"Yes, Jones, yes," replied the reverend gentleman, replenishing the glass. "Drink this."

"Bless you, sir!—bless you!" said Jones, with much fervour. "Oh! wasn't it horrid, sir—wasn't it?"

"It was an awful sight," returned the reverend gentleman, as he helped himself to a little more brandy. "But why," he added, "why should *we* fear?"

Jones shook his head and shuddered.

The door was still opened, and as the cold air rushed in, the reverend gentleman deemed it expedient to close it, and suggested the propriety of doing so to Jones; but as Jones, even then, dared not cross the room alone, it was eventually agreed that they should both go together—and together they accordingly went. But the moment they had reached the door of the parlour, they saw the outer door open too, which they held to be very mysterious, seeing that they had heard no bolt withdrawn. Finding, however, that all was then still, they closed the outer door, but they had no sooner done so, than they heard distinctly footsteps behind them, and on turning round beheld the identical figure slowly ascending the stairs. Jones in an instant rushed into the room, but the reverend gentleman remained till it had vanished—not prompted by courage—nor indeed by any feeling of curiosity—but because he had not the power to leave the spot.

"Come in, sir!" cried Jones. "Pray, come in, sir—come in!"

And when the figure had disappeared, the reverend gentleman went in, but with an expression of unmingled terror.

"Oh, do leave this house, sir, pray do!" cried Jones, as the reverend gentleman sank into his chair. "It's haunted! —I know, sir, it's haunted! If we stay we shall never go out of it alive!"

"Come what may," returned the reverend gentleman, apparently gasping for breath, "*what* may, here will I remain. But," he added, "let me not control *you*. If you wish to leave, consider yourself at liberty to do so. Go, Jones—go if you please."

Well, Jones thought this kind—very kind; he appreciated the privilege highly; but then, how was he to get out? He must necessarily go through the hall—and there the spirit *might* perchance meet him alone. Could he have vanished through one of the windows, he would have done so with all the alacrity of which he was capable, but as he could not do this, he converted a necessity into a virtue, by saying, "I shouldn't, sir, like to leave you."

"Use your own discretion," said the reverend gentleman calmly. "Until the morning dawns, Jones, here will I remain. There is much latent wickedness in this world, Jones. I mean by latent, hidden, private, secret."

"Yes, sir."

"Wickedness is in all ages wickedness, but it isn't in all ages proved to be wickedness."

"No, sir."

"Wickedness will sometimes prosper for a while."

"Yes, sir."

"But it never can prosper long."

"No, sir."

"It is certain to be found out, and when found out, punished, Jones."

"Yes, sir."

"None who deserve punishment escape."

"Very true, sir."

"This spirit which we have seen is, doubtless, the spirit of one who left the world with some secret unrevealed."

"No doubt, sir. But what do you think, sir, of ghosts in general?"

"The subject is above human comprehension, Jones, and therefore we ought not to talk on that subject."

This closed Jones's mouth effectually, and he began to reflect upon his sins. He remembered that he was indebted to the estate of a deceased landlord to the amount of sevenpence-halfpenny, which sum, as no one but the landlord himself knew of it, he had never intended to pay. The questions which he therefore proposed were—First: Was this the spirit of that landlord?—Secondly: Would it answer the purpose of any spirit to revisit the earth to enforce the payment of the sum of sevenpence-halfpenny?—and Thirdly: Wouldn't the spirit rest until that sum was paid? To these questions he could give no satisfactory answer. He thought that it would hardly be worth a spirit's while to disturb itself much about the sum of sevenpence-halfpenny, but he at once resolved to pay the sevenpence-halfpenny to the widow, in order to make all sure.

The reflections of the reverend gentleman were of a still more deeply metaphysical caste. He had, therefore, imagined apparitions to be spiritual, ethereal—beings having nothing at all physical about them; but the spirit which he had seen was enveloped in a sheet of which the material was linen—material linen. The question, therefore, was—where did it get that sheet? The attempt, however, to solve this question was presumptuous. The reverend gentleman felt it to be presumptuous, although he tried hard to get at the solution; and as he eventually thought that he must have been mistaken—as he brought himself at length to believe that the sheet which he had seen was a spiritual sheet—he turned to the consideration of the course which he felt it his duty to pursue, and upon this he was engaged until the day began to dawn, when he and Jones left the cottage and went thoughtfully home.

CHAPTER XII.

THE FEARFUL CONJECTURE.

WHEN Judkins went to the stable that morning, he found Snorter steaming and bleeding at the mouth; and feeling indignant at the idea of his being thus treated, he declared he'd give a crown if the horse could but speak.

"What devil's tricks have they been up to now?" he inquired of the animal. "What have they been doing with you? What have they been after? What do they want to spit their spite upon *you* for? Come out, old boy—come, and let's have a look at you. They've guv you a benefit this time, that's certain!" he added, on finding the horse in a worse plight than before. "Poor fellow!—poor old fellow! —*have* they been ill-using on you? Poor old boy! But I'll catch 'em—blarm their *bodies* on 'em, I'll find them out. But a'n't you a fool?" he continued indignantly, "what do you mean? Why didn't you kick 'em clean off? What did you want to let 'em sarve you out in this here way for? Do you think I'd ha' stood it? Why didn't you strike out fierce, when you saw 'em come into the stable? You might ha' knowed what they wanted—it wasn't the first time. What did you want to let 'em take advantage of your ignorance for? You know them as treats you well, don't you? Very well, then, why don't you know them as treats you ill? Poor old boy! come and let's wash your mouth out. Poor old fellow! There—you'll soon be all right again. You a'n't lame, are you? No, you a'n't *lame*. Come along in again, and make your life happy. I'll soon come and attend to you. There, old boy!—but you ought to have struck out at 'em."

Having thus by turns caressed and expostulated with the animal, he repaired to the kitchen, and having explained all to cook, asked her pointedly what she really thought of it.

"What do I think of it!" she exclaimed. "What can any one think of it? But how did they get the key? Did you leave it in the door last night?"

"No, I brought it in and hung it upon that blessed hook, where it has always hung of a night since the last go, and where I found it hanging this morning."

"Well, the fact of it is I can't live in the house, and so I shall tell missis directly she comes down. The whole place is bewitched. It's haunted. I'm sure of it. It isn't fit for flesh and blood to live in."

Mary was then informed of the circumstance, and when she had dwelt sufficiently long on the really mysterious character of the proceeding, she went up to inform her mistress, who received the intelligence with a degree of composure at which Mary was perfectly amazed.

It must not, however, be supposed that Aunt Eleanor failed to feel it. She did feel it deeply, but the expression of her feelings was calm.

"We shall find it all out by-and-by," she observed; "these practices cannot be carried on long. Time discovers all things. We must have patience."

"But isn't it horrid, ma'am—isn't it frightful that these things should go on, ma'am, night after night, without having a stopper put upon 'em?"

"It is very annoying, Mary—very. But we shall discover it all before long, I have no doubt of that."

"I hope to goodness we shall," returned Mary; "I'm sure, ma'am, it's shocking to live so. It's enough to frighten all of us out of our wits."

"Very true," said Aunt Eleanor calmly, "very true;" and while dressing and listening to Mary's expressions of fear, she at intervals repeated "very true."

Having finished her toilet, she descended to the breakfast-room, where Sylvester—who had as usual been called by Mary —soon joined her; and when she had explained to him the fact of the horse having been again taken out of the stable and treated with severity, he could not refrain from shedding tears; for as Snorter had been his dear father's favourite horse, and had been given to his aunt in the full conviction that it would be most kindly treated, a variety of fond associations were recalled, as he exclaimed, in touching accents of filial affection—

"I would not have him injured for the world."

"He has not been *injured*, my love," said Aunt Eleanor, privately reproaching herself for having said so much. "He has not been, even in the slightest degree, injured. On the contrary, they appear to have taken great care of him; still it was wrong of them to ride him so hard; indeed, it was wrong of them to take him out at all; but believe me, my love, he's not injured. We'll go and see him after breakfast, shall we? Have you kissed me this morning? I think you did," she added, as he kissed her again. "God bless you!"

They then commenced breakfast, and freely conversed on the subject which had set even conjecture at defiance: but before they had finished, their reverend friend called, impatient to communicate all he had heard and seen.

"I have, my dear madam, a tale of horror to tell," said he; but on the instant Aunt Eleanor raised her hand to enjoin silence, fearing that Sylvester, whom she fondly loved, would by any such tale be distressed.

"Have the people in the village then seen the ghost again?" she inquired.

"They have," replied the reverend gentleman.

"Then, for goodness' sake, do not tell us any more about it—Sylvester, my dear, you will have another egg?"

"Not any more; I have had quite sufficient."

"Then go, my love, and look at the horse. I know that you'll find him uninjured. And, Sylvester, dear, *will* you do me the favour to take the pony, and leave an order for me at the grocer's?"

"Certainly, aunt."

"There's a dear."

She then wrote an order, and Sylvester withdrew; and the moment he had done so, she became extremely anxious to hear her reverend friend's "tale of horror."

"My dear madam," said he, on being urged to proceed, "I scarcely know how to explain to you what has occurred; but let me, in the first place, inform you, that a spectre on horseback was seen by the people of the village last night."

"A *spectre* on horseback! The horse was mine. It was, therefore, at least a real *horse*, and I should infer, from the way in which the animal has been goaded, that the rider was a real man."

"No, my dear madam, I am constrained to believe that the spectre which appeared on that horse was the same as that which I saw about three o'clock in your parlour."

"That which *you* saw? Good Heavens! you amaze me! If *you* have seen a spectre, there is something in it, indeed! But explain, my dear sir, pray explain."

"About three o'clock this morning," resumed the reverend gentleman, with an expression of intensity, "as Jones and I were sitting near the fire, I heard the gate close, and immediately afterwards footsteps coming slowly up the path. Well, thinking it advisable to wait until some attempt were made to force the outer door, we kept our seats, but in an instant we saw the handle of the parlour door turn, and a tall figure clad in white entered the room."

"Good Heavens!" energetically exclaimed Aunt Eleanor.

"I do not mean to say," pursued the reverend gentleman, "that I was not awed by the presence of this spirit! I do not mean to say that I did not experience an unusual tremor when it appeared; but I kept my eyes firmly fixed upon it —saw it walk with great solemnity of step across the room, shake its head, as if to indicate some disappointment, and then retire with corresponding solemnity to the door, past which it slowly vanished."

"Gracious goodness!—you inspire me with terror."

"Well," continued the reverend gentleman, "having in some degree recovered my self-possession, I rose, and went to the door, and there, to my utter amazement, discovered the *outer* door open! How it became open, Heaven only knows. I heard no sound—no lock unfastened—no chain removed—no bar unlatched—no bolt withdrawn. Indeed there was not time for any mortal to have accomplished even one of these things. Still all had been accomplished at once, and in silence—all had been done by magic! Well, I closed the door, and having done so, I heard the faint sound of footsteps behind me! I turned on the instant, and then beheld the same spirit slowly ascending the stairs!"

"Gracious powers!" exclaimed Aunt Eleanor, "what can be the meaning of this dreadful visitation?"

"I gave no alarm," resumed the reverend gentleman; "I thought it would be useless—probably presumptuous. I therefore returned to the parlour and listened, and there we remained till the morning dawned, when, as all was still, we departed."

"What on earth can have induced this? What *can* it mean?"

"I have hitherto, my dear madam, been to a certain extent a disbeliever in these supernatural appearances: I have hitherto held them to be either the coinage of a diseased imagination, or phantoms set up by designing men to draw the ignorant into superstition. But, although I still believe that the majority of those cases of which we have heard are ascribable to either knavery or enthusiasm, I now know beyond all doubt that spirits appear upon earth."

"But, my dear sir, tell me," said Aunt Eleanor anxiously, "tell me, to what do you ascribe—to what can you ascribe the awful appearance of spirits here?"

"I know not, my dear madam, what to ascribe it to. I know not from what it may spring, nor to what it may tend. These things are far above human comprehension. But do you remember—believe me, I do not ask for the gratification of any idle curiosity—but do you recollect any circumstance connected with any deceased friend, or any member of your family, at all calculated to warrant the belief that that friend or relative did not depart this life in peace?"

Aunt Eleanor started, and turned deadly pale. "A thought strikes me!" she exclaimed—"a dreadful thought! But no—no—no—it cannot be! And yet that horse was his! Great Heaven! if it should be the spirit of *him!*"

"My dear madam," said her reverend friend soothingly, as clasping her temples she burst into tears. "Compose yourself: be calm. As there is one above who protects the innocent, be assured that He will protect *you*. Whatever may have befallen him, I feel that you are guileless."

"And he was guileless too."

"Then let the blessed consciousness of that fact console you."

"And yet—if he should *not* have been!—if he should have died with a falsehood on his lips. But oh!" she added, weeping with bitterness, "I cannot believe it."

"Pardon me," said her reverend friend; "you will, I know, appreciate the only motive I have in putting this question; to whom do you allude?"

"To my brother. My dear—my only brother."

"Did not *he* die in peace?"

"Yes—I must still believe it—although broken-hearted, he died in peace."

"Then of what are you apprehensive?"

"The possibility—the bare possibility—of his having, with his last, his dying breath, solemnly declared himself innocent of that of which he knew that he was guilty."

"Had you any reason to suppose that he was guilty?"

"The strongest proofs were adduced, but his word—which I had never known him to violate—in my judgment, weighed them down. It was almost impossible for any one but me to doubt the evidence of his guilt; but, placing implicit confidence in his honour, *I* doubted it; and when on his death-bed he calmly and solemnly repeated his declaration of innocence, every doubt on my mind was removed."

"Was the offence with which he was charged of a heinous character?"

"I will explain, in order that you may the better judge whether he—which Heaven forbid!—can be associated with this fearful visitation."

"Do, my dear madam, and confide in my honour."

She then made an effort to be calm, and having dried her eyes, slowly commenced—

"My brother was a physician. His practice was extensive. He was mild, gentle, sensitive, highly intellectual, and amiable in all the relations of life. He was a dear brother to me. But to all he was kind—most kind. His heart was full of sympathy and benevolence; he was a philanthropist indeed. I need not tell you how he was beloved! To the poor he was a guardian—to the orphan a father—to the widow a friend. His unassumed virtues were conspicuous to all, and by all within the sphere of his influence he was honoured. For years he retained this position, and not a syllable against his fair fame was ever breathed; but one night—one most unhappy night—the servants of a lady whom he frequently attended, and whose reputation had been, up to that period, spotless,—joined in this declaration: that long after their mistress had retired they saw him distinctly leave her chamber; that he walked down stairs stealthily, and quitted the house; and that as neither of them had opened the door to him, their mistress must have let him in herself. Nor was this all. When their master, who had attended an agricultural dinner that evening, had been informed of this on his return, other circumstances, which afforded strong collateral evidence, at once occurred to him. He had seen my brother at that very dinner; he had taken wine with him, and recollected that he had left unusually early; he, moreover, saw him as he walked home, and spoke to him, and fancied—as my brother took no notice of him—that he wished to avoid him. These circumstances tended at least to justify the suspicions with which he had been inspired; and when, on going to his wife, whom he had found fast asleep, she declared that my brother had *not* been there—although his stick was then standing near the pillow—those suspicions were confirmed. I need not describe the fearful scene which ensued. It will be quite sufficient to say that he was frantic, and that having nearly broken the heart of his wife—whom he had theretofore tenderly loved—by his fierce denunciations, he rushed to the house of my brother with the view of taking summary vengeance upon him. Here, however, he found that the whole establishment had retired; and when the servant, who answered the bell from the window, perceiving the excitement under which he was labouring, refused to let him in, he loaded my brother with the direst imprecations, and threatened to take away his life. In the morning my brother received a challenge; and although he most solemnly declared, and called his servants to prove it, that at the specified time he was in bed and asleep, he was compelled, by those laws of honour which, although prescribed by barbarism, civilisation sanctions, to accept that challenge, and they met. He who felt himself thus deeply wronged fired first, and my brother fired into the air; again he fired at him, and my brother fired into the air again; when the seconds—perceiving that my brother was resolved *not* to fire at his adversary —withdrew them from the ground. Well "——

"But what became of the lady?"

"Her husband cast her off. He was advised to bring an action against my brother, but he loved her too fondly even then to expose her thus. He has since, I have heard, been most kind to her, although she has never been restored. But from that time my brother became an altered man. He at once lost the whole of his practice; but, having some little private property, that did not distress him much; it was the knowledge that almost every one believed him to be guilty of the crime, of which he constantly declared that he was innocent, which weighed his spirits down, and eventually broke his heart. As you are aware, I was present at his death, and during his last moments he and I were alone; he was calm—quite calm and collected—and as the last words he uttered were these—'Dear sister, I die happy in the consciousness of never having broken the seventh commandment,' every doubt vanished; I felt quite sure that he was innocent, and I cannot but think so still: it is this dreadful vision that has suggested the possibility of his having at that solemn moment perverted the truth."

"He would not have done that, be assured," said the reverend gentleman fervently; "such a man as that whom you have described would not, at such a time, have done that. I do not mean to say that there is no probability of this being his spirit—albeit, I am at a loss to understand why it should be thus perturbed—it *may* be the spirit of your brother: it is possible—it may even be said to be probable—but I do not believe that you have anything to fear."

"I will myself sit up to-night; I will watch in my chamber; I will pray for his spirit to come; and if it should, I will speak to it, and fervently entreat it to remove that weight which now presses so heavily upon my heart. I feel assured that it will not harm me," she added, bursting again into tears. "In life he loved me too fondly, too tenderly "——

"Dear aunt," cried Sylvester, who at this moment entered the room, "why—why are you thus distressed? What has happened? Tell me."

"These mysterious proceedings," said the reverend gentleman, "are so annoying."

"They are annoying, very annoying," returned Sylvester. "Aunt," he added, turning again to his aunt, "you were in excellent spirits when I left you."

"I am better now, my love," she observed, making an effort to compose herself; "much better now."

"And yet you are still in tears! I cannot bear to see *you* weep, dear aunt. Come, dry your eyes. You will not let *me* fret, and I don't see why I should let you. I came to ask you to go for a drive this morning. It is beautiful out. It will raise your spirits. The air is so soft, so mild, and so clear."

Aunt Eleanor kissed him, and the subject was dropped, and as the reverend gentleman soon after left, Sylvester took his aunt out for a drive.

CHAPTER XIII.

THE EGGS AND EXOTICS.

During the whole of that day no work was done in the village. The tradesmen then did not mind losing a day, for the times were not hard. The prosperous never complain of the times: nor did they. As their wants were small, a large supply was not needed, as they then possessed all they immediately required, they met at the Crumpet and Crown with the view of discussing the varied ramifications of the mystery.

But Jones was the great card in requisition. They wanted Jones. But as Jones was a steady man, who very seldom came to the Crumpet and Crown, they didn't know how to get him.

At length, however, Obadiah Drant—who possessed far more impudence than any of his friends—offered to bet half a gallon of beer that Jones would be there in a quarter of an hour. The bet was taken, and Obadiah—seeing an old rotten sugar-loaf turnip in the road—went out, picked it up, walked with it to Jones, and offered to bet half a gallon of beer that that turnip was superior to any one of his production. Jones laughed at this of course; and when the bet had been made, he produced a turnip somewhere about seven times the size. But Obadiah Drant would not confess that he had lost—he declared that he would never give in until Legge had decided the point; and thus Jones—who well knew that he had won—was seduced to the Crumpet and Crown.

Being there, of course he was considered a fixture. Pokey—who was artful in his way—hailed him as the first horticulturist in the county; and as the majority freely subscribed to this opinion, Jones was on very good terms with himself.

They then cautiously alluded to the philosophy of spectres; and when Click, with all the energy at his command, declared his conviction that spirits never appeared upon earth, Jones looked at him with an expression of pity, and then walked out of his silent shell.

"What!" he exclaimed, "do you mean to mean that spirits never comes upon this blessed earth?"

"Brayvo!" cried Obadiah Drant.

"Why, I see one last night!" resumed Jones.

"And so did I," said Obadiah.

"But not the one as I seed," said Jones.

"Mine was a tall 'un," returned Obadiah, "a white 'un!—a white 'un on horseback."

"That ain't the one then as I seed. I seed one—a white 'un and a tall 'un."

"Where?" demanded Click.

"Where! Why, at the cottage!"

"Were you at the cottage then *last* night?" said Legge.

"In course we was there! me and master!"

"Indeed! I was not aware of that. But tell us what occurred—I am anxious to hear."

"Well," said Jones, "but mind, it mustn't go further."

"Of course not—of *course* not. No, no, no—*no!*" they exclaimed simultaneously, "certainly not."

"Well, then—a little after three o'clock this blessed morning, when master and me was consulting about rakes, horticulture, and religion, we heerd a scraping on the path that leads from the gate to the front door. Very well, says I, this'll do nicely: we'll wait till you tries to get *in*, my carrots. But before we'd time to turn ourselves round, in walks a spirit! Very well, thinks I; it's all very good, you know, as far as it goes, but what do you mean to be after? Well! the spirit takes not the leasest notice of me, but up he goes to the sideboard and looks, and presently he shakes his head awful, and turns and then stalks out of the parlour. 'I says,' says I, 'what do you think of that?' says I to master. 'Rum, very rum,' says he, 'uncommon rum.' 'Well,' says I, 'the breeze is blowing very cold,' says I, 'let's shet the door'—and I went to shet it, and send I may live, if the front door wasn't as wide open as ever it could stick! Well! this did queer us rayther more than a little, but we shet the front door, and then blow *me*, if we didn't see the self-same spirit a going up stairs, as slow and deliberate as if he belonged to the house, and paid all the rates and taxes. 'Well,' says I, 'nothing like imperance. Let's go and see what he's up to,' says I. 'Not a bit of it,' says master. 'Let's have a little brandy'"——

"Teddy Rouse all over!" exclaimed Obadiah. "Brandy's the fructifying spirit of the cloth."

"What do you mean?" said Jones indignantly. "What do you mean by that?"

"I mean that Teddy Rouse"——

"Why do you call him *Teddy* Rouse? *My* master's name is the Reverend Mr. Rouse."

"But his Christian name is *Teddy!*"

"Not a bit of it! Them as calls him *Teddy* is ignoramuses."

"Do you mean to say that I'm an ignoramus?"

"You're worser!—or you'd never have brought that there turnip to me, and have said that I couldn't produce nothing like it. He as calls my master Teddy *is* an ignoramus! I don't care who he is! I'll tell him to his face he's an ignoramus. My master's name is the Reverend Mr. Rouse, and I don't care who knows it."

"Brayvo!" cried the company. "Brayvo, Jones!"

"Talk of Teddy," continued Jones, "as if he were your equal. I'll back my master—the Reverend Mr. Rouse—to look a ghost in the face against any man in England. Teddy, indeed! When he gave you the last order for a hundred of bricks, you didn't call him Teddy then, did you?"

"But Teddy," said Obadiah, "is the short for Edward. I meant no offence."

"Call *me* Teddy, Jack, Jem, or anything you like, but I'll fight till I drop before *he* shall be called Teddy."

"Well, then, let it be the Reverend Mr. Rouse; I don't care, that's the man I meant, after all."

"I know it's the man you meant," returned Jones, who was still very indignant; "but if any man—I don't care who he is—calls him Teddy, I won't have it! I know what master is, and I know what he isn't; there ain't a man in life as knows him better than me, and am I to hear him —hear a gentleman, and what's more, a clergyman—called Teddy?"

"Don't mind him," whispered Legge; "you know what a tattling fellow he is. You should take no notice of anything *he* says."

"Well," said Obadiah, "and what did the Reverend Mr. Rouse do when he had swallowed the brandy?"

"Go and inquire!" returned Jones fiercely. "You'll not get another blessed word out of me!"

"Well, but don't go yet!" they exclaimed, as he rose—"oh, stop and have a pipe with us—don't go yet!"

Jones, however, could not be prevailed upon to stay: he left at once, and the company, of whom the majority were at first very indignant with Obadiah, began to discuss, with characteristic ingenuity and eloquence, the various bearings of the scene which Jones had thus briefly described. This discussion—interspersed as it was with an infinite variety of anecdotes—lasted the whole of the day, and when at night they departed from the Crumpet and Crown their imaginations still teemed with ghosts.

Aunt Eleanor had ordered a fire in her chamber, and, as her resolution to sit up remained unshaken, she, at the usual hour, retired with her Bible and Prayer-book, and composed herself in a chair for the night.

Before, however, Judkins retired, he conceived an idea. It struck him just after he had eaten his supper. He imagined that if he, by means of a string, were to establish a direct communication between himself and the stable door, he should, in the event of any one attempting to take Snorter out of the stable again, know it.

Acting at once upon this admirable conception, he got a ball of whipcord, and having secured one end to the handle of the door, drew it carefully and tightly towards the window of his room, when, mounting a ladder, he put as much as he thought would be required through a hole, and on going to bed tied the end thus inserted to one of his toes, and went to sleep, in the full conviction that if a discovery *were* to be made, he should make it.

But neither he nor Aunt Eleanor were disturbed. She sat reading and praying throughout the night, but no spirit appeared. This had the direct effect of subduing her apprehensions. She had prayed in the full assurance that if the spirit which her reverend friend had seen were the spirit of her brother, it would appear before her then, and hence, as it did *not* appear, she not only felt sure that it was not her brother's spirit, but cherished again the sweet belief that his spirit was then in heaven.

When Judkins awoke in the morning, and took the whipcord off his toe, he was not exactly pleased with the fact of his not having been disturbed.

"Still," said he, "at all events nothing's been wrong.

This is a capital go, this is. I'll try this here dodge every night. Safe to catch 'em by this here means; wonder I never thought on't before. Howsoever," he added, "everything's right *this* morning—that's a blessing anyhow."

And he really did believe then that everything was right, and with this belief strongly impressed upon his mind he left the room; but the moment he entered the garden he found that all was *not* right, for he perceived at a glance, that about fifty exotics had been maliciously taken from the conservatory, and more than half buried in one of the onion beds.

"Why, blarm their bodies!" he exclaimed, as he tightly clenched his fists, and looked at the plants with great severity. "Couldn't they let even *them* alone? It's *no* use," he added, thrusting his hand into his pockets, "it ain't a mite o' use doing nothing. A man may work, and tile, and slave, and sweat, till there's nothing left on him. These here warment spiles all he does, and sets him to do it all over again. It ain't a bit o' good: I see that clear. I say, cook," he cried, "cook."

"Well, what do you want now?" demanded cook, who very seldom spoke sweetly.

"*Look* here. On'y just come and look. Here you are! Here's a go! Here's the warment," he added, "been at it again."

"Serve you right," said cook; "I'm glad of it."

"Serve me right—what do you mean?"

"I'm very much obliged to Mr. Judkins," returned cook, ironically; "very much obliged to you for lighting my fire."

"What do you mean? Don't bother me about your fire: I never lit your blessed fire."

"In course not," said cook, with a bitter sneer; "in course, Mister Judkins, you didn't light the blessed fire; nor did you, Mister Judkins, bile all the blessed eggs. I wish the last had stuck in your throat, that I do."

"You're a lunatic, woman," said Judkins severely; "go and get a strait-jacket; you want one particular."

"Do you mean, then, to have the unheard-of imperance to tell me to my very face that you *didn't* light the fire, and *didn't* bile every individual egg we had in the house?"

"I tell you, you're a lunatic. Don't bother *me*."

"Oh, it's all mighty well, Mister Judkins; but missis shall know of it. *I* won't conceal it. I've kept a good many things from her, but this she *shall* know. A great, greedy, gormandising glutton. I wouldn't have such a creature about the premises."

"I know you'll get into the asylum," said Judkins; "I know you will."

"The asylum," retorted cook sneeringly; "it would be a great blessing to society if *you* were in the asylum. One was not enough for Mister Judkins—two was not enough for Mister Judkins, nor three, nor four. Oh, dear, no! Mister Judkins must swallow the whole."

"I can't talk to maniacs. Don't talk to me. I know you're not right in your head; so go away, and don't bother."

"Oh, *you* shan't get off quite so easy as you think for. Don't believe it. The very *moment* missis comes downstairs, I'll tell her all about it. *I* won't favour you a mite."

"No, I know you won't. But go away—do you hear? I've something else to think about; go away, go away, *go* away with you."

"In course, Mr. Judkins," said cook, tossing her head with accomplished mock affectation. "Certainly, Mr. Judkins. I'll go, Mister Judkins. Mister Judkins, in course, is a very great man. Oh, a very great man is Mister Judkins; a mighty great man. But *I'll* cook the goose of Mister Judkins."

"I wish, with all my soul, you'd cook yourself," observed Judkins, who, as she retreated muttering all sorts of menaces, turned to contemplate his exotics again.

"This is a blessing as far as it goes," said he; "if it isn't, send I may live." But no sooner had he given expression to this remarkable sentiment, than a man led his mistress's pony and gig up to the gate and rang the bell.

"Very *good!*" thought Judkins, as he went to the gate. "This here's the seed of *something*."

"Is this here pony yourn?" inquired the man.

"Rayther," returned Judkins. "It *is* ourn rayther;" and seizing the man by the collar, instantly added, "So, we've cotched you at last, have we? *Very* good; now, my little swell, *con*-sider yourself booked. You're my prisoner."

"What for?" cried the man, who had been absolutely taken by surprise.

"Never mind what for," replied Judkins. "Don't be at *all* particular in your inquiries. *I'm* not. You'll only just walk quietly this here way, and then possibly, perhaps, the question may be by and-by answered. Well, I shouldn't have thought it on you," he added, as he dragged the man, who felt quite confused, into the stable; "send I may live, I shouldn't ha' thought that you'd had the stuff in you to do it."

"To do what?" demanded the man.

"Never mind," replied Judkins. "You're a beauty to look at; dessay you're a beauty—no doubt. You and me shall be better acquainted, it *strikes* me."

"What do you *mean?*" cried the man.

"Don't *disturb* yourself, my friend. It's very clear you won't disturb me no more."

"I found the pony"——

"Don't trouble your intellects now at all about it. You'll have work enough for them to do when you're afore the jury. Now then," he added, as with a halter he securely tied the man's hands behind him, "if you'd like to lie down for an hour, you can. You know this horse, don't you? I wonder he doesn't snap your precious little head off."

"What do you mean?" cried the man. "I'll make you pay for this."

"Very *good!*" replied Judkins. "That's nothing but nateral. But let's have a look at you. Well," he added, having surveyed him, "you're a good sort, dessay—*of* the sort. *Very* good. You're a very clever sort too, no doubt. But couldn't you leave my plants alone? *Tcha!* that was cowardly. Well, I hope you'll have all the luck I wish you, and that ain't much; but I'll leave you to your private reflections."

"But won't you hear me?"

"Not a bit of it! What's the good! but I'll see you again, by-and-by. If you'd been a man of six foot and a half, and very stout in proportion, I shouldn't ha' minded; but you, you little muck!—however, good-bye; God bless you; take care of yourself, but if you don't, I'll take care of you, so you're safe. You *little* warment," he added, closing the door, and when he had most securely locked it, he returned to the cottage.

"Missis wants to speak to you," said Mary, as he entered.

"Very good, Polly, I wants to speak to her. So that meets the views of both parties consarned."

"Well, I must say you're imperant, Judkins," said Mary. "But missis is in the breakfast-room."

"Very good," returned Judkins. "Then into the breakfast-room I goes."

"Judkins," said his mistress, when he had been desired to enter, "I am sorry to hear so bad an account of your conduct."

"I know what you mean, ma'am. It's cook. Don't mind what she says, she's a lunatic, ma'am. She says I eat the eggs—*I* never eat the eggs. She says I lit her fire—*I* never lit her fire. But I've done something else, ma'am; I've got in my stable the very man who has been, ma'am, annoying us so long."

"Is it possible? Have you really! Is he now in the stable?"

"Secure, ma'am. I've roped him regular. He can't get away."

"Have you locked the door?"

"Fast, ma'am. Here's the key. He didn't want Snorter last night. No, he only just wanted the pony and gig."

"Well, run to Mr. Rouse with my compliments. Tell him what has happened, and beg of him to come as soon as possible."

Judkins started off at full speed, and in less than five minutes the reverend gentleman was there.

"My dear sir," said Aunt Eleanor, as he entered, "I have the happiness to inform you, that we have at length discovered"——

"I know, my dear madam, I know all about it," said the reverend gentleman; "Judkins, bring him in."

Judkins disappeared on the instant, and soon reappeared with his prisoner.

"Now, sir, what's your name?" inquired the reverend gentleman.

"John Todd," replied the man.

"John Todd! John Todd! Well, sir, what have you to say to this?"

"All I have to say is, that master found the pony in one of his meadows, and hearing that it belonged to this lady, he told me to take it home."

"Your master, sir!—who is your master?"

"Squire Lane, your reverence."

"Oh! Squire Lane. John Todd! John Todd! Don't you occupy the cottage on the left of his gate, John Todd?"

"Yes, your reverence."

"There has been some mistake here, my dear madam,"

said the reverend gentleman aside. "John Todd," he added, turning again to the man, "you are a very honest person, John Todd. I recollect you. Give my compliments to your master, and tell him that I will do myself the pleasure of calling upon him in the course of the morning. There has been some mistake, but never mind what has passed. I here present you with half-a-crown for your trouble."

John did not much like the rough treatment he had received, but as the half-crown healed every wound that had been inflicted, he respectfully bowed, and in silence withdrew.

"I know John Todd," observed the reverend gentleman; "he's a very honest man. I have known him for years, and I am perfectly sure that he is not at all involved in this mystery."

"I hope, sir," said Judkins, "that I haven't in your opinion exceeded my duty."

"You acted very correctly, Judkins, very correctly," replied the reverend gentleman. "Had I been in your position, I should doubtless have acted in precisely the same manner."

"You see," pursued Judkins, "things happened so rum. One morning one thing, another morning another—as true as I'm alive, sir, if you'll believe me, I sometimes don't even so much as know what's what. Now, look here, ma'am," he added, turning to his mistress; "I beg pardon, ma'am, for being so bold, ma'am, but jist look here. Here was this blessed morning as ever was, ma'am, when I came downstairs and went into the garden, what should I see but my best plants walked from the hothouse and sunk into one of the onion beds."

"What, this morning!" exclaimed Aunt Eleanor.

"This blessed morning, ma'am—there they was."

"How very extraordinary," said his mistress.

"Amazing," exclaimed the reverend gentleman. "Were they injured at all."

"Not the leasest," replied Judkins; "leastways they haven't taken much harm, except, p'r'aps, they've caught a little cold."

"But they were placed in the bed carefully?"

"Very. There wasn't a branch broke. That's the thing as gets over me so much. They seems not to want to hurt nothing: that don't seem to be their object, and as that ain't their object, what their object is, I can't guess. Sure-*ly* they might leave the *plants* alone; *they* can't have offended 'em in any individual way, nohow. But that ain't all, ma'am. When I was a meditating over them serious, cook comes to me, and says, 'You've lit my fire, and gormandised every blessed egg.'"

"And you mean to say that you did *not* light the fire?" inquired his mistress seriously.

"Never, ma'am. Upon my word and honour, ma'am. I wish I may never rear nothing, if I ever touched the fire. And, as to the eggs, ma'am, why, it stands to reason that I wouldn't think of touching 'em: I ain't eat a single egg this six months. I don't care a bit about 'em; and if I did, it ain't so likely that I'd go and do such a thing as that. Not a bit of it, ma'am, if you'll believe me. No; it's them fellows —whoever they are—and I on'y jist wish I could catch 'em. However they *do* it, wholly gets over me. F" instance, how did they get the pony and gig out? How could they get 'em out? Why, ma'am, I not only locked the stable door, and hung the key on the hook in the kitchen, but I had a piece of string that reached from that very door to my bedroom, and I slept with the other end round my toe, ma'am, all night; so, how they got in, I can't tell. It seems to me to be witchcraft, and nothing but."

Aunt Eleanor now very clearly perceived that these tricks were too paltry to be for one moment ascribed to the spirit of her brother; and having made up her mind to leave the village for a time, she at once resolved on spending a few weeks in London.

CHAPTER XIV.

THE DEPARTURE FROM THE VILLAGE.

THEY who have been unaccustomed to travel, find the job of preparing to leave home a strong one. However inconsiderable the journey may be, or however short the contemplated stay, the preparations which they deem essential are great. Much thought is brought to bear upon the preliminaries, much time is occupied in carrying out the scheme, and when that has been perfected and the day of departure arrives, the excitement is generally excessive.

Aunt Eleanor had been unaccustomed to travel: *she* found the job of preparing to leave home a strong job: *she* brought much thought to bear directly upon the preliminaries, and occupied much time in perfecting the scheme: nor did she expect that on the morning of her departure, she should have the slightest appetite for breakfast, for the village may be said to have been her world, and if the idea of leaving that village did not appear to her like that of leaving the world, her feelings bore a very strong affinity to those of persons who are about to visit some distant land.

On the day, however, immediately preceding that appointed for her journey to London, other feelings were inspired; for while walking alone in the garden, contemplating the change she was about to experience, and endeavouring to recollect if anything had been forgotten, she saw lying on the table in the arbour, a carefully folded note, sealed with the family crest, and superscribed "*Rosalie.*"

"What on earth have we here?" she exclaimed, as she turned the note over and over again. "The handwriting resembles that of Sylvester!—yet surely it cannot be his! Rosalie! Dear me, what can it mean? Rosalie! How very mysterious."

While anxiously dwelling upon this little incident, and considering what course she could with propriety pursue, her reverend friend entered the garden, and when they had greeted each other with their accustomed cordiality, she explained to him how she had found the note, and then proceeded to solicit his advice.

"It's very odd," said the reverend gentleman, "very odd; nay, it's remarkably odd. But let us go in, and see what we can make of it."

Into the house they accordingly went, and when they were seated, the reverend gentleman took the note, and having looked very severely at the superscription and the seal, turned it over and over and over again, with an expression of intense curiosity.

"Well," said he, at length, "let us look at the contents."

"Will it be correct," said Aunt Eleanor, "to open it?"

"Perfectly so, my dear madam!—of course!"

"It is not addressed to either of us."

"But it is the handwriting of Sylvester!"

"I think it is. It looks very much like his handwriting. But I am not sure."

"Oh, it's certain to be his; and if even it be not, you have an indisputable right to examine it, seeing that it was found on your premises, addressed to a person of whom you have no knowledge; but as it most surely is his, you have a double right to examine it, inasmuch as he is here under your especial care."

"But I should not like to wound his feelings."

"For that I would submit there is no necessity whatever. The thing may be concealed. He need not know that we have opened the note; he need not even know that you found it. The young rogue may have fallen in love. Who can tell! He may be the intended victim of some artful creature, whose object is to ensnare him. Who knows! We have heard of such things, and it hence becomes our duty to protect him—we must put him on his guard, and not allow him to be sacrificed."

"Very true, my dear sir," said Aunt Eleanor, smiling; "I fully appreciate all that you have said, but would it not be equally effective if I were to have him in, and give him the note as it is?"

"As you please, my dear madam. I of course cannot presume to have any direct voice in the matter."

"But do you not think that it would be equally effective?"

"Perhaps it might. Oh, yes. We shall be able to see the changes of his countenance, and from those changes to draw inferences which may enable us to arrive pretty nearly at the truth. Oh, yes; I can see no objection whatever to his being called in."

Aunt Eleanor then rang the bell, and directed the servant to tell Sylvester, who was in the library, that she wished to speak with him for a moment.

"That name puzzles me," resumed the reverend gentleman. "I cannot imagine who Rosalie is! I have baptized all the young persons in the village, but I do not remember the name of Rosalie! Rosalie!—Rosalie! Bless my life and soul, the name of Rosalie doesn't occur to me at all."

"My dear," said Aunt Eleanor, as Sylvester entered, "who is Rosalie?"

"I don't know, I'm sure, aunt, who Rosalie is. Rosalie, I presume, is the name of a young lady, and a very pretty name she has got, but I do not remember to have met with any one named Rosalie. Who is she?"

"Nay, my dear, I wish to know from you who she is. I have not the pleasure of knowing the lady myself."

"Nor have I," returned Sylvester. "But why do you ask *me* about her?"

"This note, my dear, I found in the arbour just now. It is your handwriting, my love, is it not?"

"It looks very much like it. Rosalie! What is it all about?" he added, breaking the seal—

"'BEAUTIFUL ROSALIE,
  Meet me to-night.
  Do not fail, Rosalie! Sweet! do not fail!'

"Well," he continued, "this *is* extraordinary. The writing is exactly like mine. I never saw two hands so much alike. Look."

"It is indeed like yours, my dear," said Aunt Eleanor.

"Exactly," cried Sylvester, who felt much amazed. "I'll just copy it, and then you will see the resemblance more clearly. Beautiful Sylvester," he added, copying the note. "No, no, 'Beautiful Sylvester' will not do at all.

"'BEAUTIFUL ROSALIE,
  Meet me to-night.
  Do not fail, Rosalie! Sweet! do not fail!'

"There," he continued, having finished the transcript; "look at this and then look at that."

"I cannot distinguish the slightest difference between them," said Aunt Eleanor.

"Nor can I," returned Sylvester. "See," he added, placing both the copy and the original before the reverend gentleman, who had been watching him with unexampled subtlety. "See what an extraordinary resemblance there is."

"Resemblance!" echoed the reverend gentleman, who couldn't at all understand this coolness. "They are both alike! The B's are the same, and the R's are the same, and so are the M's, D's, and S's. I can see no difference at all. If I fold this as that has been folded, I'll defy any man alive to tell which is which."

"Try it," said Sylvester. "Fold it in precisely the same manner, and *then* let us have a look at them."

The reverend gentleman gazed at him for a moment with an expression of doubt mingled with amazement, but as Sylvester met his gaze firmly, he did fold the copy in precisely the same manner, and having done so, exclaimed—

"There! Now, which is which?"

"I can see that this is the one which I wrote," returned Sylvester, "because the ink is not quite dry, and therefore somewhat paler; but were it not for that, I should be utterly unable to tell which of the two had been written by me."

"Then you really did *not* write them both?"

"Write them both? Certainly not. Of that I know nothing."

"Then all I can say is, it's very remarkable."

"It is remarkable. But is it supposed that the note which I have copied was written by me?"

"Why, it looked so much like your handwriting, my dear," said Aunt Eleanor mildly, "that we did think it must have been written by you."

"Then let me, my dear aunt, at once undeceive you. The resemblance which it bears to my hand is very striking; but I assure you—I feel that you will believe me—I assure you, upon my honour, that I know nothing whatever about it."

"That is quite sufficient, my dear—quite sufficient; I am perfectly satisfied; but is it not strange?"

"It is indeed extraordinary."

"Some one must have practised your style of writing with zeal to be enabled to give so close an imitation," observed the reverend gentleman, who was still extremely sceptical on the point.

"I certainly," said Sylvester, "never before saw two hands so much alike. But who sent this note?"

"I found it in the arbour," replied his aunt. "It was lying on the table."

"In the arbour! And do you not know who this Rosalie is?"

"I have not the least idea who she can be."

"Nor have I. I do not remember to have heard the name of Rosalie before."

"But the crest, my dear madam," said the reverend gentleman; "you have not mentioned the crest."

"The crest," said Sylvester, looking at it. "Why, it is *our* crest! I have one exactly like it," he added, producing a seal attached to his watch-chain, and placing it in the wax. "Why, it fits to a nicety! How very, very odd. The impression would seem to have been made by this very seal. You had one, aunt; you haven't lost it?"

"No, my love, I have it here; but mine is much smaller."

"Well, this surpasses all I ever heard of. This seal was given to me by my poor father the very day on which he died, and as I have not corresponded with any one since, I have never had occasion to use it. How, therefore, this impression of it could have been made, I am utterly unable to conceive, being certain that it has never been out of my possession."

When Sylvester alluded to his father, tears sprang into the eyes of Aunt Eleanor on the instant, and the reverend gentleman—who up to that moment had regarded the denial as a falsehood—felt that as no human being could be guilty of an act of wickedness so awful as that of deliberately associating a falsehood with the name of a parent so recently deceased, Sylvester, however strong the evidence against him might appear, must have spoken the truth. He therefore observed that in heaven, and on earth, and in the waters under the earth, there were mysteries which set all human understanding at defiance; and having made this remarkable observation, he put an end to the discussion by saying distinctly, and that with great firmness and point, that all he could say on the subject was this, that the thing was excessively odd.

But although he permitted the subject to drop for the time being thus, he would not suffer the investigation of that subject to rest there. No; he felt himself bound, as a minister and a man, to find out who Rosalie was, with the view of ascertaining beyond all doubt, whether Sylvester had spoken the truth or not. He therefore, on leaving the cottage, started on this affectionate expedition, and as he proceeded, he carefully prepared a touching lecture to be delivered with appropriate solemnity to Sylvester in the event of its being proved—satisfactorily proved—that his calm declaration having reference to his entire ignorance of Rosalie was false. But then, before this could be proved to the satisfaction of any one, and consequently before this touching lecture could be delivered, Rosalie had to be found. The reverend gentleman felt this deeply. He had not the slightest doubt that, if he found her, he should be able, by

K

an appeal—which he had also prepared, and it was one of an exceedingly powerful nature—to induce her at once to make a full confession; but he could *not* find her—no one in the village knew anything of her—not one had ever heard of the name of Rosalie before. They all knew a multitude of Maries, and all admitted that Rosalie was a much sweeter name—more melodious in sound, and in effect more *distingué* —the matrons of the village were especially delighted with it, and made up their minds with the most prompt unanimity to have the next girls they had christened Rosalie, and thus left no room for the reverend gentleman to doubt that the next generation would be studded with Rosalies; but this was not the point—his object was to discover one then; but as he found—after having travelled fairly through the village, making all the inquiries which the importance of the case demanded—that no Rosalie had ever existed there within the memory of the oldest inhabitant, she being a hundred and six years of age, he gave the thing up, and the consequence was that both the appeal and the lecture were lost.

These inquiries, however, were not without effect, although they failed to accomplish the object proposed. The reverend gentleman had omitted of course to explain to them why he sought Rosalie with so much diligence; and this omission, very naturally, and therefore very generally, suggested the question, "What can he want with her?" That she had done *something* wrong was a conclusion which, on being duly drawn from the premises, appeared to be rational to all; but then, what was that something?—what could it be?—was it an act of indiscretion or something much worse? They of course couldn't tell: their conjectures were innumerable, but as they were at the same time very conflicting, no dependence was placed upon any one of them, until the news reached the ears of Mr. Obadiah Drant, who proceeded to settle the question at once.

"I'll tell you what it is," said he to Pokey; "I can see clear through all the rampant ramifications of this fructifying manœuvre. Look here. Old Teddy Rouse wants this girl. Very well. What does he want her for? that's the point at issue! He's got no wife: he never had a wife. Very well then, can't you see? I'll bet you any money you like, that it's one of Ted's ladies."

"But," said Pokey, raising his eyes from his board, and taking snuff, "if it is, don't you think he'd know exact where to find her?"

"Not a bit of it. French!—Rosalie!—French, my boy! It's been a French name ever since Peter the Great's time. She's come over to find him out—don't you understand? Housekeeper! artful! *Now* don't you see? These are your moral men!—these are your saints!—these are the locusts that suck fifty millions a year from the sweat of the poor man's brow!—there ain't of the cloth that don't ought to be smothered. I'd hang, draw, and quarter the lot. What do we want a mob of vampires like that for. I'd send 'em all on board a man-o'-war, if I'd my will, and give 'em a good welting four or five times a day, and let 'em see how they like that. And it'll come to this at last; mark my words if it don't. People's eyes begin to be a little matter open; they only want to open 'm just a leetle more, and bang comes a rattling revolution."

"Not a bit of it," said Pokey, who always felt indignant when Obadiah spoke of a revolution. "Revolutions is mighty fine things for to talk about, but we ain't going to have 'em. Look at me, for instance. Me and my missis has got six-and-twenty pun ten in the savings bank—wouldn't I fight till I dropped before I'd lose that six-and-twenty pun ten, think you? And how many thousands of men is there in the very same predicament!"

"Fight till you dropped, for six-and-twenty pun ten!" retorted Obadiah sneeringly. "What's six-and-twenty pun ten?"

"As much to me as six-and-twenty thousand pun ten is to any of your dukes, lords, and bishops."

"Why, you ain't got a mite of patriotic spirit in you!"

"I ain't agoing to let any patriotic spirit do me out of my money."

"Do you out of your money! I'm ashamed of you, Pokey. A man of your intellects, too."

"I don't care; intellects in this world ain't of much use to a man without money."

"Then you think that such locusts as Teddy Rouse ought to be allowed to do just as they please?"

"No, I don't."

"And you'd pay 'em elevenpence-halfpenny out of every

blessed shilling you earn, that they might have their French Rosalies?"

"No, I wouldn't."

"You wouldn't! Why, look at Teddy Rouse. He's a sample of the sack. He must have *his* Rosalie, and where will you go to find one that hasn't hisn? Look at the thing logically—not through the short-sighted spectacles which always bring in view your six-and-twenty pun ten, but logically "——

"It'll take a lot of logic to convince me that I should be a better man without that six-and-twenty pun ten than I am with it."

"Well, but listen. You don't at all like these locusts. Very good! You don't at all like the idea of a revolution. Good again! But if it's impossible to get rid of 'em without a revolution, what do you say then?"

"Why, rather than stand and see my money scrambled for, send I may live, I'd fight till I dropped."

"Then you're a Tory. I know you're a Tory. You've no right to vote for the yellows at all."

"*Haven't* I no right to vote for the yellows? My father was a yellow, and he brought me up a yellow; and if ever you catch me changing my colour, expect to catch a fox asleep. If I had no money, I shouldn't care a button about a revolution; a revolution then wouldn't matter at all to me: but as I have money, and can't draw it without notice, blister *me* if ever I'll vote for revolution."

"I'm disgusted with you, Pokey!" exclaimed Obadiah. "You ought to be on Bobby Peel's side of the house. It's such sentiments as these that have drawn a matter of eighteen hundred million a year from our vitals."

"I wouldn't draw nothing from nobody's vitals."

"Then why do you sanction such men as Teddy Rouse? Why, when you see him running after his girls, don't you set your face against him? Suppose you were the father of this girl—this Rosalie—would you like it?"

"I don't say I should!"

"Very well, then. I mean to say it's monstrous that we should pay fifty million a year to enable these men to run after their Rosalies, as old Teddy Rouse has been running after his. Don't tell me about the cloth! The cloth's rotten, and always was. Even before the Pope was welted at the battle of Bunker's Hill, they were both corrupt and clerical, and anything that's clerical must of course be rotten. Look at Russia, look at Prussia, look at China, look at Spain, look at France, look at Switzerland, look where you will, they're all alike, all corrupt, all rotten, all bad. I mean to say we must have a rattling revolution in order to keep society together: we must have a regular roaring rebellion, in order to keep us from anarchy and ruin. Are we to have a parcel of oligarchies, think you, squeezing the marrow out of our very bones eternally? Do you think that this can be eternally tolerated? No!—not a bit of it. No!—they must come down!—and, mark my words, when they do come down, they'll come down with a run. All your six-and-twenty-punten men in the universe won't save 'em; come down they must and *will!* Mark my word. You may try to keep such men as Teddy Rouse on—you may encourage 'em in running about after their Rosalies"——

"I don't encourage 'em in nothing of the sort!"

"Then why don't you stand up against 'em like a man? Shall we wink at such practices as these, when they come directly under our very noses?"

"But *I* don't know nothing about practices. Look here! —this Rosalie!—what do I know about her?—how do I know that there's anything wrong?—who is she?—what's her business?—where does she come from?"

"Didn't I tell you France? She's one of the French dancers, no doubt. And as for not knowing whether there's anything wrong! Look here! Suppose you were to run about the village inquiring for Rosalie or Rosamond, or any other girl, what would Mrs. Pokey say?"

"Why, I don't suppose she'd like it."

"Very well, then. Doesn't that make the case clear? But I'll find this Rosalie out!—I'll run her down!—I'll pretty soon know who she is! Master Ted shan't be let off so easy as he has been. I'll stick to him—I'll show him up! But ta-ta! can't stop. Mind you take care of your six-and-twenty pun ten!"

"I means it," said Pokey.

"But, mark my words, my boy, it ain't your six-and-twenty pun ten that'll save this mighty country from a rattling revolution!"

Having in a strictly confidential tone given emphatic utterance to this singular sentiment, Obadiah gaily left his monied friend, and proceeded to congratulate himself on the extraordinary eloquence he had displayed.

Meanwhile Aunt Eleanor's mind was distressed. To her the note addressed to Rosalie had been the source of much pain: not because she imagined for one moment that the declaration of Sylvester was false!—she felt on the contrary convinced that it was true—but because she was deeply apprehensive that the note had some mysterious connection with her brother. She knew not why such an apprehension should be inspired: with the exception of the fact of the seal having been his, there was not the slightest link of connection between them; still the previously conceived possibility of her dear brother's spirit having been perturbed, had created this feeling of apprehension of which her mind could not be divested.

This, however, was not allowed to alter her plans having reference to her journey to London on the morrow. Upon this she had decided: all her arrangements had been made, and when the reverend gentleman—who spent the evening with them, and endeavoured to cheer them by a facetious description of that which he held to be the salubrious qualities of London smoke—had taken his leave, she and Sylvester calmly retired to rest.

During that night no voices were heard. The cottage itself seemed fast asleep, and the turnip-tops nodded and nodded until they developed the strong diagnosis of dreaming: the shrubbery was hushed, and the carrots were still, and while the caterpillars ceased to work their interesting eyeletholes, not only in the cabbage sprouts, but in the silent leaves of the savoys; the stony-hearted urns, which stood like sentinels at the gate, issued no sort of sound, which was very remarkable—very!—and as these things don't occur every night in the week, they ought to be nicely described.

This general tranquillity throughout the night was appreciated, and when cook in the morning came down and saw everything around her precisely as she left it, she began to congratulate herself on the prospect of a total cessation of that state of things by which she and the rest had been so long annoyed.

On proceeding, however, to light the kitchen fire, she found that the chimney wouldn't draw. This at first she ascribed to a change of the wind. The wood burned well, and there was plenty of it; but the smoke curled into the kitchen in volumes! She opened the door that the draught might be stronger, but the smoke became every moment more dense. She looked at the vane: the wind was south-west: the place had never smoked before when the wind was south-west!—nor did she believe that the chimney was foul.

"Hallo!" shouted Judkins, as the waves of smoke rolled into his chamber. "What are you at? Do you want to choke a fellow? What are you up to? Cook!"

"Come down!" cried cook, who kept outside the door.

"What's the matter?" demanded Judkins, on opening the window. "Is the house on fire?"

"No! but the chimney's smoking awful! Come down."

Judkins left the window, and descended the stairs; but the moment he opened the door which led immediately into the kitchen, he was met by a dense mass of smoke which almost caused him to fall backwards. His presence of mind only saved him. Suffocated as he felt—oppressed as he was—he rushed through the kitchen with all the energy at his command, and on reaching the garden, began to cough with unprecedented power and zeal.

"What—ho, o-ho, o-ho!" he cried. "What devil's—ho-o—trick is this?"

"Come and put a stop to it!" said cook, with great severity. "Don't stand rolling about and barking there like a born fool!"

Judkins would have said that she was a *nice* woman, but couldn't. He kept on coughing like a frightfully asthmatic individual, and continued to cough as if he had been thus afflicted, despite the hot remonstrances of cook, who did really indulge on this occasion in many unladylike expressions of disgust.

In the meantime the density of the smoke so much increased that it drove cook fiercely from the door; and when Judkins with coughing felt utterly exhausted, he managed to turn a tub upside down, with the view of taking a seat, but in his agony he came down upon it such a lump that he broke in the bottom and there he stuck.

Cook was now ferocious. Her rage knew no bounds. She shook her fists fiercely, and threatened to claw the eyes out of the precious head of Judkins, who had not the slightest power to extricate himself, and whose spirit of independence was too noble, too pure, to allow him to solicit her assistance.

"What do you *mean?*" she exclaimed, when the scum of her rage had boiled over. "What is it you *mean?* This is not a trick of yours!—oh! no: it isn't your trick!"

"My trick!" said Judkins, as well as he could. "Woman! you're a lunatic. I've told you so before."

"Don't provoke me!" she exclaimed, as her passion increased; "you'd better not provoke me!"

And Judkins too thought that this would not be advisable, seeing that she had all the power then in her own hands; and being thus fixed, he felt that, if she were to attack him, however fiercely, he couldn't help it; he *couldn't* defend himself; he couldn't get away.

"Call me a lunatic again, at your peril!" she continued, coming conveniently near to the tub. "*Dare* to call me a lunatic again, and I'll make you remember it the longest day you have to live. Now call me a lunatic again, if you dare!"

Judkins did not dare to do anything of the sort. He had to use his own discretion, and that discretion prompted silence; but just as he had recovered sufficient strength to make an effort to relieve himself, Mary—who, finding that she could not enter the kitchen, had opened the front door and come round the cottage—appeared, when Judkins, who was very glad to see her, said, "Polly, my girl, help me out of this pickle."

"Don't touch him," cried cook.

"I'm sure I shall!" returned Mary. "Why shouldn't I?"

"He has been the cause of all!" replied cook.

"Don't you mind her," said Judkins. "There, put your foot against the tub and take hold of my hands!"

Mary did so, and pulled him fairly up, and the tub rose with him; but he soon discarded that, and when he found himself free, he went boldly up to cook and asked her what she really meant.

"What do I mean," replied cook, who was, under present circumstances, somewhat more cautious; "why, this is what I mean—I mean to say that you or somebody else has been stuffing up my chimney."

"Stuffing up your chimney!" retorted Judkins. "Why, you ain't fit to live on a civilised scale. You took advantage of my position in society just now; but I tell you again and again you're a lunatic, and don't ought to breathe the same air as a Christian. Stop up your chimney! Why don't you go then and onstop it?"

" 'Cause I don't want to be choked," replied cook.

"Choked!" echoed Judkins; "if you was choked, it would in my mind be a blessing." And he tried to rub his blade bones, but couldn't get near them, which was lamentable, seeing that they were painful in the extreme, for as they couldn't yield to the edge of the tub, and as the edge of the tub wouldn't yield an inch to them, the pressure had really been very severe.

"Well," said Mary, "what's to be done? Missis won't be long now afore she's up, and if she comes down and finds no breakfast ready for her, she won't be best pleased."

"Pleased! no more she don't ought," returned cook. "The very morning too she's going up to London. Do you think that *I'd* have such people about me? You'd better go round and light a fire in the parlour, and bile the kettle there. There's no chance of it's ever being biled in the kitchen. Did you ever see," she added, pointing fiercely to the smoke which still continued to rush in volumes into the garden. "I shall have a pretty job after this. Every individual thing in the place will be smothered. But go, Mary; go and light a fire in the parlour."

And Mary for that purpose did go; and while cook was earnestly contemplating the smoke which, as the flames had expired, grew less and less dense, the unhappy man Judkins was silently invoking that spirit of ingenuity which he felt he had in him, with the view of replacing the bottom of the tub.

Scarcely, however, had he arrived at the conclusion that, if he could get it into the groove again it would hold, when Mary came rushing round the cottage, exclaiming, "It's just the same! they're all alike! the parlour's chock full of one solid mask of smoke."

"What!" cried cook, glancing at Judkins significantly, "has he stuffed up the parlour chimney too?"

"I wish your mouth was stuffed up," observed Judkins, with asperity; "that would be a comfort to *all* mankind. The devil's *in* the chimnies, that's my belief," he added; and just as he had finished this remarkable sentence, their mistress's bell rung violently.

"There!" cried cook, "now we shall just see who's right and who's wrong. Come along, Mary; we'll both go up to missis together."

"And if you say anything about me," said Judkins, "I'll let you know the difference."

"I shan't mince the matter a mite," retorted cook.

"No, I know you won't," said Judkins. "If ever there *was* a imp, she's one," he added, as cook and Mary went round to answer the bell. But before they reached the chamber, their mistress met them, for as the parlour chimney communicated with the one in her room, the smoke which issued from it had driven her out.

"What on earth is the matter?" she demanded. "Where does all this smoke come from?"

"The chimney," said cook.

"Is the chimney on fire?"

"No; it's stuffed up with something, ma'am."

"Send for the sweep instantly! Don't lose a moment. Tell Judkins to make the utmost haste. Good gracious me," she continued, knocking at Sylvester's door, as Mary ran downstairs to send Judkins off for the village sweep, "Sylvester, my love!" she added, knocking still louder. "*Great* Heavens!—Sylvester!—Sylvester!—come to the door."

"Is that *you*, aunt?" he cried; and on hearing his voice, she clasped her hands, and fervently thanked Heaven that he was safe.

"What is the matter?" he inquired, on opening the door.

His aunt fell upon his neck, and could not for a moment answer.

"What is it?—what has happened?" again he demanded.

"Nothing, my love," she replied, "nothing of importance. I feared that you had been overpowered by the smoke."

"What, is there a fire?"

"No, no, no—no, my love—no! The chimney's out of order—yes—the chimney's out of order—nothing more."

"Then why do you tremble so?"

"Do I tremble now? I thought the smoke might have reached your room."

"No, I've had no smoke here. I smell it now strongly. But come, come! Dear aunt, you will cause me to think that something more has occurred."

"No, no—nothing more—nothing more—believe me."

"Then compose yourself: come!—the smoke will very soon evaporate. I'll just slip my things on: I'll not be a moment."

Aunt Eleanor then descended with Mary, and on going into the parlour, in which no attempt to light a fire had been made, she examined the chimney, and being unable to see anything in it at once directed that to be tried.

And it was tried, and lo! the result was the same: they were compelled to leave the room to escape suffocation.

"How very extraordinary," exclaimed Aunt Eleanor. "It cannot be the wind."

She opened the front door; and as she did so, Judkins appeared with the sweep—a respectable and highly intelligent individual—who had been in practice more than half a century.

"I am glad that you are come," said Aunt Eleanor; "our chimneys are sadly out of order."

"It theemth ath though they voth," observed Chokes, who was blessed with a lisp of incomparable sweetness. "And yet it ithn't vethy long thinth they voth done. Vith one ith the vortht, mum?"

"They appear to be all alike."

"Then there mutht be thomethin wrong. But vith do you vont firtht?"

"The kitchen perhaps had better be done first."

"Vethy good."

"But be as quick as possible, there's a good man."

To the kitchen Chokes accordingly proceeded with Judkins, and found it comparatively clear; and while he was examining the chimney, Aunt Eleanor went into Sylvester's room, the only room in the house which was then free from smoke.

"Vy, there ithn't muth thut in thith thimbley," cried Chokes. "There theemth to be nothin amith vith thith."

"There must be *something* amiss with it," cried cook; "that's all nonsense."

Chokes would have begged of her to allow him to know his own business, but as he had no desire to be discourteous, he merely looked as if he meant it.

"I thay," said he, "there ithn't thut enough in thith thimbley to make it thmoke. But I like to go about thingth thilent and phillethophical. How did the thmoke come down? all of a heap?"

"It come down in one mask," replied cook.

"I thee," said Chokes, with intelligence beaming in his eye. "Vethy good; then there muth in that cathe be thomethin amith with the pot."

He then walked with all his characteristic coolness into the garden, and having stationed himself tranquilly, perceived that every pot had been covered with a sack.

"There it ith," said he, waving his hand gracefully; "thatth the thtate of thingth."

"Why blarm their carcasses!" cried Judkins. "What'll they be up to next, I wonder! Now, who could have done this?"

"Who!" echoed cook, with a significant glance at Judkins. "*You* ask who! I could *guess!*" she added emphatically. "Oh! I could guess!"

"Why, you don't mean to *guess* that I did it, do you?"

"Them sacks there couldn't have been put upon them pots without hands!"

"Thatth vethy clear," said Chokes.

"Clear!—it *is* clear!—and missis shall know of it this moment!"

"Go away, woman," said Judkins severely, as cook rushed in to tell her mistress all about it. "She's a imp, that woman is—a out-and-out imp."

"Vot I'm thinkin' of," said Chokes, having surveyed the cottage calmly, "ith thith: how did they get up to them there poth? Have you a ladder about the premitheth?"

"A small 'un! it'll reach up as high as my window there."

"Thatth of no uthe."

"Couldn't they get up that gutter?" said Judkins, alluding to a wooden pipe which reached from the roof to the waterbutt.

"Vy," replied Chokes, "if they didn't, I don't thee how they got up at all! But there ithn't more than room enough there for a cat! A man would break his blethed neck if he attempted to valk up there. I'd back my boy againtht the univerth for climbing, but he couldn't get up there!—a reg'lar rope-danther couldn't do it."

"Well, it's quite clear they got up somehow."

"Yeth, thatth very clear."

"And as missis is going to London to-day, the sooner we get them there sacks off the better."

"Vethy good. Ve mutht have a long ladder to do it. Whoth got one?"

"I don't know exactly; let's go and inquire."

They accordingly started; and while they were absent, cook was endeavouring to impress upon her mistress the probability of Judkins being in this case the delinquent. But her mistress would not for a moment hear of even its possibility. "I do not," she said, at length, "believe a word of it, cook; nor have you any reason to believe it. I know that you and Judkins are not friends, and if I find on my return that you are not more friendly, you must be separated. Judkins I believe to be a most faithful servant, and I would not part with him on any slight grounds."

Cook wept at the prospect which opened before her. She was deeply attached to her mistress—it may be said that she loved her—and would not on any account have left her voluntarily — except indeed to be married. This address therefore made a deep impression on her mind, and caused her to reflect upon the expediency of reforming that infirmity of temper of which every one complained.

Judkins and Chokes now returned with a ladder—the only one in the village that could reach the roof, and one which had been locked up for months—and when they had succeeded in raising it, Chokes ascended with admirable presence of mind, and having philosophically taken off the sacks, the fires when lighted burned freely again.

"Mr. Chokes," said cook, when all this had been accomplished, "you'll have a glass of ale?"

"If you pleathe," replied Chokes.

"You'll have a glass, Judkins?"

Judkins was startled! He felt quite amazed! The idea of her asking him to have a glass of ale, after what had occurred, so upset his faculties for the moment, that he seemed to have been deprived of the power of speech! She waited not, however, for his answer; she went at once and drew the ale, and absolutely placed two glasses before them!

This was touching. Judkins couldn't stand it. He looked at her for a moment, as if to be sure that he had made no mistake in the person, and then said, "Give us your hand, old girl. I don't think at all times you mean what you say, but don't let's have these here kicks up. Let's be comfortable together. Why shouldn't we be? We've got a good missis, and if we ain't happy it's all our own fault. There, give us your hand, and let's have no more quarrelling."

Cook gave her hand freely, and then left the kitchen; and when the faculties of Judkins were sufficiently restored, he proceeded to explain to Chokes precisely how the smoke had attacked him.

"Jutht tho," observed Chokes, when all had been described; "vethy true! But lithen! I've been in thith profethion now more than fifty yearth, and I flatter mythelf I know thomethin about it. Now, ven you found the thmoke tho thick in the kitchen, inthead of dathin through it ath you did, and thuth takin away all your blethed breath, you thould have dropped down inthantly upon your handth and kneeth, and then you vouldn't have had any thmoke at all. I'll tell you vy: Thmoke hath got ath muth natur about it ath we have, and knowth ath vell vot itth about. Itth the natur of thmoke to go up the thimbley, and up the thimbley ven it can it vill go, and not give no trouble to nobody; but if tho be it can't go up the thimbley, then it vill go vere it can, but alvayth up if it can. Now, thmoke vanth freth air. It'll alvayth go into freth air if it can. Vethy good. But if it can't it'll thill go up nevertheleth. Now lithen. If a room ith vethy hot, itth muth hotter at top than at bottom—that ith to thay, itth hotter near the theelin than it ith near the floor. If a room hath been heated by gath, you'll find, if you hang up your glath near the theelin, and then let it thtand for a time on the ground, it'll vathy from fifteen to twenty degreeth! Vethy good. And egthactly the same ith it vith the philothophy of thmoke, ven a room ith full of it. Near the theelin you can't breathe; it would thuffocate the devil; but near the floor you'll find freth air, upon vitch the thmoke theemth to thwim."

"There's a good deal in what you say, no doubt," said Judkins, "but if the smoke will if it can have fresh air, why don't it go down where the fresh air is?"

"Tho it would, if there voth enough of it! But it beginth at the top; it vill, as I thaid, keep up if it can, and itth vethy theldom found that a room ith tho full that thereth no freth air at all below. The freth air trieth to forth the thmoke out!—if it can, it vill; if it can't, it can't. Nevertheleth, alvath ven a room ith full of thmoke—you know vot I mean by thaying full!—I don't, you know, mean philothophically full!—alwayth crawl handth and kneeth upon the floor."

"Well, I daresay you're right about that," said Judkins; "and if you are it's a thing worth knowing."

"I know that I'm right," returned Chokes; "I know by ecthperienth, and ecthperienth teatheth vunderth. I've thaved in my time many a baby in that way. In the cathe of a houthe on fire, ven I've found a room tho full of thmoke that nobody would go near it, while the mother voth a thriekin about her babyth that voth in that room, I've crawled philothophically in on my handth and kneeth, and having pulled 'em out of bed, brought 'em to her unhurt! Many a time I've done thith, and ven the mother hath blethed me and thrieked for joy, I've felt ath a man *ought* to feel!—tho I know what it ith!"

Judkins was interested. He felt that he had a very great respect for this man; he moreover felt that Nature's God inspired even the bosom of a sweep.

Chokes, however, although a philosopher, was yet a man of business, and as he had an engagement that morning to cure a couple of chimneys in the vicinity, he rose, when he had finished his ale, to take leave, and as he did so, Judkins grasped him cordially by the hand, in the perfect conviction that he was a man!

By this time everything necessary had been prepared, and Sylvester sat down to breakfast with his aunt, who—although feeling of course that these things were extremely tiresome—was comparatively happy, for the very absurd nature of the last annoyance had had the effect of again removing that fearful impression which the idea of these mysterious occurrences having some remote connection with her brother's spirit had created.

But Sylvester—if the term may be applied to any feeling either inspired or developed by one so tranquil—was *deeply* indignant. He felt that his aunt ought at once to offer a reward for the apprehension of these people, and declared, upon his honour, that if he were a magistrate, he would, in the event of their being apprehended, punish them severely. He was unconscious of the spirit having appeared to the reverend gentleman and Jones—that had been studiously concealed from him by his aunt, lest the knowledge of the fact might alarm him—and as he viewed all the ghost stories of the village, not indeed as idle tales, but as tales induced by the tricks of the same idle persons as those by whom his aunt had been annoyed; he did think that the career of these persons should be checked, and that they should at once be punished with the utmost rigour of the law.

The time fixed for their departure now arrived, and their reverend friend, who had kindly offered to drive them to the coach, appeared in his phaeton at the gate. The trunks were then adjusted, and when Sylvester and his aunt had taken leave of the servants, they left the village with the blessings of all who saw them start. On the way, the reverend gentleman learned from Sylvester the substance of all that had happened that morning; but although he felt vexed, and would have given, at any other time, full expression to that feeling, he thought more—much more than he deemed it, under the circumstances, wise to declare. He was in fact almost silent on the subject, and endeavoured to direct their thoughts to the scenes which they would witness in London; and when they had met the coach at the point proposed, and he had handed them safely in, he gaily, yet affectionately, bade them adieu, and with many warm expressions of high consideration, they started.

CHAPTER XV.

SYLVESTER'S FIRST NIGHT IN LONDON.

LONDON! How many bosoms have swelled with rapture, how many cheeks have blushed for shame, how many hearts have been filled with joy, and how many have sunk in despair, at the sound of the magic name of London! LONDON! Well, there's no doubt that London is the Heart of the World—that its provinces are its arteries—that the issue of its ventricles gives the prevalent *tone* throughout Europe, Asia, Africa, and America; and that therefore the pulse of the world is influenced, if not indeed governed, by its action. But viewed as it is, without reference to its external influences, what a mass of all that is vicious and virtuous—pleasing and repulsive—horrible and honourable—profligate and pious—beautiful and brutal—philanthropic and ferocious—artful and amiable—

tyrannous and slavish—sceptical and credulous—solemn and absurd—profound and superficial—corrupt and correct—convivial and cold—impudent and diffident—subtle and soft—atrocious and true—cruel and confiding—sincere and satanic—benevolent and heartless—courteous and crafty—courageous and craven—obsequious and despotic—voluptuous and virginal—venerable and contemptible—in fine, what a mass—what a chaotic mass—of all that is good and bad—admirable and abominable—with all the varied shades which intervene—does this "mighty heart" of London present!

Nor is it the heart of the world only: it is a world in itself—a world in which all the existing feelings, motives, passions, and propensities, are to be found in perfection developed. To know London well is to know the world; and, albeit there are thousands of Londoners who never travelled ten miles from London in their lives, and who, notwithstanding, know but little of it—a London man strictly is a man of the world.

The first appearance, too, of London, strikes a stranger with amazement, let him enter at which point he may; and more especially effective is it if he should enter in the evening. It was evening when Sylvester arrived; and as he entered at the east, and had to go by the coach as far west as Charing Cross, the blaze of light by which he was dazzled, the noise of the various vehicles by which he was deafened, the magnificent shops which he beheld, with the myriads of human beings streaming on either side as he advanced, had the effect of inspiring him with wonder. Where could these people be driving to? What object had they in view? Upon these questions, when they suggested themselves, he had not time to dwell. The motives by which they were actuated were as various as their forms; misery, hope, joy, pride, vanity, crime, love, relaxation; and revenge, respectively impelled them on; but of this he knew nothing. The merchant who had just achieved a great commercial swindle which would stamp him a good man for life—the penny-a-liner, who had been walking all day, sustained only by the hope of an accident, praying that some important personage might fall and break his neck, that some murder might be committed before his eyes, or that some destructive fire might burst out as he passed, and thus enable him to dine on the morrow—the clerk who had just given notice to leave, in the full conviction that his "firm" could not get on without him, a mistake of which he would have the proof practically soon—the tradesman who had a bill for forty pounds due on the morrow, and had not forty shillings to meet it—the little master manufacturer who had been running after money all day and couldn't catch it, and who, for the sake of being a master, worked twenty hours anxiously out of the twenty-four, for a far less sum than he might earn by working ten hours, without this anxiety, as a journeyman—the pompous actor—the envious author—the heartless lawyer—the accomplished thief—the unprincipled gambler—the subtle, smirking, overreaching publisher—the gaudy Cyprian and the haggard milliner—the poor, but honest man and the highly respectable, because wealthy, rogue—passed on alike, for Sylvester viewed them only in the mass, without reference to their virtues, their vices, or their cares.

On the arrival of the coach at Charing Cross, Sylvester and his aunt were met by Dr. Delolme, who had been a most intimate friend of Dr. Sound, and at whose house, during their stay in town, they were to reside; and when he had received them with the warmest expressions of unfeigned pleasure, he had their luggage pointed out to his servant, who was directed to bring it after them in a hackney-coach, and then led them to his carriage and gave the word "home."

Dr. Delolme was one of the most accomplished men of the age. He was not, in a strictly professional sense, one of the most profound, albeit he had far more stuff in him than hundreds who had acquired a reputation for profundity: he was a gentleman, a highly accomplished gentleman, who repudiated with scorn those fraudulent exhibitions of eccentricity by which so many in his profession have been made, and who developed his accomplishments only with the view of inspiring with hope, emulation, or joy, those who came within the sphere of his influence.

And Mrs. Delolme was highly accomplished too; but religious enthusiasm had veiled her accomplishments, and prompted her to assume the air and language of a penitent. Her letters were studded with "D. V." in parentheses. *Deo volente* was continually on her lips. She had been one of the most lively creatures breathing, and while her elegance and amiability had enchanted the circle of which she had long been the recognised centre, her moral purity was acknowledged to be as perfect as her grace; but since a preacher who had set his whole soul on popularity—the Rev. Gipps Terre—had been the incumbent of the parish in which she resided, he, by virtue of acting and preaching for points, touching their feelings and blinding their judgment, had cleverly succeeded in turning not only her head, but the heads of all the women in the vicinity to an extent which prompted them to present him, as a matter of gratitude, with services of plate and purses of gold.

Mrs. Delolme, notwithstanding this, received Aunt Eleanor with much kindness. There was not, it is true, that warmth in her reception, that delightful cordiality, by which guests are at once inspired with the conviction, that their presence is pleasing; still the reception was kind, and as Aunt Eleanor knew of the change which had been wrought, she felt herself perfectly at home.

This, however, was not the case with Sylvester. He did not feel comfortable at all. He admired the doctor—he always had admired him—he was also much pleased with the doctor's son, Tom—a youth about twenty, whom the doctor called Tob, in consequence of Tom having acquired the habit of invariably pronouncing the *b* for the *m*, and the *d* for the *n*—but he did not at all admire Mrs. Delolme: he felt chilled by her presence; he never did attempt to say much, but her very look seemed to forbid him to speak.

It was therefore with pleasure, when Tom drew him aside and asked him if he would like to go out for an hour, that he replied, " I should indeed : " and when Tom added, " Take doe notice, I'll cobbudicate with the goverdor," he felt delighted with the prospect of escaping for a time from the apparently severe look of Mrs. Delolme.

" Well," said Tom, embracing the earliest opportunity, " I bust be off dow to by lecture, add as Sylvester beads to be a bedical swell too, he bay as well cub with be."

" Are you not too much fatigued, my dear ? " suggested Aunt Eleanor.

" Oh ! not at all," replied Sylvester.

" You will be late," said the doctor, " will you not ? "

" Oh, they never cobbedce before a quarter or twedty bidites past."

" It is now more than half-past," said Mrs. Delolme. " It will therefore be useless for you to go now."

" Oh ! we shall be id tibe to hear the barrow of it."

" But, my dear, I *wish* you to remain at home this evening."

"What for? Do you thidk it likely I shall ever pass? do you thidk it possible if I dod't attedd lectures?"

"I offered no opinion on that point, my dear. I merely said that I wished you to remain at home this evening."

"Very well! I shall be plucked!—I see how it will be! —I'll bet ted to wud that I'b plucked; add if I ah, dod't blabe he."

"Do you think it necessary for him to go?" inquired Mrs. Delolme of the doctor.

"Why, my dear," he replied, "it certaiuly is necessary for him to attend lectures."

"Of course it is," interposed Tom.

"Then I have no desire to interfere."

Tom winked at Sylvester in token of his triumph; and, as Sylvester understood it, they rose and left the room.

"What's the use of our sittidg there?" said Tom, on quitting the house. "I see do fud id it, do you?"

"There is certainly no *fun* in it," said Sylvester, smiling.

"Dot a bit! Add yet there they would have kept us as stiff as a brace of pokers the whole of the evedidg! It wod't do, Syl—I shall call you Syl, the whole of the dahe is too lodg for hubad utteradce. It isd't as if there was ady thidk goidg forward. If there were, it bight recodcile a fellow to hobe! But doe busic, doe cards, doe chess, doe backgabbod, doe gabe of ady sort do we ever have there; so if you expect ady fud id our crib, you'll be buch disappoidted."

Sylvester never had expected much fun: but he certainly had expected more gaiety. He did not, however, allow the absence of it *there* to distress him. He had quite sufficient to amuse him then. The peculiarity of Tom's pronunciation was amusing, and as Tom was not contemptible as a humorist, and as he was, moreover, very communicative, Sylvester derived during his walk as much amusement as he could have desired.

They now reached the hospital, at the entrance of which groups of students were conversing on subjects which were not strictly of a scientific character.

"Hollo, Tob," cried one. "Here's Tob Delobe," said another. "Tob's always in tibe!" exclaimed a third.

"Is he at it?" inquired Tom of one of them.

"Yes; but it's dreadfully dry."

"Dry, is it? Well, thed, let's go add wet it."

This suggestion was adopted on the instant by half-a-dozen

of them, who followed Tom into a public-house at hand, at the bar of which each of them called for a pot of porter. This order was, however, quite unnecessary. The barmaid knew in a moment what they wanted, and therefore, had they omitted to open their lips, she would have counted them and drawn a pot for each. She had had some practice at the bar, albeit still young and beautiful. She had been engaged solely as an attraction, and as an attraction she answered the purpose of her employer. She had a splendid head of hair, a pair of sparkling eyes, and a finely formed animated bust, and while her teeth were like pearls, her skin was soft and warm and clear. She was, moreover, elegantly dressed, and displayed a profusion of jewellery. On almost every finger there were two or three rings, the whole of which had been presented to her by students—who were all of course desperately in love with her—and therefore, if she saw a decent ring upon the finger of any one of them, she had but to say, "What a love of a ring!" and it was hers.

Decoy-*ducks* are not at all rare birds in London, and this one has been mentioned only in order to show what influence they have over the minds of youth. Sylvester, on being appealed to, declared that he had never seen so amiable, so elegant a creature: her eyes were so fascinating, her smile was so lovely, she seemed so delighted with everybody and everything, she was so extremely affable, so free, that really Sylvester was charmed with her; but when she placed the pot of beer before him, he looked with an expression of amazement at Tom, and said, "Is this for me?"

"Of course it is, by boy!" replied Tom; "dridk it up."

"I can't," said Sylvester; "you at all events must help me."

"It's the law id this part of the globe," returned Tom, "that doe bad shall dip into adother bad's pot."

Well! if this were the law, it was the law!—but Sylvester couldn't drink it all, that was quite clear, nor did he conceive it to be improbable that a shivering wretch, who stood behind him with a single box of lucifer matches in his hand, would object for one moment to violate that law. He therefore drank a little of it boldly, and then handed it quietly to the matchman behind, who finished it for him in very fine style, without taking his lips from the pot. As this had been effected unperceived by the rest—for they were all the time chattering with and ogling the barmaid—Sylvester thereby acquired the reputation of being—although green, palpably green—as good a man as any amongst them.

"Now," said he, when they had emptied their pots, "hadn't we better go in?"

"Id!" returned Tom, "id where?"

"Why, into the lecture-room."

"Oh! It's all over by this tibe, or dearly so."

"Well, but what am I to say if they should ask me about it?"

"Ah, I udderstadd! I say," he added, turning to the rest, "you are goidg to have wud bore fire, I suppose?"

"Oh, yes," they replied, "of course."

"Well, I'll dot be a bobedt: I'll cub back agaid. Dow thed, by boy," he added, seizing Sylvester's arm, "cub alodg. We'll just give a look id, add thed you'll be able to say with truth that you have beed there."

They accordingly entered the hospital, and proceeded to the theatre, in which the lecturer was zealously engaged on some profound demonstration, the nature of which Tom would not stop to hear, but dragged Sylvester out as soon as he felt that he had seen quite sufficient of the building to give a description of its form.

"Dow," said Tom, "we'll just go add have wud bore fire, add thed it'll be tibe for us to trot hobe agaid."

"I can't drink any more of that porter," said Sylvester. "I have already had quite enough of that."

"Well, thed, have sobethidg else. I'll tell you what you shall do—I'll stadd it: I'll pay the buddy;—call for a bottle of chabpagde. They are good fellows, all of 'em—regular trubps, and that'll stabp you at wodce as wud of us. Here's the buddy," he added, offering him a sovereign.

"No," said Sylvester, "Ill not take *your* money, I've some of my own."

"Dodsedse!" cried Tom, "I tell you I'll stadd it! Take the buddy."

"No, I'll not do that," said Sylvester; "but if you wish it, I'll order a bottle with pleasure."

"Very well, by boy; but bark!—whed I say, 'Well, what are you going to stadd?' you say boldly, 'Why, let's have a bottle of chabpagde.'"

This was agreed to before they reached the house, and

when they re-entered, Tom's friends had not only had fresh pots of porter, but had mounted cheroots and German pipes.

"Here he is!" exclaimed one of them. "Now, what do you think of it? I knew that Tob wouldn't cut us so."

"Cut you!" returned Tom, "dever! Dow, I say," he added, turning to Sylvester, "well! what are you goidg to stadd?"

"Why, let's have a bottle of champagne," replied Sylvester.

"Bravo!" exclaimed Tom's friends, "*that's* the sort of stuff after all."

And the barmaid, who was continually on the *qui vive*, waited for no direct order, but sent into the cellar for half-a-dozen at once.

Sylvester had wisely resolved not to touch it, and turning to the match-man, who still sat behind him, said, in a whisper—

"Do you like champagne?"

"Never tasted none, your honour," replied the man; "but dessay I do."

"Very well, then you shall have some; but do not let either of these gentlemen see you take it."

The man winked and rubbed his hands; and the champagne was brought, and when the barmaid had duly filled Sylvester's glass, he promptly conveyed it behind him.

When the glasses had been twice filled, the bottle was empty, Sylvester imagined that Tom would then start; but Tom would have another, and when that was drank, they would have a bottle all round.

"Now," said Sylvester to the man behind him, at the same time placing a shilling in his hand, "do not take a glass more than you think will do you good. If you do not like to drink it, you can easily throw it behind the cask."

Throw it behind the cask!—throw champagne behind the cask! In the judgment of that man the idea was monstrous. He, however, merely said—

"All right, your honour. In all my born days I never tasted nothing like it."

Bottle after bottle was now opened and drank, and Sylvester kept continually urging Tom to go; but Tom as continually said—"Ted bidites bore; there's pledty of tibe yet—off in ted bidites." But while the tall glasses continued to be filled, Tom's "ted bidites" frequently expired, indeed, so frequently, that Sylvester became extremely anxious, and at length said—

"Now, Tom, indeed I *must* go; my aunt, I *know*, is most impatient for my return."

"Well, thed," said Tom, "we'll bizzle. This is the last bottle; a couple more roudds, and thed we'll go."

The man behind Sylvester now began to sing, and although his voice was harsh, while he had not the most remote idea of tune, it manifestly fell upon his ears as sweetly as if it had been celestial music.

"Hold your doise," cried Tom, who failed to appreciate its beauty. "What do you kick up that bodstrous row here for?"

Heedless of this mild remonstrance, the fellow went on with his song, until two of Tom's friends, receiving the hint from the barmaid, seized him by the collar with the view of showing him out. They had scarcely, however, raised him from the cask on which he had been sitting, when his hat fell off, and out flew a pocket-book and a handkerchief, both of which Sylvester at once recognised as being his. He therefore picked them up in order to satisfy himself, and having done so, he said to the fellow, with great severity of expression—

"You are a bad man—a very bad man."

"What!" cried Tom, "do they belodg to you?"

"Yes," replied Sylvester; and Tom was about to inflict summary vengeance, but Sylvester held him back, exclaiming—"Pray don't hurt him. He's tipsy, Tom. He knew not, perhaps, what he was about."

"Dodsedse," cried Tom, who turned to rush at the fellow fiercely, but by this time Tom's friends had kicked him into the street.

"Now, Tom," said Sylvester, "pray let us go."

"Yes, we'll go dow," said Tom, "we'll go dow. Are you sure that you have got all you lost?"

"Yes, quite sure—quite."

"Very well, we'll just have a couple of bottles of soda-water to wash the chabpagde dowd, and thed we'll be off."

For Tom's sake Sylvester consented to this, and when they had drank the soda-water and taken leave of the barmaid, to whom Sylvester bowed with great politeness, they bade their friends good-night and started.

"Well," said Tom, "we have seed a little life."

"Life," thought Sylvester, "it is life, indeed! But," said he, "do you not feel somewhat tipsy?"

"Dot at all," replied Tom. "It would dever do to go hobe touched. They'd sbell a rat id a bobedt! I always, whed I get a little extra, cure byself before I go hobe."

"*Cure* yourself!"

"Of course; I cad always do that in five bidites."

"Indeed!"

"Oh, yes. I expected that I should have to cure *you*, but I fidd you can stadd it as well as the best of us."

"But you do not drink so much as you have drunk to-night often?"

"Oh, just as it happeds. If you associate with fellows like those, you must dridk: dot that I care about it buch."

"Then why do you associate with them?"

"I'll tell you. There was a tibe whed I was wud of the bost steady fellows goidg—whed all was right at hobe—when *hobe* was ad attractiod; I thed studied hard—attedded lectures with the utbost regularity, add so od—but always wedt hobe for relaxatiod, for thed I was fodd of my hobe; sobetibes I sat add sudg with the old lady—sobetibes she would play sub dew busic to abuse be—sobetibes we got the chessboard —sobetibes the cards—sobetibes she got be to read a dew dovel—and sobetibes we had a little party at hobe; there was always sobethidg lively goidg od, I could always fide sub sort of abusebedt; but sidce the old swell has becub so edaboured of our dew parsod, everythidg at hobe has beed wretched, dull, forbal, and cold. It is to this I ascribe by associatiod with those whob we have just left; for although they are all fide high-spirited fellows, I shouldd't do as I do, if thidgs were cobfortable at hobe."

"Then do you not study now at all?" inquired Sylvester.

"Study! I believe I *do* study," replied Tom. "Why, I wouldd't be plucked for a billiod of buddy! You shall see how add where I study, whed we get hobe. I have a couple of the bost perfect skeletods that were ever put together, with spridgs cobplete frob head to foot, which would albost idduce you to ibagide that you saw the very actiod of the buscles! Study! Why, I'b at it all the bordidg; it's odly at dight that I break loose eved for ad hour. Do, Syl; I bay sobetibes kick over the traces; but I look to the baid chadce. I have, add the goverdor kdows that I have, too buch pride to be plucked at either the College or the Hall. But here we are," he added, on reaching home, " all in good tibe. Ted to a bidite! Doctor at hobe, Jabes?" he inquired of the servant.

"No, sir."

"Tell theb we're id, add gode up to by study. Cobe alodg, Syl," he added, leading the way; and Sylvester followed to the top of the house, where they entered a room strewn with books, plates, and bones, while on the right, as they entered, stood two tall figures enveloped in bags.

"Dow, thed, look here," said Tom, taking off the bags, and displaying two really majestic skeletons. "There! what do you thidk of theb?"

"They appear to be very perfect: very perfect indeed."

"Perfect! I believe they *are* perfect. Look here!—look at the spridgs!—they'll stadd id ady attitude you please! They'll fedce with you—box with you—dadce with you—do adythidg you like. This is the bale and that's the febale: they were twids—rub-uds, wered't they?"

"They must have been finely-formed persons," said Sylvester. "I'll look at them again in the morning: I shall see them then to greater perfection. Where did you get them?"

"Goverdor gave theb *to be!*" replied Tom, covering them up again. "He gave a huddred guideas for theb; but for adatobical study they're worth a thousadd to ady bad alive. There's dothidg like theb id Europe! They are a pair of regular beauties. That's a budkcy," he added, pointing to a beautiful little skeleton. "There's dothidg codtebptible eved id that!—good forb, you see—very good forb. Do you kdow buch about cobparative adatoby?"

"Not much," replied Sylvester.

"Thed, study that. If you kdow a budkey, you kdow a bad: to parody the poet's lide—bad—of course physically—

'Bad's but a budkey of a larger growth.'

But I'll show you theb all id the mordidg. That's a cat!— capital cat, isd't it? I've killed lots of 'eb, but dever foudd ode to equal that."

"What, do you kill 'em yourself?" inquired Sylvester.

"Kill' eb? Perhaps I dod't! Why, there isd't a cat that'll cub withid a bile of this house! They *all* kdow be. Look here," he added, opening the window; "here's a beautiful parapet, gutter add all!—a capital place for 'eb, this! But do you hear ady caterwaulidg? Dot a bit of it! They dever cub here!—they dever will till I'b gode: add thed they'll have a regular jubilee, doubtless. But I cad't get a cat dow! —they all seeb to shud be! The old lady odce had a fadcy of keepidg cats; but as she lost about ted every fortdight, she cut-it!—so that I cad't get a cat dow at all!"

"Coffee's ready, sir," said James, as he entered the room.

"Very good," said Tom; "we'll be dowd id a bidite. But, Jib, I've dothidg for supper here, have I?"

"No, sir; you finished it all up last night."

"Then get me a pigeod pie; let it be a beauty. Have I ady stout left?"

"There are four or five bottles, sir."

"That will do, Jib. But let the pigeod pie, Jib, be double the size."

"Very well, sir," said James, as he left the room, and as Sylvester looked earnestly at Tom, as if he felt that some sort of an explanation would be agreeable, Tom said, "Syl, I'll tell you what it is: I like a bit of sobethidg for supper—I cad't sleep without it—add as the old swells below have dothidg but coffee, which is all very well id its way, I always sedd Jib for sobethidg dice to eat up here whed they are all gode to bed."

Sylvester thought this rational enough; and when he had given expression to his thoughts on the subject, they went down into the drawing-room together, and took coffee with Aunt Eleanor and Mrs. Delolme.

The doctor, who had been to see a patient, came in immediately after they had finished, and had coffee too; and when the tables had been cleared, he, Sylvester, and Tom discussed the prominent merits of the medical profession—while Mrs. Delolme was pointing out to Aunt Eleanor various passages in the Bible which favoured her views—till the timepiece struck twelve, when the bell was rung, and the servants came up to prayers.

Mrs. Delolme read them, and the doctor sat opposite, but all the rest turned and knelt; but, although they were read with great fervour of expression, they failed to have any other effect upon the servants than that of inducing them to pinch each other, with the view of changing that aspect of solemnity which, on entering the room, they had assumed.

The prayers being ended, the servants withdrew; and, when Mrs. Delolme had pointed out the extreme beauty of those prayers, they all retired to rest with the exception of Tom and Sylvester, who went into the study to eat the pigeon pie.

And it really was a nice pie, a very nice pie. Tom pronounced it to be "dothidg but ad oat-add-outer!"—and they ate very heartily and enjoyed it very much. The stout too was good: it was capital stout. Tom declared "there was do bistake about it!"—nor was there any: no: it was well up and soft, and two bottles went down with surpassing smoothness.

But with two bottles Tom was not content. "We'll just have wud bore," said he, "and thed we'll go to bed, for you look, Syl, as if you were nearly dead beat."

Sylvester, as Tom promptly opened the third bottle, acknowledged that he felt rather tired, but he was aroused by the production of the skeleton of a squirrel, which Tom caused to crack nuts by pinching its tail.

"I'll read you the history of this little swell," said Tom. "Whed alive he was a rub ud."

And he got his portfolio, and having placed several sheets of manuscript before him, commenced reading the life and adventures of "Moses the Squirrel."

He had, however, scarcely read the second sentence, when, on looking up, he found his friend Sylvester asleep.

"Hollo!" he cried, "Syl!"

"Really," said Sylvester, "you must excuse me."

"Well, I kdow you bust be tired," said Tom, restoring his precious manuscript to the portfolio. "Ebty the glass, add we'll be off. Travellidg idvariably bakes a fellow sleepy. I kdow what it is. I'll just put these thidgs od wud side, add thed see you to your roob. Dow thed," he added, as soon as this feat had been accomplished, and he and Sylvester left the study, and when he had pointed out Sylvester's room, he shook hands with him, exclaiming, "God bless you!—good-dight."

CHAPTER XVI.

TOB AND HIS WOBAD.

About two hours after the delivery of that remarkable sentence with which the preceding chapter concludes, Policeman D 99, an extremely intelligent and raw-boned person, whose acuteness in looking after cooks with money sufficient to take a public-house, surpassed that of any other member of the force—saw something—he could not at first see distinctly what it was, it being some distance from him, but he knew that he saw something—running along the parapet of the houses on his right.

Of course the trump of duty called him instantly to the spot, and having obeyed the call, he stationed himself opposite, from which point he clearly beheld the figure of a man, with nothing apparently on him but his shirt.

Conceiving that robbery was contemplated, and knowing that promotion sprang not from prevention but cure, he was silent, and moved cautiously into the shade of a doorway to watch the proceedings above.

He had not, however, been long in this position when his sergeant approached.

"Hist!" said Ninety-nine, as the sergeant was passing.

"Who are you?"

"Ninety-nine."

"What are you up to?"

"Here!"

The sergeant joined him in the shade.

"Do you see that fellow there?" continued Ninety-nine.

"Good God!" exclaimed the sergeant. "*Is* it possible! Why the slightest slip—a single moment's dizziness—would bring him to the ground, and dash his brains out."

"A robbery, safe," said Ninety-nine.

"A robbery; nonsense," returned the sergeant, who panted with apprehension. "He'll fall!—he'll fall presently—certian to fall."

"Not a bit of it," coolly observed Ninety-nine. "He's as safe as the bank. He's been running about in that way for a long time."

"I never saw a man in so perilous a position. What can he be up to?"

"He appears to me to be moving goods from one house to another."

"But I can see nothing in his hands."

"Nor can I," said Ninety-nine; "but he keeps on running backwards and forwards, stooping here and stooping there, as if he had. But there's more than him in it. He beckoned just now to his pals."

"Did you see *them*?"

"No, I couldn't see 'em. They keep in the background, but I know they're somewhere there."

"There he goes again!" cried the sergeant. "My life! what a devil. He's surely not after the cats?"

"Cats!" said Ninety-nine. "What man on the top of a house can catch cats?"

"He may snare them!"

'Snare 'em, he may. But I see no cats! *he's* after no cats."

"Did you see where he came from?"

"Not exactly; but I think from one of those houses down there."

"Here he comes," said the sergeant; "now watch him. He appears to have done his work. See how cool he is!—see how deliberately—how firmly he walks. Now! He has stopped! Do you see him looking in at that window? It's opened for him. He enters. He's in. Now, my boy, if plunder be your object, you're booked."

"That's safe to be his object," said Ninety-nine.

"I don't know," said the sergeant. "I think he's after one of the maids. At all events, you go off at once for another man. You'll find one at the corner. I'll remain here."

Ninety-nine started off, and soon returned with Ninety-six.

"Now, then," said the sergeant to Ninety-six, "you stand here, and keep your eyes upon that window."

"What, that?"

"No, that."

"What, that there one?"

"Yes. And if any one should come out of it, watch where he goes."

"All right," said Ninety-six.

"Now, then," said the sergeant, addressing Ninety-nine,

"we'll go over." And marking the house to which the window belonged, they went to the door of Dr. Delolme.

When the sergeant had rang the bell two or three times gently—conceiving it to be inexpedient to make too much noise—the doctor appeared at one of the windows, and called out, "Who's there?"

"Policemen," replied Ninety-nine. "There are thieves in the house, sir."

"How do you know?"

"We saw one of them just now steal in at the top window."

"Bless my life!" said the doctor. "I'll be down in one moment." And having hastily slipped on his trousers, he took a brace of loaded pistols from a case which he constantly kept in his room, and descended with one in each hand.

"What had better be done?" said he, on opening the door.

"We had better go up and secure them," replied the sergeant, as he opened his bull's-eye lantern. "I've stationed a man outside to keep a sharp look-out above. Perhaps *I* may as well have one of those?" he added, pointing to the pistols.

The doctor gave him one on the instant, and when the door had been locked and the key taken out, they proceeded upstairs—Ninety-nine going first.

As they proceeded, they took the precaution to lock every door which was not locked inside, until they arrived at the door of Tom's study, when the doctor said—

"Now, this is the room at the window of which you saw him enter; therefore prepare."

The sergeant cocked his pistol, and Ninety-nine opened the door; but he no sooner brought his brilliant bull's-eye to bear upon the skeletons, than uttering an exclamation of horror, he shrunk back appalled. The sergeant rushed forward in the twinkling of an eye, and perceiving indistinctly two figures on his right, shot one of them, as he imagined, through the heart, and produced on the instant a most tremendous rattling of bones, for the skeleton of Tom's female fell all to pieces.

"No, no!" cried the doctor, rushing in. "Don't touch them! they're merely skeletons! Bless my life," he added on perceiving the male in a pugilistic attitude, "what's the meaning of all this?"

"Hollo!" shouted Tom, who had been aroused from his

slumber by the rattling of the bones; "what are you up to? Who's there?"

"Come up, Tom, come up!" cried the doctor; and Tom, without stopping to put on a thing, rushed upstairs.

"What's the batter—what's the batter—what the devil's the batter?"

Ninety-nine trembled, and the sergeant looked pale, as the doctor replied, "There are thieves in the house."

"Thieves!" cried Tom. "Well, but I say, what's all this?—where's my wobad?"

"I shot it by mistake," said the sergeant.

"Shot it by bistake, you fool! What do you bead by shootidg it by bistake? You've dud a huddred poudds worth of dabage."

"I can't help it," said the sergeant; "you should keep such things as these covered over."

"Well, they were covered over. What did you pull the bags off for?—what the devil right had you to beddle with 'eb at all?"

"*I* didn't meddle with them!—*I* pulled no bags off."

"Who did, thed? Sobebody bust have pulled theb off."

"They were not covered up," said Ninety-nine, "when *I* entered. That there one stood as it stands now, and that t'other one was pointing at me—so."

"No, no, Tom," said the doctor, "they were not covered up."

"I tell you, I covered theb up byself, just before I wedt to bed!—I'll take by oath of it."

"Then those fellows must have uncovered them," said the sergeant.

"Where are they?" cried Tom. "If I catch 'eb, I'll break their blessed decks!—where are they?"

They looked round the room, but no soul could be seen. The sergeant went to the window and called to Ninety-six, but Ninety-six had seen no one get out.

"Then," said the sergeant, "that one at least must be in the house still."

They now commenced a diligent search, with the view of going from the top of the house to the bottom, prying into every conceivable corner, and holding themselves in readiness for an attack.

"Archibald! Archibald! What *is* the matter?" cried Mrs. Delolme, as they passed her room.

"Nothing, dear—nothing—don't be alarmed," said the doctor, on opening the door.

"But why are these men here?—pray tell me," she exclaimed, coming forward in a wrapper—"pray tell me what it is!"

"They fancied they saw some one enter the house."

"Good gracious! what, this house? And were they mistaken?"

A thought struck Ninety-nine.

"Have you, ma'am," said he, "any maid which is in any way unsteady?"

Mrs. Delolme was shocked at the thought.

"Because, ma'am," continued Ninety-nine, "the man which entered the window above hasn't been seen to get out again, ma'am."

"Give me a candle," said Mrs. Delolme. "Archibald, you come with me." And going direct to her servants' rooms, demanded immediate admittance, and obtained it; but found nothing to confirm the suspicion of Ninety-nine.

"You are mistaken in your conjecture," she observed on her return, and Ninety-nine said it was merely a thought. "Thank Heaven!" she added, "my servants, I believe, are all strictly virtuous."

"Well, I know he's somewhere about," said Ninety-nine; and when Ninety-nine had given expression to this conviction, they continued the search. They went into the drawing-rooms, but found no one there; they went into the parlours, and the result was the same.

"Strange," observed the doctor; "very strange."

"If he be in the house," said the sergeant, "we'll find him."

"Are you perfectly certain," said Mrs. Delolme, "are you sure—quite *sure*—that you saw a man enter this house?"

"Oh, quite, ma'am—quite," returned the sergeant. "We saw him cutting his capers on the parapet for more than twenty minutes before we rang the bell."

"On the parapet! Heaven preserve us!"

"How he did it *I* can't imagine. I know it made me tremble even to look at him. I expected every moment to see him fall and dash his brains out."

Another thought struck Ninety-nine.

"I don't think," said he suddenly, making a dead stand as they were about to proceed to the kitchen—"I don't think we *need* go on with this here search. It strikes me," he continued, placing his hands upon his hips, and assuming an air of infinite importance—"I say, it strikes me, and that very forcibly too, that the person, the man, the individual, which was playing off his pranks upon that there parapet, and which we saw afterwards bolt into that there top window, ain't very far off."

"What do you mean?" demanded the sergeant.

"Why, I mean as *this*," promptly replied Ninety-nine, cocking his head on one side, and looking at Tom with unexampled acuteness—"I mean to say that the man which we saw up there, now stands very near me. He had nothing but his shirt on!—very well, then. Is there no one in this room with nothing but his shirt on?"

"Why, you igdoradt raw-bode wretch!" exclaimed Tom, with indignation, "if you head to say that I ab the bad"——

"Tom! dear Tom!" exclaimed Mrs. Delolme, "pray, pray do not go on so; for my sake, dear Tom; for the sake of your own soul."

"I can pretty nigh swear to the *shirt*," said Ninety-nine to the doctor.

"Swear to the shirt!" cried Tom. "You adibal!—you doe-dothidg idcobprehedsible dodkey!"

"Don't be impetuous, Tom," said the doctor.

"Ibpetuous! Isd't it edough to bake ady bad ibpetuous to hear such ad ugly abortiod as that, with a head like a lubp of dothidg stuck upod dowhere, talk of swearidg to a shirt which he saw od a bad about half a bile off id the dark?"

"Half a mile," said Ninety-nine. "It was not a hundred yards."

"I dod't care if it were dot a huddred feet," returned Tom. "It wod't bake you a whit the less a fool."

"Don't call me a fool, if you please," said Ninety-nine, who didn't like it. "If I've done anything wrong, here's my number—Ninety-nine."

"Didety-dide!" cried Tom. "You ought to have didety-dide every bordidg before breakfast, to give you ad appetite, for swearidg to a shirt."

"That is not the shirt which we saw," said the sergeant, addressing Ninety-nine confidentially. "The one which we saw was much shorter than that. You see that comes down below the calves."

"He might have pulled it up, mightn't he, while he was running?"

"So he might," replied the sergeant. "He certainly might have done that."

"Besides," said Tom, who, during this colloquy, saw that neither his mother nor his father was satisfied, "is it codceivable that I could ever be so sedseless ad ass as to risk by deck upod that parapet! Why the copidg isd't bore thad a foot wide. He was ruddidg—*rudding* backwards add forwards, didd't you say?"

"Yes," replied the sergeant.

"I dod't believe a word of it. Doe bad could do it!—there's dot a bad lividg that would eved attebpt it! Look at the width of the stode and the height of the house! I'll bet a thousadd guideas, do bad cad be foudd to rud as *you* say you saw that bad rud alodg there. Take all St. Giles's—take all Wappidg—bridg all the sailors add bricklayers' labourers you like—take all the world—and you'll dot fidd a bad so lost—so utterly lost—to every sedse of dadger to do it."

"Certainly," said the sergeant, "I never *could* have believed it possible, if I had not myself seen it."

"You dever did see it," cried Tom. "Doe bad ever saw it. I see it dow clearly edough. I see the object which idduced you to say that you saw it."

"To what object do you allude?" inquired the sergeant.

"Buddy," replied Tom; "buddy! You thought as a batter of course that the goverdor would stadd sobethidg haddsome."

"I despise the insinuation," retorted the sergeant. "I say again, and am prepared to take my oath, that I saw a man running upon the coping of that parapet and enter the window above."

"Add do you bead to say, like your friedd Didety-dide there—the adibal!—that *I* was that bad?"

"That," replied the sergeant, "I must leave."

"And don't call me an animal again," said Ninety-nine. "I'll not be called an animal by you or any other man."

"What will you be called, thed?—a vegetable? I tell you agaid that you *are* ad adibal, add ad out-add-out ugly adibal too."

"Recrimination," said the doctor, "will never solve this mystery. I have not the slightest doubt," he continued, addressing the sergeant, "that that which you have stated is substantially correct, and that if the man entered the window above he is in the house now. The only question therefore is, 'Where is that man?' We have searched the house down to this parlour in vain; but I shall not—I cannot —feel satisfied, until we have completed the search."

"Then let us proceed," said the sergeant, "at once."

"It's *no* use," said Ninety-nine. "*We* shall find nothing."

"How is it possible for you to know that?" said the doctor.

"Kdow it," said Tom; "why, he'd swear it. A fellow who'd swear to the shape of a shirt would swear adythidg."

"Let us have no more recrimination," said the doctor. "We have had enough of that."

It is certain that as they proceeded to the kitchen, Tom did not expect that any man would be found, for he utterly disbelieved the tale of the policeman, conceiving it to be impossible for any man to run on that coping in the manner described— but at the same time equally certain is it that he hoped that some man *might* be found, inasmuch as—independently of the pleasure it would have given him to thrash the prime cause of his skeleton's fall—he perceived that both his father and his mother had inspired the conviction expressed by Ninety-nine.

"Well," said the doctor, when the kitchens had been searched, "it is perfectly clear that no stranger is in the house. I shall therefore return to my chamber with the full assurance of security. I thank you for your vigilance," he added, on reaching the hall, "but should it ever occur again, you will oblige me by ringing the bell at once, that we may go up and see what madman it is."

"We certainly *will* do so," said the sergeant. "I should have come over before, in this instance, but of course I knew not which house to come to, until I saw the maniac—for a maniac he *must* be to place himself in a position of so much peril—enter the window."

"We shall catch you yet," said Ninety-nine, addressing Tom, who, enraged at the fact of being accused of that of which of course he knew that he was innocent, and galled more especially by the knowledge of Ninety-nine having induced his father and mother to believe that in reality *he* was that "maniac," rushed at him on the instant, and struck him to the ground.

Ninety-nine drew his truncheon, but Tom, who could have crushed him, wrenched it in an instant from his hand, when the doctor rushed between them, and angrily cried, "*Tom!* are you my son, or a madman broke loose?"

"Your *son!*" replied Tom, pronouncing the *n* well; "and I should be udworthy of *being* your son, if I allowed byself to be idsulted with ibpudity by a wretch like that!"

"Here, give me this thing—give me this thing," said the doctor, evidently not at all displeased with Tom's reply; and having possessed himself of the truncheon, gave it to the sergeant, and begged of him to take Ninety-nine out of the house. "Call upon me to-morrow, and I'll speak to you," he added; and on opening the door, Ninety-nine vanished without venturing to say another word.

"Good-morning," said the sergeant, as he withdrew. "Good-morning."

"Now," said the doctor, having locked the door, and felt it to be his duty to assume an expression of anger—"Now, sir, having created the whole of this disturbance, perhaps you will deem it expedient to go to bed."

"Dot udtil I'b satisfied," replied Tom fiercely. "Father, I dever to by kdowledge disobeyed you: to by kdowledge I dever told you a deliberate falsehood: willidg as you are to believe ady bad—eved that codtebptible adibal—in preferedco to be, I would dot id ady baterial poidt deceive you."

"I am *not*, sir, willing to believe any man in preference to you."

"Well, thed, let be tell you this—it is for you to believe or disbelieve be: over your faith, I have, of course, do codtrol; but, father, I declare to you, upod by hodour, I kdow dothidg of this."

"Do you," said the doctor, "declare this upon your honour? —do you declare, upon your honour, that it was not you whom they saw upon the parapet?"

"I do," replied Tom.

"Tom," said the doctor, taking his hand, "I am satisfied, perfectly satisfied, Tom—good-night."

The doctor now believed him, but Mrs. Delolme did not. Religious enthusiasm breeds no charity, being in its essence intolerant.

"Well," said Tom privately, on getting into bed again—"this is what *I* call a go! It's a cobfort to be fortudate; but it's a blessidg to be a victib; add that I have been victibised id this affair, doe bad id Edgladd, save Didety-dide, cad doubt. That Didety-dide! Well! He's a poor fool. But look at the hischief he has caused. Here ab I, after havidg by wobad destroyed, or so shattered that it will take half a cedtury to put her together agaid—accused of goidg out at dight, add cuttidg by capers upod that appallidg parapet, whed I kdow that I'b as iddocedt as a kid id ebbryo."

Tom did think this hard—very hard;—and, while deeply reflecting upon the hardship, dropped off again to sleep.

CHAPTER XVII.

JULIA.

Of all the accomplishments by which we are charmed, true politeness is the brightest and the most admirable; seeing that while it imparts pleasure to all who come within the scope of its influence, it prompts the development of that essential goodness of heart which repudiates the idea of giving offence. It has nothing to do with formality: neither bowing nor smiling, nor the practice of any prescribed ceremonial, can prove the existence of true politeness: nor does it consist in a servile assent to every opinion that may be advanced—for that is the fruit either of folly or of subtlety springing from a mean or an immoral design: its essence is that generosity which leads us to study—not to wound, but to respect—the feelings of those around us, with a view to promote their comfort by all the means at our command; and this generosity—this germ of true politeness—conspicuously characterised Dr. Delolme. In him there was a total absence of everything bearing even the semblance of assumption. He made no display of superiority, no attempt at dictation: he would not willingly wound the feelings of any man alive: nor would he, except indeed in cases of approaching death, fail to conceal, if possible, any circumstance calculated in his judgment to create annoyance or alarm: his motive will therefore be well understood, when it is stated that, having learned that Aunt Eleanor had slept so soundly that she heard nothing of the disturbance of the preceding night, he submitted to Mrs. Delolme the propriety, under the circumstances, of keeping the whole affair a secret.

That lady, however, held that nothing ought to be concealed: that concealment was a species of deception: and that if anything occurred, and we acted or spoke as if it had not occurred, we were guilty of hypocrisy: it therefore took some considerable time, and required many powerful arguments to convince her that she was not strictly justified in unnecessarily creating alarm in the minds of her guests.

While, however, the process of conviction was going on, Tom, who could not sleep after six o'clock that morning, dressed himself, and on going into Sylvester's room, explained to him all that had occurred.

"Dow," said he, having gone completely through the scene, to the utter amazement of Sylvester, "what do you thidk of that?"

"It's very mysterious!" said Sylvester; "*very* mysterious!"

"Bysterious! But do you believe it?" cried Tom. "Cad ady bad codceive the possibility of a fellow beidg able to rud alodg a stode so darrow at such a height as that? Slip od your thidgs add cobe add look at it."

Sylvester did so, while Tom was lamenting the irreparable injury sustained by the skeleton, which he affectionately termed his "idcobparable wobad."

"There you are," said Tom, as they entered the study; "that's the state of thidgs, you see! here lies by wobad! here she is, you see, sbashed all to atobs! Dever get her right agaid: I kdow we dever shall. It will take a bad a bodth to sort the bodes. Add here you are agaid!" he added, pointing to his monkey, "that's dode for! ball, you see, wedt cobpletely through hib! That was the fidest budkey id dature. Did you ever see such havoc? Isd't it edough to drive a fellow ravidg bad?"

"It is very annoying," said Sylvester, "very. But let us look at this parapet."

"Here you are thed! this is it! a dice place to dadce upod! just look at the distadce frob the groudd! He bust be a bold bad who'd thidk of cuttidg his capers here."

"I should say that no man would ever attempt it."

"Dever! Add yet the old goverdor swallowed it all. But that I didd't care so buch about: it was the idea—the bodstrous idea—of its beidg ibagided that *I* was the bad that galled be! I dod't care about beidg victibised buch if do real disgrace is idvolved; but this was ad attack upod wud's judgbedt, ad attack upod wud's reasod, ad attack upod wud's owd self-esteeb, which I couldd't be ratiodally expected to stadd. Why, if I were to cut about here, I should say that by deck wasd't worth bore thad five bidites' purchase! As I said last dight, I dod't believe they saw ady bad at all. It's all dodsedse! Here's the goverdor," he added, as Dr. Delolme called him—

"Are you upstairs, Tom?" cried the doctor.

"Yes," replied Tom, "I'b here."

"You have," said the doctor, as he entered the study, "you have, I presume, explained all to Sylvester?"

"Yes," replied Tom, "add he thidks with be that do bad id Edgladd could do it. Look here. The stode is just a foot add a half wide. Dow, do you thidk it probable—day, do you thidk it possible?"

"Doubtless," said the doctor, "the policemen somewhat exaggerated. I do think it impossible for any man to run upon this coping in the manner described; but a man might with care walk safely behind it."

"But they said distidctly, upod it—ruddidg backwards add forwards upod it."

"But I should say that all they saw in reality was some one walking here. That they saw a man outside, I have not the slightest doubt: nor can I for a moment doubt that they saw that man enter this window."

"Well," said Tom, "that certaidly bridgs the thidg withid the scope of reasod; add if there be ady wud id the habit of cobidg here, I'll fix hib."

"You are quite sure that you left those skeletons covered?"

"Quite! I covered theb byself! Syl saw be do it."

"They were covered," said Sylvester, "when we went to bed."

"Then," said the doctor, "it's perfectly clear that some one must have entered."

"Let hib cobe agaid," cried Tom; "odly let hib cobe. He shall rebebber it—I'll fix hib!"

"We must have some iron bars put up," said the doctor. "We shall be safe enough from all intrusion then. And now," he added, addressing Sylvester, "as your aunt has heard nothing of this affair, and as the knowledge of it may unnecessarily alarm her, I think that in her presence we had better be silent on the subject. You understand?"

"Perfectly," said Sylvester. "I think so too."

"We must prevent its recurrence."

"Leave that to be," said Tom; "I'll settle that."

"Very well: do so," returned the doctor. "Now let us go down to breakfast."

"I say," whispered Tom, keeping Sylvester back, "do you kdow what a bad-trap is?"

"A man-trap? Oh, yes."

"That will be the thidg; I'll get wud of theb. I'll badage it. I thidk I kdow where I cad buy wud."

"But where will you place it?"

"Just udder the widdow: so that whed he juhps dowd he bay put his foot id it. That'll fix hib. He'll rebebber it, whoever he bay be. But dod't say a word to the old swells below. They wouldd't have it. They'd say, 'We'll dot pudish, but prevedt.' But I wadt to catch hib. By object is to serve hib out: first, od accoudt of the destructiod of by wobad; add secoddly, id codsequedce of his havidg beed the pribe cause of by being bade bost udjustly a victib. I therefore should like to catch hib very buch iddeed; add whed I do catch hib, I'll give hib codfidedtially a thrashidg, which shall redder it the happiest day of by life. Therefore, bub's the word."

Sylvester promised to be silent on the subject, and they followed the doctor into the breakfast-room, where they found Aunt Eleanor and Mrs. Delolme already seated. As he entered, Sylvester was greeted with great affection, both by Mrs. Delolme and his aunt; but Tom, having shaken hands warmly with Aunt Eleanor, sat down in silence, for, as he privately explained to Sylvester, a single glance at the other lady tended to convince him that he knew exactly what it was o'clock.

And really Mrs. Delolme did look very severe. She believed that he had told an abominable falsehood; and having resolved on introducing him in the course of the morning to the Reverend Mr. Terre, she felt it to be her duty to preface the introduction with a well sustained look of severity. But the doctor appeared to be in excellent spirits. He chatted with all of them gaily—spoke of the various exhibitions in town, of the public improvements, and so on, with an accurate knowledge of each, and in a strain which induced Aunt Eleanor to wish to see them all. Immediately after breakfast, however, Mrs. Delolme having previously intimated to Aunt Eleanor her desire to introduce her to the Reverend Mr. Terre, secured her for the morning; and when the carriage had been ordered, she requested Tom to prepare to accompany them forthwith.

"Where are you goidg?" inquired Tom.

"To various places," replied Mrs. Delolme.

"Oh! very well. Syl goes with us of course?"

"It has been decided that, until our return, Sylvester remains with the doctor."

"What for?"

"I say that it has been thus decided."

"Oh! well, if there be adythidg cabalistic goidg od, I dod't wadt to kdow adythidg about it. I'b ready whed you are."

Accordingly, when the carriage was announced, Tom entered with Aunt Eleanor and Mrs. Delolme, and when the coachman had been directed to drive them to the residence of Mr. Terre, Tom wanted to know particularly what they were going there for. The only answer he obtained, however, was that they were going for an excellent purpose; and as he found that this *was* the only answer he could obtain, he thought that he might as well be satisfied with it as not.

Having arrived at the house of the reverend lion, Aunt Eleanor and Tom were introduced to a tall, pale, light-haired, awkward individual, who, while he displayed a considerable portion of the "whites" of his eyes, proved clearly that he had cultivated that which in the Scotch Kirk is termed the "holy tone" to perfection. Tom didn't like the man; he went prejudiced against him: he felt that he had been, by him, deprived of those comforts—those innocent pleasures—of home, to which he had been from infancy accustomed, and therefore, on being introduced, he bowed as stiffly as possible.

Having received an intimation from Mrs. Delolme that she was anxious to speak to him privately for a moment, Mr. Terre, with all the grace he had in him—which really wasn't much—conducted her into an adjoining room. Here they conversed for some time, and on the return of Mrs. Delolme, she requested Tom to go in and speak to Mr. Terre.

"What about?" inquired Tom.

"He is anxious to speak to you."

"Well, cad't he say what he has to say here?"

"He wishes to speak to you privately."

"Well, but what about? I dod't wish to have ady private cobbudication with *hib!* What does he wadt?"

"You will hear, sir, as soon as you enter that room."

"Well, I daresay I shall."

"You do not, I presume, refuse to go?"

"Oh, I'll go!" replied Tom: and he went; and when he had entered the room, Mr. Terre, with an expression of dignity, and in a most authoritative tone, said—

"Young man"——

"Youdg bad!" echoed Tom, who didn't like to be thus addressed.

"In the first place," continued Mr. Terre, "I most earnestly exhort you to read, mark, learn, and inwardly digest the first ten verses of the fifth chapter of the Acts of the Apostles."

"What for?" inquired Tom.

"In order that you may understand the imminent peril to which it appears you habitually expose yourself."

"The first ted verses of chapter the fifth! Allow be to look at theb dow, that I bay see at odce what they are about."

The New Testament was handed to him promptly, and when Tom had turned to the chapter in question, and found that it related to Ananias and Sapphira, he looked at Mr. Terre, and inquired what he meant.

"You say," said he, "that I habitually expose byself to the peril here described; do you bead thed to say that I'b ad habitual liar?"

"I merely mean to say that it appears"——

"What appears?"

"That you are in the habit of telling falsehoods."

"Do you wadt be to kick you?" said Tom indignantly. "What do you bead? How does it appear? Tell be that."

"It appears, sir, from what your good mother has told me."

"Frob what by bother has told you," cried Tom. "Stop a bidite," he added, approaching the door; "I'll sood settle this affair. Bother, just step here a bobedt."

Mrs. Delolme walked solemnly in.

"Have you beed tellidg this bad," inquired Tom, "that I'b ad habitual liar?"

"I told him," replied Mrs. Delolme, "that you were in the habit of telling falsehoods."

"Bother," said Tom, "I ab, by prescriptiod, boudd to respect every word you utter; but as I ab udcodscious of *ever* havidg told a deliberate falsehood, I caddot respect the words you have just prodoudced. I kdow, of course, what you allude to—you allude to the proceedidgs of last dight; but I agaid declare, upod by sacred hodour, that every word of by dedial was true."

Here Mr. Terre turned up the whites of his eyes, until the pupils were lost to view.

"As to that iddividual," continued Tom, pointing to Mr. Terre with an expression of contempt, "I respect the sacred office which he holds, but id this case, I caddot respect the holder. Arrogadce add igdoradce forb his chief characteristics: arrogadce id presubidg to address be as he did, add igdoradce id supposidg that if eved I had beed guilty of falsehood, I could, by the beads he adopted, be boved. You are a teacher, sir; but you have buch to leard; the bubad heart should be your study."

Mrs. Delolme was shocked! and on turning to Mr. Terre, as Tom left the room, she perceived, by the awful expression he assumed, that he had given Tom up for lost. The reverend gentleman had nevertheless words of consolation for Mrs. Delolme, and when he had delivered those words in the most impressive style of which he was capable, she rejoined Aunt Eleanor—who was, alas! laughing with Tom at the time—with the view of inducing her to subscribe to a fund for the diffusion of blankets and tracts among the poor—to which fund the reverend gentleman, in order to save all unnecessary expense, kindly acted as secretary and treasurer, and which diffusion he, with infinite goodness of heart, and with the same highly laudable object in view, superintended. Of course Aunt Eleanor's subscription was obtained, and when her name had been added to the list of the faithful, she and Mrs. Delolme took leave of Mr. Terre. That Tom was overlooked by the reverend gentleman in this particular instance may be easily conceived. Mr. Terre took no notice at all of him, nor did Tom take even the slightest notice of Mr. Terre. He had no affection for him, and therefore passed him in an essentially stiff-necked style. He could have said something, but didn't; he handed the ladies into the carriage, and when he had entered himself, they drove off.

"*Isn't* he a nice man?" said Mrs. Delolme, addressing Aunt Eleanor, as they proceeded.

"Yes, he is for a sball party," said Tom.

"Thomas!" cried Mrs. Delolme, with an expression of ferocity. "I did not address myself to you. If you were half so kind, half so virtuous, half so amiable, half so pure, as the interesting person whom we have just left, you would be indeed a comfort to a mother's heart; but I fear that you are a reprobate."

"Dot a bit of it," said Tom. "I'b a victib, but do reprobate. A reprobate, bother, is a bad abaddoded to wickeddess. I ab do reprobate. As to the idterestidg creature we have just left, you'll fidd hib out by-add-by, I've do doubt, add the sooder you do so the better. Add dow," he added, "I thidk that I bay as well get out; I'b odly idterruptidg the codversatiod here, add I have a call to bake of sobe ibportadce."

As Mrs. Delolme had no other interesting creature to introduce him to, she offered no opposition to his leaving; the carriage was therefore stopped, and Tom alighted, more than ever intent on purchasing that machine which was at once to prove his innocence and enable him to be revenged on the author of all his present troubles.

For some time after Mrs. Delolme, Aunt Eleanor, and Tom had left the house, Sylvester was amused by the anatomical curiosities and lively conversation of the doctor; but having at length been summoned in haste to attend a patient, the doctor, though with manifest reluctance, left Sylvester to amuse himself in the library alone.

This, for a time, Sylvester managed to do; but while reading an elaborate treatise on the Functions of the Brain, he fell asleep, and commenced dreaming on the subject of Aunt Eleanor's marriage—a subject which had never before entered his imagination.

A gentleman, he conceived, had proposed to Aunt Eleanor—a gentleman of wealth and station—a fine, portly gentleman, who wore at the time—Sylvester saw him distinctly!—a blue coat, with yellow metal buttons, a large white waistcoat, a large bunch of seals, black silk pantaloons, and Hessian boots. Well, Aunt Eleanor had not rejected this proposal; nor had she by any means accepted it; no, she had taken time to consider. She liked his manners very well; they were graceful and elegant; she had been, moreover, induced to admire his character; he was wealthy, philanthropic, amiable, and kind, and had gained the esteem of all who knew him. There was, however, one circumstance—only one circumstance—which induced her to pause. She thought him too stout, much too stout! In Sylvester's view there was nothing about him particularly bulky; he didn't object to his appearance at all; on the contrary, he conceived him to be a remarkably fine man —handsome, full of health, and extremely well-proportioned. Still Aunt Eleanor thought him too stout, and therefore took time to consider.

The scene changed; and Sylvester opened his eyes; but he was then as soundly asleep as before, and having put the treatise aside, he mended a pen, and deliberately wrote the following letter:—

"DEAR SIR,—My dear aunt desires me to inform you that she has an idea of entering into the marriage state. She has not exactly made up her mind, nor will she until she has had the pleasure of seeing you. She is anxious to consult you. She imagines that the gentleman who has proposed to her is somewhat too stout; and as she has always had the very highest confidence in your judgment, she wishes to have your opinion upon the point, before any final answer is given.

"Independently of which, she most earnestly hopes that, if the marriage should take place, you will do her the favour to perform the ceremony.—I am, dear sir, yours faithfully and affectionately,   SYLVESTER SOUND."

This letter he directed to the Reverend Mr. Rouse, and having sealed it, rang the bell.

"James," said he, as the servant entered, "be kind enough to take this letter to the post. Go with it immediately."

"I will, sir," said James, who had no more idea of his being asleep, than he had of opening the letter to see what it contained.

Sylvester closed his eyes again, and, as the letter was off his mind, his sleep may be said to have been more profound, and thus he continued to sleep in his chair until Tom returned with a man-trap.

"Hollo, Syl!" cried Tom, as he entered the library. "Asleep!"

"I was for a moment," said Sylvester, rubbing his eyes.

"I say; here's the bachide," said Tom, pointing to the man-trap. "That's the sort of thidg, eh? It strikes me that'll hold hib."

"He'll not run a very great distance with it, I think," returned Sylvester.

"If he does, I'll forgive hib!" cried Tom. "Look here; capital teeth!"

"Rather rusty," said Sylvester.

"So buch the better," cried Tom. "But just help us up stairs with it. They bustd't see it. We'll take it idto the study, add thed all will be safe."

Sylvester accordingly assisted him up with it, and when they had affixed the chain to a staple near the window, and locked it, they tried it again and again, with the view of making sure that a man's foot would have the desired effect. Having satisfied themselves upon this important point, they began to sort the bones of the female skeleton, and thus busied themselves until dinner was announced, when they rushed into their rooms with the view of preparing to meet the awful aspect of Mrs. Delolme.

The dinner, but for the doctor, would have been dull indeed. He infused a little gaiety into the proceedings, and occasionally elicited a spark of spirit from Aunt Eleanor, to whom Mrs. Delolme appeared as if all her natural feelings had been smothered.

Very soon after dinner the ladies withdrew, and then Tom, in a most comic manner, explained all that occurred at the house of Mr. Terre.

"I shouldd't have cared," he added, having described the scene, "if he hadd't beed a parsod. I should have beed bore at hobe, especially whed he addressed be—'Youdg bad!' This cobbedcebedt did certaidly double be up, add if he hadd't beed a bidister I should, do doubt, have told hib exactly what I beadt; but, as it was, by respect for his order codtrolled oe, add caused be to feel that we were dot od equal terbs."

The doctor felt exceedingly annoyed at the fact of Tom having been placed in this humiliating position; but he made no important remark; he laughed, indeed, at Tom's quaint description of the scene; but while he wished that it had not occurred, he thought it wise to conceal his real feelings, lest his acknowledgment of the folly of the mother might tend to diminish the respect of the son. He therefore changed the subject as soon as possible, and when eight o'clock had arrived, Tom, accompanied by Sylvester, went to his lecture, having securely locked his study door.

Now much has been said about love at first sight. Some have held it to be impossible, while others have contended for its being anything but. It seems strange that this point should not have been; until the very period of which we write, settled!—very strange. But it was not. It was a perfectly open question until Julia Smart, the barmaid, saw Sylvester with Tom, when it was, beyond all dispute, settled for ever!

She saw him, and loved him. Had she been the mighty mistress of a world, and that world had been studded with brilliants, she would freely have given it for him. He had said nothing—done nothing—calculated to fascinate, or having the slightest tendency to inspire feelings of affection; he had, in fact, scarcely opened his lips to her; still she loved him—fondly, fervently loved him.

She knew that his name was Sylvester. That she had ascertained from Tom; and from that happy moment, Sylvester to her was the dearest name of which she had ever heard. Sylvester was continually on her lips. She even loved to hear the name of Sylvester sounded. Sylvester! In her judgment, what name could be comparable with that? She slept and dreamt of Sylvester. She awoke, and thought of Sylvester. Sylvester stood in imagination before her. Her blessings were lavished upon the head of Sylvester. Her prayers were for Sylvester—dear Sylvester—and she pronounced the name of Sylvester throughout the day.

When, therefore, in the evening, Tom, as usual, after the lecture, had been induced to go to the house, at the bar of which she presided, she experienced, as Sylvester entered, mingled feelings of embarrassment and joy. At first she turned pale—deadly pale—and then, in an instant, her face and neck were crimson. She tried to speak to him, but could not; and while her bosom heaved with emotion, her lips quivered convulsively as she returned his graceful bow.

Sylvester perceived this—had he failed to perceive it his perceptive faculties would have been indeed dull—he perceived it at once, and marvelled. She had interested him the previous evening, but the interest he then felt was really intense. Their eyes met constantly; both tried to avoid this, but neither could do it; one could not glance at the other without being glanced at in return. The principle of reciprocal attraction was never more clearly defined.

At length, embracing an opportunity, she approached him, and in trembling accents, expressed an earnest hope that she should frequently have the pleasure of seeing him—hinted at the happiness of which his presence was the source, and then, taking off her most valuable ring, begged of him, with an expression of fervour, to accept and to keep it in remembrance of her.

Sylvester was manifestly reluctant to do this. He did not at all like to take the ring, and explained to her that he couldn't think of doing so for a moment.

"Pray do!" she exclaimed, "for my sake: it will give more pleasure than I can express."

"Well," said Sylvester, "if I take it, it must be on this condition, that you accept from me a present of equal value in return."

"I will do so," she earnestly replied; "I care not for the value—the intrinsic value—anything that I may keep"——

"Holloa!" cried Tom gaily, who, turning at that moment, saw them in close conversation. "We are dot goidg to stadd that, you kdow; I call it a bodopoly!"

Julia smiled, and on the instant retreated.

"Well, I say," continued Tom, "tibe's up."

"I'm quite ready," said Sylvester.

"Well, thed, we'll trot."

Tom then proceeded to bid his friends adieu, and while he was doing so, Sylvester—who felt at the time somewhat embarrassed—bowed gracefully to Julia, who bowed with equal grace in return.

"Well, good-bye," said Tom, addressing Julia; "good-bye."

Julia again smiled, for she felt very happy, and Tom followed Sylvester out.

"Fide girl, isd't she?" said Tom. "Out add out. There's do bistake about her—a regular brick!"

"She appears to be very amiable," said Sylvester.

"She has a good heart, Syl—ad excelledt heart. I'll just

tell you what she did a short tibe ago. Wud of our fellows had spedt all his buddy. He was a rattler to go alodg, add whedever he had buddy he bade it fly. Well, the tibe was cobe for hib to prepare id eardest to pass; but he foudd that he couldd't raise buddy edough eved to pay for his griddidg "———

"One moment," interrupted Sylvester; "what do you mean by his grinding?"

"Why, whed a bad is dot sure of passidg—do bad cad be *sure*—but what I bead is, whed he thidks it at all probable that he shall be plucked, he goes to a gridder, whose busidess it is to put to hib those questiods which he ibagides are bost likely to be asked, add to crab hib with the adswers, that he bay dot, when he goes up, be buch at a loss. Well, he couldd't raise the buddy. He had borrowed of every fellow who had buddy to ledd, while he was able to get dode frob hobe, for his bother, who was a widow, he had by his extravagadce ibpoverished already. What thed was to be dode? Udless he passed, he was ruided for ever! He tried—constadtly tried—every bad whob he kdew; still he could get no buddy, and absolute starvatiod stared hib id the face. Fortudately, whed he foudd hibself reduced to the last extrebity, Julia heard of the circubstadces, add sedt for hib, and delicately offered to ledd hib the buddy provided he applied it to do other purpose. He probised her solebdly that he would dot, add she ledt hib the buddy; she ledt hib sufficiedt, dot odly to pay for his griddidg, but to go up both to the College add the Hall—to pay for his lodgidgs, add to carry hib home."

"He has repaid her, I hope?" said Sylvester.

"Yes! he has repaid her! He *would* have beed a scoundrel if he hadd't. He dot odly repaid her, but—as he jubpt idto a capital practice—he offered to barry her! But do; she refused his offer, codceiving that a bad who would recklessly ruid his bother, wouldd't have buch regard for the feelidgs of his wife. Oh! she's up to a thidg or two,—dowd as a habber; codverse with her, add you'll fidd she's dot a cobbod style of girl."

"She appears to have had a good education."

"A good educatiod! she's highly accobplished. I bet her at a party wud dight, add really her badders are elegadt id the extrebe. I was perfectly astodished. She plays well, dadces well, sidgs well, codverses well! If I had dot kdowd her, I should have said, that's a lady, add do bistake. She was out add out the bost graceful creature id the roob."

"I am amazed, then," said Sylvester, "that she is in that position."

"By boy," said Tom gravely, "a girl who has deither a father dor a friedd, has dot the choice of her owd positiod. *She* has deither a father dor a friedd—I bead a friedd havidg the power to probote her idterests baterially. What thed is she to do? If she eddeavours to get a berth as a goverdess, the chadces are a huddred to wud against her; add if eved she succeed, what is a goverdess? A creature dobidally above, but id reality far below, a bedial servadt. Do bedial would put up with wud half the codtubely that she is cobpelled to put up with. Her life is, id fact, a two-edged sword. She has bore to bear, with less power to bear it. A word that would woudd her feelidgs, would, upod a bedial, have do effect, while a bedial would dot eddure half the idsults which are with ibpudity heaped upod *her*."

"I see," said Sylvester, "I see."

"Very well, thed; what's a girl like that to do? For years she has had ad aged bother to support, add she does support her like a brick. But could she have supported her had she beed a goverdess? Could she have supported her by plyidg her deedle frob biddight to biddight? Do!—she therefore berged all scruples, add took this berth. They pay her well, doubtless, for she has saved a little buddy. It is dot exactly the thidg, perhaps, for so delicate a bide as I believe hers to be; but she keeps her bother, she keeps herself; she cad always keep a twedty poudd dote id her pocket; add I therefore should like to see the bad who could, udder the circubstadces, blabe her for beidg what she is. There's do dodsedse about her, you see; dor will she stadd ady dodsedse. She'll laugh add joke with the best of us; but if you wudce ibproperly step over the lide, she will delicately idtibate to you that that ibproper step has been bade. It is, hedce, that she's so udiversally respected. I dever id by life bet with a fellow who didd't like her."

They now reached home, and on being admitted, they went direct into the drawing-room, where Mrs. Delolme, Aunt Eleanor, and the doctor were taking coffee. The doctor at once inquired what sort of lecture they had heard, and Tom promptly explained to him its nature and effect. It happened to be on a subject with which the doctor himself was not perfectly conversant, and therefore the books were referred to, in order that the whole of its ramifications might appear. The examination of these books, and the arguments to which that examination led, lasted nearly two hours; during the whole of which time Mrs. Delolme and Aunt Eleanor were discussing the respective merits of the various tract societies, to the whole of which Mrs. Delolme contended every Christian lady ought to subscribe.

Immediately, however, the clock had struck twelve, the books were closed, and the conversation ended. Mrs. Delolme rang the bell and the servants appeared: and when they had taken their places, she read the prayers of the evening, in tones, by which, in the time of Oliver Cromwell, the Puritans would have been charmed.

This ceremony ended, the servants withdrew, and when Tom and Sylvester had taken their leave, they retired—nominally to rest, but actually to the study; at the door of which—as James couldn't get in—they found a cold chicken, for—as it subsequently appeared—a pigeon pie was not to be had. This, however, answered the purpose very well; and when Tom had produced two bottles of stout, they commenced in style the work of demolition.

Being anxious to have the benefit of his opinion upon the subject, Sylvester now thought that he would at once explain to Tom what had occurred that evening between him and Julia.

"Tom," said he, "you know the world better than I do; you have had more experience; you are a more close observer"——

"Here, take this leg," said Tom, "there isd't buch od it, add dod't let us have ady bore fide speeches."

"But I wish to put a question—a serious question—a question which you can, but I cannot, answer."

"Adythidg about adatoby?"

"No."

"What is it, thed?"

"I'll explain. Suppose that one of these evenings, Julia, of whom you have been speaking to-night, were to take her most valuable ring from her finger and beg your acceptance of it; *would* you accept it?"

"Suppose," replied Tom, "that this chicked, which we have just beed pullidg literally libb frob libb, were to start up whole, add, shakidg its feathers, ask us what o'clock it was; *would* you tell it?"

"Nay, that's impossible."

"I hold the wud case to be just as possible as the other. Were I to ask *her* to accept a ridg, there wouldd't be a great deal of doubt about the batter; but the idea of her askidg be to accept wud of her, is too rich for ady bad's stobach."

"I don't know that," returned Sylvester calmly; "I merely said suppose—I put it so—*suppose* she were earnestly to beg your acceptance of a ring, would you have it?"

"Well, I dod't exactly kdow—but I thidk I should."

"You *think* you would: come to the point; would you or would you not, under such circumstances refuse it?"

"Do, I wouldd't," replied Tom: "I'd take it."

"Very well. Now, while you were conversing with your friends this evening, she begged of me to accept this ring, and to keep it in remembrance of her."

"Is it possible! What, Julia?"

"Yes. I at first refused; but at length I consented to accept it on condition that she would allow me to present her with something of equal value. She agreed to this, and here is the ring. Now, what do you think of it?"

"Why, you abaze be! I thought there was sobethidg goidg od at the tibe—but I couldd't have ibagided this possible. I say, by boy," he added gravely, "be careful. This towd is studded with rub uds."

"But she is most amiable, have you not said?—kind-hearted and virtuous?"

"I do dot believe that there's a bore virtuous girl id the udiverse! Still, she bay be artful. She bay have sobe latedt desigd: what I believe her to be, add what she is, bay be diabetrically opposite. All I say is, by boy, be od your guard. This bay be but a draw. Dod't be fixed. Were she id a bore respectable positiod, it wouldd't batter so buch, but as it is"——

"A more respectable position!" echoed Sylvester. "Is it not respectable in the correct sense of the term? and have you not shown that none can blame her for being, under the circumstances, in that position?"

"Yes, by boy: still, the sphere frob which a bad takes a wife is looked at bore thad that id which he hibself bay have boved."

"Oh!" exclaimed Sylvester, "do not imagine I'm going to marry the girl! Don't imagine that I'm in love with her, for I am not. She's very amiable, very elegant, very fascinating, and very graceful, but as for being in love with her—the idea never entered my imagination."

"I'b glad to hear it," said Tom. "All I said was—add all I wish to repeat is—be od your guard!"

"Of course," said Sylvester, "you see the propriety of not mentioning this circumstance to any living creature."

"If you kdew be better, by boy," replied Tom, "you wouldd't thidk that observatiod at all decessary. But dow for the bachide," he added, going to the trap. "Let's see this gedtlebad, add thed we'll go to bed."

"You'll lock the door when we go out, of course?" suggested Sylvester.

"Do! dot a bit of it! It bay, you kdow, be wud of our fellows. If we leave the door oped, we shall catch hib either way—dod't you see?"

Sylvester acknowledged the wisdom of pursuing that course, and they set the trap so that the slightest touch would cause the spring to operate at once; and when Tom had earnestly expressed his conviction that that machine would vindicate his honour, he set aside the things and saw Sylvester to his room, at the door of which he bade him adieu for the night.

CHAPTER XVIII.

THE MAN-TRAP.

That night, Ninety-nine kept a sharp look-out; his look-out, in fact, was remarkably sharp: he never looked out more sharply. He crept into doorways, peeped round corners, and ran behind cabs, that he might not be seen. He was very wide awake—nay, enthusiastic! Didn't he wish for about half a chance!—didn't he pray for Tom's appearance upon the parapet! He had, it is true, been paid for the blow he received from Tom on the preceding night; but he panted for revenge! Revenge was his object: the attainment of which would have made him happy. Oh! if he could but have caught him!—but he couldn't: he couldn't see him: he couldn't see any one there. Still, he inspired a most lively hope—the hope of catching him some blessed night in a state of intoxication.

Wouldn't he serve him out then — wouldn't he stick his knuckles into his throat—wouldn't he knock him about with his truncheon—wouldn't he drag him to the station like a dog! Perhaps he wouldn't—which, being interpreted, means that there is nothing apocryphal about it. That night, however, he was doomed to disappointment. The object of his hot and inextinguishable hate would not even appear at the window—he therefore concluded that he was afraid, and said so with an air of triumph.

The morning came. Tom had slept soundly. He had not been disturbed: he had heard no noise. He, therefore, on waking, feared that he should not have the power that day of taking his honour out of the gaol of suspicion, knowing well that his mother would not accept bail. He, however, thought it right to go up and have a look, and having slipped on his things, he did go up, and beheld with amazement his man —his own man—his own skeleton—in the trap, leaning deliberately upon the sill of the open window with a book in its hand, a German pipe in its mouth, and an empty stout bottle and glass by its side.

Tom looked—of course he looked!—but he looked with an expression of mingled marvel and mirth. He couldn't tell at all what to make of it.

"I say, old fellow," he at length exclaimed, "what are you up to there?"

The skeleton answered him not.

"You seeb," said Tom, "to be doidg it rather browd!"

The skeleton made no reply.

"Have you hurt your leg at all, old fellow?"

The skeleton maintained a most contemptuous silence.

"Well," said Tom, "if ever there was a rub go this is wud!" and, approaching the skeleton, he burst into a loud roar of laughter.

"Syl bust see this," said he, as soon as the first burst had subsided; and rushing down, he dashed into Sylvester's room, and, on finding him asleep, shook him violently.

"What's the matter? What's the matter?" cried Sylvester.

"Here's a go, by boy!—cobe alodg."

"Have you caught him?"

"Yes, *he's* id the trap!—cobe alodg."

Sylvester instantly drew on his trousers and followed Tom, who continued to roar.

"There you are!" said Tom, as Sylvester entered the study. "There he is! That's the swell!—fast as a four-year old! That's a go, isd't it? What do you thidk of that?"

Sylvester knew not exactly *what* to think of it! He thought it very odd. He examined the skeleton from head to foot. Its leg was fixed in the trap fast enough—but how did it get there? That was the only problem to be solved.

"It's very strange," said he. "I can't understand it!"

"Udderstadd it!" cried Tom; "who cad? Surely *this* was dot the swell that was cuttidg his capers od the parapet! Yet it seebs as if he'd beed about to repeat the sabe gabe, got caught, add thed ibagided that he bight as well edjoy hibself id this way as dot! As to his sbokidg: that's hubbug. He hasd't the bellows to do it."

"Nor could he hold much stout," said Sylvester; "and yet the bottle's empty."

"There's sobe trick here," said Tom; "safe to be a trick. But dod't touch hib—let hib be as he is. The goverdor shall see hib: perhaps *he'll* be able to bake sobethidg out of it. Let's go add dress: by that tibe he'll be dowd. Dow," he added, addressing the skeleton, "if you have ady more of your dodsedse—if you bove to your old quarters before we cobe back agaid—I'll burder you."

They then left the room, and having locked the door securely, proceeded to dress; and when that operation had been simultaneously achieved, they went downstairs together, and found in the breakfast-parlour Mrs. Delolme, Aunt Eleanor, and the doctor.

"Odly just cobe up," said Tom, addressing the doctor; "odly cobe. Such a gabe."

"What is amiss?" inquired Mrs. Delolme.

"Odly cobe idto by study. I've caught hib."

"You have?" cried the doctor.

"Just cobe add look."

The doctor followed him and Sylvester on the instant, and Mrs. Delolme took the arm of Aunt Eleanor and hastily followed the doctor.

Having reached the room door, Tom unlocked it at once, and having thrown the door open, exclaimed, "There dow, what do you thidk of that?"

The doctor looked at the skeleton and smiled.

"What is all this?" said he; "what is the meaning of it, Tom?"

"The beadidg," replied Tom, "is this. Beidg adxious to catch that idsade swell who was cuttidg about the other dight od the parapet, I bought this bacbide, add havidg set it last dight, this is all I, at presedt, have got for by buddy."

"O Thomas—Thomas!" cried Mrs. Delolme, raising her hands in a state of mind bordering on despair.

"What's the batter?" said Tom.

"Oh!" replied Mrs. Delolme, with a sigh. "O Thomas —Thomas!"

"Why, what do you bead?"

"That ever I should have such a son!"

"Very good," said Tom; "but what is it you bead?"

"Do you mean to say," replied Mrs. Delolme, "Thomas! *do* you mean to say that you did not *yourself* place that figure there, in order that we might believe that it caused that unhallowed disturbance the night before last?"

"Well," exclaimed Tom, "that beats all. I'd better go to bed add sleep, add keep there. I'b victibised every way. What! Do you bead to say that you believe that I could bake byself such a codsubbate dodkey as to cobe up here id the biddle of the dight to place by bad id such a positiod as that, to idspire the belief that it was he who was cuttidg about od the parapet?"

Of all people on earth religious enthusiasts are at once the most credulous and the most sceptical; they really believe everything ascribable to human nature that is vile, and as readily disbelieve everything connected with human nature that is good. Mrs. Delolme, therefore, did believe that Tom had placed the skeleton there with a view to deceive them, and when she had told him she believed this, Tom said that he was done.

"I'll dot say adother word," he added; "dot adother syllable. If you'll believe that, there's dothidg bad you'll dot believe."

"Of course," said the doctor, "you found this skeleton in that position?"

"Of course I did," replied Tom. "Do you thidk that I should be such ad idiot as to throw away by buddy upod this bachide for the purpose of stickidg by bad id it thus? I call it hard to be suspected id this badder: very hard: it isd't the thidg—it's dothidg like the thidg; I wod't have it!"

"If, as you say," observed the doctor—"and I've not the slightest doubt you speak the truth, Tom—if, as you say, you found things as they are, there is something mysterious about it."

"I declare to you, upod by hodour," said Tom, "that thidgs were as they are whed I edtered the roob, add that frob the tibe Syl add I left it last dight, till I foudd the thidgs here as they are, I dever got out of by bed."

"Oh, *I* am quite satisfied, Tom," said the doctor, "as far at least as you are concerned; but it's strange—very strange! Just ring the bell."

The bell was rung and James appeared.

"James," said the doctor, "have you been in this room during the night?"

"Me, sir? No, sir."

"Now, speak the truth, Jib," said Tom fiercely, "or I pitch you out of the widdow od suspiciod."

"Upon my word, sir, I haven't: I haven't, as true as I'm alive."

"Very well," said the doctor; "that will do."

James then retired, and they looked at each other with varied expressions of doubt and dismay.

"It is," observed Sylvester, "of course inconceivable that the skeleton could have got there by itself."

"As idcodceivable," said Tom, "as that he was the swell who was cuttidg about od the parapet."

"What is the meaning of this?" inquired Aunt Eleanor. "You speak of a person having been on the parapet. What do you mean?"

"Since you know so much, dear," replied Mrs. Delolme, "I'll explain all to you by-and-by."

"Well," said the doctor, "I can make nothing of it at *present*. Perhaps after breakfast some light may appear. Come," he added, "let us go down. Lock the door, Tom, and keep the key in your pocket."

Tom did so, and as they were going downstairs, he said privately to Sylvester, "Victibised agaid! Sure to have the luck of it! If there's ady luck stirridg, I'b just as safe to have it as St. Paul's Churchyard is to have the widd."

Now it strangely enough happened, that while *they* were

at breakfast, the Rev. Mr. Rouse was at breakfast too, and it also happened that he had no sooner finished his first cup of coffee than Sylvester's letter arrived.

"London," said he musingly, looking at the post-mark; "from that kind creature of course! And yet," he added, turning to the superscription, "it is not her writing. Tut! bless my life; now whose hand can it be? I've seen it before! —I know the hand well!—well, now, that's very strange. The seal, too—a boar's head—that is not her crest! But the writing!—that's the point! Now, whose can it be?"

The reverend gentleman took up an egg—not conceiving that that would assist him; but he took up an egg and broke it, chiefly in order that his memory might have some refreshment. But no: that memory of his failed him: he could *not* remember whose writing it was, nor could he conjecture: but as it occurred to him, at length, that if he were to break the seal he might in an instant ascertain, he opened the letter, and when he saw from whom it came, he at once recollected the hand.

But of all the extraordinary expressions into which a man's countenance ever yet was tortured, his were the most extraordinary, and at the same time perhaps the most rapidly varied, when he saw what that letter contained.

Having read the first sentence—which opened the whole case—he turned to the fire and violently poked it. He then read the next, and, albeit the word "stout" provoked something like a smile, while the expression of the highest confidence in his judgment was, as far as it went, agreeable, the strongest feelings he experienced—the feelings which prevailed—the feelings which were in the ascendant throughout—were those of wonder and vexation. He knew not why he should be vexed. It was amazing, certainly—at least to him it appeared amazing—that she should have entertained the thought of entering into the marriage state; but then why should the circumstance vex him? He really couldn't tell. He didn't know. And yet one of the strongest feelings with which it had inspired him was that of vexation.

"Tut! bless my life!" he exclaimed; "who would have thought it? Tcha!—well!—married. Bless my heart alive. Tche! What a singular thing. Married! God bless me. Tcha!—I must be off, sir!—be off. Tchu! the strangest thing I ever heard of. Tche!—I never was more surprised.

Well, that does astonish me. Tcha! Bless my soul. Well, so it is. There's no time to be lost!"

Having delivered himself fitfully thus, the reverend gentleman rang the bell, and when he had hastily directed the servant to fill his carpet-bag with shirts, stockings, shoes, cravats, shaving machinery, and so on, he wrote a note to a reverend friend in the vicinity, requesting him to officiate during his absence.

Again he rang the bell.

"Tell Jones," said he, when the servant appeared, "to put the horse in. I'm going to town. Tell him to be quick, or we shall miss the coach."

He then went up to dress; and when all had been prepared, he dashed through the village at a more rapid rate than *he* had ever dashed through that village before.

"Hollo!" said Obadiah, as he and Pokey saw him pass. "What's Ted up to now! There's something in the wind. You saw his carpet-bag, didn't you? What's the odds he isn't going after his Rosalie? I'll bet you what you like she's been down here, incog.!—I'll bet you what you like, he has seen her, and finding that he couldn't carry his games on in a place like this without exciting observation, sent her to London, where he is off to now. Come, I'll bet you what you like of it—come!"

"He's off somewhere," said Pokey.

"Of course he is! And isn't it disgusting? Isn't it enough to make one's hair stand on end? I see it all clearly. It fructifies in my mind readily enough. *I* see the manœuvre. Yet these are the men we bow and scrape to—these are the men we pamper and praise. But just look you here, if we haven't before long a rattler, my boy, I'll eat grass like a cow! Sure to have it—safe—it must come: and do you mark my words, let it come when it will, all of that kidney may look out for squalls. What, do you suppose that because Johnny Bull is an ass now, he'll be an ass always? The idea is rotten! No; just look you here now, and do you mind this; no sooner are the people's eyes a little matters open—no sooner have they got out the dust that has blinded them ever since Peter the Great's time—than down comes a regular amalgamating battery, that'll stalk through the land, and sweep everything before it. There'll be no swindles—no petty-larceny plundering proud pick-pocketing pensioners—no placemen—no priestcraft—no poverty then; bribery and corruption will then be struck flat; and if ever they're suffered to rise again, it'll be the people's fault. We shall then see how such men as Teddy Rouse'll stand. They won't have 'em at no price—no more they don't ought. They'll be swept clean away—as old Boney once said, when he went out to welt the invaders—swept clean from the face of the earth, and sent after their French girls —their Rosalies—pretty dears! There, if I'd *my* will, I'd have a rope to reach from one steeple to another, and string 'em all up in a lump. I'd do it wholesale—*I* wouldn't mince the matter with them; I'd rid the earth of them at once, and then the mass of money which they swallow up would go into the pockets of the poor. As for Teddy Rouse—why, it's awful to see a man in his situation at *this* game. Here's a man running after French girls openly and in the face of day, and yet—look you here—we *pay* that man expressly to teach us morality. I mean to say it's monstrous. Isn't it, now, dreadful! When you come to look at it, isn't it disgusting?"

"It's all very well what you say," replied Pokey; "but you've been a preaching without any text."

"Text!" exclaimed Obadiah. "Ted is my text—corruption's my text—immorality's my text—national swindling's my text—revolution's my text! Everything's my text, when I see men like Teddy Rouse going at this rate."

"At what rate?"

"At what rate? Why, running after Rosalies!"

"You don't know, in this case, that it is so."

"Not know? You're a Tory: I always thought you were a Tory—not know?"

"You only guess."

"I'll tell you what I'll do; I'll bet you what you like of it."

"Bet me? You know I never bet."

"I'll bet you five shillings of it; now, there."

"But how can you prove it?"

"Never you mind—*I'll* prove it."

"But when?"

"Within eight-and-forty hours."

"Then, blame my *buttons*," cried Pokey, "if I don't take you. *Now*, then—there's my crown."

"No, I shan't put down the money; let it be till the bet's decided. Mind you, I'm to prove that Ted's now gone to London."

"You are to prove that he's now gone after some girl, and that that girl's name is Rosalie."

"Not a bit of it—there you quibble. No; the bet's off—I'll not bet with any man who quibbles."

"I don't at all quibble: but I didn't think you *would* make such a bet as that."

"Look you here," said Obadiah, "you'll turn up a Tory—now mark you that. I've long had my suspicions; but if you don't vote for the fructifying Tories, at the very next election, you'll wholly surprise *me*. I'm ashamed of you, Pokey, as true as I'm alive; and so I'll leave you to your reflections. Good-day."

As Obadiah left, Pokey smiled, knowing well that although he couldn't compete with him in talking, he had but to pin him to a point and he was done.

During the whole of that morning, Mrs. Delolme and Aunt Eleanor were conversing on the subject of supernatural appearances, which is at all times, and especially with the ladies, a prolific and highly interesting theme. The conversation sprang, of course, out of that morning's marvel; and although Mrs. Delolme had entertained the belief that Tom had himself placed the skeleton there, she felt herself eventually constrained to admit that it was possible—just possible—that the spirit which formerly inhabited that skeleton had caused it to walk to the window alone. She would, however, give no opinion on the point: that she reserved until she had consulted Mr. Terre. She was sure that *he* would be able to settle the question; and, as she felt that he was inspired—as she religiously believed that he had divine authority for every word he uttered—it was, in her judgment, altogether impossible that any opinion which he might express upon *any* subject could be wrong. She therefore calmly waited to consult her oracle. But the feelings of Aunt Eleanor were of a more distressing caste: the mystery affected her far more deeply. The idea of a spirit —if a spirit it really were—following her thus, and being visible only when she was near—inspired her with the most intense feelings of alarm. Her thoughts again reverted to her broken-hearted brother. The death-bed scene was again before her: she again heard his last declaration of innocence; and as her former apprehensions, that, to comfort her, he had uttered a falsehood with his dying breath, again came strong upon her, her affliction was poignant in the extreme. This, however, she thought it prudent to conceal from Mrs. Delolme. She had no confidence in her judgment. She could not speak to her as to an affectionate friend; she could not unbosom herself freely; she was not a friend to whom she could open her whole heart, knowing well that if she did, instead of deriving consolation, she should be rendered still more wretched. She was, therefore, on that point silent. She conversed, indeed, freely, on the subject of supernatural appearances in general, but the immediate source of her own peculiar sorrows she did not disclose.

At the same time the doctor, Tom, and Sylvester were conversing on the same subject, but in a more philosophical strain, in the study. The idea of there being anything supernatural in the removal of the skeleton from the position in which it usually stood to the trap, they unanimously repudiated as being utterly absurd. They all felt that it had been removed by some one: on that point they had not the slightest doubt; the only question with them was, who had removed it? Various were their conjectures, and, as is customary in such cases, very conflicting; but those which appeared to them to be most probable, were at length reduced to two: one being, that it was a trick of one of the servants; and the other, that the thing had been done by the man whom the policeman saw the previous night on the parapet. The latter was suggested by Sylvester himself.

"For," said he, "although it is clear that had he jumped straight down from the window he would have been caught in the trap himself, it is also clear that, by going on one side, or even over the trap, he must necessarily have escaped it. I have no doubt that he did either one or the other, and that, subsequently finding the trap set for him, he placed the skeleton in it, and made it assume the position in which it was found."

"Well," said the doctor, "that certainly appears to be reasonable, so far as it goes; but what could be the man's object in coming here? That is the point which puzzles me."

"It might be idleness merely," said Sylvester; "or what, perhaps, he would call fun. He is clearly a fanciful fellow. The position in which he placed the figures before, and especially that in which this is now, tend to prove that if his object be not purely fun, he imagines he has some fun in him."

"If I catch hib," said Tom, "I'll show hib a little bore fud. He shall hibself look fuddy before I've dode with hib."

"Well," said the doctor, "we have come to this point, and it appears to be the most reasonable at which we can arrive. We must endeavour now to prevent a recurrence of these tricks, and I think that we shall at once attain that object by having the window barred."

"Do," said Tom, "dod't bar the widdow yet. I wadt to catch hib; add that I shall catch hib, I'll bet ted to wud."

"Well," said the doctor, smiling, "if you should happen to catch him, and you find that fun *is* his only object, you must, in the administration of your justice, be merciful."

"Oh! I'll be berciful," replied Tom. "Dothidg that he ever had id the shape of bercy shall surpass it. I'll give hib such ad out-add-out dose of bercy, that a bile of people shall hear hib proclaib how peculiarly berciful I am."

The doctor smiled, and left the study, when Tom and Sylvester replaced the male skeleton in its former position, and busied themselves about the bones of the female until they were summoned to dinner.

As usual, the dinner went off flatly: for although the doctor chatted—and that sometimes gaily too—no one else did; Mrs. Delolme *would* not; Aunt Eleanor *could* not; and while Tom *dared* not, Sylvester thought he *ought* not. When, therefore, the ladies had retired, not only Tom and Sylvester, but the doctor himself felt much relieved, and, after a pleasurable and profitable discussion—profitable especially, in a professional point of view—Tom and Sylvester left to attend that evening's lecture.

"Well," said Sylvester, on leaving the house, "what am I to present to this poor girl? The thing had better be done at once. What is it to be?"

"Oh!" replied Tom, "bake her a presedt of adother ridg."

"She appears to have an abundance of them already."

"What id the jewellery lide has she dot ad abuddadce of?" returned Tom; "chaids, brooches, decklaces, earridgs—I cad't thidk of adythidg of the sort that she has *dot* got."

"Had she a bracelet on last night?"

"The very thidg. I rebebber dow she has do bracelets."

"Then we had better go and buy a pair at once."

They went accordingly into the first jeweller's shop they came to, and having fixed upon a pair of a chaste and elegant pattern, they purchased them, and then went direct to the hospital.

Now, before they arrived—before they could have arrived there, a cab drew up to the door of Dr. Delolme, and when the driver had given his customary knock—a knock which quite frightened the occupant of the cab, who felt really very nervous on being announced in a style which he conceived to be so dreadfully *distingué*—James came to the door, and then went to the cab, and having satisfactorily answered to two questions, was presented with the card of the Reverend Edward Rouse. James opened the door for the reverend gentleman to alight, and he alighted, and drew out his purse. The fare was a shilling, but as he had been, by that knock, convinced that the driver conceived him to be some highly important personage, he gave him half-a-crown; which was very incorrect of the reverend gentleman, for had the cabman known why the extra fare was given him, he'd have subsequently split, if he hadn't smashed in every door it became his duty to knock at. The reverend gentleman, however, unconscious of that fact, gave the half-crown, and having followed James in, was shown into one of the parlours.

"Good gracious!" exclaimed Aunt Eleanor, when James had delivered the card; "is it possible?"

"Anything the matter, my dear?" inquired Mrs. Delolme.

"I fear there is something," replied Aunt Eleanor; "I very much fear it, for Mr. Rouse, of whom you have heard me speak, dear, has come unexpectedly from Cotherstone."

"Indeed!" exclaimed Mrs. Delolme; "I'm quite delighted. Pray do not let him go, dear, until you have introduced him."

Aunt Eleanor left the room; and on entering the parlour, she at once grasped the hands of the reverend gentleman, with an expression of cordiality mingled with apprehension.

"My dear, dear friend!" she exclaimed, "why, when did you arrive?"

"I came by the coach," replied the reverend gentleman; "the same coach as that which you came by."

"Well, I'm much pleased to see you; is all right at home?"

"Oh! quite right; quite right! Why, really," he added, with a playful expression, "you must, indeed you must, be very wicked; for since you left us the village has been as tranquil as possible; no noises, no annoyances, no apparitions; no; nothing at all of the sort,"

Aunt Eleanor was sad. She could have wept; but would not do so then.

"Well, now," he continued, "I only came this evening just to say how d'ye do, and to let you know that I had arrived. I'll call in the morning; what time shall I call?"

"Oh, as early as you please! but you are not going yet?"

"Yes; I'll call in the morning; we shall then be more tranquil. You have much to say to me, and I have much to say to you. In the morning we'll talk over everything calmly."

"But I really cannot permit you to leave me in such haste. Come into the drawing-room—come."

"No, no, my dear madam; you perhaps have a party."

"No, indeed, we have not; there's only Mrs. Delolme, who is exceedingly anxious to be introduced to you. The doctor is unfortunately out now, but he will be in presently; Sylvester, too, will be in very soon; therefore, come, my dear sir—nay, you really must come. Mrs. Delolme, I know, will scold me, if you go without allowing me the pleasure of introducing you to her."

"Well, my dear madam, if you are sure that I'm not intruding, I shall be happy to be introduced to that lady. I cannot," he added playfully, and at the same time pressing both her hands in a style which, for him, was extremely unusual, "I cannot—nor will I cause *you* to be scolded. I may scold you myself—that, perhaps, I *may* do—but you must not be scolded by any one else."

Aunt Eleanor smiled—she didn't at all understand what he meant, still she smiled; and having conducted him into the drawing-room, presented him at once to Mrs. Delolme, who received him gracefully, it is true, but with that excessive formality which freezes. The reverend gentleman was awed! The severity of her expression had at first the effect of blocking up all conversation. Aunt Eleanor, however, at length broke the ice, and until the return of the doctor a stream of religious discourse flowed freely.

While they were thus engaged, Tom and Sylvester were listening with laudable attention to a highly important pathological lecture, during the delivery of which neither Julia nor the bracelets were, for one moment, thought of. At the conclusion, however, both were instantly remembered, and Sylvester, taking Tom's arm, proceeded at once to the bar of the Bull, accompanied, as usual, by half-a-dozen friends.

As they entered, Julia was looking anxiously at the clock, for about the fiftieth time in the course of ten minutes, but when she saw Sylvester, her heart leaped with joy, although she felt more than ever embarrassed.

Sylvester bowed and slightly smiled, and as he smiled she blessed him.

Having managed, mechanically, to supply the demands of the noisy students, she retreated to the other end of the bar, when Tom, perceiving that Sylvester had not been supplied, cried, "Hollo, here! what do you bead? What's by friedd dode? Isd't he to have ady?"

"Really," said Julia, coming forward in a tremor, and addressing Sylvester, "upon my word, I beg pardon; pray forgive me."

"I see how it is," said Tom, as Sylvester was endeavouring to convince her that it really was a matter of no moment; "you are in love with Bob Topps."

"Why, of course," cried Bob Topps, a short, stout, stumpy student, who sported a comical conical hat; "that all the world knows. We are going to tie up as soon as I've passed."

Julia smiled and retreated again.

The students now entered into an animated discussion upon a point to which, in the course of the lecture, particular reference had been made, and when Sylvester found that they were much too intent upon the subject to notice *him*, he made a signal for Julia to approach.

"Now," said he, "you must perform your promise by accepting these from *me*."

Julia took the bracelets, placed them in her bosom, and pressed them to her heart, and having taken his hand with a fervent expression, exclaimed—

"God bless you!"

Tom, although apparently engaged in the discussion, saw all that passed, and shortly afterwards expressed himself precisely to this effect—

"Dow, by boy, tibe's up; we bust bizzle—are you ready?"

"Quite," returned Sylvester; "quite."

"Thed we'll be off. Good-dight!" he added, addressing the students; "I shall see you to-borrow."

"To-borrow bordidg," said Bob Topps, "or to-borrow dight, Tob?"

Hereupon there was a laugh—a loud laugh—among the

students, and during its continuance, Sylvester shook hands with Julia, who was in consequence overjoyed, and having said " *Good*-night ! " left the house with Tom.

"I'll tell you what it is," said Tom, "that girl's id love with you. Dothidg cad be clearer thad that. But it wod't do, Syl. Do, that'll dever do."

" What will never do ? "

" Why, it'll dever do for you to be caught, Syl, id that trap."

"Caught in that *trap !* " echoed Sylvester. "There's an end of it. I have accepted a present from her, and she has accepted a present from me : that settles it."

"Yes, by boy, that settles it certaidly as far as it goes; but if you codtidue to go there, by boy, you'll cause her to believe that you are desperately id love with *her*."

" Well, then, I had better go there no more."

" Why, do bad has a right to cause a girl to believe that he's id love with her udless he idtedds to barry her."

" Very true; and as of course I have no such intention, I had better not go there again."

" Why, I should *say*," observed Tom, " that you'd fly at a little higher gabe thad a barbaid."

"I have no contempt for her because she is a barmaid. That which you told me last night, Tom, convinced me that she ought now to be in a better position. I would not trifle with the feelings of such a girl; I would not raise hopes which could never be realised. I am sorry now that I went there at all; but the matter is settled—I go there no more."

"She's ad artful card, do doubt," said Tom; "add if you give her a chadce she bay addoy you, which wouldd't be pleasadt : it wouldd't, for instadce, be pleasadt at all were she to cobe sobe fide bordidg to have a chat with the old ladies ! 'Where do you live, dear ? ' by bother would ask. 'At the Bull.' 'What's the Bull ? ' 'A public-house.' 'Add what are you, dear ? ' 'I'b the barbaid.' *Wouldd't* the old swell oped her eyes ! Sedd I bay live, what a look she'd have for her ! Do, it wouldd't do at all to give her a chadce of goidg there, which she bight, add perhaps would do, to addoy you."

That Tom did not do justice to Julia is clear; but he gained his point, and the subject dropped.

On reaching home, Sylvester, when he heard of the arrival of his reverend friend, was delighted and amazed.

" *Who* is it, Syl ? " inquired Tom.

"Mr. Rouse."

"Mr. Rouse—ah! who is he?"

"The Reverend Mr. Rouse."

"Oh, a parsod; ah! *I* shall go idto by study. Jib, bridg be sobe coffee up there."

"But you'll come in and speak to him, of course," cried Sylvester.

"Do, Syl, I dod't like parsods id private. They are all very well id the pulpit, but id a roob I cad't bear theb."

"Oh, but he's such a very nice fellow. I'm sure you'll be pleased with him. Do come in."

"Well, I'll go id with you; but if he be adythidg at all like the crew whob we used to have here, I shall cut it id a bobedt."

They then entered the drawing-room, and Sylvester seized the reverend gentleman by the hand, and having shaken it heartily, introduced Tom.

"Well," exclaimed Sylvester, "this *is* unexpected. Why, I'd no idea of your coming to town."

"I had no idea of it myself till this morning," returned the reverend gentleman, inferring at once that they wished it to *appear* that his visit was quite unexpected.

"And did you leave the village pretty quiet?" resumed Sylvester. "Have any ghosts been seen by the people since we left?"

"No; all has been tranquil—perfectly tranquil."

"By-the-by, Mr. Rouse," observed Mrs. Delolme, "what is your opinion of supernatural appearances—of visions—of ghosts? Do you think that they are really ever seen?"

"I have not the slightest doubt upon the subject," replied the reverend gentleman.

"Do bad," said Tom, to whom the reverend gentleman seemed to appeal, "that is, do idtellectual bad, I should thidk, cad have dow the ghost of a doubt about that."

"I have myself seen one," resumed the reverend gentleman —and Tom privately intimated to Sylvester that he had *nearly* put his foot in it—"I have seen one enter a room, walk deliberately across it, look about, turn, and then walk deliberately back—as distinctly as I see you before me."

"And it is, I suppose, impossible," said Mrs. Delolme, "for you to have been in a reverie at the time?"

"Quite impossible—quite."

"I mean, you could not have seen it in imagination merely?"

"Certainly not. Had I been alone I might have doubted—I might have doubted even the evidence of my own senses—I should have been then inclined to believe that I *had* seen it merely in imagination; but I was not alone: I was with one who had no imagination in him!—pardon the expression—I mean my gardener, whose mind I believe to be as destitute of imagination as it is possible for the mind of a man to be."

"And may I ask, did *he* see it?" inquired the doctor.

"He did, as distinctly as I saw it myself."

"And had you any proof that it was not flesh and blood?"

"Why I cannot say that I had any actual *proof*."

"Neither you nor your servant attempted to touch it?"

"No, neither attempted to touch it."

"Did it make any noise as it walked along?"

"Not more than you or I should make without our boots."

"But as much, you think?"

"I should say quite as much."

"Then there must, I submit, have been something more than spirit about it."

"I believe not. The noise indeed might have been imaginary; but the appearance of the figure I am satisfied was not."

"Well," said the doctor, "these things are extraordinary: many equally extraordinary things have been accounted for; but as many have occurred for which we cannot account, we must view this as being one of them."

The time had now arrived when the reverend gentleman thought it prudent to depart. He had previously been engaged by the doctor to dine with them on the morrow, but while taking leave of Aunt Eleanor, he promised to call upon her early in the morning.

Almost immediately after he had left, Mrs. Delolme, who was very highly pleased with him, rang the bell for prayers, and when they had been read, Tom and Sylvester retired to the study. James had provided a pound of German sausage for them this time, and a couple of bottles of Burton ale, the whole of which they managed between them, of course!—and when Tom had set the trap again, and placed a piece of string across the window, so that even the slightest touch would bring down a shelf laden with empty bottles, they left the study and retired to rest.

CHAPTER XIX.

THE DELICATE DISCLOSURE.

IN the morning, Tom, on awaking, found the skeleton by his side. He started, of course, when he saw it first, and opened his eyes and his mouth. There it stood—within a foot of him—pointing directly at him with its right hand, and making a fist of its left.

Tom got out of bed—on the other side of course—and he wasn't long about it. He didn't at all like the look of the thing. Nor did the expression of his features denote the existence of unmingled joy. He felt queer. He couldn't understand it. There it stood in a menacing position, with a white pocket-handkerchief tied round its shin.

"Dodsedse!" cried Tom, at length. "Pooh! I wod't have it! I say, old fellow, what gabe do you call this?"

The skeleton was, as usual, silent, and Tom went round to inspect it more closely. "I'd sbash you, old fellow," said he indignantly, "if I thought you had adythidg like life id you!" And having given utterance to this remarkable expression, he went as he was into Sylvester's room.

"Adother gabe, Syl," said he. "Cobe add look here."

"What now?" exclaimed Sylvester.

"*Just* cobe add look. There!" he added, as Sylvester entered his room. "There you are!—what do you thidk of *that?*"

"Good gracious!" cried Sylvester. "What, was it there when you awoke?"

"Exactly id that positiod. I haved't touched it."

"Well, this *is* strange!"

"Do you see its leg tied up, as if it were idjured whed caught id the trap?"

"Really, this surpasses all!"

"Dow, we wod't tell the womed about this," said Tom;

"if we do, I'b safe to be victibized agaid; but the goverdor shall see it, add thed we shall hear what he thidks of the batter."

Again and again Sylvester expressed his surprise, and feeling in reality all that he expressed—for he hadn't the most remote idea of the manner in which the skeleton had been removed—he returned to his own room to dress.

During breakfast, not a syllable on the subject was uttered; but afterwards, Tom took the doctor upstairs and showed him the thing as it stood.

"And do you mean to say, Tom, you know nothing of it?" said the doctor, who began to suspect Tom himself.

"All I kdow of it," replied Tom, "is this: that there add thus it stood whed I woke."

"But were you not disturbed at all during the night?"

"Dot at all. Add I defy ady bad alive to cobe idto by roob while I'b asleep without wakidg be up."

"Whose handkerchief is that round the leg? That, perhaps, may give us some clue."

Tom took off the handkerchief; and having examined it, found that it was his own.

"Ah!" said the doctor suspiciously. "Well, all I can say, Tom, is, that it's strange. We may, perhaps, find it all out by-and-by."

He then left the room; and, as Tom perceived clearly that he was again suspected, he struck the intruding skeleton in the mouth, and knocked its head off.

As the doctor was thoughtfully going downstairs, Aunt Eleanor's reverend friend arrived; and, on being announced, was welcomed with warmth by all, save Tom, who was privately engaged in delivering a deeply indignant soliloquy. Even the features of Mrs. Delolme were relaxed when the reverend gentleman appeared; for all the virtues he possessed, with all those which he could be imagined to possess, had been by Aunt Eleanor duly set forth.

There was, however, one fact which puzzled him exceedingly, and that was, the absence of all anxiety on the part of Aunt Eleanor to have a private conference. He couldn't understand it. He had fancied that her anxiety to converse with him privately would have been most intense; instead of which, he found that even the most favourable opportunities were lost, and that, in fact, she was not at all anxious about the matter. He was not, it is true, displeased with this; it didn't in the slightest degree distress him; it, on the contrary, tended to convince him that the stout individual in question was one whom she really didn't care much about; but he did think it strange—exceedingly strange—that after having summoned him to London, expressly in order to consult him on the subject, she should not in any manner, either directly or indirectly, allude to it. It was true she *might* be waiting until he had seen this stout gentleman; certainly this struck him as being extremely probable; it moreover struck him, that as bulk was the point at issue, he couldn't form anything like a just judgment upon that point *until* he had seen him; still, although these might be the real causes of her silence, and although he thought it likely that he should meet him at dinner, he could not but feel, notwithstanding the delicacy of the subject, that a few brief preliminary observations would be agreeable, and by no means whatever incorrect.

In the course of the morning Mrs. Delolme expressed an earnest desire to introduce him to Mr. Terre, and as the reverend gentleman—conceiving that *he* was in reality the man who had proposed—was equally anxious for the introduction, the carriage was immediately ordered, and they went.

He now thought he saw clearly how the case stood: that this great gun was the stout individual, that Mrs. Delolme knew all about it, and that she had been deputed by Aunt Eleanor to manage the introduction, in order that he might at once be able to pass judgment upon the point at issue.

Instead, however, of finding Mr. Terre the stout person he had imagined, he found him particularly thin, which at once upset all his ideas on the subject of *his* being the man, and tended to remove those prejudices against him which he had almost involuntarily inspired.

In bringing these two reverend persons together, Mrs. Delolme, perhaps naturally, anticipated a high intellectual treat; but, as this anticipation was not based upon any profound knowledge of the men, she was doomed to experience disappointment. They were both superficial, and therefore both cautious. They were afraid of each other, and knowing that there exists much virtue in silence—seeing that it leaves an immense amount of eloquence, genius, tact, and erudition to be imagined—prudence prompted them both to avoid every subject upon which they conceived a discussion might arise.

But although disappointed in this respect, their silence had a great effect on Mrs. Delolme; it caused her to believe that they were both profound, and hence to raise them in her estimation, for she felt it to be the true silence of wisdom; and so, indeed, it was, as far as that wisdom went.

Well, that Mr. Terre was not the individual in question, the reverend gentleman now felt convinced; he therefore resolved to wait till dinner time with patience, in the full expectation of seeing him then, and being anxious to call upon a friend or two in town, he, on their return, took leave until five.

Meanwhile Tom and Sylvester were busily engaged in devising means by which they might solve that mystery, the effect of which upon the minds of Dr. and Mrs. Delolme had wounded Tom's private feelings deeply. He knew that he was unjustly suspected, of course; he also knew, that unless the whole affair was satisfactorily cleared up, his reputation must suffer. He admitted that, in the absence of all proof to the contrary, the suspicion that he had invented these tricks with the view of clearing himself of the accusation of Ninety-nine, was neither irrational under the circumstances, nor strained; but he did think it hard—knowing his innocence—very hard, that everything he did for the purpose of removing that suspicion, should have a direct tendency to confirm it.

"But I'll dot give it up," said he, having invented and repudiated fifty schemes which at first appeared likely to achieve the object in view. "I'll dever give it up till I fidd out the cause, although we had better keep it to ourselves ndtil the gradd result is discovered. Dow, I'll tell you what I'll do to begid with: I'll sedd Jib out for a couple of bells, add as the skeletod seebs to be either directly or iddirectly the great swell, I'll hadg theb ibbediately over by head, add have stridgs attached to its legs, so that if it be reboved, however slightly, the bells bay ridg udkdowd to hib who reboves it."

"Very good," said Sylvester. "But why send James for the bells? Why let *him* know anything about them? You'd better get them yourself; or I'll run and get them for you. We shall however have to go out by-and-by, and then we can bring them in with us."

"That will be the best way, certaidly," said Tom; "but what do you thidk of the schebe?"

"I think it a very good one. But *I* should advise sitting up, here in the study. I'll sit up with you with pleasure."

"It wod't do, Syl—I'b sure it wod't do. Whed they see a light they'll cut back."

"Then let's sit in the dark."

"Id the dark! What bortal cad keep hibself awake throughout the dight id the dark? Hubad dature hasd't the power to do it."

"*I'd* do it. I'd keep myself awake, especially on such an occasion—I'd stake my existence upon it."

"Well," said Tom, "suppose we try the bell dodge first. The thidg cad't be boved without causidg the bells to ridg, dor cad the bells ridg without wakidg be. I therefore thidk that we had better try that dodge to-dight, the result of which bay, perhaps, guide us to-borrow."

"Very well: then let it be so. We'll bring the bells in with us when we go out."

Having decided on pursuing this course, they left the study to prepare for dinner; and on going into the drawing-room shortly afterwards, found that the reverend gentleman had arrived. He did not, however, appear to be at ease. He was evidently anxious about something. He kept fidgeting about, and glancing at the door, and starting when any one entered.

"Your aunt and I," said he at length to Sylvester, aside, "have had no conversation on that subject yet."

"Have you not?" said Sylvester, who conceived that he alluded to the mystery which still occupied *his* thoughts.

"I don't think she likes to allude to the subject."

"Very likely not. But did you ever hear of anything so extraordinary—so unaccountable?"

"I never was more astonished in my life than when I heard of it."

"All in the house were astonished."

"Do they all know of the circumstance?"

"Oh! yes. But whatever may now occur will be concealed from them all till the point has been gained."

"Do you think that his object *will* be attained?"

"I've no doubt of it."

"Well!" said the reverend gentleman thoughtfully, "it is *altogether* the strangest thing I ever heard of."

Dinner was announced: and although no stout individual

had arrived, the reverend gentleman felt very nervous. This feeling, however, while they were at dinner, wore off: indeed the doctor, who was at all times anxious to make those around him happy, at length put him in high spirits by his lively and interesting conversation. He was delighted with the doctor. He had never met with a man whom he admired so much. And the doctor was equally delighted with him; for simplicity of manners is appreciated most by those who are most conversant with the world's hypocrisy.

At eight o'clock Tom and Sylvester left; and as the ladies had previously retired, the reverend gentleman fully expected that the doctor would allude to the contemplated marriage, seeing that Sylvester—as he imagined—had told him that the whole affair was known to them all. But the doctor, of course, knowing nothing about it, did not say a word upon the subject; which the reverend gentleman thought very strange, feeling convinced that he was perfectly cognisant of the cause of his coming to town. As, however, the subject was not alluded to by him, *he* did not like to allude to it, and therefore no allusion was made to it at all.

About nine, the doctor was summoned to see a patient, and having taken the reverend gentleman up to the ladies, apologised and left; and as, shortly afterwards, Mrs. Delolme quitted the room to give some instructions to the servants, Aunt Eleanor, addressing her reverend friend, who was anxious for her to begin, said, "Well, and when do you think of leaving town?"

"Why," replied the reverend gentleman, "that depends upon circumstances entirely."

"I see. But you do not think of leaving us yet?"

"Why—no. Until something has been settled, of *course* I shall not think of leaving. When do *you* think this affair will be arranged?"

"What affair do you allude to?"

"Why, of that affair of course—which has brought me to town."

"Oh! I beg pardon. I didn't ask as a matter of curiosity. I thought it might be something in which I was concerned."

"And so, my dear madam, it is."

"Indeed! Why, what *do* you mean?"

"I know your delicacy," replied the reverend gentleman,

with great deliberation, "and I appreciate it highly; but when am I to be introduced to him?"

"To him! To whom?"

"Why, this gentleman."

"What gentleman?"

"Why, the gentleman who has made you an offer."

"Oh!" exclaimed Aunt Eleanor gaily, being quite disposed to keep up that which she conceived to be a very pleasant jest, "I understand. *You* shall be introduced: I'll promise you *that*."

"Is he—very—*remarkably*—stout?"

"Not very—not remarkably so—at least, not that I know of. But you shall see him one of these days."

One of these days! This, under these circumstances, struck the reverend gentleman as being a most extraordinary expression. One of these days! Had he come between sixty and seventy miles, nominally for the purpose of being introduced to this man, but virtually in order to be told that he *should* see him one of these days?

"He is in town, I presume?" said he, after a pause.

"Really," returned Aunt Eleanor, still keeping up the assumed joke, "I don't know exactly where he is at present."

"Indeed! But, of course, he'll be here in a day or two?"

"He may be; and when he does come, I'll at once introduce him—you funny man, be assured of that."

Funny man! Well, in the judgment of the reverend gentleman, it was a funny affair altogether. He didn't know that *he* was particularly funny: he might be—he wouldn't undertake to deny that he was: nor did he deny it—but he thought the whole proceeding of course very odd.

"But," said he, "in the event of your accepting this offer, when do you *think* the affair will take place?"

"Well, I really cannot say; but, when it does take place, you will, I hope, do me the favour to officiate?"

"I shall feel, on the occasion of your marriage, great pleasure in being *present*. But I suppose it will be settled now in a very few days?"

"No, I don't think it will be so soon."

"In a week, then, or so?"

"I think not so soon as that."

"Well, my dear madam," said the reverend gentleman, who really felt very much embarrassed, for, while he could not but think that he had not been exactly treated *well*, he was anxious to conceal the fact of his being annoyed, " you know best, certainly—you ought to know best. But I presume, from what you have said, that you intend to accept his offer?"

"Why, really, that is a question which I *cannot* answer now. I shall, however, be in a position to do so *immediately* after the offer has been made."

"*After* it has been made! Has it not already been made?"

"Not yet, no! it has not been made yet."

"Oh! I beg pardon! I thought it had been."

"Why, what *do* you mean? There is nothing in your countenance facetious; and yet you are jesting, of course?"

"Jesting! Bless my life, no; I'm not jesting at all."

"Do you really mean to say that you are serious?"

"Perfectly so."

"Then what *do* you mean?"

"You have had—or rather you expect to have—an offer of marriage: do you not?"

"No!"

"But a gentleman has proposed, or is about to propose to you?"

"Not that I am aware of."

"Tut!—bless my life: a stout gentleman!—one whom you think somewhat *too* stout?"

"I know nothing of it."

"Well, but—really, my dear madam—is that a fact?"

"I know nothing whatever, my dear sir, about it."

"Bless my heart alive! Well, but did you not direct a letter to be sent to me, stating that such was the case?"

"*Most* certainly not."

"The young dog—the young rascal. I'll give him a lecture. I shouldn't have supposed it. I shouldn't have thought he would have done such a thing. The young scamp."

"To whom do you allude?"

"To Sylvester."

"Sylvester! Well, but, my dear sir, you don't mean to say that our Sylvester sent such a letter as that?"

"Here it is!" replied the reverend gentleman, searching all his pockets with astonishing rapidity. "Here it is!

No, it isn't: it's in my other coat. But Sylvester sent me a letter—which letter you shall see to-morrow morning—to this effect: that you had desired him to inform me, that you thought of entering into the marriage state: that you hadn't exactly made up your mind: that you would not do so until you had consulted me: that you fancied that the gentleman, who had made you an offer, was somewhat too stout "——

"Too stout!" cried Aunt Eleanor, laughing.

"Yes, somewhat too stout: that you would not decide until you had had my opinion upon the point: and that, if that opinion were favourable, you wished me to perform the marriage ceremony."

"Why, you amaze me!"

"That is the substance of the letter which I received yesterday morning."

"And signed by Sylvester?"

"Signed by him—in his own handwriting."

"Impossible!"

"It's a fact. I'll take my oath to the writing. I'd just commenced breakfast when the letter arrived, and when I read the contents you may imagine my surprise."

"You might well be surprised," said Aunt Eleanor, smiling.

"I *was* surprised, because I never imagined for one moment that you contemplated anything of the sort. However, it appeared to me quite clear then, and therefore I came up to London at once."

"And was this the sole cause of your coming to town?"

"I had no other object than that of seeing you."

"Then, really, I am very sorry for it."

"I am not—*I* am not! On the contrary—now that I find that it's nothing, but what they, in London, call a hoax—I'm quite pleased—I'm delighted! It seems to have struck into my mind a new light: it has given animation to feelings which have long lain dormant. I candidly confess to you that I am much pleased: nay, I'll also confess to you this, that I came up fully determined to oppose that man's claim, by declaring—if I found that he was anything of a size—that he *was*, in reality, much too stout."

"What!" said Aunt Eleanor gaily; "and thus to prevent me from gaining an affectionate husband?"

"No; to prevent you merely from having him. But we'll

speak more of this by-and-by. The idea of my leaving that letter at the inn! I wish that I had brought it. I changed my coat, you see, when I went to dress."

"Well, but are you quite sure," said Aunt Eleanor, upon whom the observation of the reverend gentleman, having reference to those feelings which had long been dormant, had a very peculiar effect; "are you certain that that letter was written by Sylvester?"

"Quite. But you shall see it in the morning, and form your own judgment. I feel quite clear upon the point."

"Then, really, I must scold him well."

"Leave that to me, my dear madam: just leave that to me. Although I cannot be angry with him for it, *I'll* give him a lecture. We had better not, however, say a word to him to-night. I'll bring the letter with me in the morning, and then we shall have all before us."

Mrs. Delolme now re-entered the room, and shortly after, the doctor returned and recommenced chatting to the reverend gentleman, while, at intervals, Aunt Eleanor merrily laughed at the idea of her having objected to a lover on the ground of his being too stout.

Soon after the return of Tom and Sylvester, their reverend friend took his leave, and when prayers had been read, they went as usual into the study to supper, and when they had eaten to their hearts' content, they adjusted the bells, and went to bed.

CHAPTER XX.

THE BELLS.

So much has been written and said about LOVE, that were not his beautiful features ever varying and ever new, the subject *must* have been ere this exhausted. One of the peculiar attributes of Love is his perpetual juvenility—his immortal youth. He was created with the Creation: he was the favourite boy of Eve: Eve was remarkably fond of Love; and he has been ever since the first favourite of her daughters. From the Creation he lived till the Deluge: he was in the Ark with Noah, and welcomed back the dove.

From the Deluge he lived till the commencement of the Christian Era, and in the whole of the proceedings of the eventful period which intervened, took an active and a most conspicuous part. From the commencement of the Christian Era he continued to live; and he is alive now, and full of health, joy, and beauty, and albeit six thousand years old, doesn't look more than six.

This, however, may be said to be a painter's view of Love. Let us view Love philosophically. Stop! Philosophically? No: that is impracticable—quite. Love repudiates Philosophy, and Philosophy repudiates Love. They are, and ever have been, at war: they are, in fact, the greatest enemies that ever had existence—each breathes *destruction* to the other: they are very inveterate foes. Love frequently upsets Philosophy, even in the very streets; which is very incorrect of Love, certainly; but then Philosophy is constantly endeavouring to upset Love! Sometimes, however, Love—in his most amiable moments—will meet Philosophy calmly, and try to effect something like a reconciliation; but Philosophy will not be propitiated, conceiving that Love can never love Philosophy. Nor can he; nor can Philosophy ever love Love. Love may be beloved by millions dearly; but never can Philosophy be a lover of Love.

It being, therefore, impossible to take a philosophical view of Love, suppose we take a common sense view—and yet what on earth has Love to do with Common Sense? Absolutely nothing. Love doesn't even know Common Sense. We cannot, therefore, take a common sense view of Love. No; if we view him at all, we must view him as he is—a monarch reigning in the hearts of his people: a mighty monarch—the King of Hearts: a king without revenues sufficient to find him even in shirts—an absolute and a naked king!—a king, moreover, glorying in his nakedness, of which, being pure, he is never ashamed: a king whose dominion is illimitable, and whose prime minister is so impartial, that he strikes the light of Love into the souls of all, without reference to either caste, colour, or creed.

He doesn't, however, always inflame the thrilling bosoms of youth; he'll sometimes let people alone for forty or fifty years. This may be held to be an extraordinary fact, but it is a fact nevertheless—a fact which must not be denied; nor, for more than a moment, even doubted, seeing that

P

Aunt Eleanor and her reverend friend supplied at this period a case in point.

Aunt Eleanor was upwards of forty years of age, and the reverend gentleman was upwards of fifty, while neither had, up to this time, really loved. The germs of love were in the hearts of both, but they had never struck root. And in speaking of love, it must be understood as love, not certainly *contra*-distinguished, but distinguished from affection; for while Aunt Eleanor was one of the most affectionate creatures that ever breathed, the affections of the reverend gentleman were strong. It will hence be seen that love does not necessarily co-exist with affection: in other words, that affection may exist without love; for certain is it that the reverend gentleman never inspired the passion of love until he received Sylvester's letter, and that Aunt Eleanor never really felt that she loved, until her reverend friend spoke of those feelings which had in his bosom lain dormant so long. Then, indeed, the flame burst forth to amaze them with the consciousness of their having been formed to love each other; and that consciousness, coupled with the amazement thereon consequent, kept them awake—on the morning that followed the eventful day of which the preceding chapter treats—until half-past two o'clock.

At half-past two o'clock—it was a singular coincidence—they both fell asleep, and they hadn't been asleep more than fifteen minutes when Tom heard his bells.

"Hollo! very good!" said he, getting out of bed. "Stop a bidite, add I'll give you pepper!" And grasping a stick, a blow from which would have made the head of any man ache for a month, he went up stealthily into the study.

"Who's there?" he demanded in tones of indignation. "Do you hear?"

All was silent.

"I've got you, have I?" he continued. "Very good. Wait a bidite: let's strike a light, add have a look at you. Dow thed," he added, having lighted the candle; "dow thed, where are you? Do you hear? It's of do use, you kdow —codcealbedt is vaid. Do you *hear?* I'll sbash you, if you dod't cobe out! Where have you got to? *Hollo!*"

All was still silent. There was not a breath to indicate the presence of a soul.

"I'll tell you what it is, old fellow," resumed Tom, "you've poked yourself sobewhere; but dod't believe I'b goidg to give you up; dot a bit of it. I'll have you, add *do* bistake; you'd better cobe out of your hole; d'ye *hear?*"

Tom examined minutely every cupboard and every corner; he looked round and round, but no creature could he see. He also examined the skeleton. There it stood—it didn't appear to have been removed—it didn't appear to have been touched, and yet he heard the bells ring. He surely could not have been mistaken in that? The very thought induced a doubt. He felt that he might have been mistaken: he thought it possible—just possible—that he had been dreaming, and, while dreaming, fancied he heard the bells.

"Well, if it is so, it is!" he at length exclaimed. "I certaidly *thought* that I heard theb. However, it's clear that there's dobody here, so I bay just as well go to bed agaid as dot!"

He therefore descended, and put out the light, and having established his stick near the pillow, got into bed again calmly. He had scarcely, however, covered himself comfortably up, when the bells began to ring again merrily.

"That's sobethidg dear the bark, at all evedts!" cried Tom, who was out of bed again in the twinkling of an eye. "There *cad* be do bistake dow! Wud bobedt, by friedd," he added, grasping his stick—"odly stop *wud* bobedt, add you'll oblige be."

Again he stealthily ascended to the study, and with feelings of hope looked round and round. There wasn't a corner—there wasn't a hole sufficiently large to admit a mouse—that then escaped minute examination. He looked everywhere again and again, but the result was destruction to the hope he had inspired.

"If," he exclaimed, "I *do* dail you, Heaved have bercy upod your bodes, for they shall bake the sweetest busic bodes ever had the ability to bake."

Having given emphatic expression to this sentiment, he again descended and got into bed; but his head had not been on the pillow three minutes, when the bells again recommenced ringing.

"Go it!" he cried, "by all badder of beads. There's dothidg like bakidg edough doise. But if you thidk I'b goidg to cut up add dowd stairs *all* the blessed bordidg, you'll fide yourself bistaked, by friedd, do doubt! Dow thed," he added, in the depths of thought, "what's to be dode? That fellow's sobewhere—there cad't be two opidiods about that. But where? That's the questiod. He's havidg a gabe, add a dice gabe it is. But sedd I could catch hib! Pull 'eb *dowd!*" he added, as the bells continued to ring: "dod't be dice about it—dod't bidce the batter; pull 'eb dowd! Well, I'll go up agaid—*wodce* bore; add if I *should* dail this idgedious gedtlebad, it strikes be as beidg extrebely probable that he'll kdow it!"

Once more, accordingly, Tom left his room, and, on going upstairs, he fell over a string, which not only brought the bells and the skeleton down, but pulled Sylvester half out of bed and awoke him.

"Who's there?" cried Sylvester, in startling tones—"*Who's* there?"

"I!" replied Tom. "Dod't be alarbed—dod't be alarbed!" and he rushed at once into the study.

"Tom!" cried the doctor, who had heard the noise, "what on earth are you about?"

"Adother gabe!" replied Tom. "Here's adother dice gabe! Just cobe up—odly cobe; frob this spot I'll dot bove ad idch."

The doctor, who really felt very much annoyed, slipped on his dressing-gown at once; and as he was proceeding upstairs, with the view of speaking to Tom very severely, Sylvester, who was somewhat alarmed, came cautiously out of his room.

"What is the meaning of this?" said the doctor.

"Upon my word, I don't know," replied Sylvester. "Some one pulled me nearly out of bed just now."

"Pulled you nearly out of bed? Oh! we must investigate this. Now, sir," he added, on reaching the study, "what *is* all this about?"

"It's a gabe," replied Tom. "But he's here—I kdow he's here."

"Who's here?"

"He whob I'd give ady buddy to see."

"Nonsense!" cried the doctor. "I demand an explanation."

"You shall have it," said Tom. "But just wait a bidite: just wait till I've foudd hib. I'b adxious to give hib ad expladatiod first."

"What do you mean, Tom? Surely you are mad. There's no one here."

"Sobe wud was here, add that dot two bidites ago."

"I don't believe it; I cannot believe it."

"I'b sure of it. If dot, how cabe by bells to ridg?"

"What bells!?"

"Why, by bells; the bells which I hudg up id by roob last dight?"

"Tom, what do you mean?"

"I bead that the bells which I hudg up id by roob last dight, add which cobbudicated with the legs of by bed, have beed ridgidg away for the last half hour; add I also bead that those bells would dot have rudg if the stridgs had dot beed pulled: that by bad would dot have falled if he had dot beed touched, add that, therefore, sobe wud has beed here."

"Tom," said the doctor, with an expression of severity, "I'll not be disturbed thus night after night. We must, I see, get lodgings for you somewhere else."

"The disturbadce is dot of by creatiod. You dod't thidk that I have disturbed you?"

"Who else *could* have done it?"

"That's the very poidt I'd give a billiod to ascertaid!"

"As far as I alone am concerned, it's a matter of sligbt importance, but when the whole house is disturbed, it's most unpardonable. Even Sylvester must have his rest broken. What was your object in pulling him out of bed?"

"Out of bed?—Syl!—pull hib out of bed? Why, I haved't beed idto his roob!"

"If *you* didn't, who could have pulled him out of bed?"

"That's the poidt—that's the very questiod! But were you thed pulled out of bed, Syl?"

"I was very nearly."

"But you dod't bead to thidk that I did it?"

"It's a matter of little moment, Tom, whether you did or not."

"But I didd't! I haved't beed dear you."

"Then it must have been some one else. I only wish that he hadn't cut my hand quite so much."

"Has your hand been cut?" inquired the doctor, taking it immediately in his. "It appears to have been cut with a string. Tom," he added sternly, "go to bed, sir, and let us have no more of this folly."

"Well," said Tom, "but do you bead to bead"——

"I have nothing more to say," observed the doctor.

"Well, I suppose you'll let be explaid?"

"I don't require any explanation," said the doctor, who left the study, and in silence returned to his room.

"Victibised agaid!" exclaimed Tom, as the doctor left him. "Shouldd't I be happier id the grave? I do believe that if you were to go frob us roudd to our Adtipodes, you wouldd't beet with a bore udfortudate swell. If there be ady luck afloat, it's perfectly sure to cobe idto by harbour. I'b wud of the elect to receive addoyadces. I'll back byself agaidst ady bad id the udiverse to have byself bisudderstood, add by botives bisidterpreted. Dow look here, Syl, you kdow the purpose for which I put up those bells. Well, about half ad hour ago, I heard theb ridg, add I cabe up daturally with a sball stick, expectidg to fide a bad of sobe sort. But do; he'd cut it; add I wedt dowd agaid; add the bells radg agaid, add agaid I cabe up add had by usual luck agaid; add agaid I wedt dowd, whed the bells radg agaid; add just as I was cobidg up here for the last tibe, to see if I *could* dail this varbidt—what would I dot give to see hib dow!—I fell over sobethidg, add grazed by shid—brought dowd by bells, add brought dowd by bad—add 'for all these courtesies' I ab dedoudced! If this be dot edough to bake a bad love his bother, I dod't kdow what is!"

"Then did you fall?"

"Fall! slap! over sobethidg; I dod't kdow what, dor do I care—but I fell, add I suppose it was the doise I bade that woke you?"

"No," returned Sylvester, "some one had hold of my hand!"

"Is that a fact?"

"Oh! there's no doubt at all about it. I was pulled more than half out of bed!"

"Add did you see do wud dear?"

"Not a soul! I was somewhat alarmed at the moment, and called out to know who was there, and you answered me."

"Thed I suppose I'b let id for *that?*"

"Not at all. You stated just now that you didn't come near me; I am, therefore, quite satisfied on *that* point; but that some one was near me at the time, is quite clear."

"Well, but where could he have gode to? I saw do wud

cobe frob your roob! I wish I had—it would have beed a happy idcidedt! How could he by ady possibility have got out? Add if he could have got out, he couldd't have rushed past be without by seeidg hib; and if eved he could have rushed past be idvisibly, he couldd't have pulled you out of bed dowd there, add kdocked by bad dowd here, at wud add the sabe tibe."

"There may be two of them."

"Good! so there bay. But if I odly caught wud, I'd give hib edough for both. I dod't thidk, however great a gluttod he bight be, that he'd hesitate for wud sidgle bobedt to codfess that he had had bore thad his bodicub—bore thad he could, with ady great degree of cobfort, digest. But isd't it stradge, dow, that we cad't get to the bottob of this? Isd't it barvellous, Syl?"

"It is indeed. I know not what to think of it."

"Well," said Tom, "I suppose they are pretty well satisfied dow! I presube they dod't idtedd to do ady bore bischief this bout! we'll therefore go to bed. But I'll try adother dodge or two. Of course, I'b safe to be bade a bartyr; I've suffered three bartyrdobs already, but I'll dot give it up. If they *are* to be caught, I'll catch 'eb; add if I do catch 'eb, I strodgly recobbedd theb to look out! I'll reward theb haddsobely—they shall be paid! I feel dow as if I could half burder a couple with all the pleasure that appertaids to life. However, let's pludge idto bed agaid. I feel so biserable, Syl, that I've a good bide to say I'll go to sleep for a bodth!"

They then returned to their respective rooms, and were disturbed no more.

In the morning, almost immediately after breakfast, the reverend gentleman called; and Aunt Eleanor, with all that tact by which ladies are commonly characterised, arranged matters so that they were alone. The reverend gentleman was in excellent spirits—he had not, indeed, been for some years so gay; but Aunt Eleanor felt tremulous, and anxious, and odd; her pulse did not beat with anything like regularity, nor did she speak with any certainty of tone; she knew not, in fact, what to make of her feelings; they appeared to her to be so extraordinary—so droll—there was, in a word, a certain novelty about them which she could not at all understand.

"Now, my dear madam," said the reverend gentleman, when all the preliminaries to conversation had been arranged,

"I'll show you my credentials." And taking Sylvester's letter from his pocket, he presented it with an air of confidence perfectly consistent with the feelings he entertained.

"Dear me," said Aunt Eleanor, on glancing at the letter, "this is indeed his handwriting! And yet how extraordinary it is, that he should have sent such a letter. I cannot account for it at all!"

"The young rogue! like a young colt or a young kitten—full of play, my dear madam, full of play!"

"But it is so contrary to his general character and conduct."

"Youth, youth!" said the reverend gentleman. "Youth always was, and always will be youth!"

This remarkable observation settled the point as far as it went, and Aunt Eleanor proceeded to read the letter; but while she was reading, the reverend gentleman—who watched her with an expression of anxiety mingled with delight—could not perceive the slightest change in her countenance; at which he marvelled—and naturally; seeing that he was at the time perfectly unconscious of the fact that, although she was reading with great apparent care, she was in reality *thinking* of something else. Had the reverend gentleman the previous day omitted the observation having reference to the resuscitation of certain feelings, which had long been lying dormant, she would, while reading this letter, have laughed heartily; but as that observation had been made, she looked at the fruit, of which she conceived it to be the germ—her thoughts were not upon the cause, but the effect—and therefore, while reading it, she didn't laugh at all.

"Well, my dear madam," said the reverend gentleman, "what is your impression now?"

"It certainly is Sylvester's handwriting," she replied; "but what his object could have been, I cannot possibly conceive."

"Fun was the young rogue's object, no doubt! It is clear that he thought it an excellent jest."

"But such jests, my dear sir, are highly incorrect; he must be scolded!"

"Leave that to me, my dear madam—leave all that to me. I'll give him a lecture. Shall we have him in now?"

"I think that we had better."

The bell was rung, and Sylvester was summoned; and when he appeared, he greeted the reverend gentleman precisely as if unconscious of the existence of any such letter as that which Aunt Eleanor held in her hand—which was thought very remarkable.

"Sylvester," said the reverend gentleman, assuming a somewhat stern expression, "I am anxious to have a few words with you calmly. Sylvester, there are jests which are venial, and jests which are not; there are jests which are harmless, and jests which are not; jests which are harmless, are those which I hold to be venial; jests which are not harmless must be condemned. But there are, independently of those which I have named, jests which, although in themselves unimportant—or, I should rather say, apparently unimportant—are calculated to lead to important results, and it is to this particular species of jest that I now wish to call your attention. In all ages jesting has been known. History, both sacred and profane, speaks of jesting. The pagans' chief jester was deified: Momus was the heathen god of jesting. Kings and princes have kept their jesters, sometimes with the view of being rebuked for their follies, but more frequently, I fear, for the purpose of being applauded for those follies—sometimes, that their passions might be regulated by wit, but more often that it might pander to those passions. Jesting has, therefore, antiquity to recommend it; but this is not the point at which I am anxious to arrive. Jests or jokes—they are strictly synonymous—may be divided into two distinct classes: those which are salutary, and those which are pernicious—I use the term 'salutary' advisedly, seeing that a well-timed jest has frequently been known to do much more good than a sermon. Again, there are white lies, and there are black lies; there are also white jokes and black jokes; but albeit a lie, whether white or black, is still a lie; and a joke, whether white or black, is still a joke; lies are at all times highly reprehensible, while jokes at all times are not. There are practical jokes and theoretical jokes; moral jokes and physical jokes; there are, moreover, jokes which are based upon falsehood, and jokes which are based upon truth; but the jokes to which I am anxious to direct your attention are those in which falsehood is involved. Now, it seems to me to be perfectly clear that you would scorn to tell a deliberate falsehood; but it is—nay, it must be—equally clear that you imagine that when a falsehood is involved in a joke, it loses its reprehensible character."

"Not at all," said Sylvester, who had been throughout

utterly at a loss to understand what the reverend gentleman was driving at. "A falsehood, no matter what colour it may assume, or however ingeniously it may be disguised, is, as you have said, a falsehood still; and I should no more think of telling a falsehood in jest than I should of telling an absolute falsehood in earnest."

"My dear madam," said the reverend gentleman, "just oblige me with that letter. Sylvester," he added, "my anxiety is to impress upon your mind that a falsehood is a falsehood, and nothing but a falsehood, if even it be playfully enveloped in a joke. Now, allow me to read this letter: 'My dear aunt desires me to inform you that she has an idea of entering into the marriage state.' Is there not a falsehood involved in this? Were you ever desired by her to inform me of anything of the sort? But to proceed"——

"Nay—I beg pardon—what letter is that which you are reading?"

"What letter? This letter—your letter."

"My letter?"

"The letter you sent to me!"

"You are mistaken. *I* have sent you no letter."

"But this letter is yours?"

"Not if it be addressed to you. I never wrote to you in my life."

"Well, but look at it. That is your writing, is it not?"

"It looks like my writing—most certainly; but I never wrote it."

"My dear," said Aunt Eleanor, "if it be yours, confess it. I will not be angry—indeed I will not; although it is certainly very incorrect, yet I pledge you my word that I will not be angry."

"My dear aunt," said Sylvester, "if it were mine, I should feel myself bound to confess it at once; but I assure you most solemnly that it is not. I never had occasion to write to Mr. Rouse, nor have I ever written to him. The resemblance which this writing bears to my own is amazing; but I pledge you my honour that it is not mine."

"Well, but really," said the reverend gentleman, "it seems to me to be almost impossible to have been written by any one else."

"If I cannot induce you to believe me," said Sylvester, "I am, of course, sorry—exceedingly sorry; I can, however, say no more than I have said, the substance of which is, that that letter never was written by me."

"But you perceive it bears your signature! He who counterfeits the signature of another is guilty of an act of forgery, and forgery is a crime which is punishable by law—it is, in fact, a transportable offence—it used to be, indeed, a hanging matter; but even now a man who commits an act of forgery may be taken up and treated as a felon; he may be tried in a criminal court, and if the jury find him guilty, the judge may pass upon him a sentence of transportation. It is therefore improbable—most improbable—that any man could, for the sake of a joke, be so awfully reckless as to place himself thus in a position to be torn from the bosom of his family—to be branded as a felon—a common felon—and compelled to work in ignominious chains."

"However improbable it may appear," said Sylvester, "that any one besides myself wrote that letter, I repeat—most firmly and most solemnly repeat—that it never was written by me. You remember the note that was found at the cottage—the note addressed to Rosalie—the hand in which that was written resembled mine as strongly as this does, and I have not the slightest doubt that the person who wrote the one wrote the other."

"Well, it's very mysterious," said the reverend gentleman. "Of course, I am bound to believe you on your honour; still I must say it's very mysterious."

"It is," returned Sylvester, "very mysterious. But I assure you, my dear aunt—I do assure you both—that I would not be guilty of so great an act of folly."

"I am sure that you would not, my dear," said Aunt Eleanor. "I'm perfectly satisfied now, but I thought—I did think—that you might perhaps have done it by way of a jest. I am now, however, firmly convinced you did not, and you must therefore forgive me for supposing that I was justified by that letter in believing that you did."

The reverend gentleman scarcely even then knew what to make of it; nor did he much care about saying another syllable on the subject: he saw more clearly than he had ever seen before that Aunt Eleanor was an amiable, affectionate creature, who was anxious to take the most charitable view of everything that could be said to involve a doubt, and was therefore most anxious for Sylvester to leave; but before he was able to give an intimation of this anxiety, they were joined by the doctor and Mrs. Delolme, whose presence prevented an interesting scene which the reverend gentleman had in contemplation.

CHAPTER XXI.

THE PROPOSAL.

The forms in which proposals of marriage are made are as various as the views, thoughts, and passions of those who make them. It may at first sight appear strange that there should be so many ways of doing one and the same thing; and yet, perhaps, of the myriads of millions who have proposed, no two men ever—either in ancient or modern times—managed this matter precisely alike. Nor is it at all probable that any two men ever will; for, independently of the infinitely varied characters of lovers, the minds, forms, features, and feelings of those whom they love are so diversified, that every proposal, whether romantic or rational, ardent or cold, pathetic or comic—and the comic style is by far the most popular among the ladies—will have some little novelty about it.

Without, however, dwelling upon this, it is certain that one of the easiest things in the world for a man to do, is that of proposing to a widow. She understands it so well. She knows so exactly what you mean, and what you are anxious to say; and helps you over any little difficulty with so much tact, that it's really quite delightful. Yes; a widow most certainly affords every possible assistance to a man in this position. But while it is certain that the easiest proposal a man can make is that which is made to a widow, it is equally certain that by far the most difficult is that which a man has to make to an old maid.

Now, albeit Aunt Eleanor was an old maid, it is highly correct to cause it to be distinctly understood that she was not so particularly antiquated as some may imagine. No! she was upwards of forty; but although the exact age of a single lady above forty is conventionally apocryphal, it may be said that she was much nearer one than one hundred with safety, seeing that no man in Europe can prove that she was not.

The reverend gentleman, however, did not look at her age —he looked at her virtues: her amiability, her piety, her benevolence, the sweetness of her disposition, and the purity of her heart. Still he conceived it to be extremely difficult to propose; and that apparent difficulty increased as the time drew near at which he had determined that the proposal should be made. How hard he studied, few can tell; how many times he rehearsed that which he had fixed upon as his opening speech, few have the power to form anything like a correct conjecture; there are, however, many who can tell precisely why, when the time for the delivery of that speech had arrived, his recreant memory abandoned his will; there are also many in a position to understand how it happened that, having resolved on the immediate pursuit of his object, he at once, notwithstanding that desertion, commenced.

At this time he and Aunt Eleanor were in one of the doctor's drawing-rooms alone; and as there appeared to be no prospect of any immediate interruption, he coughed— slightly coughed—and thus began—

"Have you seen the papers this morning?"

"I saw one in the breakfast-room, but I merely glanced at it."

"You didn't read the debate in the House of Commons, I presume?"

"Parliamentary debates I very seldom read: I am not sufficiently conversant with political affairs to read those awfully long speeches with any degree of interest. Was there anything of importance brought forward last night?"

"Why, the Chancellor of the Exchequer, I perceive, announced that the expenditure exceeds the income."

"Indeed! Some bad management, I presume?"

"He says not—and he ought, I think, to know as well as any man in England. But it strikes me that I could suggest to him the means by which the revenue might be increased!"

"He would be glad, I should say, if you were to do so. But what is the nature of the means you would suggest?"

"Merely the imposition of an additional tax."

"Are we not sufficiently taxed already?"

"It appears that we are not. If we were, the income would be sufficient to meet the expenditure."

"In private life it sometimes happens that the expenditure exceeds the income, even when, for all just and legitimate purposes, that income is ample; but I suppose that in public affairs the case is different. I do not, of course, pretend to understand that difference, but I *should* like to know what description of tax you would suggest to the Chancellor of the Exchequer."

"Well," said the reverend gentleman, with a peculiarly bland expression, "that which I contemplate is a tax upon all single men above forty!"

Aunt Eleanor smiled and blushed. She knew what he meant: she knew what would follow—she understood him as well as he *could* have been understood, even by a widow, but was silent.

"I would," he continued, "I would tax those fellows to the extent of five-and-twenty per cent. upon their incomes. What business have men of that age to be single? Do you not think it disgraceful? Don't you think that a tax of the kind ought to be imposed?"

"Why," said Aunt Eleanor, "it would be a *novel* tax."

"As far as men are concerned, it certainly would be; but in the feudal times the ladies who held fees or estates which required military services were thus taxed, with the view of inducing them to marry, in order that their husbands might perform those services themselves."

"But no tax in this case can be imposed on those grounds."

"Very true: still I'd tax them! I'd make them either marry or pay."

"They had better pay than be unhappy."

"Granted! But I do not associate unhappiness with marriage: it is, I admit, often the result; but there are men who will, when there is a bright prospect of happiness before them, continue to live in the shade."

"In such a case they cannot, I submit, see that prospect."

"No; that's the point. They are blind—morally blind, sand-blind, as I have been—selfishly blind. But I'd open their eyes. I'd tax them; there's nothing in life like taxation, when the object is to bring men to their senses. Nor would I permit them to occupy a whole house: they should merely have lodgings. Look at my house; it's a nice house, a good house, a capital house. *You* might make it a comfortable house, but I can't; and as I can't, *what* right have I to live in it alone?"

"You cannot be said to live in it alone."

"Conventionally, an unmarried man is single, and a single man lives in the world morally alone. Now, I want to know why *I* should live in the world alone: in other words, I want to know why I should remain unmarried?"

"I see no reason why you should: except, indeed, that you are happy."

"But, my dear madam, I am not happy. I used to be happy, certainly; but ever since I received that note I have felt a certain sort of something like a wish to be married. Now, I do not belong to the Church of Rome—I belong to the Church of England—and therefore I do not see why I should not enter into the marriage state. Do *you* see any just cause or impediment?"

"Oh, dear, no: none whatever."

"Do you see why I should not marry, when marriage presents a bright prospect of happiness?"

"No: I really do not."

"Then I want your advice."

"But I have had no experience in these matters."

"So much the better: I'd rather, my dear madam, have your advice—upon this point especially—than that of any other creature breathing. Now, suppose that I were in love —that is to say, suppose that I had so firm—so ardent—an affection for a lady, that I imagined marriage to be absolutely essential to my happiness: suppose this, I merely say suppose it, and then tell me what you'd advise me to do?"

"Really," replied Aunt Eleanor, smiling, "I'm so perfectly unacquainted with affairs of this character, that I feel quite incompetent to offer advice."

"But how, in this case, do you *think* I ought to act?"

"Well, really—I scarcely know: but I should think that if you are in the position you describe, you ought at once to *propose* to the lady."

"Very good. But how is it to be done?"

"I cannot give you *any* information upon that point."

"Well, but how do you imagine it ought to be done?"

"Upon my *word*, I cannot say. I have had so little experience in these affairs, that it may almost be said that I am ignorant of them."

"But you *have* had offers?"

"Oh, yes! I have had many offers, certainly."

"Will you do me the favour to explain to me how *they* were made?"

"My dear sir—really—I scarcely know how it is possible for me to do so."

"If you would, you would oblige me. I should then know exactly how to manage it myself."

"Well: but upon my word, the idea of your asking me for information on the subject appears so excessively odd."

"My dear madam, whom should I ask for information but one who is able to give it? I pledge you my honour, I never proposed to a lady in my life; I cannot, therefore, be expected to know anything about the matter: whereas, you having had offers made you, know well how the business is done."

"I really do not pretend to know anything about it."

"I am aware that you do not *pretend* to know; and this absence of all pretension, in my judgment, constitutes one of your most admirable characteristics, but you nevertheless *do* know all about it; do you not?"

"Upon my word—it seems so strange that *I* should be thus applied to."

"To whom else can I apply? Now do let me know all about it."

"Well, but what do you wish to know?"

"How to propose! that's the point. I merely wish to know how it's done."

"But, my dear sir, unless I have some little knowledge of the character of the lady, it will be quite impossible for me to tell what style will be likely to suit her."

"You know her," said the reverend gentleman, with a smile: "I fancy that *I* know her well; but you know her infinitely better."

"Indeed. Dear me: why, whom can it be?"

"Whom should it be? to whom is it likely I could wish to propose? There is but one in this world, my dear madam, and—you are that one! Yes; that's the point—that's it; I wish to propose to you!"

"To me!" exclaimed Aunt Eleanor archly. "To me?"

"To you, my dear madam; to you."

"Dear me! why, how came you to think of such a thing?"

"I'll explain: when I received that letter, which I then

of course believed had been written by Sylvester, I privately asked myself two or three questions. First, what had I been about? secondly, what could be done? and, thirdly, what ought I to do? I answered these questions, and those answers were—to the first, that I had been very stupid; to the second, that this stout fellow might be supplanted; and to the third, that if he could be, I ought to supplant him. I inspired the spirit of rivalry on the instant, and came up resolved on defeating this porpoise: I felt that he was no friend of mine, and I do really think that if he had appeared, I should not have been particularly courteous. Again. I examined my heart; I examined it minutely; and the result of that examination proved that it was in reality full of affection. I had before no idea that that heart of mine possessed such a treasure of beautiful feelings. I found pearls of happiness—pearls, of the very existence of which I had been previously unconscious. I dived into the depths, and brought them from the caves in which they had been so long concealed: they were rough but pure, and being pure, you are the person to polish them up. I now, therefore, repeat, that I am anxious to propose, my dear madam, to you; and if you'll explain how it is to be done, I'll buckle on my armour, and do it at once."

"Upon my word, I cannot give you any such explanation; nor do I think that you in reality need it."

"I never did such a thing in all my life. I never before thought of doing such a thing. I cannot therefore be expected to know much about it. But I suppose that there's a fashion in these matters—a sort of style—a kind of form—which society prescribes; is there not?"

"I really cannot say."

"Well, but pray do assist me a little!"

"Why, what assistance can you possibly require?"

"I require, in an affair of this description, every conceivable assistance. I feel altogether at a loss. I know no more what to say than an infant would know, were it possible to place one in a similar position. What am I to say? What can I say?"

"My dear sir! say whatever your feelings may prompt, and be assured of this, that nothing that you may say, will be at all displeasing to me."

"Well, now that's very kind. It's exactly like you. I

appreciate it, believe me, as I appreciate every feeling and every principle by which you are guided; but then, I'm no nearer the mark—not a bit! However, do me the favour to listen for a moment, and I'll make something like an attempt."

The reverend gentleman then drew his chair nearer to the couch upon which Aunt Eleanor sat, and having taken her hand affectionately in his, thus proceeded:—

"The parsonage—the house in which I live—is, as you are well aware, a nice house—a substantial, well-built, roomy house, with a garden attached—a beautiful garden—surrounded by a capital wall: very well. Now, the cottage in which you reside is a very nice cottage; there is also a garden attached to that, and, albeit it is not surrounded by a wall, it is still a very beautiful garden. But do you not think, that if you were to leave this cottage and come to live with me in that house, you would make me one of the happiest men alive? and, do you not believe that I would endeavour to promote your happiness by all the means at my command?"

"That I do most fervently believe."

"Very good! Again. The affair, I apprehend, might thus be managed: I might, some fine morning, proceed to this cottage and take you to church, and when the marriage ceremony had been performed, we might leave the village for a month or so, and then return to that house together, and live in peace, harmony, and love. Do you not think it might be managed thus?"

"Certainly, it *might* be thus managed."

"And do you not also think that we had better thus manage it?"

"That is another question altogether!"

"I am aware of it; but what are your feelings upon the point—that is to say—what is your impression?"

"Why, my impression is that—to use parliamentary language—this debate had better be adjourned: in other words, that we had better wait until we get back again to Cotherstone, and calmly talk the matter over there."

"Very good! I am not an impetuous man: I have no desire at all to be precipitate; but you really must promise me this, that if in the interim any stout individual should in reality solicit your hand, you will not let him have it."

"I will promise this, and more: I will promise that if *any* individual should do so, no matter whether he be stout or thin, I'll not marry without your consent."

The reverend gentleman hereupon kissed the hand he held, and, having done so, felt perfectly happy.

"And now," said he, after a pause, during which they most affectionately reciprocated each others' glances, "when do you think of returning?"

"Why, I scarcely know," replied Aunt Eleanor; "I am anxious to see Sylvester settled before I leave town."

"Exactly. He is to be a surgeon, of course?"

"Yes; that has been decided upon, and Dr. Delolme, who is a kind, good creature, is now gone to have an interview with a gentleman whose talents are distinguished, whom he holds in high esteem, and to whom he is anxious that Sylvester should be articled."

"This may be arranged then in three or four days?"

"Oh, yes; it will, I expect, be very soon settled."

"And will you, when this has been settled, have anything at all to detain you in town?"

"Nothing. I think of returning on the following day."

"Oh, then we had better return together—that is, if you have no objection?"

"I *can* have no objection. I shall, indeed, be most happy to accompany you."

"Then let it be so—I need not explain to you how happy *I* shall feel!—let it be so."

"You will dine with us to-day of course?"

"I scarcely know. I dined here yesterday."

"Oh, but if you are not engaged, you must. The doctor, I know, expects that you will."

"Then I will. I have scarcely time," he added, on looking at his watch, "to run back to the inn, but I will. The doctor's a fine fellow, and you are a fine fellow—that is to say, I don't mean exactly that, but—you know what I mean. Adieu, until dinner-time! Eleanor!" he added, taking both her hands in his, and gazing upon her with an unfeigned expression of fervour, "God bless you!"

He then left the room, and Aunt Eleanor, who felt very happy, went upstairs to dress.

CHAPTER XXII.

TOM APPEARS TO GIVE EVIDENCE IN A CASE.

AFTER dinner, at which they were joined by Mr. Scholefield—the surgeon to whom Sylvester was about to be articled, and who ate nothing but fish, bread, and pastry, and drank nothing but pure cold water—Sylvester, as well as Aunt Eleanor and the reverend gentleman, was so delighted with his conversation, that Tom experienced the utmost difficulty in inducing his young friend to accompany him, as usual, to the hospital. He did, however, eventually succeed, and they started, and heard the lecture for the evening delivered; and, at the conclusion, Tom received a short message from Julia, of which the substance was, that she wished to see him for one moment.

"What's id the widd dow!" exclaimed Tom. "There's sobethidg bovidg. What does she wadt with *be ?*"

"You'll go in, of course?" said Sylvester.

"Yes, I'll go id. I bust go id!"

"Then shall I walk about here, or go towards home?"

"Oh, just walk about, I shall be but a very few bidites: I odly wadt to hear what's the batter."

"Very well, then I'll walk up and down here until you return."

Tom then went into the house, and as he entered, Julia was evidently disappointed; she did not at all expect to see him alone, having heard from one of the students that Sylvester had been in the theatre with him.

"What's up?" inquired Tom. "Is there adythidg the batter?"

"Oh, dear me, no!" returned Julia, when, as several students were impatient for porter, she added, "I'll speak to you in a moment."

Having supplied the immediate demands of the thirsty, she returned to Tom, and said, "How is your friend?"

"Which?" inquired Tom. "Do you ibagide I've odly wud?"

"I mean your young friend: him whom you call Sylvester."

"Oh! he's well edough."

"He will not be here to-night, I presume?"

"Do, he cad't stadd dridk: he's dot beed buch used to it."

"Is that the only cause of his not coming?"

"Why, what other cause do you ibagide he could have?"

"I was fearful that I had been unfortunate enough to offend him."

"Offedd hib! Pooh! dodsedse: you cad't offedd *hib!*"

"Are you quite sure that I have not done so?"

"Quite."

"Then I am happy. I thought that I might perhaps have given him some offence, and if I had, the consciousness of having done so would have been indeed very, very painful to me."

"Bake your bide easy," cried Tom, "about that. I dever kdew you to give offedce to ady bad alive, add I'b perfectly sure that you have dot offedded hib."

"Then bring him again with you, that I also may be sure. There is no necessity for him to drink, not the slightest. Will you bring him in with you to-morrow evening?"

"He'll dot be here, I kdow, *to-borrow* evedidg. But *I'll* see about it."

"Do, there's a good creature, and then I shall be satisfied."

"Well, but I say, old girl, is this all you wadted be for?"

"I merely wished to be assured upon that one point."

"Oh, that's all right edough. Let's have wud pull at the pewter, add thed I'll be off."

The porter was brought, and Tom had "one pull," and managed to pull it all out of the pot, and when Julia had begged of him not to forget, he bade her adieu for the night, and left.

"Well," said Sylvester, when Tom had rejoined him, "was it anything of importance?"

"Oh, she berely wadted to ask about a youdg fellow whob she fadcied she had offedded."

"How does she look?"

"Buch as usual; just about the sabe."

Tom thought it wise to keep Sylvester unconscious of Julia's anxiety, and he did so; and, in order that the subject might not be dwelt upon then, he reverted to the conversation of Mr. Scholefield, and thus turned the current of Sylvester's thoughts.

That night Tom decided upon sitting up alone. He had

privately decided upon this, feeling certain that if his intention were known to Sylvester, he should never be able to get him to bed; while he thought that it would be highly incorrect to keep him out of it, so languid as he almost invariably appeared to be.

When, therefore, they had had their usual supper in the study, Tom saw Sylvester to his room, shook hands with him, and bade him good-night; and then, making all the noise he conveniently could, bounced into his own room, and slammed the door, and locked it, of course with the view of inducing all whom it might concern to believe that he was in reality gone to bed. But it was not so; he remained in the room a short time—say ten minutes—and then, having carefully unlocked the door, crept noiselessly back to his study.

And there he sat, and there he continued to sit, with a little dark lantern shut up by his side—sometimes smoking and sometimes drinking—but constantly thinking, and earnestly wishing that some one might do him the favour to appear. He was fully prepared, both morally and physically, to receive any guest who might honour him with a visit; he had resolved on doing all in his power to serve him—that is, to serve him out—and it is extremely rational to cherish the belief that, if any one *had* appeared then, his reception would have been most warm; but the prospect which Tom had with pleasure portrayed, and which he viewed and improved with peculiar delight, began about half-past two to recede. He had, with the utmost fortitude, sat for two hours, proposing and solving an infinite variety of surgical questions, having direct and immediate reference to the dislocated joints and broken bones of his contemplated victim—and, as no one had appeared, he certainly did begin to think that the pleasures of his imagination were not about to be realised.

He was not, however, at all disposed to give the thing up. No, he filled his German pipe again, and ignited his German tinder, in order that the room might not even for an instant be illumined, and again philosophically enveloped himself in clouds. He had, however, scarcely sent forth twenty whiffs, when he fancied that he heard a noise below, and starting up on the instant, grasped his stick, and felt that the time was come.

But the sounds—which he believed were those of footsteps —receded, and gradually died away; when, as he imagined that he might have been mistaken, he resumed both his seat and his pipe.

Now it strangely enough happened, that about an hour after this—that is to say, about half-past three—policeman Ninety-nine did, on going his rounds, perceive that the street door of Dr. Delolme was slightly open.

"What's the odds," said Ninety-nine, confidentially to himself, "that there isn't a burglary here? I shall make something of this; I should like a burglary, and I ought to have one, for I haven't had any luck lately. Let's have a look," he added, going very quietly up to the door; "that'll do—that'll do. I shall nail at least one of 'em. Burglaries always look well on the sheet."

He then glided to the opposite side on his toes—the proximity of a policeman being betrayed by his heels—and having established himself in the shade of a doorway, drew forth his truncheon and watched. Nothing in nature could surpass the vigilance with which he kept his eye upon that door, nor could the ears of even a cat prick up and expand more instantaneously than *his* ears pricked up and expanded on hearing the slightest unusual sound. That a burglary had been committed he fervently hoped, and felt that if it should prove to have been accompanied by murder, it would be all the better for him. *He* would give no alarm—not a bit of it. Had he even known that murder might thus have been prevented, he was too wide awake to spoil such a fine chance by any premature interference.

Having for nearly half an hour kept his eyes, ears, mouth, and imagination on the stretch, he heard some one approaching, and on looking up the street saw the figure of a man walking leisurely down on the opposite side with his hands in his greatcoat pockets. Under these circumstances Ninety-nine, of course, took but very little notice of him; but when he saw him enter the house of Dr. Delolme, and heard him, when he had entered, close the door and deliberately bolt it, he felt in an instant prepared to swear that that man was his enemy Tom.

Having deliberated for a moment, and recollecting that the doctor had told him to ring a certain bell in the event of his seeing any one again upon the parapet, he opened his bull's-eye and rang the bell, and the doctor in due time appeared at the window.

"Who's there?" he demanded.

"Come down, sir," replied Ninety-nine, in a confidential tone; "there's a dodge, sir."

"A what?"

"A dodge, sir; you'll find it all out, if you will but come down, sir; you'll soon see who's who, sir, and know what's what."

The doctor closed the window, and having slipped on his pantaloons and dressing-gown, descended, expecting, of course, that the parapet was again the scene of action.

"I am sorry, sir," said Ninety-nine, on being admitted, "I'm indeed very sorry to inform you that your son, sir, is endangering your property very strangely. This door, sir, has been open for more than two hours, sir—wide open. Of course it was my duty to watch it, and I did so: I watched it until your son returned, which was just about a minute before I rang the bell."

"Is it possible!" cried the doctor; "and left the door open? Just come up with me—I'll investigate this; but quietly—don't make the slightest noise."

"All right, sir; a mouse shan't hear me."

The doctor then—followed by Ninety-nine—ascended, and on going into Tom's room found, not only that Tom was not there, but that he had not been in bed at all.

"Well," exclaimed the doctor, "this is, at all events, conclusive. But where can he be?"

"Upstairs perhaps, sir," suggested Ninety-nine.

"Very likely. But let us go up quietly."

Ninety-nine then took the lead, and as Tom—who was still at his post, and who had heard sounds below which could not be mistaken—had prepared himself to receive any friend who might happen to look in upon him, Ninety-nine no sooner entered the study than he received a blow which felled him in an instant to the ground.

"Who's there?" cried the doctor.

"'Tis I," replied Tom, amazed on hearing the doctor's voice.

"Tom! *what*, in the name of Heaven, do you mean?"

"O-o-o-o!" cried Ninety-nine.

Tom opened his little dark lantern, and having seen Ninety-nine stretched upon the floor, felt that he had made some mistake.

"I ask you again," said the doctor, "what you mean by this abominable conduct?"

"What abobidable codduct?" cried Tom. "I've beed sittidg up here with the view of catchidg that scouddrel whose budkey tricks have so much addoyed us."

"It is false," cried the doctor.

"What's false?"

"Every word that you have uttered. You have not, sir, been sitting up here. You have been out, sir."

"Out! what, out of the house, do you bead?"

"Yes, sir!"

"What, do you bead sidce I cabe id frob the lecture?"

"Yes."

"Do, I'b blest if I have."

"How *can* you deny it, Tom? This policeman here saw you enter just now."

"Iddeed! What, this fellow? Well, if he did he did, add *if* he did, he's a datural curiosity! I bust have a look at *hib*."

Ninety-nine, on being rolled over by Tom, conceived it to be his duty, as a policeman and as a man, to pretend to have been dreadfully injured; but having been in reality more frightened than hurt, Tom soon made him assume a sitting posture on the floor: and, having done so, exclaimed, "Didety-*dide!* Why, this is Didety-dide! What does *he* pretedd to kdow about the batter?"

"Policeman," said the doctor, "is this, or is this not the person whom you saw just now enter the house?"

"It is, sir," replied Ninety-nine; "and I'll swear it."

"You will," exclaimed Tom.

"*Yes*," cried Ninety-nine, who was seized with so strong a fit of energy, that he started to his feet on the instant: "I will."

"Why, you wretched, cadaverous, udhappy lookidg adibal, what do you bead? what's your botive id cobidg here prepared to swear to a falsehood so bodstrous? You're too codtebp-tible to be revedged upod, or I'd take it out dow; I cad but spurd you, add treat your accusatiod with scord."

"This will not do, Tom," said the doctor severely. "This will no longer do for me. I'll at once put a stop to it. I'll not be thus annoyed night after night."

"Well, but *I* have dot addoyed you!" cried Tom: "you've dot beed addoyed by *be!*"

"I have, sir, and you know it."

"I kdow," replied Tom, "that I have dot."

"But here is proof of it."

"What proof? the proof idvolved id the evidedce of this codsubbate wretch? The bagistrate who would believe hib od his oath ought to be deprived of his cobbissiod."

"The idea," continued the doctor, "of prowling about in the middle of the night, and leaving the street-door open. I'm ashamed of you—perfectly ashamed of you. I couldn't have supposed that you would be guilty of an act so monstrous."

"It's of do use," said Tom, "I kdow it's of do use! but I tell you, father, agaid add agaid, that sidce twelve o'clock I've dot stirred frob this roob."

"I'll not believe it," said the doctor: "I will *not* believe it."

"I should think *not*," interposed Ninety-nine.

"Siledce, you ugly abortiod!" cried Tom, whom the sneer of Ninety-nine had enraged: "if I have adother word od the subject frob you, I'll walk id."

"You shall walk *out*, sir," said the doctor; "you shall not remain here; I'll not have the house disturbed in this way."

"The disturbadce has *dot* beed created by be."

"Go to bed, sir, and let me have no more of it; I'll no longer tolerate such practices. Go to bed."

The doctor and Ninety-nine then left the room—Ninety-nine, with great discretion, taking the lead—but he had no sooner reached the top of the stairs, than that discretion forsook him, and, turning to Tom, said, "*I'll* nail you!" an observation which so excited Tom's ire, that he rushed at him on the instant; but, before he could reach him, Ninety-nine, in his anxiety to get away, slipped, and glided to the bottom —not smoothly, no; but bumping in his progress the bottom of his spine, and causing him not only to call out, "*Oh!*" but to pull a face, of which the prevailing expression would have puzzled Lavater himself.

"Keep back!" cried the doctor, "I command you:" and Tom, who felt that Ninety-nine had had quite enough of it, did not follow him up—or, rather, down: but the doctor descended, and assisted him to rise, and, having done so, led him into the drawing-room, and gave him some brandy, and placed in his hand a small piece of that metal which has, in this sublunary sphere, more influence than either mind, honour, religion, or love.

In falling, however, Ninety-nine awoke Sylvester, and as he came to the door, in order to ascertain what was the matter, Tom went into his room with the lantern in his hand, and placing himself upon the edge of the bedstead, looked as if all had been lost.

"What is the meaning of this?" inquired Sylvester. "What has occurred?"

"Get idto bed, Syl," said Tom, "add I'll tell you all about it."

Sylvester accordingly got into bed, when Tom, having struck the lantern in the face, commenced—

"Syl," said he, "I'b a victib. But that you kdow. I was always a victib. I was bord to be a victib. I shall becobe id a short tibe wud of those predestidariad swells who believe that a bad's actiods are chalked out by Fate, add that he must walk Fate's chalks, whether he likes theb or dot. Just look here! Last dight I decided od sittidg up alode, id order to catch that scabp who has created so buch addoyadce. I didd't tell you a word about it, because I kdew that you'd wadt to sit up with be, add thought that you'd buch better dot. Well I sat up; I sat frob the tibe you wedt to bed, till about half ad hour ago, whed, plaidly hearidg footsteps od the stairs, I prepared to receive, as I fadcied, the fellow by whob the whole of these disturbadces have beed created. Well, presedtly the study door opeded, add id walked a bad, add I gave hib wud which laid hib low, whed, of course to by utter abazebedt, I heard the voice of the goverdor! It's a blessidg the goverdor didd't edter first!"

"Then whom did you strike?"

"Didety-dide the policebad! the fellow who said he could swear to by shirt!"

"Well, but what brought *him* there?"

"I'll tell you. I dod't thidk he likes be; at all evedts I feel codvidced he doesd't like be buch, add if he does, he likes the goverdor's buddy buch bore; add hedce, id order to get a little of it, he trubped up a tale to the effect that our street-door had beed oped—wide oped—for two hours; that he had kept his eye upod it, id order to ascertaid what was goidg od; add that evedtually he saw *be* edter the house, add thed heard be close the door, add bolt it?"

"Is it possible!"

"Did you ever hear of adythidg so abobidable? Well, with this tale artfully prepared, he radg the dight bell—which I couldd't hear—add whed the wretch had related all that his thick pig's head had allowed hib to codceive, up cabe the goverdor idto by roob, add, of course, whed he foudd that I had dot beed id bed, the tale of the wretch was codfirbed!"

"I see."

"But beidg daturally adxious to kdow where I was, he cabe up to the study: add as I said before, it's a bercy he didd't cobe first, for if I'd gived hib the blow, which luckily fell to the lot of Didety-dide, I should have beed wretched for life. However, Didety-dide got it, add it served hib right; I dod't care a straw about that; all I care for is this, that as I was dot id bed, as I'd dot beed id bed, add as he foudd be id the study with by clothes od—the goverdor firbly believes Didety-dide, add thus ab I victibised agaid!"

"Well, it certainly did look suspicious."

"I kdow it—I feel it—I see that, udder the circubstadces, the goverdor is perfectly justified id believidg the tale of that biserable fat-headed wretch; it is the very codsciousdess of that which bost galls be!"

"But, of course, you have not been out?"

"Certaidly dot! Frob the tibe you wedt to bed, till the tibe they cabe up, I dever, for a sidgle bobedt, boved frob the study. Besides, is it likely—is it like adythidg likely—that I should be such a codsubbate dodkey as to go out and leave the door oped for ady wud to walk id that pleased? Is the idea of by doidg such a thidg at all ratiodal?"

"Such conduct would certainly have been very indiscreet."

"Iddiscreet! Why, if I thought that it would ever be possible for be to cobbit such ad act of iddiscretiod as that, I should deeb byself fit for a ludatic asylub."

"I cannot imagine how he came to think of such a thing."

"Oh, these fellows will do adythidg for buddy; it's a batter of little ibportadce what."

"Well, it certainly is strange—very strange—that he should have fixed upon this particular morning."

"Exactly! That's where it is! It is that very thidg which gets over be! Had he fixed upod ady other, I should have beed, of course, id bed add asleep. But it was to be, I suppose. I kdow I shall sood becobe a predestidariad. But isd't it edough to bake a bad hit his head off?"

"It is, certainly, very unfortunate."

"By usual luck! Dothidg bore cad be said of it. I always have luck. I cabe idto the world to be lucky. I'll have by dativity cast wud of these days, add see udder what lucky pladet I was bord. But I'll have do bore of it. The thidg is settled dow, Syl; do bore watchidg for be; dor will I attebpt after this to discover the cause of our recedt addoyadces. Dot a bit of it. I'll give the thidg up. If a legiod of ibps were to haudt the house dight after dight, Syl, I'd dot bove a peg! The very efforts which I bake to clear byself tedd but to idvolve be bore deeply; like the fly id the web, the bore I try to get out, the bore firbly I'b held. I'll give it up, cobe what bay I'll pludge idto bed at by usual tibe, add get up at by usual tibe, add dot before. Do batter what capers bay be cut, or what pradks bay be played; that bischievous devil, whoever he is, bay stick a hot brick upod wud of the chibdey-pots, add dadce upod that if he likes; the bood bay be abused, add the stars bay be abused, but he sbad't abuse *be*; I've had edough of his abusebedt; he dod't get be to rud after hib agaid; I'll borally *seal* by head to the pillow, although I should dearly like to catch hib! You see it plays vedgeadce with *be*—it destroys at wodce all the goverdor's codfidedce; add places be id the position of a thoughtless, reckless, characterless scabp! That's the poidt, Syl—that's what I look at! Up to this tibe, the goverdor has reposed the bost udlibited codfidedce id by hodour; but dow, of *course*, he ibagides that I seek to deceive hib, add that, too, by tellidg bead, deliberate falsehoods."

"Well, but when you have explained all to bim," suggested Sylvester, "surely that confidence will be restored?"

"I fear dot, Syl: day, I cad hardly expect it, the circubstadtial evidedce is so strodg agaidst be. Bady a bad has beed hadged upod collateral, or circubstadtial, evidedce far less codclusive. However, sobethidg bust be dode. I'll go to bed add thidk about it. Call be whed you rise: I bay dot be awake; add, udless I put id by appearadce at breakfast, the *great* swell will kdow all about it, if she doesd't kdow all about it dow. Therefore, dod't forget to call be."

"I'll not."

"Thed I'll be off add get a widk or two, if I cad: I cad't expect to have *buch* rest, indeed—

"'There's do rest, but the grave, for the pilgrib of love.'"

Poor Tom! He shook hands with Sylvester and left him, and turned into bed with a heavy heart; but he soon went to sleep, very soon; and slept soundly, until Sylvester summoned him to breakfast.

The doctor had not explained the affair to Mrs. Delolme. This Tom perceived the moment he entered the room, and, in consequence, felt comparatively comfortable; but he saw that the doctor was angry with him still, although the expression of that anger was concealed from the rest.

Now, as this was the day on which Sylvester was to leave the doctor's house, and make that of Mr. Scholefield his home—it having been arranged the previous evening that he should live with him a month before the articles were signed—the talents of Mr. Scholefield, and the prospects of Sylvester, formed the chief topics of conversation during breakfast. With Mr. Scholefield himself, Aunt Eleanor was delighted, and so, indeed, was Sylvester, although that delight was in some degree subdued by a variety of youthful apprehensions; and while even Mrs. Delolme confessed that she thought him an amiable person, the doctor bore testimony not only to his high professional abilities, but to his excellent qualities as a man. All were therefore satisfied that Sylvester's prospects were, as far as they could then be viewed, bright; and when the doctor had endeavoured to impress upon Sylvester the propriety of pursuing whatever course of study Mr. Scholefield might suggest, he rose from the table and withdrew.

He had scarcely, however, entered the library, when his servant came to inform him that a policeman had called, and was anxious to see him immediately. The doctor of course imagined that this was Ninety-nine, and directed the servant to show him in at once; but when he found that it was not, he was filled with apprehension; it struck him in an instant that something had happened to Ninety-nine, and that probably his fall had proved fatal.

"I beg pardon," said the policeman, with appropriate respect; "your name, sir, is Dr. Delolme?"

"It is," replied the doctor.

"You have a son, I believe, sir!"

"I have."

"His presence is required at the police-office, Bow Street, immediately."

" For what purpose ? "

" To give evidence in a case of robbery and assault."

" A case of *robbery* and assault ? "

" Yes, sir. He is, I believe, the only witness."

" Well, but when did it occur ? "

" About three o'clock this morning, I believe, sir ; I don't know the whole of the particulars, but I think that it happened about that time."

The doctor rang the bell, and desired the servant to send Tom in. As far as his fears for Ninety-nine were concerned, he felt greatly relieved ; but every doubt having reference to the truth of Ninety-nine's accusation against Tom vanished.

" Now, sir," said the doctor, when Tom appeared, " you are wanted at Bow Street police-office immediately."

" What for ? " inquired Tom.

" You witnessed a robbery this morning, did you not ? "

" The odly robbery I witdessed, was a robbery of reputatiod, add that reputatiod was by owd."

" But you witnessed a robbery in the street, about three o'clock this morning ? "

" Who says so ? " demanded Tom fiercely. " Do you ? " he added, turning to the policeman.

" I know nothing of it myself," replied the man.

" Do you kdow Didety-dide ? Has this, too, beed got up by hib ? "

" I know nothing of the particulars," returned the policeman. " All I know about the matter is this, that I was sent here to request your immediate attendance at the office."

" Oh, *I'll* go ! " said Tom. " I see how it is. Add," he added, addressing the doctor, " I hope you'll go with be."

" *I* will go with you, sir."

" Do so : I wish you to do so ; add if I fide that that wretch has beed trubping up adother charge agaidst be, I'll have the dubber off his coat, add the coat off his back. I'll write to the cobbissioders at wudce : I'll dot be thus addoyed by a fellow like that."

The doctor again rang the bell, and having ascertained that the carriage was at the door, he directed the policeman to get on the box, and they started.

During their progress to Bow Street not a word was uttered by either the doctor or Tom : the doctor was anxious for silence to be preserved, and Tom felt no inclination to break it; nor, when they had arrived, did a syllable pass between them. The carriage door was opened, and they alighted in silence; and on passing through a passage heard a fellow bawling " Mr. Delolme!" The policeman then led the way into the office, and found that the case was then on—that the prosecutor had already given his evidence, and that he had then just gone out of the office to look for his witness—the magistrate having consented to wait a few minutes, in order that he might be produced. An intimation was therefore given that the witness was in attendance, and Tom was ushered into the box and sworn.

During the performance of this solemn ceremony, the magistrate was relating, across the table, an anecdote, which caused the clerk, as a natural matter of duty, to roar; and when Tom had kissed the book, he looked well at the prisoner, who was dressed in the most fashionable style, but whom he didn't know from Adam.

"Well," said the clerk, addressing Tom, when he felt that he had laughed sufficiently long to satisfy the magistrate, "what's your name?"

"Thobas Delolbe."

"What d'you say?"

"Thobas Delolbe."

"Speak up, sir!"

"Thobas Delolbe," repeated Tom, in a voice of thunder.

"I'm not deaf," said the clerk.

"Oh!" replied Tom, "I thought you were."

"Thobas Delolbe," said the clerk, as he proceeded to write it down. "Thobas: how do you spell Thobas—with a *b*?"

"With a *b*?" said Tom. "*You* cad spell it with a *b* if you like; I always spell it with ad *eb*!"

"Oh, an *eb*!" said the clerk, as he winked at the magistrate. "*Very* good: and do you spell Delolbe with an *eb* too?"

"Why, of course."

"I only ask for information—Thobas Delolbe. Well, Mr. Thobas Delolbe, what are you?"

"A studedt of bed'cide."

"A student of what, sir?" demanded the clerk, who could not resist laughing; nor could the magistrate—nor, indeed, could the doctor, although he felt vexed at the time—"a student of what?"

"Of *bed'cide!*" replied Tom indignantly, and thereby set the whole court in a roar.

"Of *bed'cide!*" said the clerk, when the laughter had in some degree subsided. "I see! A student of bed'cide—very good. How do you spell bed'cide?"

"How do I spell bed'cide?" cried Tom, who felt highly indignant; while the court was convulsed with laughter, in which even the prisoner joined; "what do you mead?"

"I mean," said the clerk, having recovered the power to speak, "I mean to ask how you spell bed'cide?"

"Add do you bead to say that you dod't kdow how to spell it? If so, I should like to dose you with it till you do. I should feel great pleasure id thus curidg you of the *igdoradce* with which you are afflicted."

"Well," said the clerk, who didn't much like this, "but is bed'cide spelt with a *w* or a *b*?"

"A *w* or a *b*, you fool!" said Tom, looking contemptuously at the clerk, who really began to feel himself wounded.

"Like Thobas, it's spelt with an *eb*, no doubt!" observed the magistrate; and this—*being* the magistrate's joke—was on the instant hailed with the loudest burst of laughter ever even heard within *those* walls. The clerk, the policeman, the turnkeys, the crier, and the fellow who administered the solemn oaths, *roared;* while the prisoner — who was a student of human nature—shook his sides on speculation, conceiving, of course, that the magistrate's gratitude would prompt him to repudiate the evidence.

"Well, I suppose it *is* spelt with an *eb*," said the clerk, when he and the other impartial judges of a joke had become exhausted. "You are a student of bed'cide, you say?"

"Is this the court of Bobus?" inquired Tom, looking round with an expression of imperturbable gravity, which threw the whole court again into convulsions. "Cobus presides here if Bobus does *dot!* Ab I," he added, addressing the magistrate, as soon as his voice could be heard, "ab I id a place sacred to justice?—a place id which solebdity is supposed to reigd, add of which digdity is supposed to be wud of the chief characteristics?—a place id which obediedce to the law is taught, add respect for those who admidister the law idspired? I ab—I presube that I ab—add yet I who have taked a solebd oath to ibpart with truth that which I kdow, ab bet with dothidg but buffoodery, ragged jokes, add silly

R

laughter. That bad's life," he added, pointing to the prisoner, "his very life bay, for aught I kdow, be id peril, add yet you teach hib, add all who are here, to view the adbidistratiod of justice as a jest."

The officials again felt it to be their duty to laugh, but the magistrate clearly didn't like it at all, and more especially as Tom's rebuke was hailed in the body of the court with applause. He therefore, assuming an aspect of gravity, said, "Let us proceed with the business of the court."

"I thidk it high tibe that we should," said Tom, and another laugh burst from the officials.

"*Silence!*" shouted the magistrate sternly; and "Silence!" was indignantly reiterated by the crier, who had been making more noise than any other man in court.

"Now, sir," said the magistrate, determined to be severe upon Tom, who, however, was not at all afraid of him, "what do you know about this?"

"About what?"

"About what! Why, this robbery?"

"Dothidg."

"Nothing! You are a witness in this case, are you not?"

"I ab placed id the positiod of a witdess."

"Then what do you mean by saying that you know nothing of it?"

"I bead, by sayidg that I kdow dothidg of it, that I kdow dothidg of it."

"Then what did you come here for?"

"That's the very poidt which I ab adxious to ascertaid!"

"What's the meaning of all this? Do you know, sir, that I have the power to commit you?"

"Cobbit *be!*" cried Tom.

"Ay, sir; commit you."

"You bay have the power, but you dare dot, I apprehedd, exercise that power without sufficiedt cause."

"I shall be justified, sir, by your refusal to give evidence."

"I have do evidedce to give! I have sword to speak the truth, the whole truth, add dothidg but the truth: I respect that oath, add whed I solebdly declare that I kdow dothidg whatever of this robbery, the truth, the whole truth, add dothidg but the truth, is idvolved id that solebd declaratiod."

"Have a care, sir! have a care!" exclaimed the magistrate. "How long have you known the prisoner?"

"How lodg have I kdowd hib?"

"Yes, sir: that's the question. How long have you known him?"

"Well," said Tom, deliberately taking out his watch, "sobewhere about twedty bidites."

"Come, come, sir; I'm not to be trifled with: these *ingenious* evasions will not do here."

"What idgedious evasiods? You asked be how lodg the prisoder had beed kdowd to be: I told you about twedty bidites. Is there ady evasiod id that?"

"Are you not one of his associates?"

"Wud of his associates?"

"Ay! one of his associates. Come now, answer that question."

"It is albost too codtebptible to be adswered; but I'll adswer it by statidg, with all the iddigdation at by cobbadd, that I ab dot."

"Oh, none of your indignation, sir; it will not do here. Answer my questions plainly. You have never been in any way connected with him?"

"Dever."

"You don't know him?"

"I do dot."

"You never saw him before in your life, I daresay?"

"I dever did."

"No: I don't suppose you ever did."

At this stage of the proceedings the doctor would have interfered, with the view of expostulating with the magistrate, but that he felt that Tom would be a match for him yet.

"Is he known to the police?" resumed the magistrate, with infinite significance; and, doubtless, had Ninety-nine been there, he would have given Tom a character; but he was not, and the rest knew nothing at all of him.

"How do you get your living?" inquired his worship.

"What do you bead by by lividg?" said Tom.

"How do you support yourself?"

"Dohow. I dod't support byself at all."

"Who supports you?"

"By father."

"Oh, then you have a father, have you?"

"I have."

"Ah! and what is he?"

"A doctor of bed'cide."

"Oh! he's a doctor too. A respectable man, I daresay?"

"He is a bad who occupies, add who deserves to occupy, a far higher social positiod thad ady other bad in this court. *He*," added Tom, with a sarcastic smile, "*he* is a gedtlebad."

"Oh! no doubt. Is he here?"

"I believe so: he cabe id the carriage with be."

"Oh! the carriage! Ah! what carriage?"

"What carriage!—why, our carriage. Is it at all probable that we should cobe to see so courteous add so distidguished a persod id a jarvey?"

The clerk here privately expressed his conviction that notwithstanding all Tom had said, he and the prisoner belonged to the same gang; and when the magistrate had winked at the clerk with great significance, he suddenly said—

"Where's the prosecutor? You are a very clever fellow," turning to Tom, "but I think that we shall know each other better by-and-by."

The prosecutor, who had imagined that this was altogether another case, was then directed by one of the officers to step forward, and he did so.

"I think I understood you," said the magistrate, "that this robbery was committed about three o'clock?"

"About three."

"Very well. Now, how far was your witness from the prisoner at the time?"

"A very short distance! He was, in fact, walking just behind him."

"I thought so!"

"What!" exclaimed Tom, addressing the prosecutor fiercely, "do you bead to say that *I* was walkidg behidd hib?"

"You!" cried the prosecutor, in a state of amazement. "No! *You* are not my witness!"

"What's the meaning of it all?" said the magistrate. "I don't understand it. If," he added, addressing Tom, "if you are not the prosecutor's witness, why did you come here?"

"I cabe here because a policebad called to idforb be that by presedce was required ibbediately. That's all I kdow about the batter."

"Well, but why did you get into the witness-box?"

"Because I was ushered id the bobedt I edtered the court."

"I am sorry that this mistake should have occurred," said the prosecutor. "But certainly that gentleman is not the witness whom I expected."

"It's well for that *gentleman*," said the magistrate, "that he is not. As it is, I have a great mind to detain him until he brings forward some respectable person"——

"You will, sir, detain him at your peril!" said the doctor, coming forward with an air of calm dignity, and speaking in tones which commanded attention. "I am his father—my name is Delolme; and if you wish to have evidence of *my* respectability, I can refer you not only to some of the first families in the kingdom, but to many of your own immediate friends."

"I regret," said the magistrate, whose countenance fell the moment the doctor mentioned his "immediate friends"—"I regret exceedingly that so great a mistake should have occurred; but we really have so many persons here who pretend to be that which they are not, that we are compelled to look upon almost all with suspicion."

"It may be so," calmly retorted the doctor; "still the course which you have pursued in this case has been, in *my* judgment, highly incorrect."

"Well," said Tom, "I suppose I bay go?"

"You may," replied the magistrate.

"Very good. But before I retire, allow be, as a batter of gratitude, to ackdowledge the courtesy with which I have beed received id this Suprebe Court of Jollity add Justice."

The magistrate was silent, and Tom withdrew; and as he did so, he was greeted with a buzz of applause, which fell harshly, of course, upon the ears of his worship, who, determined on taking his revenge out of some one, indignantly demanded the prosecutor to explain.

"I am really very sorry," said the prosecutor, who was evidently a highly respectable man, "but I can give no other explanation than this, that that gentleman was sent for by mistake and placed in the witness-box, during my absence from the court."

"But how came he to be sent for?"

"I sent for him, because the person who witnessed the robbery gave me *his* address."

"Well, is that person here?"

"I am sorry to say that he is not."

"Very well; then the prisoner must be discharged."

"You will, I hope, remand him, and thereby give me some time to produce this witness."

"I have no evidence before me to justify a remand."

"You have *my* evidence, and you have also the evidence of the policeman."

"Don't dictate to me, sir. I say that I have no evidence before me to justify me in remanding the prisoner, and that, therefore, he must be discharged."

"Well, but am I to be deprived of my property and assaulted by a man whose character is known to be infamous, without having"——

"It's your own fault; you have no one to blame but yourself. You should have had your witness here."

"Well, if this is the way in which justice is administered, Heaven protect me from its administration!"

"Understand that I am invested with authority here, and that I will not suffer you or any other man to bring that authority into contempt."

"I hold it to be quite unnecessary for me to do so. You bring it sufficiently into contempt yourself."

"Leave the office, sir! If you do not know how to conduct yourself properly, leave the office!"

"I will do so; and I hope that while *you* preside over it, I shall never have occasion to enter it again."

The prisoner, who was a well-known member of a numerous and highly respectable-looking body, yclept in those days "the swell-mob," was then discharged; and as the prosecutor was leaving the office in disgust, Tom, with a view to the vindication of his own honour, arrested his progress.

"Will you do be the favour," said he, "to explaid to be how this stradge bistake occurred? By object id requestidg this favour is to satisfy by goverdor that I ab dot the bad."

"In any case you are entitled to an explanation," said the prosecutor, "after having been put to so much trouble and annoyance."

"Oh, I dod't care a straw about that. I'b odly adxious to rebove whatever doubt bay exist id by goverdor's bide, about by beidg out at that tibe id the bordidg."

"Well, then, about three o'clock, as I was returning from a party, I was accosted by the fellow whom this Midas has discharged, and, as I conceived him to be a respectable man, we walked on together for some considerable distance, when suddenly he gave me a blow which nearly stunned me, drew my watch from my pocket in an instant, and made off. At this time a young gentleman was walking behind us, and witnessed the whole transaction. I did not, however, stop to speak to him then, but pursued the scoundrel, who was eventually secured, and while the policeman held him, I returned to this gentleman, and begged of him to accompany me to the station. This, he said, would put him to great inconvenience, but he assured me that he should be most happy to appear and give evidence at the police-office, when called upon to do so. Being satisfied with this assurance, and knowing that my evidence alone, without even that of the policeman, would be sufficient to cause the prisoner to be detained, I did not press him to accompany me then, but took his address, which he readily gave me, and it certainly is my impression that he told me that he was the son, or the nephew, of Dr. Delolme. I was, of course, somewhat excited at the time, and being so, I may have misunderstood him: indeed, I now feel that I *must* have misunderstood him; but certain am I that, in some way, either directly or indirectly, he mentioned the name of Dr. Delolme. He might have said that he was known to Dr. Delolme, or that he was in some way connected with Dr. Delolme, but he certainly mentioned the name of Dr. Delolme, for the moment I heard that name mentioned, I was satisfied."

"Might he not," said the doctor, "have been, as the magistrate suggested to us, one of the associates of this man?"

"I do not believe that he was. I cannot believe it. He was a young man, upon whom I fancied at the time I might with safety place the utmost reliance. I may have been deceived; it is possible: but certainly my impression is that he knew no more of the fellow than I did. And now," added the prosecutor, turning to Tom, "having explained how it happened that I sent for you this morning, I hope that you will accept my apology for"——

"Dodsedse!" cried Tom; "dod't bedtiod it. I'b odly sorry that the fellow was dot pudished. You have dot recovered your watch, I suppose?"

"Oh, yes; I found it this morning in the area of one of the houses; but, as a watch, it's valueless. This is it, broken all to pieces, you see ; I saw him throw it away just before he was secured."

"Well," said Tom, "although the gold is odly worth it's weight, I'b very glad that *he* hasd't got it. But did you ever see such a bagistrate ?"

"He's a disgrace to the bench," replied the prosecutor indignantly. "I have heard of him frequently, but with his conduct this morning I am perfectly disgusted. That fellow is as well known to him as any pickpocket in London, and yet, because his dignity was wounded by the calm and correct observations of the doctor, he must let him loose to prey upon society again, although he had ample evidence upon which to commit him. However, the affair is now at an end, and I have but to repeat my expressions of regret that I should have given you both so much trouble."

He then left the office with the doctor and Tom, and having seen them into the carriage, was about to take his leave, when a fellow came up to the door, and inquired if they would like to have the proceedings reported at length.

"You are a reporter, I presume ?" said the doctor.

"I am," replied the man.

"With which of the newspapers are you connected ?"

"Oh, several. But *I* report specially for the *Times*, *Standard*, *Herald*, and *Globe*."

"Well," said the doctor, who was anxious, of course, that Tom should not be publicly ridiculed, "I see no necessity for the publication of that nonsense; it had nothing whatever to do with the case."

"Then you would like to have all that suppressed ?"

"Why, I cannot conceive any sufficient reason for its insertion."

"I have *taken* it in full, and the whole of it will be inserted, unless, indeed, you wish to have that or any other particular portion suppressed."

"Well, I certainly should like *that* portion to be left out."

"Very well, sir; then not a single word of it shall appear. You are, of course, aware that we are paid by the line, and that, therefore, whatever we suppress is a dead loss to us, unless, indeed, the sum we should receive for its insertion be paid to us for its suppression."

"I understand," said the doctor; "and it is but correct that you *should* be paid the sum you would have for its insertion by those who wish to have it suppressed. What would be the sum in this case?"

"I think it would make about sixty lines, and I manifold seven—that is to say, I send the report to seven papers, each of which pays me three-halfpence a line; but a couple of sovereigns will be sufficient: say a couple of sovereigns."

"You must allow *me* to settle this," said the prosecutor; "I have given you *trouble* enough; you shall not through me be put to any expense."

"I beg pardon," said the doctor, "your loss has been greater than mine. But what security have I," he added, turning to the reporter, "that that which you promise to suppress will not appear?"

"I am well known here, sir, and I may say, with pride, that my reputation is without a single stain. I shall be happy to refer you to the magistrate. He has known me for years. You will, probably, before you leave, do me the favour to apply to him, in order"——

"No," said the doctor, smiling, "that I am sure I'll not do; but here is my card, and if nothing should appear in either the evening or the morning papers, I shall be happy to give you a couple of sovereigns."

"Oh! if my honour is doubted, there's an end of the matter. It is not of the slightest importance to me whether I receive the money of you or the proprietors of the papers to which I send the report. I am always, of course, anxious to oblige; but it is to me, as you must perceive, a matter of no moment whatever."

"Now, do let *me* settle this affair," said the prosecutor.

"No," returned the doctor, "that indeed I will not. You promise," he added, addressing the reporter, "that if I give you two sovereigns, not a syllable having reference to my son shall appear?"

"Let it all appear," cried Tom; "*I* dod't care a buttod about it!"

"That," resumed the doctor, heedless of Tom's observation, "that is, of course, understood."

"Of course."

The doctor drew out his purse, gave two sovereigns to the reporter, shook hands with the prosecutor, and gave the word—"home."

"Why did you give hib that buddy?" cried Tom. "Why did you dot give it to be?"

"I gave it to him," replied the doctor, "because I had no desire to see you ridiculed in the public papers."

"Ridiculed! Well, that's rich! How could I be ridiculed? The bagistrate was the swell, I apprehedd, to be ridiculed. It strikes be that I bade a hit whed I asked hib if I was id the court of Bobus!"

"Bobus!" cried the doctor. "Yes, you did make a hit! Do you know what produced all that laughter?"

"Of course. The codsubbate igdoradce of the clerk."

"No, Tom; that laughter was produced by your Bobuses and Cobuses."

"What do you bead by Bobuses and Cobuses? I didd't say Bobus! I said Bobus! Id the produdciatiod Bobus add Bobus, the differedce is ibbedse."

"I cannot perceive any difference at all."

"What! Dot betweed Bobus add Bobus?"

"Bobus is Bobus, and nothing but Bobus."

"Well, but I didd't say Bobus! Bobus is a beastly produdciatiod of Bobus!"

"I wish that I could induce you to think so."

"Well, but do you bead to say that I prodoudce Bobus, Bobus?"

"I do."

"Well, I bust look idto this. I begid to suspect that there bust be sobethidg id it. I dod't, of course, wadt to be bade a laughidg-stock of!"

"But a laughing-stock you ever *will* be, Tom, until your absurd pronunciation of the *m*'s and the *n*'s be corrected."

Tom became thoughtful; and as they were then near home, the subject was, for the time being, dropped.

CHAPTER XXIII.

THE LOVERS' RETURN.

IGNORANCE is universally contemned, and yet ignorance itself is universal. There is nothing more fiercely denounced than ignorance; yet, in general, they are most ignorant who denounce it most fiercely. All men are ignorant; and yet mankind is not a mass of ignorance; all men have knowledge; but man is not omniscient. Ignorance is comparative; there is not a man breathing who does not know something of which every other man breathing is ignorant. The great art is to conceal our ignorance; and this art is highly valuable, seeing that it constitutes the germ of knowledge; nay, the man who endeavours to conceal his ignorance, is already in possession of a most important branch of human knowledge—the knowledge of the ignorance he is anxious to conceal. Some men have a talent for the display of their ignorance. Such men are ignorant of their ignorance, and are consequently much to be pitied. To be ignorant of one's own ignorance is to be in the most profound state of ignorance in which a man can be involved. The common answer, "I don't know," is candid, but it is at the same time a very palpable manifestation of ignorance—and yet where is the man who knows everything? There is not such a man upon earth. The lowest species of ignorance is that which prompts a man to *think* that he knows everything; and the highest caste of knowledge is that which makes him feel that in reality he knows only this—that he knows nothing. There are, however, men who are expected to know everything; but of this expectation disappointment must always be the fruit. Take our greatest men—men of the mightiest minds—men most highly distinguished for wisdom—how ignorant they are of those common things with which common men are conversant. A journeyman barber would curl his lip and look with feelings of contempt upon a head of hair cut by an astronomer; his exclamation doubtless would be, "He *must* be a hignoramus as cut this ere 'air!" Nor is it unworthy of belief that there is not one statesman in a thousand, either native or foreign, who knows how to cut out a pair of short gaiters. Place Wellington and Napier in the kitchen, and Gunter and Ude in the field, and what consummate ignorance would be displayed by them all! But this term ignorance is applied with more indiscrimination than any other. A is said to be ignorant by B, because he happens not to know that which B knows, albeit he knows that of which B himself is ignorant. Tom thought the clerk at the police-office ignorant, because he professed not to know exactly how to spell " bed'cide;" he thought the magistrate ignorant; he thought the officers ignorant; indeed, the only man in court whom he imagined to be wise was the doctor; and yet the doctor, as will be seen, was, as far as the practices of penny-a-liners are concerned, one of the most ignorant men there.

It will be in all probability remembered that he gave one of these genuine " gentlemen of the press " two sovereigns for the suppression of Tom's evidence. Well! the doctor of course thought that it would be suppressed, and so did Tom; although he felt at the time, and strongly too, that those two sovereigns would have paid for a box of cigars, and *innumerable* pots of porter. The *Standard*, however, was no sooner in, than Tom saw the whole proceedings reported at length; and, with feelings of deep indignation, perceived that he, and he only, was ridiculed!

"A dice bad," said he confidentially—" a very dice bad. I bust have adother idterview with you, by friedd—I bust, id fact, have that hodour id a very short tibe."

Having expressed that which he felt in these cabalistic terms, he rang the bell, and when James appeared, he said, with an air of mystery, " Jib, rud for the evedidg papers."

" The evening paper's in, sir," replied James promptly.

" What do you bead? Do you thidk I'b such a codsubbate ass as dot to kdow that the paper's id, whed I hold it id by hadd? I wadt the others—the *Globe*, the *Sud*, add the *Mood*, if there be a *Mood!*"

"I shall have to go out with the carriage, sir, directly; the ladies are dressing for dinner."

" Dab the didder, Jib! Rud for the papers—bridg be the lot as soon as possible!"

James accordingly went for " the lot," and Tom again read the report in the *Standard*. He had previously conceived an idea that there must in reality be something peculiar in his style of pronunciation; but he had never before imagined that that peculiarity would appear so ridiculous in print. He read it aloud again and again, but as he pronounced his *m*'s and his *n*'s, he was really unable to detect anything wrong. The substituted *b*'s and *d*'s looked absurd enough, but in his ear they sounded all right.

"Bobus," said he—"Bobus. Well, that's correct! Bobus —dothidg cad be bore distidct thad Bobus! Add bed'cide. Well, bed'cide; what cad possibly be plaider thad bed'cide? I wod't have it!" he exclaimed; "it's a regular codspiracy —a dead take id!" And just as he had arrived at this conclusion, James returned with the *Globe* and the *Sun*.

"Well, Jib," he cried; "got 'eb?"

"Yes, sir. There are only two, sir, besides the one you have."

"Very well. Two are two too many. That'll do, Jib— that'll do."

James then left the room, and Tom very soon found that the reports in these papers were literally the same.

"Very *good*, Bister Reporter," said he sarcastically. "*Very* good. It *strikes* be I shall serve you out to-borrow. I dod't know exactly, add therefore I cad't say; but if I dod't get that buddy back, I'll do byself the pleasure of takidg it out. *I'll* see you to-borrow bordidg, you literary wretch. Here you are," he added, as the doctor entered the library—"here's the full chadge for your two sovereigds. All id."

"Indeed!"

"Every word of it."

"Very dishonourable: very."

"Add yet the fellow didd't like to have his hodour doubted! Why didd't you give *be* the buddy?"

The doctor very gravely commenced reading the report, but as he proceeded, his features relaxed, for the thing had been well done, and every point told.

"Well," said Tom, when the doctor had finished, "what do you thidk of it dow?"

"Why, I think it most dishonest on the part of the reporter, but as I feel that this report will induce you to correct your defective pronunciation, I am not very sorry to see it in."

"Well, but *do* you bead to say, dow, seriously, that I prodoudce by *ebs* add *eds* id that ridiculous fashiod?"

"I do."

"Add are the *ebs* add the *eds* the odly letters which I prodoudce idcorrectly?"

"Your pronunciation, Tom, of every other letter in the alphabet is perfect. The substitution of the *b* and the *d* for the *m* and the *n*, alone renders your conversation comical, or, as you would say, *cobical*."

"Well! I'll certaidly see idto it. If this be the case, I'll sood get over those two fellows."

"I hope you now see the necessity for doing so. Your professional success, Tom, as I have before frequently explained to you, depends in a great measure upon that."

"Oh! I'll get over it. I'll sood badage it. But what are you goidg to do with that fellow?"

"The reporter?"

"Yes; of course you'll debadd the buddy back?"

"Not I. If I were to see him, I should certainly expostulate with him, for such practices are highly dishonourable; but I shall take no trouble about the matter."

"*I* bay get it, I suppose, if I cad?"

"If you can, Tom, you may," replied the doctor, with a smile. "But I have an impression that you will find that there is, in that quarter, 'no money returned.'"

The impression on Tom's mind was of a different character, but he thought it inexpedient to explain how he intended to proceed; he, therefore, allowed that subject to drop; but, being anxious to have a point of far more importance settled, he said, with a countenance which denoted that anxiety, "Add dow let be ask you wud serious questiod. We all dide together at Scholefield's to-day. Very well. Dow, I shall feel of course buch bore cobfortable if you tell be that you are satisfied, perfectly satisfied, that I was dot out of the house frob the tibe I left the drawidg-roob last dight till we left id the carriage together this bordidg. Are you or are you dot satisfied of this?"

"I am satisfied now, Tom—perfectly satisfied—that you are not the person who witnessed the robbery; but the door, Tom—the fact of the door being found open—that's the point!"

"Yes. But that poidt is berely assubed. I dod't believe a word of it! I dod't believe the door was foudd oped at all!"

"*I* feel justified in believing that it was; and if it were, the question is, who *could* have left it open if you did not? It surely could not have been Sylvester?"

"Syl! Do: I'll adswer for hib with by life. I saw hib idto his roob; add I kdow he wedt to bed: I also kdow that if he had gode dowdstairs after that, I bust have heard hib. Besides, he isd't at all the style of fellow to do it!"

"Well, all I can say is, that it's a mystery, which time may perhaps unravel."

"But look here, father! Dod't believe that I ever have told, or that I ever will tell you a falsehood. Dod't believe it."

"Well, Tom, I am not at all anxious to believe it. I certainly cannot *prove* that you ever told me a falsehood, but you are aware that these circumstances are fraught with suspicion."

"Exactly! That's the poidt! That is the very thidg which galls be! But *we* shall fidd it out by-add-by."

"And, until we do find it out, Tom, I am perfectly willing to be silent on the subject."

Mrs. Delolme and Aunt Eleanor then entered the library, and shortly afterwards they, with the doctor and Tom, repaired to the house of Mr. Scholefield. Here they met the reverend gentleman, by appointment; and here Aunt Eleanor was delighted to find that Sylvester already felt perfectly at home. Of Mrs. Scholefield he had at once become a favourite; she treated him, in fact, with as much kindness as if he had been her own son; and as she was in reality a most amiable person, Aunt Eleanor, feeling satisfied that everything would be done to promote his happiness, decided on returning to Cotherstone on the morrow.

Accordingly, in the morning, she and the reverend gentleman, accompanied by Mrs. Delolme, Mrs. Scholefield, Sylvester, and Tom, went to the office at Charing Cross, and when she had had some private conversation with Mrs. Scholefield, having reference to Sylvester, she left town perfectly happy in the conviction that the utmost possible care would be taken of both his morals and his health.

Immediately after the coach had started, Tom proceeded to Bow Street alone; and, on entering the office, looked round with an anxious hope of again seeing that literary gentleman who received the two sovereigns of the doctor. That gentleman, however, was not then there; but, conceiving that he might be there anon, Tom waited two hours for him with exemplary patience, and then spoke to one of the officers of the court.

"I ab adxious," he observed, "to see a reporter."

"There they are," returned the officer, "in that there box."

"Are they reporters?"

"All on 'em."

"But I wadt to see the wud whob I saw here yesterday."

"All them was here yesterday."

"But there was wud here yesterday, who is dot here dow?"

"With all *my* heart."

"Very good. But perhaps you cad tell be where to fidd hib?"

"Don't bother. How should I know where to find him?"

"Do you thidk it likely that they cad tell be?"

"Ax."

"Why, you surly, low bred, ill codditioded"——

"Silence! or I puts you out of the office."

Tom looked at him contemptuously from head to foot and up again, and said something about his being a nice man, he *didn't* think! but as one of the reporters at the moment left the box, Tom turned from the fellow to address him.

"A reporter," said he, "was here yesterday whob I dod't see id the office to-day. Cad you tell be where to fidd hib?"

"What paper is he connected with?"

"He reports for seved papers, he told us."

"Seven! You are the gentleman, I believe, who was yesterday in the witness-box."

"I ab."

"I thought so. But there was no person connected with seven papers here."

"He certaidly told us seved."

"What was his object in speaking to you on the subject?"

"Why, he cabe to the carriage-door to idquire if we were adxious to have ady portiod of the report suppressed, add as by goverdor thought that that dodsedse bight as well be left out, the fellow offered to suppress it for two sovereigds."

"But of course you didn't give him the two sovereigns?"

"The goverdor did. He gave hib two sovereigds to leave out the lot, add the wretch put it all id."

"I see," said the reporter, smiling. "But he had nothing whatever to do with it. He is not a regular reporter: he is

"What's it! What! Don't your ideas fructify?"

"What do you mean?"

"What do I mean! There! That any man in the nineteenth century should be able to see the world wag as it does, without having any ideal fructification! Pokey, you're a flat. *You'd* never do to sit in the House of Commons. Even Bobby Peel would beat you. Why, just look here, didn't you see Teddy pass just now with the old maid?"

"Yes. Well?"

"Well. Don't you see?"

"See what?"

"Why, the dodge!"

"What dodge?"

"What dodge! Pokey, you were never born to be the Lord Chancellor. Amalgamate your ideas, man. Let 'em flow and fructify! What! Well, as true as I'm alive! Why, just look you here! Do you mean to tell me—a man of your scope, and sense, and fructifertility—do you mean to tell me, point blank, without any reservation of ideas, that you don't see as clear as mud what Ted's been up to?"

"Can you?"

"*Can* I! Who can't! It's as plain as the sun at twelve o'clock. Look you here: when Harry the Eighth married Nell Gwynne, did they marry in public? No! *They* married privately. *Now,* don't you see?"

"I can't say as I do," replied Pokey.

"You can't! Well, I never see such a job in my life. What! Can't you see there's been a private marriage here?"

"No, I'm blest if I can."

"Pokey, you ought to go to school again, and have them ideas of yours put under a course of fructification. Not see it. Send I may *live*, if ever I see such a job before! Where are your eyes? what's become of your notions? are all your ideas asleep or what, that you can't make nothing out of this?"

"Well, what do *you* make of it?"

"What do I make of it! Just look you here. Hasn't the old maid been up to London, and didn't Ted follow her, and haven't they been there all this time, and *now* haven't they come back together?"

"Well, and what of that?"

"What of it! *Have* you lived all these years in the world and can't see what they've been up to! They couldn't marry here. Oh! dear me, no: they must go up to London, and be married by special licence. This is your aristocracy of humility! this is your parsonic pride! Mark my words, Pokey, that pride must come down. *We're* not going to let it much longer ride rough-shod over the eternal principles of the people. We must tear from their eyes what I call the film of folly. We must make them understand these amalgamating dodges. We must do as they did in France under Peter the Great, when Robespierre towelled the Dutch, we must give the aristocracy a blessed good welting. That'll bring 'em to their senses; and mind you this, they'll never be happy till they get it. We must have a revolution all over the world; things are now on a rotten foundation! your kings, and your queens, and your bishops, and parsons, and all the lot of aristocratic leeches, who suck the best blood of the eternal people, must be swamped: they must be swept clean away from the face of the earth, as they were in the time of the Romans. What do we want with an amalgamating mass of corruption fructifying upon our very vitals? Why should we give eighty millions a year away for nothing? What good do the aristocracy do us? If you can't pay your taxes, away go your sticks; and what for? Why, to fatten up your flaming aristocracy. Do you mean to call that eternal justice? Do you mean to call that the glorious principles of everlasting liberty? What did we sign the Magna Charta for? Why, for fructifying freedom. If we had no aristocracy, we should have no taxes; and if we had no taxes, we should be free. I'll take you, then, upon your Magna Charta, and show that you are nothing but slaves. Would the Russians stand it, think you? Would the Chinamen stand it? No! The Jews wouldn't stand it under Moses. Look at the history of the world, and you'll find that nobody stands it but us. When Solomon built his temple among the gods, the Solomonians wouldn't stand it: they said, point blank, 'Here you've got about a thousand wives, of one sort or other, and when we come to look at the mobs of kids, we are not going to support so expensive an establishment.' Even the very workmen struck! and we must strike, and when we do strike, the blow will be a stunner. It's of no use half doing the thing. We'll go in like rattlesnakes, my boy, as they did at Nova Scotia. *We'll* let them see what we're made of! we'll show 'em from which point of the compass the wind blows: we'll go in a burster; and when we do, the lesson shall last 'em their lives. *We'll* not much longer be plundered in this way! we'll not be ground down to the earth, and have our substance squeezed out of us thus, by the iron hand of an iron-hearted aristocracy. Not a bit of it! What did Johnny Russell say in the House the other night? 'I tell the noble lord,' said he; and Johnny can speak up sometimes if he likes—'I tell the noble lord that he'd better look out. There's a spirit abroad that won't have it. It's fructifying now, and will soon break loose; and when it does, there'll be pepper.' And so there will: mind you that. Down with them!—that's my sentiments—down to the dust! A rattler, my Briton—a rattler for me. Now, just look you here"——

"Well, but what are you talking about?" inquired Pokey.

"What am I talking about?"

"Ay! What has all this about Peter the Great, Solomon, Moses, and Magna Charta to do with our parson? What have the Russians to do with him, or the Frenchmen, or the Chinamen?"

"What! are you so thick-headed, so pugnaciously stupid, as not to see that all this tends to show you the system?"

"What system?"

"What system! Why, the system of extortion—the system of plunder—the fructifying system of downright dead robbery, which grinds the people's vitals into dust."

"But we wasn't a-talking about nothing of the sort. We was talking about a private marriage."

"Well, I know it. But can't you make your ideas fructify beyond *one* point of the compass? I know we were talking about Teddy Rouse being privately married in London: and just look you here"——

"Well, but what makes you think so?"

"What makes me think so! Why, can there exist two opinions about it? Didn't she sneak off to London; and didn't he go sneaking after her? Why didn't he take her up with him, like a man? They have come back together because it's all over; but why not do things in a straightforward way? It's disgusting to see a man like him—a man, paid as he is for teaching simplicity—to go dodging about in that manner."

"But this is all guess-work, you know?"

"Guess-work! Pokey, Pokey, when *shall* I get you to fructify your ideas a little?"

"Yours, I think, fructify a little too much. You said when he went up, that he was going after his French girl, there—what's her name—Rosalie!"

"I know I did; and what does it prove? Why, that he'll run after every one he takes a fancy to. Depend upon it, Ted's not particular. None of them are. No one expects it in a parson. They're a clerical lot; and you know what I mean by the term clerical. I say, Quocks," he added, as that gentleman joined them, "did you see Teddy Rouse and his woman come in?"

"Teddy Rouse and his *woman!*" said Quocks. "What do you mean? I saw him set down Mrs. Sound at the cottage."

"He didn't take her then to the parsonage?" observed Pokey.

"The parsonage! No. Who said he did?"

"Drant says they're married!"

"Married! Rubbish. It isn't likely!"

"Why not?" demanded Obadiah.

"Why not! Do you think he'd have taken her to the cottage, and shaken hands, and left her there, and then driven home by himself, if they'd been married?"

"Well, I was only taking a charitable view of the thing; because if they're not married they ought to be, that's all about it."

"What do you mean? I shouldn't mind well thrashing any man who says there's anything a mite wrong about Mrs. Sound. She's as straight as an arrow, *I'll* warrant!—right up and down, and no nonsense—not a mite."

"You know she's been to London?"

"I do; what of that?"

"You know he's been to London too?"

"Yes; and what of that?"

"Well! Look you here, I only know it doesn't look well."

"What doesn't look well?"

"Why, it doesn't look well for Ted to run after her, and then to bring her back with him; now, does it?"

"Why not?"

"Why not! Why, it looks as if there must be something in it."

"In what?"

"Why, as Harry the Eighth said, just after the French Revolution, 'I'll tell you what it is,' said he, 'if'"——

"Never mind what Harry the Eighth said! I want to hear what you say."

"Well, but this is a case in point. 'If,' said he, 'honourable gentlemen think that I'm to be done in this way, I must fructify their intellects a little.'"

"Never mind fructifying!—give me a plain answer to a plain question."

"He never did such a thing in his life!" observed Pokey.

"Pokey," said Obadiah gravely; "what would you have been if it hadn't been for me?"

"What do you mean?" demanded Pokey indignantly, for he felt that he was quite as good a man as Obadiah, who never in his life had twopence that could be said to be his own; "what should I have been if it hadn't been for you?"

"Ay! what would you have been if it hadn't been for me? Look you here, now; I'll tell you; you'd have been like one of the rattlesnakes in the wilderness; you wouldn't have had a fructifying idea about you."

"Well," said Quocks, "but what have you to say against the character of Mrs. Sound?"

"What have I to say against her character?"

"Ay! You said just now that it didn't look well—that there must be something in it, and that if she were not married, she ought to be. Now, I just want to know what you mean by all this?"

"You do, do you? Well, then, just look you here: when I said that if she and Teddy Rouse were not married, they ought to be, I meant what I said; and do you mean to say they ought not?"

"But what did you mean to insinuate?"

"What did I mean to insinuate! Why, of course, that they ought to be married."

"And why?"

"Why! When Peter the Great fructified the Greeks"——

"Never mind Peter the Great; the question is, why ought they to be married?"

"I was going to tell you. Peter"——

"I won't have it. Answer my question."

"'Answer my question.' Are you one of the ragged aristocracy? Do you want to come Billy the Conqueror over us? 'Answer my question.' A fructifying tyrant could say no more to his slave. I'm the slave of no man; not a farthing's worth of it. Come to fair argument, and I am your man. I'll go with you into the history of the world; but if you want to come any of your haughty aristocracy, it won't do for me, mind you that."

"Obadiah," said Quocks, "you're a fool. I don't flatter you when I say that you are only one remove from an idiot; because I'd much rather talk with an idiot than with you. Independently of which, an idiot—a perfect idiot—is infinitely more harmless. You take delight in stabbing the reputation of those around you: you glory in the practice of founding falsehoods upon truth: you are too vain to see that you are despised, and too ignorant even to know that you are ignorant: you are one of society's butts—a creature who has not a single friend in the world, for what man in the world can feel justified in either opening his heart to you, or trusting you with a secret? You are a dangerous man, Obadiah—dangerous, not because you have any high intellectual power, but because you are utterly destitute of it. I don't mean to say that you are malignant. No: you are ten times worse than a man who is actuated by malignity: you have not the tact to perceive what is calculated to injure a man, and what is not. You lose friends, Obadiah, as fast as you make them, because they soon find that you are not to be trusted."

"Well," said Obadiah, "you have been fructifying, certainly, to an *amalgamating* extent. Have you done?"

"Quite. My object is merely to induce you to study your own character."

"Thank you: you're very kind—you always were; but I know my own character as well as any man in Europe, Asia, Africa, or America."

"I am very sorry for it."

"No doubt. But just look you here: just allow me, if you've done now, to ask you one question. You said just now that I take a delight in stabbing the reputation of those around me. Mark you that!—those were the very words you put in juxtaposition."

"Well."

"Well, just look you here, now; whose reputation have I ever endeavoured to stab?"

"Whose reputation have you *not?* That's the exception, if there be one: the other's the rule."

"Well, but whose reputation have I been endeavouring to stab now?"

"That of a lady whose goodness is known and has been appreciated by all but you, and that of a gentleman—for he *is* a gentleman—whose honour and benevolence none but you ever doubted."

"I deny it!"

"Deny what?"

"Deny what! Deny that I've been endeavouring"——

"Oh!" exclaimed Pokey, with uplifted hands; "oh!"

"Oh! You fool, what do you mean by *oh?*"

"*Didn't* you walk in before Quocks came?"

"But I'm speaking of now! It has been said that—when I made the observation, that if they were not married, they ought to be—I endeavoured to stab their reputation. Now, I'll prove that I endeavoured to do nothing of the sort."

"Do so."

"I'll prove it by logic, and I defy all the mathematicians in the habitable globe to knock it down. I'll prove it by the regular mathematical construction of the English language, and will any man tell me there's any constructed language in the universe more mathematically regular than that? I'll prove it in juxtaposition"——

"Well, prove it."

"Prove it! Well, just look you here, and if your ideas *can* fructify, let 'em. Just look at the grammatical character of the words: if they are not married, they ought to be. Isn't that a correct amalgamation?—and *being* amalgamated, what do the words mean? Is there any man in nature so lost to every sense of grammatical transubstantiation as not to see that they mean this, and nothing but this, that they ought to be married, if they are not?"

"But why ought they?"

"*Why* ought they! Isn't one a bachelor and the other a spinster? And is there any law in life to prohibit such a marriage? What would be said if Johnny Russell or Bobby Peel were to bring in a bill to render marriages of that sort illegal? Wouldn't it be kicked out of the House neck and crop? I said they ought to be married; and I say so still. I'll not flinch from what I said. I'm not ashamed of what I say. I'd say it just as soon before their faces as I would behind their backs. They *ought* to be married, and what objection can we have to such a marriage, if they like it? For my part, I think that they'd just suit each other."

"Ah!" exclaimed Pokey, "it won't do, you know. That's not what you meant."

"What do you mean by saying that's not what I meant? Can you tell the fructifications of my bosom? Can any man alive dive into another's heart, or see what's going on in another's private brain? It will take a wiser man than you, Pokey, to do it. I refer you to the words—if the words don't mean that, they mean nothing!"

"You shuffles," said Pokey.

"He always did shuffle," said Quocks.

"Shuffle!" exclaimed Obadiah, who was perfectly disgusted with Pokey's ingratitude. "You'd have shuffled through the world an ignoramus, if your weak ideas hadn't been fructified by me. What do you mean by shuffling?"

"Why, you've shuffled in this!" returned Pokey, who wasn't aware that Obadiah had done anything to his ideas, with the exception of confusing them occasionally. "I don't care a button about the words, I look at what you meant, and you meant this"——

"*We* know what he meant very well," observed Quocks; "and I'd strongly recommend him, if his ideas must 'fructify' on matters of this character, to keep the 'fructification' to himself. It may be true that his slanders are not of much importance, because no one who knows him believes a word he utters. Were he a man with any pretensions to respectability, the consequences might be serious as well to others as to himself; but he is not: he is at best but a half-witted butt, without a particle of manly pride about him."

"You're going it," exclaimed Obadiah. "Now, I daresay that you think I *care* a great deal about what you say, don't you?"

"If I thought that, I would, both for your own sake and that of society, say more: I would then take some pains to show you exactly what you are; but I know that you *don't* care—that you haven't the sense to care: if you had, you would scorn to go prowling about as you do, picking up loose scraps of slander to 'fructify;' chuckling over the misfortunes of your neighbours; magnifying their follies, and making those follies the bases of lies. I really don't know a more contemptible character than that of a lazy "——

"Do you mean to say that *I'm* lazy?"

"Lazy! Why, what do you do besides lounging about barbers' shops? You don't do twenty-four hours' work in a week. I have nothing, of course, to do with that; but when a man has a family, and squanders away, newsmongering, three-fourths of his time, when that time might be occupied in benefiting his family, what is he but a lazy man? I should be ashamed to lead such a life."

"Oh, don't you trouble your head about me."

"I don't *want* to trouble my head about you. I only want to show how much better it would be if you were not to trouble your head—such a head as it is—about others. Not that I imagine that I shall be able, by showing this, to do you any good—you're past that; you must talk, and I'm not at all surprised at your talking; all that I'm surprised at is, that you should still find people to listen to your talk. You *have* pretty nearly tired all the old ones out: Pokey, I believe, is the only one of the lot that will listen to you now, and the sooner *he* sends you to Coventry the better."

"Let him do it!" exclaimed Obadiah. "What do I care for Pokey? Who's Pokey placed in juxtaposition with me?"

Pokey, who didn't at all like this contemptuous observation, drank up his beer and departed; and as Quocks, who had already finished his, went with him, Obadiah was left to "fructify" alone.

CHAPTER XXIV.

LOVE.

DURING Sylvester's residence with Mr. Scholefield, his career as a somnambulist was checked, and as his history *as* a somnambulist is all that we have to contemplate, it will be necessary to leap over a space of five years, with a brief explanation of the means which induced the development of his somnambulism to cease, and a description, somewhat less brief, of an incident for which, perhaps, many will be quite unprepared.

And first with respect to the means by which his career as a somnambulist was checked. It has been seen that Mr.

Scholefield was an abstemious man; it has been stated that when he dined at the doctor's, he neither ate nor drank anything calculated to heat the blood or to produce any unnatural excitement; it will, therefore, be sufficient to add simply, that his arguments in favour of that practice were so strong and so convincing, that Sylvester adopted it at once; and having done so, he felt throughout the day so much lighter and more lively, that he adhered to it during the whole of the time he resided in Mr. Scholefield's house. It will, however, here be correct to observe that his adherence to this system must not be ascribed to any consciousness on his part of the cause of his having previously felt so languid—he had not even the most remote idea of the fact of his physical energies having been during the night exhausted: he attributed his gaiety and lightness of heart solely to the regimen he had adopted, and hence he continued to adhere to it firmly.

Now it happened that when Sylvester had been articled about twelve months, Mr. Scholefield was summoned to attend a female who was reported to be in the very last stage of consumption. He accordingly went, and was shown into a plain but clean and neatly-furnished room, in which he found a poor wasted, yet beautiful girl on a bed, near which her broken-hearted mother sat weeping.

The old lady rose as he entered, and tried to conceal her tears, but as the effort deprived her of the power to speak, he pressed her hand in silence and went to the bedside.

"My poor girl," said he, with a benevolent smile, on taking her hands, which were like gloved bones, "why, your eyes are bright and sparkling; you must not be in this state long."

"I feel," she observed faintly, "I feel that I should be *well* if I were not so weak. I have no pain—no absolute physical pain—and yet I am prostrated thus."

"Well, well," said he soothingly, as a deep sigh escaped her, "you must not be sad. We must hope for the best, and see what can be done. I will send you that which will raise your spirits; but your mind must be tranquil—you must be quite calm. In the morning I'll see you again."

He then gently pressed her thin, weak, fleshless hand, and, as she fervently breathed forth her thanks, he left her.

On leaving the room he was followed by her heart-stricken mother, who exclaimed, with an expression of anxiety which denoted the existence of those feelings which mothers only can experience—

"Pray, sir, tell me—*are* there any grounds for hope?—or will my poor dear child be lost to me for ever?"

"My dear lady," replied Mr. Scholefield, who, although he perceived clearly that the case was hopeless, felt perfectly justified in concealing the fact then, "when I call in the morning I shall be able to express a more decided opinion. For the present, be assured that there is no immediate danger."

The poor lady cherished the hope thus inspired, and, clasping her hands with deep fervour, thanked God.

"But," he added, "how long has your daughter been ill?"

"She has been sinking, sir, gradually for nearly twelve months."

"Has anything of very great importance ever occurred to her? Do you *know* of any circumstance at all calculated to prey upon her mind?"

"Alas! yes. I ascribe it all to that. She became, sir, about twelve months since, enamoured, deeply enamoured, of a gentleman—a medical student—who"——

"I perceive, my dear lady. I do not wish to pry into any private matter: that medical student, I perceive, was a villain."

"No, thank Heaven! She is virtuous, sir—pure as an angel! And he, I believe, was virtuous too. But having —I do not say intentionally—I do not believe that the slightest blame can attach to him—but having fascinated my dear child, she saw him no more."

"Was he aware of the fact of his having made this impression?"

"I think not: and even assuming that he was, he perhaps acted wisely in the view of the world, for he was young— very young; while my child was then in a position far, very far, below the sphere in which she had been accustomed to move."

"Did she write to him at all?"

"She, unfortunately, knew not where to write. She made every possible effort to ascertain—not with the view of being importunate, but merely in order to see him once more—but, alas! she could gain no intelligence of him. There was one student at the hospital who knew him; but although she applied to him frequently, all that she could learn from him was, that he had left. She then began to fade and pine, and has been pining ever since. She remained in the situation she occupied then until she became too weak to perform its duties, and now, sir, although once a lovely girl, she is as you have seen her."

"Did he leave her unkindly?"

"Unhappily, no, sir. Had he been unkind, her pride would have sustained her. But he was, on the contrary, most kind and courteous. You probably perceived that she wore bracelets. Those bracelets were his gift. She wears them constantly; she would not part with them for worlds!"

"I wish that I knew where to find him. You, of course, know his name?"

"His name we could *never* learn; my child never heard more than his Christian name mentioned."

"That's very unfortunate—very."

"I do believe, sir, that if she could see him once again, her recovery even now would be almost immediate."

"Well, then, let us hope that she will again see him."

"I fear that that is hopeless."

"Things apparently more impossible have occurred."

"Very true, sir; very true."

"Well, then, do not despair. Hope still, and conceal your distress as much as possible from her."

"I will do so," the poor lady exclaimed, as fresh tears gushed from her eyes; "as much as possible, I will."

Mr. Scholefield then promised to send to her immediately on his return, and to see her again in the morning, and having reassured her that there was no immediate danger, he left her re-inspired with hope.

During dinner that day, Mr. Scholefield alluded to this distressing case; merely stating, however, that the poor girl had formed a romantic attachment to a young man, whom she had since never seen, and that she was then in consequence pining away in a hopeless state of consumption. This statement, brief as it was, interested Sylvester deeply, and as he had never witnessed a case of the kind—as he had never seen the hectic flush, and the various other symptoms of approaching death, which are, in such cases, commonly developed—it was suggested by Mr. Scholefield—who was, at all times, anxious to advance Sylvester's professional knowledge—that, in the morning, they should visit the poor girl together.

In the morning they accordingly went, and, on entering the room, found the old lady much more tranquil; but the very instant Sylvester approached the bed, the poor girl started as if from a dream.

"Mother! mother!" she exclaimed; "look! *there!* Have I my senses still, or have I lost them? Is this a vision?—Sylvester!" she added, as he extended his hand, for, in an instant, he recognised Julia. "Oh, this is joy beyond expression," and, seizing his hand with all the energy at her command, she passionately kissed it, and wept.

"My poor girl," said Sylvester tenderly; and, while his eyes were filled with tears, her mother stood struck with amazement. "How is it with you?"

"Oh! I am happy now—quite—quite happy—Sylvester! Oh! how I have prayed to behold you once again. Blessed be God!" she added devoutly, "my prayers have been heard."

"And now," said Mr. Scholefield, having somewhat recovered from the state of surprise into which this unexpected scene had thrown him; "you and I must come at once to an understanding. I have," he added, with a smile which caused her to bless him, "I have brought him, whom I perceive you were rather anxious to see, with me; but, understand, I must bring him no more, unless you promise me faithfully that you will be henceforward calm."

"I do promise faithfully: I will be calm."

"I must not allow him to come here and throw you into this state of excitement, when my object is to keep you as tranquil as possible."

"I will be tranquil; indeed I will. I am not excited *now!* I am only happy."

"Very well; then he shall again come to see you."

"Heaven will bless you for this!" exclaimed Julia; and Mr. Scholefield and her mother retired to the window. "Sylvester!" she added, with a look of unspeakable fondness; "can you forgive me?"

"Forgive you, my poor girl, what have I to forgive?"

"My boldness; my forwardness."

"How can I forgive that of which I am unconscious?"

"You are kind," she replied. "But tell me, have you been well?—and happy?"

"I have; and sorry indeed am I to find that you have not."

"I have not been; but I am happy now, and hope to be soon again well. But you will not despise me? I cannot conceal from you that which I know that I ought to conceal. But, oh! how I have longed to see you. Do you remember that happy evening — the evening on which you gave me these?"

Sylvester, who then, for the first time, noticed the bracelets, replied that he did.

"You were smiling then," she continued; "why do you not now smile?"

Sylvester burst into tears.

"Do you weep for me?" she faintly inquired. "God bless you! Do you not think, then, that I shall recover?"

"Well," said Mr. Scholefield, coming forward, "we must now for the present leave you; but, remember, you must be quite calm."

"I will be calm—quite calm," replied Julia, who still held Sylvester's hand in hers; and when Mr. Scholefield was leaving the room, Sylvester said, "I will see you this evening."

"You will," she exclaimed, with an expression of ecstasy.

"I will."

She kissed his hand, and he left her happy.

On leaving the house, Sylvester explained to Mr. Scholefield the circumstances under which he had previously known her, and having related the history of the bracelets, and all that had been said of her by Tom, he earnestly inquired if her recovery were hopeless.

Mr. Scholefield replied that it was—quite hopeless. "She may," he added, "live four or five days longer; but your interview with her has, in all probability, exhausted nearly the whole of her remaining strength. Poor girl! I am, indeed, very sorry for her. She has been, it appears, the sole support of her mother; her death will break the old lady's heart."

"Do you think," inquired Sylvester cautiously, "do you think that they are in poverty now?"

"I should say, not in absolute *poverty*—that is to say, not in a state of actual destitution—but that they are poor, very poor, I've no doubt."

Sylvester was silent and thoughtful. He had in his desk a ten-pound note, and as he felt quite sure of being able to borrow another of Tom, he resolved on sending them twenty pounds, anonymously, in the course of the morning.

In pursuance of this resolution, he, on leaving Mr. Scholefield, called upon Tom, who was at that period preparing to pass the college.

"Tom," said he, "I want ten pounds. I wish you'd let me have it, till I can hear from my aunt!"

"Ted what!" cried Tom.

"Ten pounds."

"Is there such a sub id the world?"

"Why, it isn't a very enormous sum."

"I dod't thidk there is such a sub; *I* dever had such a sub id by possessiod. I should like to see the bad who has got ted poudds. There *was* a swell, and his dabe was Crœsus, who bight have had ted poudds by hib; but I dever yet heard of a Crœsus *secuddus*."

"Nay, but joking apart, Tom; *will* you let me have ten pounds for a few days?"

"By dear fellow, ask be for ted drops of blood, add I'll give 'eb to you freely; but what state of bide do you ibagide the old people would be id if they fadcied I had the sub of ted poudds by be? They have dever yet let be have such ad aboudt of buddy. Ted poudds! *Wouldd't* I have a flare-up with ted poudds!"

"Well," said Sylvester, "it's a matter of slight importance. I did want twenty, but as I've only ten, I must make ten do for to-day."

"Stop!" cried Tom; "a thought strikes be. Did you ever go to by udcle's?"

"No; I never knew that you had one."

"Greed, Syl; still extrebely greed. *I* dever saw hib; but all our fellows have; he is, I believe, dearly related to the lot. Dow, I tell you what it is, Syl, I haved't ted poudds, but I've a watch which did, I believe, originally belodg to by graddbother's graddfather's secodd wife's bother, add which I udderstadd is worth thirty. If, therefore, you thidk that we cad buster up courage edough to take this to the pawdbroker's, I've do doubt he'll ledd us the sub of ted poudds upod it."

"Oh, I've a watch too! But I don't know how to manage it."

T

"We'll badage it sobehow. Let's take theb both, add if bide isd't valuable edough, you kdow, he cad hold yours as well."

"Mine's worth more than twenty pounds."

"Well, but there's dothidg at all like beidg sure. Cobe alodg, add let's try our luck. I should like to see what sort of a swell this udiversal relatiod of madkide is."

They accordingly went to a pawnbroker's shop, and looked artfully in at the window for a time, and then walked on a little, and turned and returned, and examined the goods in the window again; and then anxiously looked up the street and then down, with the view of ascertaining if any one were watching them.

"Well," said Tom, at length, "shall we go id?"

"Why," returned Sylvester, "I don't at all like the idea. Suppose any one were to see us?"

"That would be awkward, certaidly. But bight they dot thidk that we wedt id to buy sobethidg?"

"Well, it is true they *might* think so. But really I don't at all fancy the thing."

"Well, I'll tell you what I'll do," said Tom. "Perhaps it doesd't look well for two fellows like us to go id together; I'll toss you for the chadce—such a chadce as it is: heads, I go id; tails, *you* go."

"Agreed," said Sylvester; and when they had removed from the window Tom tossed, and the result was a head.

"By usual luck," he exclaimed. "But dever bide, *I'll* go."

And he did go, boldly—up to the window; and stopped, and examined the little articles exhibited therein, and then went back to Sylvester fraught with an idea.

"Syl," said he, with a doubtful expression, "I say: will it look well, do you thidk, for wud fellow to go id with *two* watches?"

"Perhaps not," returned Sylvester; who began to wish that he hadn't embarked at all in this expedition.

"Who kdows," resumed Tom, "they *bay* thidk that I stole theb. I'll tell you what, Syl; let's go idto this public-house, add talk over the batter calbly."

Into the public-house they accordingly went; and when Sylvester had ordered a bottle of soda-water for himself, and Tom had called, of course, for a pot of porter, they sat down with the view of having a calm discussion on the intricate ramifications of the case.

"Dow," said Tom, "the questiod is, what's best to be dode? Add id the first place, what do you suggest?"

"Why, I think that we had better give it up," replied Sylvester.

"Give it up! Dever! We'll have the buddy. Stop a bidite," said he, as the waiter entered; "there, that'll do: we'll oped that. Dow," he added, having pulled out two-thirds of the porter, "I'b ready for adythidg id life. I'll tell you what I'll do; I'll go over with wud, add thed they cad have *do* suspiciod."

"Well, then, take mine," said Sylvester.

"Do, *that* wod't do. Suppose they ask if the watch is by owd? Dod't you see? I cad't say yes. Add if I were, add it should cobe to a search, add the officer were to fide adother watch id by pocket—but that I could leave here; yes, I bight do that; still, I'd better take my owd. I wudder what sort of questiods they usually ask. I'll bet ted to wud I'b bowled out."

"Then don't go."

"Dodt go! What are you talkidg about? What have I to fear? 'I wadt you to ledd he ted poudds upod this.' That's all I have to say: add a child could say that. I have seed childred frequedtly go id alode. If they should have ady doubt about the batter, I'll bridg theb over here. But thed it bight cobe to a pair of haddcuffs; we bight thed be barched off together on suspiciod."

"We had better give it up," said Sylvester. "You had better not go."

"Go! *I'll* go!" cried Tom valiantly; and having finished his porter, he left the room with the air of a man who fully expected to meet an enraged rhinoceros.

During his absence, Sylvester was filled with apprehension. He conceived that Tom *might* be suspected of dishonesty—that he *might* be detained—that he *might* be given into the custody of a policeman, and that the result would be a humiliating exposure. He tried to subdue the fears thus inspired, but as Tom was absent a very long time, they every moment acquired fresh strength.

At length, however, Tom returned, and on entering the room he dashed his hat upon the table, and exclaimed—

"It's of do use, Syl, I cad't do it! I did just dow work by-self up into a fit of desperatiod, but just as I was bakidg a rush id, a fellow cabe to the door with a ped behind his ear, add looked at be exactly as if he suspected that I was goidg to cut a pade of glass out of his widdow. Dow, I'll tell you what we'll do: I kdow a fellow who's up to everythidg of the sort; we'll go to his lodgidgs—*he'll* do it id a bobedt. Cobe alodg!"

"No," said Sylvester, "I shouldn't like that. Don't you think that the doctor would lend me ten pounds?"

"Id ad idstadt. I dever thought of that!—of course he would."

"I do not like to have it of Mr. Scholefield, because *he* would know at once what I wanted it for."

"Thed have it of the goverdor! Shall I ask hib for you?"

"No. I think it would look better for me to ask him myself."

"Very well; thed cobe alodg; we shall just about catch hib at hobe. I'd ask hib to ledd it to *be*, but that would be do go at all."

They then left the house, and as they returned to the doctor's residence, Sylvester said—"Have you seen Julia lately?"

"Do," replied Tom; "I've dot beed to the house for a lodg tibe. But I believe she has left. Ill health, I believe, was the cause of her leavidg. The last tibe I saw her—that was sobe bodths ago—she wadted to kdow where *you* lived, but, of course, I didd't feel at all justified id gividg her your address."

Sylvester was silent; and as the subject was not pursued by Tom, they returned in silence to the residence of the doctor, who was then in the library alone.

"You had better go id at wudce," said Tom. "I shall be id by study. Dod't leave, you kdow, without cobidg up."

Sylvester promised that he would not; and on going into the library was received by the doctor, as usual, with the utmost cordiality and kindness.

"Doctor," said he, "I have to ask you a favour. It happens that I want ten pounds until I receive a remittance from my aunt, which will be the day after to-morrow."

"Very good."

"Will you do me the favour to let me have it?"

"Of course! I am quite sure that the purpose for which you want it is a good one."

"It is. I do not like to ask Mr. Scholefield"——

"My good fellow, not another word. Here is a cheque for fifteen."

"Ten will be quite sufficient."

"I have written it now; and whenever you happen to want money, come at once to me."

He then inquired after Mr. Scholefield, and when he had made a few remarks having reference to professional matters, Sylvester withdrew, and went upstairs to Tom.

"Well," said Tom, "he let you have the buddy, of course?"

"In a moment," replied Sylvester. "I asked him for ten, and he gave me a check for fifteen."

"What ad out-add-out systeb that cheque systeb is. It saves a bad the trouble of puttidg his hadd idto his pocket, which is very addoyidg whed there's do buddy there. I dever wrote wud id by life. I should like to write a few. I'b sure it bust be a cobfort."

"When you know that they will be cashed."

"That's of course what I bead. If ady badker id dature would cash by cheques, I'd give hib add all his clerks twelve-bodths' hard labour."

"But you are not short of money, are you?"

"Dot a bit of it! I dod't *wadt* buch; but I'b dever without a sov. Whed I cobe dowd to wud that's the sigdal for actiod; I dever let 'eb rest till they bake it up five. Five's the *baxibub;* wud's the *bidibub;* but the goverdor owes me two, which I *cad't* get."

"He *owes* you two?"

"Of course. About twelvebodths ago a swell swiddled hib out of two—which two he said I hight get if I could; but I cad't fide the fellow—add as I therefore cad't get the buddy of hib, the goverdor owes it of course!"

"Well, if you can convince him that he owes it by such a line of logic as that, I have not the slightest doubt that he'll pay you."

"I expect he'll give it be wud of these days id a state of disgust, to get rid of the addoyadce. But I say, you'll stop add have a bit of ludch with be?"

"No; not this morning."

"I've got sohe *pribe* stout, add the bortal rebaids of a capital pie! Have a look at it."

"No, I *must* be off."

"Well, if you bust, why, you bust! But whederer you

wad't to go to by uncle's, you cad't do better thad take be with you. That's a dodge I *shad't* forget."

Sylvester smiled, and left him; and when he had got the cheque cashed, he enclosed the whole of the twenty-five pounds, with a delicate note, signed simply "*A Friend*," and privately sent it to Julia's mother.

In the evening — having previously intimated to Mr. Scholefield that he had promised to call upon Julia—he performed that promise, and the moment he entered the room, the old lady—who felt sure that the money had been sent by him—fell upon his neck, blessed him, and sobbed like a child.

On reaching the bed, he found Julia much weaker. Her eyes, indeed, flashed as she beheld him, and the blood rushed at once to her cheeks; but her glance soon changed to an inexpressive glare, and her cheeks became deadly pale.

"My dear girl," said Sylvester, perceiving at once that Mr. Scholefield's conjecture was correct: "I fear that you are not quite so well this evening?"

Julia had not the power to speak above a whisper, and that was too faint to be heard.

"But, come," resumed Sylvester tenderly; "you must not be sad. All may yet be well. Julia, I have come to sit with you—to converse with you, Julia."

Julia sighed, and slightly smiled, as she pressed his hand to her pallid lips.

"Julia," said Sylvester, after a pause, during which her eyes continued to be fixed upon him; "will you for a moment excuse me?"

Her lips moved, and Sylvester, on bending his ear to them, heard faintly the words, "You will not leave me long?"

"I will not be one moment," he replied, and, on leaving the room, he sent a man off to Mr. Scholefield, to request his immediate attendance.

On his return, he resumed his seat, in silence, by her side, and again took her weak hand, and met her fond gaze; and thus he continued to sit in silence until Mr. Scholefield arrived.

Mr. Scholefield, who, in a moment, saw how the case stood, gave Julia a few drops of wine, which, in some degree, revived her: and having instructed Sylvester what to do in an event which he clearly perceived to be inevitable, he sat for some time with the poor old lady—who was overwhelmed with grief, and whose heart was then ready to break—and when he had affectionately taken leave of Julia—as he felt, for the last time—he left them, with Sylvester's hand still clasped in hers.

It was then eight o'clock, and for nearly an hour Sylvester sat watching her, almost in silence, without perceiving the slightest change. About nine o'clock, however, she intimated a wish to have a little more wine, and—as Mr Scholefield had privately told him that whatever she wished for then she might have—Sylvester tenderly raised her head and gave her a few drops more.

Again she revived and was able to speak, although but in a whisper, and that so faint, that it could scarcely be said to have violated silence: still, finding that she had *this* power restored, she moved her lips slightly, and Sylvester listened.

"Sylvester," he heard her say, "I soon shall be no more. I feel that every hope of my recovery has fled: the only hope I cherish still is, that we may meet in heaven! God for ever bless you! I die happy, Sylvester—quite happy—now that you are near me! Pray for me, Sylvester—pray with me. Angels of light are waiting now to bear our prayers to heaven!"

Sylvester, who was deeply affected, knelt and prayed with fervour: her mother also knelt and prayed—and Julia ceased to breathe!

They were, however, for some time unconscious of this, for her eyes continued bright, and her features were unchanged, while she still pressed Sylvester's hand; but when they at length found that her spirit had fled, her poor, devoted, broken-hearted mother gave one convulsive shriek, and instantly fell upon the bed a corpse!

For some time Sylvester stood by the bed motionless. His faculties were paralysed. He seemed struck with horror! Eventually, however, he recovered himself, and summoned assistance from below.

The person who kept the house—a kind, honest, motherly creature—no sooner ascertained what had occurred, than she begged of him, as a favour, to remain—for she had heard from Julia's mother how kind he had been—until he had seen what property had been left.

To this Sylvester consented; and, at the earnest request

of this poor but honest woman, took charge of all the papers, money, and jewellery found.

"I feel that you will do all that is necessary," said Sylvester, "and be assured that you will not go unrewarded."

"I do not think of reward, sir," replied the good woman. "I *will*, sir, do all that is necessary, for I loved the young lady as if she had been my own child, and her mother I regarded as a sister."

"Those bracelets"—— said Sylvester.

"I have heard of them, sir; you wish them to remain on?"

"I do."

"They shall not be removed. Be assured that I will pay every possible attention."

"I feel assured that you will," said Sylvester, who left the house with a heavy heart, to explain at home all that had occurred.

Mr. Scholefield was not much surprised: he knew when he left the house that poor Julia could not live more than a few hours; and although he imagined that her mother might linger some days, he felt sure that her daughter's death would break her heart; but Mrs. Scholefield, who of course did not view it as he did, professionally—took the deepest possible interest in the case, and went with Sylvester in the morning to superintend the arrangements; and that day week poor Julia and her mother were—followed by Sylvester—borne to the grave.

CHAPTER XXV.

THE MAIDEN SPEECH IN PARLIAMENT.

HAVING related in the preceding chapter the only incident of importance connected with this history which occurred during Sylvester's residence with Mr. Scholefield, it will be necessary now to proceed from that period at which he passed with *éclat* both the college and the hall.

Finding a strict adherence to that regimen, to which he had been accustomed while under Mr. Scholefield's roof, now most inconvenient, he gradually reacquired the habit of living as those whom he visited lived; and as he did so his somnambulism—of which he was still unconscious—returned.

It did not, however, develop itself strongly at first; but by degrees he could eat, drink, walk, converse, read, write, compose, and translate with as much facility while asleep as he could when awake. It frequently puzzled him, when, on rising in the morning, he found a mass of matter on the table which had been composed by him in the course of the night; indeed, he had not left the house of Mr. Scholefield more than a month, when he discovered in one of his drawers an elaborate Treatise on the Functions of the Heart, of the composition of which he had no recollection, although it had been manifestly written by himself.

Nor was this all: essays and other articles, with which he occasionally furnished the various medical journals, were written during sleep; he had but to commence or think about one in the evening, no matter how difficult the subject, to find it completed in the morning when he rose.

These circumstances, constantly occurring as they did, engendered a peculiar species of superstition. He imagined that he was under the influence of genii, and this idea led him into abstruse speculations on supernatural influences in general; in which speculations, as a matter of gratitude, those genii rendered him some powerful assistance, but only, of course, when their slave was asleep.

He had, however, too much knowledge to progress in the black art to any great extent; his reasoning powers were too acute to allow him to embrace that pseudo science; still he felt involved in a mystery, the solution of which he held to be beyond all human power, and while with reason he annihilated the temples of the genii, he without reason clung to the ruins still.

But even then his somnambulism was not confined to his chambers. Sometimes he would walk when the moon was up with a lamp in his hand, which, although extinguished, he fancied illumined all around; sometimes he would rise about three o'clock, walk to the Serpentine fast asleep, bathe for an hour, dress himself, and then return to bed; and frequently, when he had been to a ball, would he return in an hour or two, recommence dancing, and stop till the last, while all whom he met, or with whom he conversed, were unconscious of the fact of his being asleep.

On one occasion four of his most esteemed friends called at his lodgings about five o'clock—the hour at which he invariably dined—and acted and talked precisely as if they had made up their minds to stop. He would, at any other time, have been very glad to see them; but, as he wanted his dinner, he felt their presence then to be extremely inconvenient, and soon began to feel most impatient for their departure. But they had not the slightest notion of starting—not they. There they were, and there they stuck, wondering what highly important personage had been invited to meet them, for they all felt that he must be a person of great distinction to induce Sylvester to keep them waiting so long.

"I say," inquired one of them, about six o'clock, "whom are you waiting for?"

"Whom am I waiting for!—no one," said Sylvester.

"Oh, thought you were waiting for some one."

"No. What induced you to think that I was?"

"I thought so merely because it's six o'clock—that's all."

"It is six," said Sylvester, looking at his watch, and, as he did so, he privately wished they'd be off; but of this they had not even the most remote idea, and their manifest tenacity to the place was, in his view, amazing. He couldn't understand it. They never called before at such an hour, nor had he ever known them to linger so long. Had one, or even two, of them dropped in upon him, he wouldn't have thought much about it; but the idea of four having called at the same time—and that, too, at *such* a time—certainly did strike him as being most strange.

Half-past six arrived, and there they were still—impatient but merry—hungry but gay—indulging in pointed but lively allusions to maiden dinners and wolfish guests, which, to Sylvester, were wholly incomprehensible.

"Is your *cook* ill, old fellow?" said one of them.

"Not that I'm aware of."

"I thought that she might have been seized with something suddenly."

"She may have been, for aught I know," said Sylvester, who joined in the general laugh. "I have not had the pleasure of either seeing her lately, or receiving anything from her."

They now thought that something must have occurred in the kitchen, and attributed Sylvester's obvious impatience to some peculiar species of domestic mortification. They therefore resolved on waiting till seven without making any further allusion to the subject; but before that hour had arrived, Sylvester—finding they *wouldn't* go—said boldly, " I'll tell you what, gentlemen, I *must* have my dinner ! "

" Do so, by all means," said one of them ; " oh, yes ; have it up at once."

Well. Sylvester certainly thought this cool ; but as it was then quite clear that they meant to see him eat it, he turned and rang the bell.

" Bring up the dinner," said he, when the servant entered.

" Here, sir ; in this room ? "

" Yes."

The servant looked, and frowned upon them all, which was, perhaps, but natural, seeing that cook had, for nearly two hours, been frowning upon her. She left the room, however, immediately ; and on her return laid the cloth for one ! The guests glanced at each other, as if they didn't understand this—nor did they ; but conceiving that the servant might feel confused, and that in her confusion she had become quite oblivious, they were silent. When, however, the girl—whom they now watched narrowly—brought up the tray, and placed on the table nothing but a small calf's tongue, and a couple of chickens done to rags, the case became, in their judgment, serious.

" I say, old fellow, how's this ? " said one of them ; " are you going to dine alone ? "

" Unless you'll have a cut in with me," replied Sylvester.

" A cut in ? What ! four or five fellows, as hungry as wolves, cut into a couple of chickens ! You know, I suppose, that we came to dine with you ? "

" Dine with me ! No ! Why didn't you tell me you were coming ? I'd no idea of it ! "

" Not after having invited us ? "

" What *do* you mean ? "

" Did you not send notes to all of us this morning, inviting us to dine with you at five ? "

" No ; certainly not ! "

" Well, but I received one."

" And so did I !—and I—and I ! " cried the rest.

"But not from me. Have you one of them with you?"

Their hands were in their pockets in an instant, but they found that not one of the notes had been brought.

"And have you been waiting all this time for dinner?"

"Of course."

"And I have been waiting for you to go! It's a hoax! But come along, we'll soon make it all right."

"Stop a minute," said one, "for I'm ready to drop!" And seizing a chicken, he *had* a "cut in." The rest followed his example, for their appetites were keen; and when they had managed to pick all the bones, which they did in the space of three minutes, Sylvester took them to the nearest hotel, and ordered the best dinner that could be served up at eight.

The "hoax," as they all now conceived it to be, was a source of much merriment during the evening. It gave a zest to the dinner, a zest to the wine, and a zest to every joke that was uttered. They enjoyed themselves exceedingly —infinitely more than they could otherwise have done; and on leaving, they all pronounced it to be the merriest evening they had ever spent.

It was about twelve when Sylvester returned to his lodgings, and in ten minutes after his return he was in bed and asleep. He had not, however, been asleep long, when— his imagination being somewhat heated by wine—he commenced dreaming; and as this led to results which will be anon explained, it will be as well for the dream itself to be at once related.

In the first place, then, he imagined himself a candidate for the representation of his native county. A requisition, signed by all the freeholders in the county save one, had been forwarded to him, and as he had therefore consented to stand, the whole of the scenes which are held to be inseparable from a contested election then passed in review before him. The formation of the committee—the preliminary meetings—the nomination—the election—the declaration—the chairing— and the ball, followed each other in rapid succession. He was returned, of course; for there was only one man who voted against him, and that was the other candidate, whom he challenged in consequence; fought with two pieces of ordnance carrying twenty-four pounders, and wounded in the ear; and having accomplished all this, came to town, where he then was engaged in the preparation of various highly important bills, which he intended to submit to the House without delay.

Having arrived at this interesting point, he imagined that that was the very day on which his presence in the House was expected, and as it soon came down to the hour at which two honourable members would be waiting to introduce him, he rose, and having dressed with care, walked down to the House, with one of his "bills"—which was, in reality, a "Treatise on the Ear"—under his arm.

This was about half-past twelve; for the whole of the dream had not occupied more than three minutes; and on reaching the House, into which he well knew the way, having been frequently under the gallery, he looked about the lobby for the honourable members whom he expected would be waiting to receive him; when, being unable to recognise them there, he walked boldly into the House, bowed to the Speaker, and took his seat.

The confident air with which he entered, would alone have been sufficient to disarm all suspicion of his being a stranger, if even any such suspicion had been excited; but as it occurred just after a general election, when a host of new members are almost invariably returned, the doorkeepers thought of course that he was one of them.

Nor did the members themselves for a moment suspect that he was not; in fact, the idea of his being an intruder, never occurred to any one of them. They all thought that of course he was one of the new members; and being interested in his appearance, inquired anxiously of each other who he was.

Sylvester, however, took no notice of them; that is to say, individually; he viewed them only in the mass: his attention was fixed upon those who addressed the House; the arguments adduced by some of whom he rose to answer, but being unable to catch the Speaker's eye, others followed, and he resumed his seat.

The question before the House on that occasion had reference to the practice of baking the dinners of the poor on the Sunday, and Sylvester felt disgusted with the wild fanaticism by which the speeches of some of the opponents of that practice were characterised. It was hence that he rose to reply to them, and was sorry when he found himself compelled to resume his seat. He was still, however, on the *qui vive;* and as the honourable member who was then speaking was the most malignant, bigoted, superficial, self-sufficient, persecuting, narrow-minded Puritan of them all, the very moment he had finished, Sylvester, fired with indignation, started up, caught the eye of the Speaker, and commenced.

He was, however, for a moment compelled to pause; for the House, as a matter of courtesy, cheered him; and when the cheering had subsided into the most profound silence, he felt himself much more calm, and said—

"Sir,—In every society, and in every circle, in every house, institution, or assembly, in which religious enthusiasm has been tolerated, it has engendered dissensions, bitterness, heart-burnings, and hatred—severed friendships, subdued affections, destroyed brotherly love and sympathy—converted harmony into discord, happiness into misery, and filled the mind in which sweet peace reigned, with fearful apprehensions. (Cheers.) Sir, religious enthusiasm, as it is called, but which I call fanaticism, is as distinct from religion itself, as intolerance is from charity, as humility is from pride, as meekness is from arrogance, or as Christian forbearance is from cruel persecution. Its essence is tyranny; its history has been written in blood. Ignorance is one of its chief characteristics, and even where the germs of genius have struck root in the soil, it has sprung up, and waved and bloomed but to be blasted. Its presumption shocks heaven. It would impiously wrest the sword of Justice, and the sceptre of Mercy, from the hands of the Eternal God. (Great sensation.) To the advancement of human knowledge it has been opposed; to the progress of science it has ever been a bitter foe. The pretence of the Puritans is, and always has been, that they fear that science will compass the destruction of religion! Science compass the destruction of religion! It is false that they have any such fear; and if it were true, the inspiration of that fear is of itself impious. Religion derives its light from truth, even as the moon derives her lustre from the sun. It is based upon truth, and truth is eternal:

> 'The stars shall fade away, the sun himself
> Grow dim with age, and Nature sink in years;
> But *Truth* shall flourish in immortal youth,
> Unhurt amidst the war of elements,
> The wreck of matter, and the crash of worlds.'

No! (continued Sylvester, when the cheering had subsided).

It is not that they fear the destruction of religion; they are apprehensive only of the destruction of that fanaticism which stands between darkness and light. It therefore behoves us, as the chosen representatives of the people, whose morality and whose happiness it is our duty to promote, it behoves us, I say, when we see this religious enthusiasm, or rather this fanaticism, thus endeavouring to creep in here, to repudiate it *in limine*. (Cheers.) They who are anxious to introduce it may be pure—I say that they may be—I do not know that they are not; but this I know, there's nothing looks so much like a good shilling as a bad one. (Loud laughter.) Let us throw out at once this fanatical bill; let us crush this and every other attempt to circumscribe the already too limited comforts of the poor, and instead of sowing religious dissensions among the people, creating discord, and inspiring them with hatred of each other; let us legislate with a view to promote the cultivation of those kindly, beautiful, generous, philanthropic feelings which impart a zest to life, and which bind man to man."

At the conclusion of this speech, which was hailed with loud cheers, and which really was delivered with much point and energy, Sylvester at once resumed his seat; but while the members around him were crying—"Who is he?" in vain—for none could tell them—he rose and left the House.

CHAPTER XXVI.

THE ACCUSATION.

In the morning, while at breakfast, the eye of Sylvester rested upon the speech which he himself had delivered, and which he found ascribed to "An Hon. Member." He was struck with the speech; not because it developed any extraordinary talent, but because the words employed were those which he had been in the habit of employing, while the sentences were of his own construction. No man, perhaps, ever was, or ever will be, able to pass a speech of his own unnoticed. Both in speaking and writing, every man has a peculiar style—a style, of which the peculiarity of it cannot be at once perceived by others, is very soon discovered by himself. Hence, though unconscious of its being his own, Sylvester dwelt upon this speech, notwithstanding it was but an outline of the question at issue—an outline which left the filling up to the imagination. Still it is questionable whether even this piece of declamation could have been delivered by him in the House when awake. Had he been in reality a member—albeit he might have felt equally indignant at the mode in which the subject was discussed—his calm, retiring, diffident nature would, in all probability, have prompted him to be silent; but, while asleep, every feeling, every idea of fear, was absent; he experienced no nervousness, no trepidation; whatever his imagination suggested, he did, regardless of all unfavourable consequences, seeing that Danger never presented itself then to his view.

Having read this speech again and again—suggesting improvements as he proceeded, precisely as if he had been conscious of its being his own—he was amazed by the sudden arrival of Mr. Scholefield, whose countenance denoted the most painful anxiety.

"Good God!" he exclaimed—"Sylvester, what have you been doing?"

"Doing?" echoed Sylvester, with an expression of wonder. "Explain."

"Where were you last night—or rather this morning?"

"Last night I was at the hotel just above, with some friends."

"At what time did you leave those friends?"

"About twelve o'clock."

"Well, and where did you go then?"

"Where did I go. I came home and went to bed."

"Immediately?"

"Immediately."

"Sylvester," said Mr. Scholefield, with deep emotion, "confide in me. Disguise nothing from me. I have," he added, as tears sprang into his eyes—"I have towards you the feelings of a father."

"Why, how is this?" interrupted Sylvester. "What is the meaning of it all?"

"Sylvester, you have known me sufficiently long, I hope, to know that I am your friend; therefore conceal nothing from me."

"What have I to conceal? I am perfectly unconscious of

having done anything which renders concealment necessary, or even expedient."

"*Did* you not visit Lady Julian last night?"

"Most certainly not. I have not seen Lady Julian since I left you."

"What! were you not there until three o'clock this morning?"

"There!—where?"

"At Sir Charles's house."

"No."

"Sylvester," resumed Mr. Scholefield solemnly, "Sir Charles himself, on his return at that hour, saw you pass out at the garden-gate."

"No such thing!" exclaimed Sylvester indignantly.

"He declares it to be a fact."

"Then he declares that which is false."

"But Thompson, his butler, saw you too."

"Neither of them saw me. Neither could have seen me, for I was not there."

"Sylvester, their evidence is strong, and, I fear, too conclusive. Thompson undertakes to swear that he saw you coming from the ante-room which leads to Lady Julian's chamber."

"He does!"

"He does; and is, moreover, prepared to swear that he let you out. His statement is this: that being anxious to see the butler at the next house, he went and conversed with him, until he heard Sir Charles's carriage approaching; that he instantly returned, and on his return, found the door as he had left it, slightly open; that he then closed the door, until the carriage should be announced, and having occasion to go upstairs, saw you coming from the ante-room alone; and that on seeing you he descended and let you out, just as the carriage drew up to the gate."

"It is false! every word of it! utterly false."

"He declares every word of it to be true! He also declares that he should have spoken to you had he not felt that one of the other servants had let you in. In fact, having seen you there so frequently, and at almost all hours, both with me and alone, I don't suppose the idea of there being any impropriety in the visit for a moment occurred to him."

"Well, but why did not Sir Charles himself speak?"

"He did do so: at least, he says that he called to you before he could alight, and that you bowed and passed on; when, fearing that Lady Julian—who is in a delicate state still—had had a relapse, he went immediately up to her chamber, and had she not at once denied that you had been there, no more would have been thought of the matter."

"She was justified in denying it! She was bound to deny it! I had not been there. If I had, be assured that to *you* I would, under existing circumstances, confess it."

"I *thought* that you would!"

"And think so still. Either Sir Charles and his butler have been grossly mistaken, or they have conspired to blast her reputation and mine."

"That they have both been mistaken is certainly possible; but in the possibility of Sir Charles having entered into any such conspiracy I cannot believe. I know him to be devotedly attached to his wife. I have known him privately, and under almost every variety of circumstances, for years, and if any man *can* be said to know another's heart, I know his. No, Sylvester: be assured that he is incapable of entering into such conspiracy."

"What then is to be thought of it? He knows me well! I am perfectly well known to them both! And is it not almost inconceivable that either of them could, under the circumstances, have mistaken any one else for me?"

"It does *indeed* appear to be almost inconceivable."

"Well!" exclaimed Sylvester, "the thing begins to assume a serious aspect!"

"Serious! I contemplate the consequences with feelings of horror. Unless you can break down the evidence against you, your death may be the immediate result; and failing that, your ruin as a professional man will be inevitable. Sir Charles is in a state of mind bordering upon madness. He has ever since been raving for revenge. He cast Lady Julian off instantly; and, but for the interposition of the servants, would have killed her; and now he has sent a friend to you to demand immediate satisfaction."

"Is it possible?"

"That friend is now in the room adjoining, where, as he called upon me first, not knowing your address, I begged of him to remain until I had seen you."

"Well," said Sylvester thoughtfully, "the thing appears

to be coming to a crisis! But, be assured of this, that I was *not* there. Will you," he added calmly, "do me the favour to introduce him?"

Mr. Scholefield, with an expression of sorrow, then rose and left the room, and, having been absent for a moment, returned with Sir William D'Almaine.

"This," said Sir William, on taking a seat, "is indeed a most unhappy affair; but as I can have no desire to harrow your feelings, I will, if you will favour me with the name of a friend, go immediately and consult him."

"Sir William," returned Sylvester, "Sir Charles is mistaken. He imagines that I was at his house last night, or rather this morning. I was *not*."

"You were not! Do you intend, then, as a defence, to adopt a denial?"

"I do; and, in doing so, defend myself with truth."

"Well, but Sir Charles himself saw you, and so did his butler."

"It is a mistake. They did not see *me*."

"Oh, that will not do at all. Sir Charles assures me, upon his honour, that he saw you, and I am, of course, bound to believe him."

"You may perhaps believe that which he himself believes; but I deny that you are *bound* to adopt the belief of any man."

"This is not belief, merely; he *knows* that you were there."

"How is it possible for you to know that?"

"He declares that you were, upon his honour."

"And I, upon my honour, declare that I was not."

"Equivocation, you must allow me to observe, in affairs of this kind, will not do."

"I scorn equivocation, and despise the man who is mean enough to have recourse to it. I state upon my honour that I was not there, and to that statement—based, as it is, upon truth—I will adhere, let the consequences be what they may."

"Pardon me. You are a young man, and therefore you will, perhaps, allow me to observe, that in cases of this description you have but one course to pursue."

"I am aware of it. I *have* but one course to pursue, and that is the course of truth, which I will pursue."

"Then am I to understand distinctly that you refuse to refer me to a friend?"

"No, certainly not; I refer you at once to Sir Charles."

"Ay, but that is a most extraordinary reference."

"This proceeding appears to me to be extraordinary altogether. I refer you to him; consult him, and I will at that consultation be present."

"That, I apprehend, sir, would not be quite safe."

"Not safe! Why not? What have I to fear, conscious, as I am, of my own integrity? I will meet him with all the confidence truth can inspire, and I feel that my presence will induce the conviction that he has been mistaken."

"Sylvester," calmly interposed Mr. Scholefield, "allow me to suggest that you had better depute me to see Sir Charles, and explain to him the feelings to which you have given such earnest expression."

"Mr. Scholefield," returned Sylvester, "I have, as I believe you are aware, been always anxious to adopt any suggestion of yours; but I submit—this being a matter of professional life or death to me—that I ought to see Sir Charles, and explain to him *myself* that he is labouring under a most serious mistake."

"Well," replied Mr. Scholefield, "I can have no objection to your seeing him."

"I fear," observed Sir William, "that he is not now in a fit state to view the matter calmly."

"I am sure," said Sylvester, "that when Sir Charles sees me, he will be at once satisfied that I am not the man."

"Well," said Sir William, who really began to think that Sir Charles must have been mistaken, "if that be the case, why, by all means come with me. Mr. Scholefield perhaps will accompany us?"

"I will do so with pleasure," replied Mr. Scholefield; and without loss of time they left Sylvester's chambers, and proceeded to the house of Sir Charles.

"Now," said Sir William, on their arrival, "I think that Mr. Scholefield and I had better go up first, and soothe Sir Charles, if possible."

Sylvester did not object to this, and they accordingly left him in one of the parlours; but the moment they had explained to Sir Charles that Sylvester solemnly denied the accusation, and that he had come expressly to deny it in person,

Sir Charles rushed below, entered the room in which Sylvester had been left, and seizing him by the throat, would have strangled him, but for the prompt interference of Mr. Scholefield, who, suspecting his object, had followed him on the instant.

"Mean, base, cowardly, contemptible liar!" exclaimed Sir Charles, absolutely foaming with rage. "If you have not the courage to *fight* with me, I'll ruin you—ruin you—ruin you for ever."

"I'll not be thus insulted with impunity," cried Sylvester. "The accusation is false."

"What!" exclaimed Sir Charles, seizing the poker on the instant—"what!"

Sylvester was about to confront him, when Mr. Scholefield hurried him from the room, and when he had given his card to Sir William, with the name of Mr. Scholefield as his friend, he left the house, solemnly and most indignantly declaring his innocence of the charge.

CHAPTER XXVII.

THE MEETING.

SYLVESTER, on leaving the house of Sir Charles with mingled feelings of indignation and alarm, proceeded at once to the residence of Mr. Scholefield, with the view of awaiting his return. He knew not of course what would be the result; but having deputed Mr. Scholefield to act as his friend, and feeling prohibited from taking any step without his direct sanction, he summoned all the patience at his command, and took a seat in the surgery alone.

While he was here, tortured with anxiety and brooding over the probable consequences of that which he felt of course conscious of being a mistake, Mr. Scholefield, whose apprehensions were even stronger than those of Sylvester, being determined if possible to ascertain the whole truth, and having learned that Lady Julian was at the house of her father, went, in order to have an interview with her, unknown to Sir Charles and D'Almaine.

On his arrival, he found her father in a dreadful state of excitement and somewhat uncourteous, conceiving, as he did, that a message had come from Sir Charles.

"What is your object?" he demanded, when Mr. Scholefield had inquired if he could see Lady Julian. "Why do you wish to see her? What have you to communicate? By whom were you commissioned to come? My daughter is innocent! Sir Charles shall know to his cost that she is innocent. I'd stake my life upon her word. If, therefore, you are charged with any insulting or humiliating message, she is not to be seen. I'll not have her insulted: I'll not have her humiliated. She is as virtuous now that she has *returned* to her father's house, as she was when she left it. Sir Charles, by whom I presume you have been sent"——

"General Lloyd," calmly interrupted Mr. Scholefield, "I have not been sent by Sir Charles."

"Do you come then in the character of a mediator?"

"No. My object is to have an assurance from Lady Julian that Mr. Sound was not the gentleman whom Sir Charles saw."

"Then you assume that she must have been visited by some one?"

"I merely assume that Sir Charles must have seen some one."

"Assuming that, does it follow that she knows whom he saw?"

"Not necessarily; but"——

"Sir, she knows nothing whatever about it; nor do I believe that he saw any one at all. It is a trick, sir—a conspiracy—an infamous conspiracy. But *I'll* sift the matter; I'll get to the bottom of it. He shall not with impunity blast the reputation of my daughter."

"General Lloyd, I came here with no other view than that of ascertaining if this young man—whom I regard as a son, and upon whose honour I have always placed the most perfect reliance—has been seen by Lady Julian since he left me. I am aware of its being an extremely delicate question, under the circumstances, to put to Lady Julian"——

"Not at all—not at all. If she has not, she will say so; if she has, she will declare it."

"That is my only object in seeking an interview with her."

"Very well."

"I feel that you will appreciate my anxiety, when I explain to you that this young man's very existence is at stake."

"Has Sir Charles called him out, then?"

"He has."

"And does he intend to go?"

"I see no alternative."

"The meeting *must not* take place. If Sir Charles should happen to fall, the reputation of my daughter will be for ever lost! It must by some means be prevented."

"I am most anxious to prevent it; but how can it be done?"

"Who is his friend?"

"Sir William D'Almaine."

"But the friend of the accused?"

"He has referred them to me."

"Good. You are anxious to prevent it. You pledge me your honour that you wish to prevent it?"

"I do."

"Very good. Then it shall be done. Continue to act. I'll take care that *you* are not compromised. Continue to act. Under no other circumstances would I interfere, but in this case I feel bound to do so. And now come and speak to my daughter."

The general then led the way into the drawing-room, and on finding Lady Julian in tears, he exclaimed—

"Are you my daughter, Louise, or are you not? Are you innocent, or are you not? If you are, act like the daughter of a soldier, and let us have no more tears."

Lady Julian seized the hand of Mr. Scholefield, and sobbed bitterly.

"Louise!" shouted the general, "is this the way to repel the attacks of an enemy?"

"Mr. Scholefield is no enemy, father," she replied.

"I didn't say that he was. If he had been, I shouldn't have brought him up here. But be firm. Be a woman. Don't act like a child. Mr. Scholefield wants to know whether you have or have not seen that young fellow since —since when?"

"Since he left me," said Mr. Scholefield. "You remember when he left me?"

"I do, perfectly," replied Lady Julian; "I have *not* seen him since."

"Neither last night nor at any other time?"

"Neither last night nor at any other time since he came with Mr. Scholefield."

"Very well," replied the general; "*that* point's settled. Is there any other question you wish to have answered?"

"My object," replied Mr. Scholefield, "was merely to ascertain that fact. Of course," he added, turning to Lady Julian, "you have no idea whom Sir Charles could have seen?"

"I have not, indeed."

"How should you have?" interposed the general. "You were in bed, were you not?"

"Yes; and had been asleep, but awoke just before Sir Charles returned. But what does he say, Mr. Scholefield? You have seen him, of course?"

"I have but just left him."

"Is he still labouring under this cruel delusion?"

"He appears to be very much excited."

"Of course!" cried the general. "He *appears* to be excited! That's an indispensable part of the plan."

"You wrong him, father: be assured that you wrong him. This is no *plan* of his. I feel that he is incapable of any such meanness."

"Of course you do. I'm aware of that. And were he to crush you, you'd feel so still. You were a fool to marry him; and I was a fool to consent to the match. We're a couple of fools, and as fools he wishes to treat us. However, we shall see: we shall see about that: we shall *see!* We are not to be struck down so easily as he imagines. Mr. Scholefield, a word or two with you, alone."

"You will call and see us?" exclaimed Lady Julian, seizing the hand of Mr. Scholefield, as he rose. "You will not believe that I'm so guilty a creature. I am innocent! indeed, indeed, I am innocent."

"There, there!" cried the general; "that will do; that will do. Don't be a fool!" he added, kissing her affectionately, as the tears sprang to his eyes. "There: now be calm— quite calm: let us have no more of this."

Lady Julian, as they left the room, sank upon the couch, and when her maid had been summoned, they returned to the parlour.

"I was told how it would be," said the general; "I was warned long ago."

"Warned of what?"

"Of jealousy being the fruit of the match. If I had fifty daughters, and they were all as ugly as the devil, I'd never again consent to the marriage of any one of them with any man twenty years older than herself. Still I thought that Julian was really a man of honour."

"And I think that he is so still. That he has hitherto loved Lady Julian fondly, I have had opportunities of knowing."

"Well!" exclaimed the general, "we shall see! I'll go to him as soon as I feel fit to go. I'm only waiting until I get cool. It's of no use going to a man in a rage. But now, as regards this challenge. Will you promise to communicate to me the time and place of meeting?"

"I will."

"That is all I require. This you promise, upon your honour as a gentleman?"

"I do."

"Very good. That's settled. Let the affair go on. I shall hear from you in the course of the day?"

"You shall."

"No one shall ever know from me how I obtained the information, nor from whom."

"I depend, of course, upon your secrecy."

"You may do so with confidence. Until this matter has been satisfactorily cleared up, I would not have Julian fall for the world. Fix any time you like, but let me know."

"That there may be no mistake, I will see you myself."

"That's better! Now, mind, I depend upon you."

"And I depend upon you: for I would not, on any account, have that young man injured."

Mr. Scholefield then left, and as he felt that the contemplated meeting would be harmless, his mind was more at ease, although he was still apprehensive that the consequences to Sylvester would be, in a professional point of view, ruinous. Hoping, however, that these consequences might yet be averted, he hastened home, but before he arrived, Sylvester —whose anxiety had so much increased, that he found it impossible to remain there alone—had left, with the view of calling upon Tom, having previously written a note to Mr. Scholefield, stating where he was to be found.

At this period Tom was in practice for himself; and that practice, moreover, was extensive: for, notwithstanding he had the same peculiarity of pronunciation as before, he had a high reputation for skill—a reputation which he had, by the legitimate exercise of his talents, acquired, and which experience and constant study enabled him to sustain.

"What's the batter?" he exclaimed, as Sylvester entered his library; "why are you thus excited? Has adythidg very bobedtous occurred?"

"Yes," replied Sylvester; "I have been drawn into a mess."

"A bess! Well, well, sit dowd add be calb; add let's see if we cad't draw you out of it. Dow, thed, what is its dature?"

"You know Sir Charles Julian?"

"Yes."

"He declares that he saw me leave his house about three o'clock this morning."

"Well!"

"And his butler declares—and is, moreover, prepared to swear—that he saw me at that hour absolutely coming from Lady Julian's chamber!"

"I say, old fellow," said Tom, shaking his head significantly; "a bedical bad, too!—a bedical bad!"

"But it was not *me* whom they saw!"

"It was dot?"

"No: upon my honour!"

"That's a blessidg. Where were you at that tibe?"

"In bed."

"Cad you prove that you were?"

"I can prove that I went home at twelve."

"That's sobethidg, certaidly; but that's dot edough."

"It's impossible for me to prove that I was in bed at three."

"Which is awkward, very awkward. Well," he added, after a pause, "what has beed dode?"

"In the first place he has cast Lady Julian off, and in the next he has sent me a challenge."

"Well! That's doidg busidess. Do you bead to go out?"

"I have left the affair entirely in the hands of Mr. Scholefield."

"Very good; add what does *he* bead to do?"

"I've not seen him since I left him with Sir Charles."

"Do you bead to say that *you* have beed to speak to Sir Charles?"

"I went in order to convince him that I was not the man; but the moment he saw me he seized me by the throat, and tried to strangle me."

"He did! Well, id that case, Syl, out you *bust* go! I dod't buch adbire this bode of settlidg batters; but as it is the odly bode prescribed by society, society bust establish adother before it cad expect that which is dow in existedce to be repudiated. But whed are you goidg to see Scholefield agaid?"

"I expected to see him an hour ago. I waited at his house till I was tired of waiting, and then left a note stating that I should be here."

"Well, old boy, you bust keep up your spirits! Let's have a glass of wide od the stredgth of it."

"There he is," exclaimed Sylvester, on hearing a knock.

"That's the goverdor," said Tom. "That's his kdock for a thousadd. Dow the questiod is, will it be wise to explaid all to hib?"

"Why will it not?" demanded Sylvester.

"Why, he has a thorough hatred of the practice of duellidg; he holds it id utter abhorredce; add were it to cobe to his kdowledge that you had beed called out, I do believe that he would idduce you to suffer ady iddigdity rather thad go. The questiod therefore is, shall we tell hib or dot?"

Before Sylvester had time to answer this question, the appearance of the doctor, with Mr. Scholefield, sufficiently proved it to be unnecessary, for he at once took Sylvester by the hand, and enjoined him to be tranquil and firm. "I am," he added, "strongly opposed to this practice; but, under existing circumstances, the challenge must be accepted. We are all friends here; but, of course, not a syllable must be said on the subject to any other party. I shall see you again in a few minutes. Do not leave till I return."

"Well," said Tom, as the doctor left the room with Mr. Scholefield; "if ady bad had sword that the goverdor would, udder ady circubstadces, sadctiod the acceptadce of a challedge,

I should have said that that bad had cobbitted perjury. Why, he has heretofore dedoudced the practice of duellidg vehebedtly, as a barbarous, brutal, cowardly, cold-blooded practice. I have heard hib agaid add agaid codtedd that every bad who happeded to kill adother id a duel, whether he idtedded to do so or dot, was a burderer. I'll dever applaud hib for codsistedcy agaid. But I say, old fellow, whed does the thidg cobe off?"

"I know nothing about the arrangements."

"Well, but dod't you kdow where you are to beet?"

"I've not the slightest idea. Mr. Scholefield has, on my part, the entire arrangement of the affair: beyond that I know nothing."

The doctor and Mr. Scholefield then returned to the library, and when Tom—who entertained the kindliest feelings towards Sylvester, and who had made up his mind to embrace the earliest opportunity of giving information—had been taken aside, the doctor communicated something which induced him to abandon the course he had meant to pursue.

"You will dine with me to-day?" observed the doctor, addressing Sylvester.

"I had much rather not. I'd rather dine alone. I do not feel that I am a coward; but I am of course thoughtful. I have, moreover, a letter or two to write."

"Write theb here, add dide with be thed," said Tom.

"Dine where you please," interposed Mr. Scholefield; "only let me know where I can find you."

"I will remain here then. You will find me here. I'll not leave the house till you return."

"Very well," said Mr. Scholefield. "Then that's understood;" and, on leaving the house with the doctor, he proceeded to keep his engagement with Sir William D'Almaine.

"I don't think," observed Sylvester, on being left with Tom, "that society has any right to place a man in this position. It appears to me to be dreadful, that the life of one man should be thus coolly staked against that of another. Life against life! and with it all earthly hopes, prospects, and affections! Henceforth, be the result of this affair what it may, I'll never either give or accept a challenge. Were I guilty of the offence with which I am charged, I should not of course have the slightest reason to complain—although that would be, in effect, placing the accuser on the same footing as the accused: subjecting the man who has been injured to the same consequences as the man by whom the injury has been inflicted—but, as I am innocent, I do think it monstrous that society should force me to peril my life for the satisfaction of him by whom I have been falsely accused."

"Society does dot absolutely force you," said Tom.

"Its influence has precisely that effect. Were I not to go out, it would denounce me as a coward."

"Still it leaves you free to choose the alterdative."

"And a pretty alternative it is."

"The paid idflicted by society's cedsure—add bore especially the cedsure of that portiod of society who take ibbediate cogdisadce of battles of this descriptiod—depedds, id a great degree, upod a bad's susceptibility. Sobe there are who despise it; add I dod't kdow but such bed display as buch courage as they do by whob it is feared."

"But a man in society—unless, indeed, he be independent of society—must go with society's stream. If he attempt to stem the tide thus established, he may struggle and struggle, and with all his struggling, be scarcely able to keep up to the point from which he started: while he who contentedly goes with the tide, glides smoothly along without an effort."

"That's true, Syl, as far as it goes; certaidly they who go with the tide fide it the *easiest* way to get alodg, but it is extrebely questiodable whether it be at all tibes the wisest. Prejudices are to be reboved, for exabple, odly by oppositiod; frob oppositiod the whole of our great add glorious schebes, both political add social, have sprudg; oppositiod is the gerb of ibprovebedt; we bust have beed id a state of igdoradce the bost profoudd had there beed do such thidg as oppositiod. It is easier, doubtless, to go with the tide thad to oppose it; but our object should be to divert the streab whed we fide that its course is perdicious."

"But I am not in a position to turn the stream now against me."

"Do bad alive probably *could* do so alode. He bust, to be successful, have the idfluedce add the exabple of a dubber to back hib."

"Do you wish me, iu this case, to be one of that number?"

"Why, suppose that you were dow to leave towd"——

"Had I *fifty* lives, and had to peril them all, I wouldn't do it."

"It was dot by idtedtiod to advise you to do it; I berely said *suppose* you were dow to leave towd, what"——

"Nothing could justify such a step now. Independently of compromising one of my best friends, I should be for ever branded as a coward. No! be the result what it may, I'll go through it."

"Well," said Tom, whose sole object in discussing this subject was to prove that Sylvester in reality possessed that firmness for which he had previously given him credit, "if that be your fixed deterbidatiod, we'll say do bore about it. I'll dow, for a short tibe, leave you. You have letters to write, add I've a call or two to bake; I shall dot be gode bore thad ad hour."

"Tom," said Sylvester, taking him by the hand, "I have one request to make; it is this: that before you go out, you will pledge me your honour that you will give information of this affair to no one. I ought not, I know, to have named the subject even to you; but, remember, I have done so in the most perfect confidence."

Tom pressed his hand warmly and smiled, and having given the required pledge, left him.

Sylvester then sat down calmly to write an affectionate letter to Aunt Eleanor, to be delivered to her only in the event of his falling; and while he was thus engaged, Mr. Scholefield and Sir William were settling the preliminaries of the meeting.

The general was also at this time engaged. He had, with the view of getting "cool," been running up and down stairs, pacing the rooms with extraordinary rapidity, and hurling fierce denunciations at the head of him whom he imagined had conspired to blast the reputation of his daughter; and when by these vehement means he had become, in his judgment, *sufficiently* "cool," he started off to have an interview with Sir Charles, in a state of intense perspiration.

On his arrival, Sir Charles was "not at home." He had given instructions to be denied to all save Sir William D'Almaine. But when the porter told the general that Sir Charles was not at home, the general *looked* at the fellow, and asked him if he knew who he was. "Attention!" he shouted, as the porter muttered something in reply to him—"announce me!" And the porter, who in this his extremity scarcely knew how to act, did announce him, and the general was eventually shown up.

As he entered the room in which Sir Charles, who was still much excited, had been anxiously awaiting Sir William's return, the general walked stiffly up to the table, and, on taking a chair, sat immediately opposite Sir Charles, and looked at him for a moment with an expression of severity.

"Sir Charles—Sir Charles Julian!" said he, at length, "I am here—calm and cool as you may perceive—to demand an explanation."

"General," returned Sir Charles, more in sorrow than in anger, "I have nothing to explain—*nothing* more than that which, I presume, you already know. That your daughter has dishonoured me, is lamentable, but true."

"It is false, sir—atrociously false!"

"Could I reasonably entertain a *doubt* upon the subject, I would abandon every feeling of suspicion at once; but as her paramour was actually seen coming from her chamber: as my man let him out; and as I myself saw him leave the house as I approached it, *doubt* is impossible."

"I don't believe a word of it—not a single word."

"Of what?"

"Of what! Why, of the statement you have made with the view of justifying your abandonment of my daughter."

Sir Charles rang the bell, and when the servant appeared, he ordered Thompson up immediately.

"I'll prove it," said he. "Unhappily I can prove it. Thompson is my witness: interrogate him yourself."

"Oh!" retorted the general sarcastically, "I have not the slightest doubt of his having duly learned his lesson."

"What do you mean to insinuate by that?"

"We shall see—*we* shall see," returned the general, as the butler entered. "Now, sir," he continued, addressing Thompson fiercely, "I have to ask you a few plain questions—questions which, doubtless, you will have to answer upon your oath."

"I will answer them now," said the butler, "as truly as if I were on my oath."

"We shall see—we shall see, sir. Now, then. The very first question I have to ask you is this: did Sir Charles, or did he *not*, sir, instruct you to make the statement which you have made against Lady Julian?"

"I have made no statement against Lady Julian."

"No equivocation—no quibbling! I ask you a straightforward question, sir, and I expect that you will give me a straightforward answer. I ask you again, whether Sir Charles did or did not instruct you to make the statement which you *have* made against Lady Julian?"

"And I answer again that I have made no statement against her ladyship."

"What! Have you not declared, and are you not prepared to swear, that she is an adulteress?"

"No," replied Thompson, "certainly not. I don't believe that she is; I never said that I believed it."

"Why, how is this?" demanded the general of Sir Charles. "What am I to understand?"

"Pursue your own course, General Lloyd," returned Sir Charles. "Pray proceed in your own way. I have no wish to interfere with your mode of interrogation."

"All I have stated," resumed Thompson, "is this: that about three this morning I saw Mr. Sound coming slowly from the ante-room which leads to Lady Julian's chamber, and that I let him out of the house."

"And are you prepared to *swear* to this statement?"

"I am, sir—I am."

"And will you also swear that you received no orders—no instructions from Sir Charles"——

"General Lloyd," vehemently interposed Sir Charles, "I'll no longer sit here and be thus insulted. Thompson, leave the room. If," he added, when Thompson had left, "if you have any charge to bring against me, let it be brought at once *plainly*, that I may meet it. You have insinuated against me one of the basest and most abhorrent practices by which it is possible for a man to be disgraced. Do you mean to accuse me distinctly of such baseness?"

"I mean to accuse you of this, Sir Charles Julian—I am not a man to mince my words, or to shrink from the avowal of that which I feel—this it is of which I accuse you: I accuse you of having heartlessly conspired with that despicable wretch—whose oath I perceive is entirely at your command—to crush a woman, a fond, devoted fool of a woman, whom you know to be as virtuous and as pure as a child."

"General Lloyd!" cried Sir Charles, "General Lloyd, you amaze me! Were any other man upon earth to charge me with anything so infamous, I should at once denounce him as a villain. What right have you to insult me with so monstrous an accusation? What grounds have you—what real grounds—for believing me *capable* of acting so shameful a part?"

"Sir Charles Julian, you amaze *me!* Were any other man upon earth to charge *her* with anything so infamous, I should at once denounce him as a villain. What right have you to insult *her* with so monstrous an accusation? What grounds have you—what real grounds—for believing *her* capable of acting so shameful a part?"

"I have evidence."

"You have: and I have evidence, too—evidence of a much purer caste. I have *her* evidence, upon which I'd stake my life—I have the evidence of him who is charged with her—I have my *own* evidence, and I have yours—for I defy you to show, that since you unhappily married her there has been anything in her conduct to justify suspicion."

"There has not been. Until this occurred I fondly believed her to be pure. She had my entire confidence—no man could have reposed more confidence in a woman than I reposed in her; and even now that she has betrayed it"——

"She has *not* betrayed it! I'll not have it so."

"I'd give up station, wealth, and all to have it proved that she has not."

"To have it *proved* that she has not! How can it be proved? What woman can *prove* that she has not been false? You well know that to be impossible. It is for you to prove that she *has* been—and what proof have you of that?"

At this moment Sir William D'Almaine was announced, and the general—who, inferring that the preliminaries had been settled, was anxious to receive the communication from Mr. Scholefield—rose on the instant, and having briefly said—"Sir Charles, I shall see you again on the subject," left the room.

X

It was about four when Sylvester received the intelligence that the meeting was to take place that evening at seven, and the firmness with which he received it proved clearly that cowardice formed no part of *his* composition. He was thoughtful, it is true, but tranquil. There was no display of any reckless devil-may-care spirit; he viewed the affair like a man who perceives the importance of the part he is about to perform, and although he was willing to converse calmly on the subject, he was indisposed to treat it with levity.

"I say, old fellow," observed Tom, gaily, soon after they had sat down to dinner, "where's your appetite?"

"I have it still," replied Sylvester.

"Well, cobe—get od. Do bad should go idto the field with ad appetite!"

"I am doing very well."

"I hope you'll do better whed supper-tibe cobes."

"I hope so, too."

"But, I say, old boy, I wish you'd take be with you."

"That, I apprehend, would be *rather* incorrect."

"Dot at all. I bight go as your surgeod."

"I hope that no surgeon will be required."

"Well, I hope so, too. But if I were to go, I dod't thidk that the *practice* I should have would buch ibprove be. As to Sir Charles hittidg *you!*—that's quite out of the questiod. If he *cad*, why thed he cad hit a lath; day, I'd back ady bad who cad hit you at twelve paces to go through the eye of a deedle. It's *dot* to be dode! The idea is ridiculous. Add, thed, as regards your hittidg hib?"

"I shall not attempt it."

"You'll dot? What, do you bead to say, thed, that you'll fire id the air?"

"It is my intention to do so."

"Thed of course you wish to kill hib!"

"Certainly not."

"Thed dod't attebpt to fire id the air. You are buch bore likely to hit hib if you do so thad if you were to fire directly at his head."

"How so?"

"You have had doe pistol practice?"

"I have not."

"You dever, perhaps, fired off a pistol id your life?"

"I never did."

"Well, thed, let be tell you this; if you fire at his head, you'll cut the groudd frob udder hib: you bay, perhaps, take off the sole of wud of his boots, but the chadces are ted to wud id favour of your cuttidg up the turf; whereas, if you bake ad attebpt to fire id the air, add you do but fire straight, you'll be as safe to put the bullet through his head, as if the buzzle of the pistol were placed betweed his eyes; for, of course, you'll have to deal with hair triggers, add if you have, add you *raise* the pistol, *off* it goes sobe codsiderable tibe before you kdow where you are. Look at that pier-glass; it seebs at twelve paces to be rebarkably easy to hit; but fire at it—you shall do so if you like after didder—fire right at it; you *bay* kdock the kdob off the todgs—you bay sbash the fedder—you bay crack the hearth-stode, or bake a sball hole id the rug—but you'll fide, udless you take a bost burderous aib, that you'll dot go dear the glass. The buzzle of a pistol, id the hadd of a dovice, is perfectly certaid to drop: just try it after didder."

"I've no desire to do so."

"Well, but thed you will see the effect!"

"My dear fellow, I've no ambition to become a duellist. I shall be able to fire as well as I wish to fire, for I'll take especial care that before I touch the trigger, the pistol shall point directly upwards. I have been grossly insulted by Sir Charles, it is true; but it is also true that when he insulted me, he imagined that I had seriously injured *him*. It was an error on his part: he had been deceived. I would not deprive any man of life because he happened to be labouring under a mistake."

"But Sir Charles would deprive you of life."

"If he should do so, the crime will be his, not mine."

"You will be, eved id that case, *particeps cribidis*. You kdow—you have, at all evedts, a right to assube—that his object is to kill you; add yet you voludtarily place yourself in a positiod to be killed! The cribe would dot be cobbitted were you dot to go out: you have id your owd hadds the power to prevedt it, and if you do *dot*, you are to all idtedts and purposes ad accessory."

"So are you—so is your father—and so is Mr. Scholefield? We are all accessories, in that sense: we all have the power to prevent it. But at the same time we all know that society would hold the exercise of that power to be dishonourable."

"If, thed, society thus *forces* a bad out, I codtedd that he is justified id firidg at his oppodedt. If I were to go out to-borrow, add I kdew that the object of by adtagodist was to kill be, I should fire as he fired, add if I killed *hib* I should call it justifiable hobicide. He who does dot idtedd to fire at his oppodedt has do right to go out at all. I cad ibagide a case id which a bad would be justified id goidg out add firidg id the air: for exabple, that of a bad who had deeply idjured his friedd, add who felt it deeply, add who wished to give a tacit *ackdowledgbedt* of the wrodg he had idflicted; but id a case like yours, a bad has do *right* to go add stick hibself up like a target, add say to his oppodedt, in effect, 'Fire away! I have dot idjured you: dor shall I fire at you. I cabe out edtirely for your satisfactiod; therefore kill be if you cad.' It isd't a *fair* positiod for a bad to be placed id. It is, id fact, adythidg *but* a fair positiod."

"The position," said Sylvester, "is certainly unfair; and one point which you have suggested, will be sufficient to induce me not to fire as I intended. I'll not fire in the air lest it *should* be considered a tacit acknowledgment of guilt. No, I'll fire on one side."

"Id that case, the *secodds* had better look out. If you dod't bide, you'll burder wud of theb."

Sylvester smiled; and from this time till six Tom did all in his power to amuse him, and when Mr. Scholefield arrived with the chaise, he found him as calm and as firm as ever.

"You'll dot let be go, thed?" said Tom.

"I should like you to go," returned Sylvester; "but of course it would not be *exactly* correct."

"Not exactly!" observed Mr. Scholefield.

"I *could* hadg od behide! But I'll dot do that. I suppose you bust have all the fud to yourselves. Adieu, old fellow! I'll wait at hobe for you. Drive back here ibbediately all is over. Adieu!"

Sylvester pressed his hand with warmth, and having said calmly—"Tom—God bless you!" he joined Mr. Scholefield, who was apprehensive still, and they entered the post-chaise together.

The meeting had been arranged to take place at Wormwood Scrubs, and on their way Mr. Scholefield was constantly looking back. This Sylvester ascribed to an anxiety to ascertain if *Sir Charles* were behind them; and when he heard him order the postboy to drive more slowly, he suggested that Sir Charles might be ahead.

"He may be," replied Mr. Scholefield; "I have no doubt he is."

He, nevertheless, continued to look anxiously behind until suddenly his countenance assumed a gay expression, and he ordered the postboy to drive on fast.

On their arrival at the appointed spot, they found Sir Charles on the ground, and Mr. Scholefield, on alighting, went up to Sir William, with whom he for some time conversed. Everything bearing the semblance of an arrangement was of course out of the question, and as such was the case, the pistols were loaded and the ground was measured, but just as the principals were about to be placed, the general, with two officers, sprang upon the ground, exclaiming, "There are your prisoners!"

"What right, sir," demanded Sir Charles fiercely, "what earthly right have you to interfere?"

"What right!" returned the general. "Independently of my common right as a man, I have the right of a father, firmly resolved to vindicate the honour of his child."

"Can the honour of your daughter be vindicated thus?"

"We shall see: we shall see. It never *could* be vindicated were you now to fall. No, no, Sir Charles; I can't spare you yet."

"From whom did you obtain your information?"

"Did I not hear Sir William D'Almaine announced? and did you conceive that I was *totally* blind?"

Sir Charles looked at Sir William, and evidently inferred that that announcement had been the cause of the general's interference.

"This," resumed the general, addressing the officers, "this is Sir Charles Julian, and this is Mr. Sylvester Sound. You have seen what they contemplated: you know for what purpose they have met. Arrest them."

The officers bowed; and as one of them followed Sir Charles to his carriage, the other accompanied Sylvester and Mr. Scholefield; and when the general had rejoined the friend with whom he came, and whom, despite his anxiety to conceal himself, Sylvester discovered to be the doctor, they returned to town, and went at once before a magistrate, who bound the parties over to keep the peace.

CHAPTER XXVIII.

PIER-GLASS PRACTICE.

That evening Sylvester supped with Tom, and on being urged to stop there all night, he, having no anxiety about returning to his chambers, consented; and after sitting up till one, conversing gaily about the occurrence of the day, went to bed pretty nearly exhausted.

Tom went to bed too; but as the night-bell rang soon afterwards, and he was summoned to assist in augmenting the surplus population, he intimated the interesting fact to "Jib"—whom he had seduced from the doctor's—and left the house.

Jib was a most especial favourite of Tom, and had, in consequence, become a great man: quite a confidential card. Whatever Jib said in that house was law. He was the superior swell of the establishment. Nothing could be done without Jib. He was a species of domestic oracle; and as he felt—and very naturally—that he knew what was what, about as well as any man in the realm, he wouldn't allow the "bedials" to advance a syllable in opposition to his views. Whatever he wished to have done, was done, and he'd have it done, too, in a tidy style; and while he had an extremely deep sense of his own importance, he felt it correct to look fierce.

When, therefore, he received Tom's important communication, he knew as well as any man in England what it meant, and having grunted and yawned, and eventually turned out, he went down to fasten the door.

While returning, however, he was struck—struck with amazement, paralysed—perfectly paralysed, on beholding a tall figure slowly descending the stairs, with a pistol in one hand, which Jib didn't see, and a very dim light in the other.

Jib was silent, breathless, and *looked*—oh, how he looked

at the figure. His eyes were nearly out of his head, and, while his hands were uplifted, and his fingers were extremely wide apart, his lips described a perfect circle, and his knees smote each other, as if each patella wished to knock the other out.

As the figure—which looked very ghastly—approached, Jib retreated—correctly, retreated; and when he had got as far as he *could* get, without going through the street door, he saw the figure—which treated him with the utmost contempt, taking no more notice of him than if he had been nothing—stalk into the dining-room as coolly as if he absolutely paid the rent and taxes.

The position Jib occupied then was awkward. The figure—which of course he believed to be a ghost, for Jib's faith in supernatural appearances was firm—had left the dining-room door wide open, and situated as he was then, nature swindled him into the belief that he must of necessity pass this door, which appeared to him, then, to have an unexampled appetite. It never, for a moment, struck him that he might open the front door, and let himself out. No; he felt that he must pass *that* door, and how to manage it he couldn't exactly tell. He never before felt so much confused. His intellects were usually clear enough—he had, at all events, been accustomed to flatter himself that they were commonly as clear as those of any man in Europe—but at that particular period they really did appear to be completely upset. He couldn't tell what to make of it. He felt very ill. A faintness came over him, and yet he was conscious—perfectly conscious—at least of this, that the figure was then in the room.

"Courage!" he exclaimed confidently to himself, and the word seemed to have a great effect upon his nerves; for he stood upright boldly and breathed again, and absolutely made up his mind to pass the door; but no sooner had he taken the first courageous step, than he heard the report of a pistol and fell.

That he had been wounded he firmly believed; *where*, he couldn't tell; nor did he much care then to know, but that he had a wound somewhere about his person, was in his view abundantly clear.

"Mur*der!*" cried the cook, at this moment, above. "James!—master—mur*der!*"

The sound of a voice reinspired Jib, and he felt quite valiant again, and rose, and actually darted past the dining-room door, and rushed upstairs in a fit of desperation to the cook, who, conceiving him to be some other gentleman, backed in and fastened the door.

"Cook, cook!" he cried, "cook!"

"Who's there?" she demanded, for she did not immediately recognise his voice.

"Me! me!—James!—me!" he replied; "let me in."

At any other time cook would not have done this; but her characteristic delicacy was overcome by fear. She wanted protection: she knew she did; and therefore, having thrown a flannel-petticoat round her, she adjusted her nightcap, and opened the door.

"Good Heavens!" she exclaimed; "what on earth is the matter?"

"Horror!" cried Jib, with an appalling expression; "I've seen—I've seen—a ghost!"

Cook shuddered and echoed, "A ghost!"

"A ghost!"

"My gracious!" exclaimed cook; "where?"

"Some water—some water," said Jib, "I feel faint."

And so he did; and looked faint; and cook gave him some water, and wiped the cold perspiration off his forehead with a towel. And Jib drank the water, and felt a little better; and when cook had urged him to tell all he knew, he proceeded in trembling accents thus—

"Cook! heaven and earth, what a sight it was!"——

"Good gracious!"

"I went down to fasten the door after master"——

"I *thought* I heard the night-bell."

"Well, I'd no soon effected this accomplishment, than what should I see—Oh! horror!"——

"Good Heavens preserve us!"

"I saw—I beheld—a long, lanky, pale, horrid, ghastly-looking ghost, with eyes starting right out of its head, coming towards me."

"Oh! my goodness!"

"Well—I never was a coward, and so I wasn't then—I stood and watched it, and where should it go, but deliberate into the dining-room, where it is now!"

"Heaven forgive us all our sins!"

"Well, there I stood—I didn't move—when presently something went *bang!* just like the tremendous roar of a cannon."

"Yes, that's what I heard."

"Well, just after then you called out, and as I knew you was frightened, I came up to ease your mind."

"That was very good of you. What I *should* have done if you hadn't, James, Heaven only knows. I'm sure that I should have gone right out of my senses. Have a little more water; you look very pale."

"The smell of the brimstone made me faint."

"Well, I thought I smelt brimstone—I smell it now!—dreadful!—don't you?"

"I do—I do!" sighed Jib, and fainted.

Of all the horrid feelings by which the human breast is animated, those which cook now inspired were perhaps the *most* horrid.

"James, James!" she exclaimed, "oh, for goodness sake! James, there's a *good* man! James!—Oh, Heaven have mercy upon me!"

Susan, who slept in the next room, and who, although she had been awakened by the cry of murder, dared not venture out before, no sooner heard these fitful exclamations than, prompted by an extremely natural species of curiosity, she came to the door and peeped.

Was it possible—could it *be* possible? There was James on the bedside, supported by cook. His head was resting on her bosom, and she was chafing his temples. He had nothing on but his trousers and shirt, and she had nothing on but her night-dress—the petticoat having slipped off. The scene was awful. Susan was shocked. She couldn't have thought it. She couldn't have believed it. She *wouldn't* have believed it, if she hadn't herself seen it with her own eyes.

"Hem!" she cried, and bounced into the room.

"O Susan!" sighed cook; "I'm so glad you're come."

Susan, with a sarcastic smile, and at the same time, tossing her head contemptuously, replied, "Very pretty; *very* pretty, upon my word!"

"O Susan!"——

"Don't talk to me. Master shall know of all this, if I live."

"But, Susan "——

"I'll have no communication with such a creature."

"Well, but hear me!"

"I'll not hear a word, ma'am. No, ma'am; I'll not bemean myself, ma'am, to talk to you. You ought to be *ashamed* of yourself, you *ought!* Fine doings, indeed. But master shall know, and either you or I leave to-morrow morning."

"Susan, *will* you hear me?"

"No, I'll not," replied Susan, with a look of disdain, and having sufficiently extended her nostrils, bounced out of the room in a high state of virtuous indignation.

Cook now felt the extreme delicacy of her position, but her very first object was to bring Jib round. This she tried to effect by all the means at her command, but for some time her efforts were quite unavailing. Had he been absolutely dead, he couldn't have appeared more inanimate: indeed, at one time she thought he *had* departed this life, and began to turn the probable consequences over in her mind. As a *dernier ressort*, however, she seized the ewer, which happened to be very nearly full, and having violently dashed the whole body of water in his face, Jib struck out, and from that moment consciousness gradually returned.

"Where am I?" he faintly inquired at length, looking round with the aspect of a most unhappy wretch, for the water had obliterated every trace of the characteristic respectability of his appearance, "Is that you, cook?"

"O James, James!" replied cook, with a sigh; "you have, I fear, ruined me—ruined me for ever."

"Ruined you!" exclaimed Jib, making an effort which rendered his restoration almost complete; "how, how have I ruined you?"

"O James!" replied cook; "Susan has been here"——

"She has!" cried Jib; "and saw *me!*"

"Yes; and called me all the names she could lay her tongue to."

"Oh, I feel very ill. But I'll soon settle that. She is jealous, I suppose—she's jealous. But the ghost, cook—how about the ghost? Have you seen it?"

"No, it hasn't been here."

"Then it's there."

"Where?" demanded cook, looking round with a feeling of horror.

"In the dining-room—the dining-room; not here—not here; but there where I left it."

"Heaven be praised. If it were to come here, I should sink."

"Hark!" exclaimed Jib.

"How you frighten me. What is it—what do you hear?"

"Listen! Don't you hear that?"

"That. No. What?"

They both listened with anxiety the most intense, and, while listening, they heard the bell ring.

"That's master," said Jib; "he's come back."

"Then run down, and let him in at once," said cook.

Run down. Yes. Nothing could be much more easily said, but Jib, at the time, felt that he couldn't do it.

"I'm afraid," said he, "of that nasty brimstone. I know it will overcome me; I'm quite sure it will."

"But I don't smell it half so much now. In fact, I don't smell it at all!"

"Not smell it! Oh, it's enough to knock you down."

"Well, but what's to be done? Master must be let in. There you are!" she added, as the bell rang again. "He'll be in a passion presently."

"Cook," exclaimed Jib, "I can't help it!"

"Well, but somebody must go, you know. *I* can't go."

"Nor can I," replied Jib; "it's quite out of the question."

The bell rang again, and with increased violence.

"I knew how it would be," observed cook; "I knew he'd soon get in a passion. He'll pull the bell right down presently. You'll see if he don't."

"I wish he would," said Jib; "and then I couldn't hear it."

"Well, but what's to be done! You know something must be done."

"Something must be done; but what I don't know. Did you name the ghost to Susan?"

"Not a word."

"That's lucky. Perhaps *she'll* go, for I don't feel well—indeed, I'm anything *but* well. I wish you'd go and ask her."

Cook didn't at all like to leave the room; but as the bell rang again with greater violence still, and the case became, therefore, most urgent, she offered to compromise the matter by going with Jib, to which compromise Jib most reluctantly consented.

They accordingly went, with trembling steps, to Susan's door, and having looked round anxiously, knocked.

"Who's there?" demanded Susan.

"Me, Susan—only me," replied cook.

"What do you want?"

"Open the door; there's a good girl, open the door."

"I shan't! I'll do nothing of the sort. I'll have nothing at all to say to any such creature. But master shall know all about it, mind that!"

"*Will* you go and let him in?"

"Me go—me? Where's your fellow? Let him go; *I'll* not go—the ideor, indeed! Let *him* go—that is, if you can spare him."

"You wrong me, Susan—indeed you do."

"I don't care a pin about what you say, *ma'am*—I'll not go."

The bell rang again, and continued to ring, for the wire sawed to and fro with unexampled violence; and as it was then clear that Susan was inexorable, cook actually offered to go down with Jib!

"Why, it's madness you utter!" exclaimed Jib—"madness! If you were to see it, you'd be frightened to death."

"It won't harm me, James; it won't harm me. Come, come—be a man!"

This appeal to Jim's manhood awakened his courage, and seizing the ewer—the only available weapon in the room—he inspired a little of the spirit of desperation, and descended, closely followed by cook.

As they passed the dining-room, Jib was amazed, but at the same time relieved, on finding the door closed; but they had no sooner passed, than Tom, whose patience was exhausted, thundered at the street door with such startling violence, that, as the sound reverberated, cook flew upstairs, leaving Jib in the hall alone.

Having recovered those faculties which had thus been astonished, Jib nerved himself once more, and opened the door; and as Tom very angrily entered, he was about to tell him exactly what he meant, but he no sooner saw Jib's deplorable aspect, than his anger was wholly supplanted by mirth.

"Why you biserable, udhappy lookidg *wretch*," cried Tom, "what have you beed at? Puttidg your head udder the pubp, or dividg idto the water-butt?"

"Oh!" said Jib, "I've seen a ghost!"

"You've seed a what?"

"A horrid ghost!"

"What had you for supper last dight?"

"Bread and cheese, sir."

"Dothidg else?"

"Oh, yes; I did have a little bit of pork."

"Of course you did. Your stobach's out of order: you've beed dreabidg."

"No, it isn't that, sir; oh, no, it isn't that. I saw it as plain, sir—as plain as could be."

"Did you really. Well, add what did it say? It threw a bucket of water over you, I suppose, to begid with?"

"No, sir; nor did it say a word; but I saw it stalk horridly into that room: and it's my belief that it's in there now."

"Well, let's go and have a look at it, Jib. Let us see what it's bade off."

Jib duly delivered the lamp to Tom, and allowed him to enter the room alone; but the moment he entered, Tom, perceiving the pier-glass shattered to atoms, exclaimed—

"*Hollo!* why, what's all this!" with so much vehemence, that Jib, who imagined the ghost was there still, started off, and rushed upstairs with feelings of horror.

"Where are you off to?" cried Tom. "Jib, what do you bead. Do you hear? Jib!"

"Ye-e-e-yes, sir," replied Jib, almost unable to utter the word.

"Cobe dowd, thed. What do you bead by ruddidg away id that state of bide? Cobe dowd, sir, ibbediately. Do you hear be? Cobe dowd."

"Oh, sir," replied Jib, trembling, "I dare not."

"Dare dot. Dod't tell *be* that you dare dot; cobe dowd this bobedt, I desire you."

Jib, who felt very ill indeed, and who also felt that he *must* go down, descended anxiously, and with great deliheration, while Tom more minutely examined the room.

"Dow, Jib, what's all this about?" demanded Tom, rather angrily; "who broke this glass?"

"Glass, sir. What glass?"

"What glass! why, this glass."

"Oh!" exclaimed Jib, as he fixed his eyes upon it, "it is broke, indeed."

"Well, how did you do it?"

"Do it, sir? I didn't do it."

"By whob *was* it dode?"

"Oh, sir, it must have been the ghost!"

Tom, for a moment, looked at him fiercely, and then exclaimed—

"Why, you idsoledt, lyidg, darrow-bided, idcobprehedsible dodkey, what do you bead? What do you take be for? Ad idiot? Have you beed fool edough to swiddle yourself idto the belief that I should take id *that*, you codsubbate ass?"

"If it wasn't done by the ghost, sir, I don't know who did it. But it was the ghost: depend upon it, sir, it was the ghost."

"That you *bead* to say you wish be to believe?"

"It must have been the ghost, sir; *I* didn't do it!"

"You bead to stick to that?"

"It's the truth."

"That's edough! Pack up your traps add be off. I'll have do bad id by house id whob I'b udable to codfide. I have hitherto reposed the utbost codfidedce id you, but dow that I fide you cad tell the bost ibpudedt falsehoods, that codfidedce is gode: therefore, start."

"Indeed, sir, this isn't a falsity? it isn't, sir; as true as I am standing here alive."

"What!" exclaimed Tom, indignantly.

"Cook knows it isn't, sir. Cook heard the noise."

"What doise?"

"The noise of the ghost, sir; which was, for all the world, as if heaven *and* earth was a coming together."

"Is cook id bed?"

"I think not, sir. She came down with me to let you in; but when you knocked loud, she ran away frightened."

"Tell her to cobe dowd agaid, thed. I'll have *this* affair

cleared up at wudce ; add remebber, udless it be cleared up satisfactorily, off you go. Dow, tell cook I wadt her, add dod't be lodg about it."

Jib—whom the idea of leaving appalled—was *not* long about it : he went up to cook, who slipped on her dress, and changed her cap, and came down in a singularly short space of time ; but mark ! followed by Susan, whose deep indignation had had the effect of keeping her on the *qui vive*.

"Cook," said Tom, "I do dot care buch about the glass : by chief object is truth, to which I expect you will adhere. Dow, what do you kdow about this ?"

"All I know, sir, about it, is this : that I heard a tremendous noise like an earthquake, and got up, and called out, and found it was a ghost."

"Did you see this—ghost ?"

"No, sir; I didn't see it exactly ; but James did."

"How do you kdow that ?"

"He told me so."

"Is that all you kdow ?"

"I don't know nothing more, sir."

"But I do," said Susan ; " and a good deal more, too."

"Well, what do *you* kdow ?"

"Why, sir, I know this ; I'll not live in any house where there's such goings on."

"What do you bead ?"

"I mean, sir, that I heard a noise, but a very different sort of a noise from that of an earthquake ; and when I came out to ascertain what it was, *who* should I see but *Mister* James comfortably sitting on *Missis* Cook's bed, and she a cuddling of him with very great affection."

"Cook," said Tom ; "I fadcied that you were a strictly virtuous persod."

"And so I am, sir. I'll defy the world to prove that I am not. This envious creature's jealous, sir ; that's it."

"Jealous !" cried Susan.

"Yes, jealous ! But if you will but listen, sir "——

"I feel boudd to do so."

"Then, sir, I'll tell you exactly how it all occurred. I heard a noise, as I before said, and called out to know what it was, when James ran up and told me he'd just seen a ghost. I was frightened, of course—very frightened—so frightened, I didn't know what to do ; and as James felt ill and wanted some water, I gave him some, and he sat on my bed. We then talked about the ghost, and while we were talking, James fainted away, and it was as I was trying to bring him round that Susan entered the room and saw us."

"You have spoken the truth, cook?" suggested Tom.

"I have, sir, indeed. I'd repeat the words if they were the last I had to speak."

"He faidted, you say? absolutely faidted?"

"He did, sir; and I *couldn't* bring him to until I'd thrown the whole jug of water over him."

"It's all very fine," observed Susan, who was not at all satisfied; "very fine indeed."

"This affair," said Tom, "shall be fully idvestigated ibbediatedly after breakfast; add if I fidd that your statebedts are false, dot wud of you shall rebaid in the house. Go to bed."

They then retired to their respective rooms with manifest feelings of dissatisfaction; indeed, so dissatisfied were they, that neither Jib, cook, nor Susan could go to sleep again.

While at breakfast that morning Tom related the whole affair to Sylvester, and the relation was productive of a most hearty laugh.

"I might as well have had a shot at the glass yesterday," said Sylvester; "I couldn't have shattered it more."

"I dod't believe you could have hit it at all," returned Tom. "Try it dow. You *cad't* do ady more dabage. Where are the pistols?"

"I took them up with me last night."

"Thed we'll have theb dowd at wudce," said Tom, ringing the bell; "you'll thed see the effect of pier-glass practice. Jib," he added, when Jib had appeared, "you'll see a case id the roob id which Mr. Soudd slept, bridg it dowd."

Jib, who was particularly active that morning, very soon produced the case; when Sylvester, who had the key in his pocket, unlocked it and took out one of the pistols.

"Dow," said Tom, "aib at the bull's eye; there's a capital wud established. Stadd here."

"The cap's off," said Sylvester, on cocking the pistol.

"Is it?" cried Tom. "I wudder how *that* got off. Here's adother."

Sylvester, having put on the cap, pointed steadily at the

bull's-eye indicated, but, on pulling the trigger, the pistol flashed in the pan.

"Hollo!" cried Tom. "Well these are pretty pistols to go out with, certaidly. Why, where did you get theb?"

"Scholefield got them. I don't know where."

"He who sedt them out ought to be *ashabed* of hibself. However, try adother cap."

Another cap was tried, and the result was the same.

"Why," cried Tom, "what's the beadidg of this? There bust be sobethidg wrodg. Look here," he added, "the thidg isd't loaded at all."

"Not loaded!"

"Do. I'b afraid there was foul play codtebplated here."

"Is the other loaded?"

"Let's see. Yes, that's all right edough. Were these the pistols you were to have fought with?"

"Yes."

"Thed that's the wud which *you* were to have had. Scholefield ought to have seed to it. Certaidly, he ought to have seed that all was right."

"I don't suppose he knows much about affairs of this kind."

"Probably dot; but do bad should uddertake to do that of which he is igdoradt, especially id a batter id which life is idvolved."

"I believe that he scarcely knew what he was doing; he appeared to be very much excited throughout."

"It is excitebedt, thed, to which this deglect bust be ascribed; but it certaidly was a bost ndpardodable trick od the part ob Sir Williab D'Albaide."

"Do you think it was done intentionally, then?"

"It looks very buch like it."

"But is he at all the sort of man to act so dishonourably?"

"Why, iddepededtly of beidg a duellist, he is a gabbler, ad id the hodour of a gabbler, I've dot buch faith."

"I suppose that I can do nothing in it?"

"I'd bedtiod it to Scholefield. But I dod't thidk that, as the batter has terbidated, I should take ady further dotice of it."

"Well, I must say that it was a most unfair proceeding."

"Udfair!" cried Tom; "the desigd was burderous!"

Y

The pistols were then restored to the case, and shortly afterwards Sylvester proceeded to his chambers, where he found a message from Sir Charles's attorney, by whom he was served with a notice of action.

CHAPTER XXIX.

SYLVESTER REVISITS COTHERSTONE GRANGE.

FIVE years! What a variety of changes take place in five years! What aërial castles are built but to fall—what hopes spring up and bloom but to wither—what fears are inspired but to prove that they are baseless—what beautiful bubbles are blown but to burst.

The great majority of mankind find the space of five years rich in incident; but there are individuals to whom, during five years, scarcely an incident worth recording occurs. For example, nothing of importance had occurred to either Aunt Eleanor or the reverend gentleman. They were, moreover, in precisely the same relative positions as they were five years before. It may have been imagined that they *might* have managed matters between them by this time; and so, indeed, they might, but they didn't. He had obtained her consent, it is true, and continued to visit her daily; nay, he had even on three occasions spoken of the contemplated "happy day;" but he never could get her to *name* that day, until just before those events occurred which have been detailed in the preceding chapter.

Nor had anything of importance transpired in the village. It is true that the barn which stood opposite the cottage had been, about twelve months before, newly thatched; it is also true that Obadiah had twice made an assignment, marvelling how it could possibly be that, while all around him were prosperous, he should be constantly involved—sometimes ascribing it to the measures of "Bobby Peel," and sometimes to those of "Johnny Russell;" but, beyond this, nothing worth recording took place.

When, therefore, Sylvester—after having placed his defence to the action in the hands of the doctor's attorney—went down to Cotherstone, with the view of explaining all that had occurred before the case should appear more pointedly in the papers, he found nothing there to strike him with any great degree of astonishment. But conceive the amazement of his aunt and her reverend friend, when he stated to them the fact of his being the defendant in an action for criminal conversation. Conceive the horror with which they heard that statement made, and the relief which they experienced, when he wound up all by a solemn declaration of his innocence? Nothing could be more touching, or more sincere, than the expressions of their belief in this solemn declaration. And yet, to them, how extraordinary it appeared that precisely the same thing which occurred to the father should thus have occurred to the son.

"There must be," observed Aunt Eleanor, when she and her reverend friend were alone, "some deep mystery in this."

"It is, certainly," said the reverend gentleman, "the most mysterious thing I ever heard or read of."

"Heaven grant that the consequences may not be the same."

"I say Amen to that. But, if he be innocent, I do not see how they can prove him to be guilty. The case must be tried before a judge, and no judge *could* allow a young man like him to be cast unjustly."

"That I apprehend depends entirely upon the evidence, does it not?"

"Exactly. But what evidence—what clear, substantial evidence—can be brought against an innocent man? For example: suppose I were accused of burning a house down; would I not, if I were innocent, defy all the world to prove me guilty? What evidence *could* be brought forward to prove me guilty of that of which I was innocent?"

"Circumstantial evidence," said Sylvester, who at the moment re-entered the room.

"Circumstantial evidence, I grant, has frequently led to conviction; but then it must be very strong and conclusive. What circumstantial evidence could be sufficient in, for instance, a case like yours?"

"In cases like mine, the proof, almost invariably, *depends* upon circumstantial evidence."

"But what evidence—what sufficient evidence—of any kind, can they bring against you?"

"There is the evidence of the butler, who is ready to swear that he saw me in the house at the time."

"I must go to town and talk to that butler. I must see that man. His soul is in peril. It is necessary that he should *know* that. I have a great mind to go to-morrow morning."

Sylvester smiled at his reverend friend's simplicity, and observed that he feared that that would be of little use.

"I don't know that," resumed the reverend gentleman. "Men have been induced, under similar circumstances, to turn from the pursuit of evil. It may be that this man has been bribed by his master—I do not say that he has been—but such things are possible: indeed, if my memory serves me right, I have read in some book that such things have been done. If, therefore, it be so in this case—if this man's master has wickedly bribed him to swear that that is true which he knows to be false—he should be seen and talked to, and expostulated with; the position in which he is about to place himself ought to be clearly laid before him; the awful nature of the sin he is about to commit should be explained to him seriously and solemnly; and who knows that, when he has been made duly sensible of the consequences which must of necessity follow the commission of so dreadful a sin, he may not become wise in time and repent? I hold it to be the duty of every Christian minister to endeavour, by all the means of which he is capable, to rescue unfortunate souls from perdition; and if I could save this unhappy man—if I could in time convince him of the error of his ways—if I could show him that his immortal soul is now in jeopardy—strike into his mind the light of truth—inspire him with confidence in Him to whom all hearts are open—bring him to the throne of grace and mercy, and teach him to sin no more: if I could but in time effect this, I should think no journey too long, no trouble too great; no pains nor expense should, on my part, be spared."

"I appreciate the feelings by which you are actuated," said Sylvester; "and I am by no means insensible to the power of your appeals; still I think that, under the circumstances, such a journey as that which you contemplate would be unprofitable."

"Oh, there is no knowing what might be done. The

heart of the man might be altogether turned; his ideas of good and evil might be completely changed, and therefore, I might be successful. However, we'll think the matter over. I don't like in any case to act with precipitation. *Our* views may change; but I must say that my present impression is, that an hour's conversation with that unhappy man would do good."

During the whole of that evening nothing was discussed or even thought of but the forthcoming trial; and soon after the reverend gentleman had left, Sylvester and his aunt retired.

He had not, however, been asleep more than half an hour, when the company, assembled at the Crumpet and Crown, were thrown into a most intense state of consternation by the sudden re-appearance of Pokey, who declared that the ghost had re-visited Cotherstone Grange.

"I see it," said he, with an aspect of terror; "I see it, as plain as I see you here now!"

"Where?" demanded Obadiah.

"Just down the road. I was going home quiet, when, all of a sudden, what should I see but a monstrous tall figure—taller than the t'other by more than a yard—breathing white smoke from his nostrils, and looking with an eye of real fire."

"It won't do," said Legge; "at least it won't do for me. I suppose you saw a man with a cigar in his mouth."

"Not a bit of it."

"How many eyes of fire had he?"

"I saw but one, and that was a blazer—I never before see such an eye in my life—but, of course, he has two, although I didn't see 'em."

"No; you saw but one, and that was a cigar; and the man was puffing away at the time: that was it."

"I know better! Do you think I'm such a fool as not to know a real man from a ghost?"

"*That* was no ghost!"

"It was, I tell you. Can't I believe my own eyes?"

"It won't do, Pokey! I won't take it in! If you saw anything *but* a man, you saw it in imagination merely."

"As Peter the Great did," observed Obadiah, "at the time he imagined he'd welted the Dutch."

"Peter the Great!" retorted Pokey contemptuously "What has this to do with Peter the Great?"

"What has it got to do with it? It's got all to do with it! mind you that! When the Dutch, in the reign of old Harry the Eighth"——

"Blister the Dutch, and Harry the Eighth, too! What do you think we want to know about the Dutch! I tell you again that I see a ghost! It was all in white, from head to heel; and what's more, it had an umbrella."

"An umbrella?" cried Legge.

"I say an umbrella! And what's more, he had it up, as if it rained pouring."

"Well!" said Legge, "I've heard of many things, but I never before heard of a ghost with an umbrella!"

Whereupon a loud roar of laughter burst from all but Pokey, whom their utter incredulity rendered indignant.

"I don't care a button about your laughing," said he: "I know what I know; and I'll bet you half a gallon it was a ghost, and nothing but!"

"Who's to prove it?"

"If you can't believe me, come and see it yourself! Now, then!"

"We should be great fools to do that!" said Obadiah; "as big fools as the French was at the battle of Bunker's Hill, when Charley the Second"——

"I don't care about what they was at Bunker's Hill; I only know this: you daren't come and see."

"Daren't!" echoed Obadiah valiantly; "daren't!"

"Ay, daren't! I'll bet you half a gallon you daren't!"

"Do you know what Cæsar said when Pompey told *him* he daren't? 'Pompey,' said he"——

"Pompey be smothered. What's Pompey to do with it? I tell you I'll make you this bet, if you like, and I'll put the money down."

"Do you think that, for the sake of half a gallon of beer, I'll allow you, or any other man in the universe, to place me in the juxtaposition of being laughed at? *Not* exactly. My ideas don't fructify in that way, and so you needn't think of having the laugh against *me*."

"I don't want to have the laugh against you."

"But it would be against me if I were to go out on such a fool's errand as that. It won't do, Pokey: it won't do, my boy. You're a very clever man at your needle, no doubt, but you mustn't at all expect to get over *me*."

"There is certainly something white moving about," said Legge, who had been to the door.

"Is it a fact?" cried Obadiah.

"Come and see!" replied Legge, who returned to the door, and Obadiah rose and followed him, and Quocks, Bobber, and Pokey rose and followed Obadiah; and, after straining their eyes for some time towards the cottage, they all indistinctly perceived something white.

"*Now*, will you believe me?" cried Pokey.

"It's strange," observed Legge; "it is certainly strange! —but we have yet to learn that that which we see is a ghost."

"What else *can* it be?" demanded Pokey.

"It isn't the old maid's white horse?" suggested Obadiah, pointedly.

"No: that's no horse," returned Legge. "Will any one come with me and see what it is?"

"Oh," said Quocks, "if we go at all, we had better go altogether. What do you say?"

Obadiah seemed very unwilling to go, but as all the rest consented, he felt, of course, ashamed to hold back. They, therefore, moved slowly towards the cottage; and as they moved, the figure became more and more distinct; but they had scarcely got more than half way, when Obadiah exclaimed, with a start, "Here it comes!—Don't you see? —It's coming towards us. There—there!" and having uttered these startling exclamations, was about to rush back; but Legge seized his arm on the instant, and stood to watch its movements with comparative calmness. When, however, he found that it was absolutely approaching, even he receded—gradually, it is true—but his retreat kept pace with the advance of the figure, upon which he still kept his eyes constantly fixed.

On reaching the door—to which Bobber, Quocks, and Pokey had previously rushed—he stood for a moment to ascertain whether the figure really meant to come on, and on being sufficiently convinced that that *was* its intention, he darted in, closed the door, and locked it.

"Heaven save us!" exclaimed Mrs. Legge, who was then with the rest in the passage.

"Hark!" cried Legge, as footsteps approached; "hark—*hark!*"

The next moment, to their horror, they saw the latch rise. Their hearts sank within them. They were stricken with terror. There was not a man there who appeared to have sufficient strength to move. They could, in fact, scarcely breathe—while poor Mrs. Legge, who had fallen on her knees and covered her face with her apron, fainted.

Again the latch moved, and a knocking was heard: and Legge, unnecessarily, whispered, "Hu-s-s-s-h!" seeing that they would not if they could, at that moment, have made the slightest noise for the world.

The footsteps receded—slowly, and apparently with some degree of irresolution—and then a slight cough was heard—a sort of clearance of the throat—which on their ears fell like a groan. But after that they heard no more: they listened still, and breathed again; yet, although they felt better, they continued very faint. They called for brandy, but Legge, who was endeavouring to bring his wife round, could not then attend to that call; nor was it until that lady had recovered that the brandy-bottle made its appearance.

During the whole of this time not a single observation, having reference to the ghost, was made. They were thoughtful, but silent, and looked at each other with expressions of amazement and alarm; but when each had had a glass of Legge's brandy, they began to discuss the subject openly, yet cautiously, until indeed each had had a *second* glass, when Obadiah boldly declared that he didn't believe it was any ghost at all.

"What!" exclaimed Pokey, on hearing this monstrous declaration. "Do you mean to tell me, after what we've heard and seen, that it could by possibility be anything *but* a ghost?"

"Yes, I do. Look at the nature of ghosts in general. What are they? Spirits—that's what they're made of. Now fructify your ideas a little; just look you here:— Do you think that if that had been a ghost, and it had wanted to come in here, it *wouldn't* have come in?"

"How could it?"

"How could it!"

"Ay, when the door was locked?"

"What's the odds about the door being locked? Couldn't it have come through the keyholes?"

"What, a ghost of that size!"

"What's the size to do with it? Ghosts—real ghosts, can go anywhere they like, and through anything they like. It makes no odds to them what it is. Talk about a keyhole; why, they'll go through the smallest conceivable crevice. What does it matter to them? If that had been a ghost, rather than suffer himself to be done, he'd have sunk into the earth on one side of the door, and come up on the other, at once!"

"What do you mean? What, clean through the flag-stones?"

"Flag-stones! Of course! What do ghosts care about flag-stones?"

"Well, if they'll do that"——

"That! They'll do anything, those fellows will. It's no odds to them what they do."

"But do you mean to say"——

"Yes, I do! I mean to say that that was no ghost."

"I don't believe it was myself, now," interposed Legge.

"Nor do I," said Quocks.

"Nor don't I," observed Mr. Bobber.

"Well, but, look here," cried Pokey, "if it wasn't, what made you all so frightened?"

"There's times," said Obadiah, assuming a profoundly philosophical expression, "when the ideas of men don't fructify as they ought; there's also times when the amalgamating juxtaposition of those ideas is not *boney fidi non compas*. When, therefore, the intellects is either nem. con., or sine die, and the fructification of ideas in the brain is at its maximus, why, we're just like the Romans when the Greeks stormed Turkey, we don't know what to think; but when the supernatural excitement is over—when the mind comes fructifying round to its own proper juxtaposition—then, my boy, we can look at the whole of the ramifications of the case calmly, and see what out-and-out fools we have been."

"I know what you mean," said Pokey, "exact; although I don't understand them hard words; you mean to say that when we're frightened, we're different to what we are when we are not."

"That's just what I do mean."

"Very good. And I agrees with you. But what puzzles me is, that you should have both heard and seen it, and thought it a ghost, and then when it's gone, say it's no ghost at all. For my part, I still think it was one, and a real one, too. If it was not, what was it?"

"That's the point. That's just what I should like to find out."

"Do you think it was a man dressed up like a ghost?"

"I do."

"Then why don't you go out and tackle him? You're big enough."

"If it be a man," said Legge, "I should only just like to catch him. *I'd* serve him out. I'd break every bone in his skin!"

"Well, why don't you go and do it? If *I* thought it was —little as I am—I'll be blistered if I wouldn't go out and tackle him. But I don't—I can't think it. The very fact of it's coming right up to the house, convinces me that it isn't a man."

"I think it is now," observed Legge.

"And so do I," cried Obadiah.

"*I* don't think it was a ghost," said Quocks.

"No more don't I," said Mr. Bobber.

"Well, then, look here," cried Pokey, "if that's it, look here. Here's four men here as believes it to be nothing but a man dressed up as a ghost—four strong, powerful, bony men—why, do you think that if I was one of you four, and believed, as you believe, that I wouldn't be after him in double quick time?"

"If he is a man," cried Mrs. Legge, who had privately had a little brandy-and-water, "I should like to catch the villain—I'd scratch his very eyes out!"

"But just look you here," resumed Pokey, who wanted to go home, but didn't at all like the idea of starting; "here's four of you here as does believe it, and yet there isn't one that'll move a peg!"

"Oh, I'll go," said Legge, "if you'll all come with me; or if any one of you will come, I'll go."

"You don't stir out of the house again to-night," said Mrs. Legge, "if I know it. You know, I suppose, what you've got to do in the morning? Let them as likes to go, go: *you* can't. Here's the brewer, here, coming here at four."

"I know it, my dear—I know it," said Legge.

"Very well, then; what do you want to go out for?"

"I don't want to go, my dear. Still if I were quite sure of catching this fellow, I should feel myself bound to go out with the rest."

"I only just wish I had him here," cried Mrs. Legge energetically; "I'd teach the villain, I'll warrant!"

"You had better, I think, go to bed, my dear," said Legge, who perceived that his spouse was excited—"you had better go to bed; I shall be with you shortly."

"I shall not go till you go," replied Mrs. Legge; "and I think it's time for all married men to be at home."

"Let us have some more brandy-and-water," said Quocks, who invariably, when he received a hint of that description, stopped an hour longer, at least. "Suppose," he added, "we have glasses round?"

"What do you want any more for?" inquired Mrs. Legge.

"Oh, we must have another glass apiece."

"*I* shan't draw any more. Legge may do as he likes; but, if I was him, not another drop should be drunk in this house to-night, if I knew it."

"Now then, Legge! Come, where's this glass? Now, gentlemen, give your orders."

"I must go," said Pokey.

"Nonsense, man. What, go alone? The ghost is safe to chaw you up. Wait till I go, and then you'll be safe. Come, order another glass like a man."

Pokey, who *didn't* like to go alone, ordered another glass; and so did Obadiah, and so did Bobber, and so did Quocks; and Legge attended to their orders, while Mrs. Legge intimated plainly that she thought him a fool.

Legge, however, took no notice of this. He was used to it. There was, therefore, no novelty whatever about it. He replenished their glasses, and took their money, and then philosophically filled another pipe.

He had, however, no sooner done so, than they again heard a knocking at the door: not the same description of knocking—no, but a knocking which clearly intimated that he who knocked really meant it.

"Shall I go?" said Legge, doubtfully.

"Certainly not," cried Mrs. Legge. "No."

"Oh, go," said Obadiah. "Only don't let him in."

"Why not?" demanded Pokey. "You say if he's a ghost he can get in without you; and if he isn't you should very much like to catch him: why, then, should he not be let in?"

"Who's *there?*" cried Legge, on approaching the door.

"Oh, for Heaven's *sake*, let me in—oh, pray let me in!" replied the man who had knocked.

"Who are you?"

"I'm a traveller—a poor traveller. But pray let me in."

"Oh, let him in," said Quocks. "If he means any nonsense, we are more than a match for him. Let him in, Legge."

"I'll not have him here," cried Mrs. Legge. "Keep the door closed: I'll not have him here."

But before the last words had been uttered, the door was opened, and in rushed a poor man, with cheeks blanched with terror, exclaiming—

"A ghost—a ghost!"

"What do you mean?" demanded Legge. "Come into this room. Now, then, what do you mean by a ghost!"

"Pray give me some water," said the poor man faintly. "Please give me some water."

"Here, take some of this," said Pokey, offering his glass; "it'll do you a little more good."

The poor man drank from Pokey's glass, and appeared to approve of the flavour of its contents.

"Now, then," said Legge, "what was it that alarmed you?"

"A ghost," replied the traveller. "I never saw one before in all my life."

"Are you sure it was a ghost?" inquired Pokey.

"Quite," replied the traveller—"Oh, quite sure."

"You don't think it was a man dressed up like a ghost?"

"If it was, he ought to be shot. But I can't think it was, no, I don't think that that was any man."

"Nor do I," observed Pokey.

"What, have *you* seen him then?"

"Yes; I saw him about half an hour ago: we all saw

him. He had an umbrella then. Had he one when you saw him?"

"No, he'd no umbrella. But it struck me—though, of course, it couldn't be—but it struck me that he had a cigar in his mouth smoking."

"Then it *is* a man!" cried Legge. "Whereabouts did you see him?"

"Just down the road, there. He's not a hundred yards from us now."

"Then, as true as I'm alive," said Legge, "if any one will go with me, I'll see what he's made of!"

"Indeed," said Mrs. Legge, "you'll do nothing of the sort."

"Will you go, Drant?"

"I don't think it worth *while*," replied Obadiah. "Not that I'm a mite afraid—only I don't exactly think it worth while."

"Well, will *you* go, Pokey?"

"I tell you I don't think it *is* a man at all. If I did, I'd go at once, but I don't."

"That's no man," observed the traveller.

"Not a bit of it!" cried Pokey. "If I thought it was I'd go in a moment."

"*I'll* go!" cried Quocks.

"Then come alone," said Legge; "come along!" and, despite the remonstrances of Mrs. Legge, they started.

On reaching the road, they looked cautiously round. Legge was armed with a thick stick, and Quocks with a poker; and, doubtless, had they seen any ghost at that moment, they would have attacked him; but they didn't: they walked down the road, and all was still; but just as they came within sight of the cottage, they saw the same figure glide slowly towards the door, and apparently vanish through one of the panels.

"No man could do that," observed Quocks, "that's quite clear."

"Strange," said Legge, mysteriously; "very strange, indeed."

"Shall we go up to the gate?"

"I'll go to the door, and knock them up, if you like."

"Well, but let's first go up to the gate, and have a look."

Legge consented at once; and they went to the gate, and looked anxiously round, but saw no "ghost." The door was closed, and all was still: there was, indeed, a light in Aunt Eleanor's room; but that they both knew to be usually there.

Aunt Eleanor, however, was restless that night; the duel and the action both preyed upon her mind; and, therefore, when she heard Legge and Quocks talking at the gate, she came to the window and looked.

"What's that?" exclaimed Quocks, as he saw the blind move.

"That's Mrs. Sound," returned Legge. "Stop a bit. Perhaps she'll open the window."

She did so; and having cried "Who's there?" Legge answered; and she knew his voice at once.

"Is there anything the matter, Mr. Legge?" she inquired.

"Why, ma'am," replied Legge; "they say it's a ghost."

"Good Heavens. What again! Did *you* see it?"

"Why, ma'am, I saw something very much like one; and if it be, it has just now entered your cottage."

"Heaven preserve us!" exclaimed Aunt Eleanor.

"You shouldn't have told her that, Legge," said Quocks.

"I don't wish to alarm you, ma'am," cried Legge. "My only object is to render every possible assistance, if any assistance be required."

"You are very kind — very kind. *Will* you wait a moment?"

"Certainly, ma'am, with all the pleasure in life."

Aunt Eleanor then rang the bell, and continued to ring until Mary appeared.

"Mary," she cried, "tell Judkins to get up this moment."

"Anything the matter, ma'am?"

"Tell him to go down and speak to Mr. Legge."

Mary conveyed the message to Judkins, who was up in a moment, and lost no time in running down to the door.

"What's the row?" he inquired; "what is it?"

"Have you heard any noise?" cried Legge.

"Noise! no. What noise do you mean?"

"We thought that you might perhaps have heard some noise."

CHAPTER XXX.

THE SUSPICION.

AUNT ELEANOR, notwithstanding her apparent tranquillity while speaking to Legge and his friend, no sooner returned to her chamber alone than she burst into tears, for the recollection of her brother's death came again full upon her, and all her former painful apprehensions were renewed. She felt that his spirit still hovered around her—that it had something dreadful to communicate, and that it could not rest until that communication had been made. She wished it would appear to her then—she absolutely prayed that it might then appear; and, while contemplating with feelings of dread the possibility of its appearance, her imagination, being excited strongly at the time, at once created a figure—the very figure of her brother—which stood with an expression of sorrow before her.

She started, and for a time ceased to breathe, and while she glared at the spectre, she became cold as death. There it stood, perfectly motionless and silent, and there it continued to stand, until, inspiring sufficient courage, she exclaimed, in a thrilling whisper—

"*Dear* brother, why are you here?"

This broke the charm. The spectre instantly vanished. But it came again when all was still, and she then saw it even more distinctly than before.

She rose to approach it with feelings of awe, but, as she advanced, it receded, until it completely disappeared beneath the bed-clothes. This was strange, certainly—very strange indeed. She couldn't at all understand it. Could it be possible the she had been deceived? Could she have beheld it in imagination merely? She passed her hands over her eyes, and then, in order to be *sure* that she was perfectly conscious, proceeded to bathe them.

Again she looked round. The spirit had fled. She turned down the bed-clothes. No spectre was there. But the idea of getting into a bed in which she conceived a spirit had taken refuge, appeared to her to be monstrous. She therefore resumed her seat in her easy-chair, and, having looked in vain for the spirit's reappearance for nearly an hour, she involuntarily dropped off to sleep, and slept soundly until Mary at the usual time came to the door.

The reverend gentleman, soon after this, heard that the ghost had revisited the Grange, and having made minute inquiries of which the result was the startling information that it had again entered the cottage, he proceeded to call on his dearest friend in a state of intense anxiety.

As he passed through the gate, she descended the stairs, and when they met, he pressed her hand with affectionate warmth, but her pale face inspired him with fearful apprehensions.

"Dear Eleanor," said he, "you are not well. Have you been *much* alarmed?"

"I have been somewhat alarmed," she replied, as she slightly smiled, and led him into the parlour. "Then you have heard," she continued, "you have heard of this mysterious occurrence?"

"I heard that the people in the village were alarmed by the appearance of a spirit which they saw enter here. At least they imagined that they saw it. Whether they did or not of course I must leave. I presume that *you* saw nothing of it?"

"I saw it as distinctly as I now see you here."

"Is it possible?"

"Not at the time it was seen by them, but subsequently, while I was sitting in my chamber."

"Heaven preserve us!"

"I saw it twice: and, as I feared, it was the spirit of my poor, dear brother."

"What, and did it speak to you?"

"No. I spoke to it, but it instantly vanished; and when it reappeared I rose to approach it, but again it vanished, and I saw it no more."

"You amaze me! Then you absolutely saw its countenance?"

"Yes; and it was that of my poor, unhappy brother."

"Bless my heart alive—why, what on earth can it mean? There must be some dreadful mystery at the bottom of all this. It was silent, you say—quite silent?"

"Quite."

"Did it not intimate anything by gestures?"

"Nothing. It was perfectly motionless."

"Strange—very strange. It could not have appeared without an object, and one would have thought that that object, whatever it might be, would have been, of course, communicated in some way. You could not have been mistaken? You were not, I presume, at the time, dreaming?"

"Oh, dear me, no; I was sitting in my chair."

"Well, there *are* strange things, both in heaven and on earth. Did Sylvester see it too?"

"No; in this house it appeared to me only. He does not even know that *I* have seen it; nor do I wish him to know, feeling perfectly sure that the knowledge of my having seen the spirit of his father would break his heart."

"Don't you think it would be prudent to put him on his guard? It may appear to *him*, and that with the view of revealing some highly-important secret, and, if taken by surprise, he may be too much excited and confused to understand it. What do you think?"

"I am at all times anxious to be guided by you; but it strikes me that when you reflect upon the probable consequences, you will wish to conceal it from him, at least for the present."

"You may be right; I am quite inclined to believe that you *are* right. Let it be so. We may know more anon."

At this moment Sylvester entered the room, and having greeted both his aunt and her reverend friend warmly, proceeded to ascertain what had occurred.

"Was there anything the matter last night?" he inquired.

"Do you mean, my dear, when I knocked at your door?"

"Yes; why did you knock?"

"I merely thought that you might have been disturbed."

"What induced you to think so?"

"Why, the people in the village imagined they saw a ghost"——

"What, again?"

"Yes; and some of them declared that they saw it come here."

"How very extraordinary. Mystery follows me, go where I may. Do you know the persons who fancied they saw it come here?"

"Legge was one — the person who keeps the public-house."

"I'll go over and speak to Legge immediately after breakfast. He is rather a superior man, too; is he not? I speak, of course, with reference to his position."

"Exactly," returned the reverend gentleman. "He *is* a superior man; a man of strong mind, and good, plain, common sense."

"And a kind creature, too," said Aunt Eleanor, "I'm sure. He came over last night, in order to ascertain if he could render me any assistance."

"Well, I'll go and speak to him," said Sylvester; "and then I shall hear all about it. It certainly is most mysterious. I can't understand it at all."

It will not be incorrect to observe that these observations were induced by the thought that he might, unconsciously, have been the cause of all. He had previously no conception of being a somnambulist, but, as a remarkable case of somnambulism had just before been published, he thought it possible — just possible — that he was in reality a somnambulist himself. He did not — he could not — believe that he was; but feeling, of course, anxious — as the thought had been conceived — to ascertain whether he really was or not, he at once resolved on viewing every circumstance that had occurred in immediate connection with that.

In pursuance of this resolution, he immediately after breakfast left the cottage, and went to the Crumpet and Crown. Obadiah, and Pokey, and Quocks were there, with Bobber, and several others, and as he was perfectly unknown to them all, he was, of course, minutely examined from head to foot as he entered.

"I say," whispered Pokey in the ear of Obadiah, "who's he?"

"A government spy, you fool. Don't your ideas fructify?"

"Is that a spy?"

"Of course. Hold your tongue."

"But how do you know?"

"I know by the cut of him. Mind what you're after,

Bobby Peel has sent him down to feel the pulse of the eternal people. You'll see now I'll cook his goose for him presently. Fine morning, sir," he added, addressing Sylvester, who had taken a seat immediately opposite.

"It is, indeed," said Sylvester, "a beautiful morning."

"Barleys want rain, sir."

"You have not yet been able to get much barley in, have you?"

"Not get it in, sir! What not here the latter end of May!"

"They haven't got much barley in about here," observed Quocks.

"What, not barley?"

"No, not barley. Look at the drought we've had. How *could* they get it in? The land's as dry and hard as the road."

Sylvester called for a glass of ale, which Mrs. Legge brought with a most winning smile.

"Is that the way you means to cook his goose?" whispered Pokey.

"Stop a bit, my Briton," replied Obadiah; "you'll know more about it, my boy, by-and-by. He who deals with a deep 'un must be deep himself; you can't get all out of a spy in a hurry. The drought, sir, I believe, has been pretty general," he added, turning to Sylvester; "how are the wheats in your part of the country?"

"That which I saw along the road looked well."

"The heavy-land wheats about *here* don't look so much amiss, but those on the light lands are perished. Which road, sir, do you allude to?"

"The road between here and London."

"Oh, London. Ah, exactly. Didn't I tell you so?" he added, turning to Pokey; "I'd have bet ten to one of it. I knew what he was the very moment I saw him. I don't want to look at a man twice to know who and what he is. Not a bit of it. Have you just arrived from London, sir?"

"I came yesterday."

"Oh, indeed. And what, may I ask, do you think of the spy system generally?"

"The *spy* system?"

"Ay; you know in Harry the Eighth's time they did the trick very deliberately."

"Upon my word, you give me credit for more knowledge than I possess."

"What, don't you remember when Peter the Great came over here just before the French Revolution, when Buonaparte threatened to welt the whole world, and sent Robespierre after the Dutch?"

"Really," said Sylvester, smiling, "you are much too learned for me. I never before heard that Peter the Great, Buonaparte, and Robespierre were so intimately connected."

"Why, they all lived in juxtaposition."

"Obadiah," said Quocks calmly, "don't be an ass."

"What do you mean?" cried Obadiah indignantly.

"Hold your tongue. Don't expose yourself before strangers."

Obadiah thought this very severe, and was about to inflict upon Quocks an extremely cutting observation; but as Legge, who had been hopping down some beer, entered the room at the moment, Quocks escaped that infliction.

"Good morning, sir," said Legge, addressing Sylvester, whom he had quite forgotten.

"Good morning," returned Sylvester. "You were somewhat alarmed last night, were you not?"

"Well; it's true we were, rather. You have heard of it, of course?"

"I heard of it this morning."

"A mysterious piece of business, sir, that. I can't understand it."

"Nor can I. It is indeed mysterious."

"He's the ghost for a thousand," whispered Obadiah.

"And a spy, too?" said Pokey.

"Both, my boy. I'll bet ten to one of it. Now, you'll just see how I'll pump him. You didn't see the ghost then, yourself, sir?" he added, addressing Sylvester; and then, turning to Pokey, with a wink of great significance.

"No," replied Sylvester. "I wish that I had. By the way, I have to thank you, Mr. Legge, for your attention to my aunt."

"Your aunt, sir?" said Legge. "Upon my word, sir, I haven't the pleasure of knowing you."

"My name is Sound."

"Oh! I beg your pardon, sir. I hope you're quite well, sir. Upon my word, I'd quite forgotten you. I knew I'd seen you somewhere, too! How is Mrs. Sound this morning?"

"Not quite so well."

"I don't wonder at it. A thing of this sort must be very alarming to her. I know it gets over me. I can't make it out at all!"

"He's a government spy, isn't he?" whispered Pokey to Obadiah.

"How do you know that he isn't?"

"And the ghost, too!"

"He may be! You can't tell he's not."

"You saw this ghost, I believe?" said Sylvester.

"Oh, we all saw it!" returned Legge.

"Distinctly?"

"As distinctly as a thing of the kind *could* be seen."

"And what shape did it assume? What did it look like?"

"Why the figure was that of a man: tall—very tall: it stood, I should say, seven feet high."

"Seven *feet!*" cried Pokey; "more nearer yards."

"Imagination probably added to its height," observed Sylvester. "But how did it act?"

"Why, sir," replied Legge, "when it was first seen, it was walking up and down just before the cottage gate: and, from the description, I imagined it might be smoking a cigar; for only one eye, it was said, could be seen, and that was an eye of fire."

"It was no cigar," said Pokey; "not a bit of it. It *was* an eye—safe!"

"Well," resumed Sylvester, "and did it continue to walk up and down?"

"For a time," replied Legge; "but it afterwards came here—to this very door—and knocked, and lifted up the latch; but somehow or other, I felt afraid at the time to let it in."

"I wish that you *had* done so!" said Sylvester.

"Then do you not think that it was really a ghost?"

"Why, the thing is so extraordinary, that I scarcely know what to think! But had you opened the door at the time, you would have seen at once whether it was a ghost or not."

"I'll do so if it should come again. I've made up my mind to that."

"That's the only way to satisfy yourself on the point. Take hold of it, if you can. You need not have recourse to any violence. Touch it; and if it *be* tangible, you may then, of course, be quite sure of its being no ghost."

"But if I were to find that it was not a ghost—if I were to catch any fellow playing such a trick as that—I'd make him remember it the longest day he had to live."

"And so would I!" cried Mrs. Legge. "I'd scratch his very eyes out!"

"I'd murder him right off!" exclaimed Pokey.

"And serve him right, too," said Quocks. "Hanging's too good for him."

"If," observed Sylvester calmly, "a man in a state of consciousness, and with the view of creating alarm, were to be guilty of so disgraceful and dangerous an act, he would deserve to be punished with the utmost severity; but, if even the figure which you saw last night *be* a man, it does not of necessity follow that he deserves the rough treatment you contemplate. There are men who are in the habit of walking in their sleep, and who perform acts of the most extraordinary character while in a state of somnambulism; and it certainly would not be just to treat a man of that description with as much severity as you would treat a heartless, impious scoundrel, whose sole object is to inspire the most appalling species of apprehension."

"Very true: very good," said Legge. "That's right: quite right."

"If I were to see this figure," resumed Sylvester—"I'm not in the habit of boasting, nor do I pretend to any extraordinary valour—but if I were to see it, I should go right up to it at once. I should soon, of course, be able to discover what it was; and if I found it to be a man, and not the shade of a man merely, my very first object would be to ascertain if he were asleep. If I found that he was, I should take the utmost care of him; but if, on the contrary, I found that he was not, I'd secure the villain instantly, and bring him to justice."

"That's a very proper view to take of the matter," observed Legge.

"Ay; but that's no man," cried Pokey. "There an't a mite of flesh and blood about it."

"I can scarcely believe that it is a man myself," said Legge. "No man could have gone through the panel of a door as that did—eh, Quocks?"

"No," replied Quocks, "not a bit of it. I don't mean to say that no man could go through; but I do mean to say that if he did, he'd make a hole in it, which wouldn't be closed up by magic, as that was."

"Well," said Sylvester, rising, "it is altogether a most extraordinary occurrence; still, were I to see the figure, I certainly should ascertain, if possible, what it really was. Good morning, gentlemen," he added, "good morning."

"That's no fool," observed Legge, when Sylvester had left.

"Not a bit of it," said Quocks. "He knows a thing or two, and takes more than one view of a question."

"Drant offered to bet ten to one about his being a government spy," observed Pokey; and this observation produced a hearty laugh.

"Laugh away!" cried Obadiah. "Laugh away, my boys! But just look here! Can you prove that he isn't? Come now! It's easy to laugh: any fool may laugh; but can any of you *prove* that he isn't a spy?"

"Can any one here prove than you are not one?" said Quocks.

"Me!" cried Obadiah indignantly. "Me a spy? Me? Where's the gold that could buy me? I scorn the vile fructifying insinuation. What! place me in the juxta-position of a wretch who would do any cold-blooded business for money—a fellow who'd swear a man's life away just as soon as look at him—a villain, a boney fide villain, whose trade is that of tempting men merely to betray 'em! I call it a most amalgamating insult! No man alive has a right to insult another by such a monstrous insinuation as that!"

"Then why did you thus insult the nephew of Mrs. Sound?"

"I didn't *tell* him that he was a spy!"

"Nor did I tell you that you were a spy. You asked if

any one could prove that he was not: I asked if any one could prove that you were not. I believe one to be as much of a spy as the other; but you forget that when you denounce men for insinuating that which you have insinuated, you, in effect, denounce yourself."

"Well; but look you here: he was quite a stranger."

"What of that? Did that justify you in setting him down for a spy?"

"But he looked like a spy; he came in like a spy, and acted as much like a spy as I ever saw a man in my life."

"Did you ever see a spy?"

"Why, I can't say that ever I did *see* one."

"Then how is it possible for you to know when a man either looks or acts like one? Besides, the idea of a spy being sent down here, is too absurd to be thought of."

"Bobby Peel might, you know, send one down just to see, you know, which way the wind blows!"

"Bobby Peel!—psha! What do you think Bobby Peel cares about the wind in a place like this?"

"What! Do you mean to say, then, that you think he don't care?"

"Not a straw! Why should he?"

"Why should he! What, then, are we to be tyrannised over and trampled upon by a plundering lot of oligarchical pensioners, and not have a voice in the matter at all?"

"Obadiah," said Quocks. "You'll *excuse* me; but, as true as I'm alive, Obadiah, you're a fool."

"It's all very well to get over it in that way: there's nothing more easy than to call a man a fool: there's no argument in it! But prove me to be one: that's the point of the compass! Place me in juxtaposition with any man in Europe—I don't care who he is!—and if he knows anything of history, he'll find I can tell him what's what. You may call me a fool just as long as you please: I don't care a button about what you call me. Prove me to be one—that's the teaser, my boy!—prove me, if you can, to be a boney fide fool, and I'll stand glasses round."

"What do you mean by boney fide?" inquired Pokey.

"Boney fide! Send I may live! What, don't you know what boney fide means? Where did you go to school? Who had the fructification of your ignorant ideas? Boney fide means out-and-out, of course. A boney fide fool is an out-and-out fool; and I should like to see the man who can prove *me* to be one."

"I should like to see the man who can prove that you are *not* one," said Quocks, who indignantly finished his beer, and then, without condescending to utter another syllable, left them.

"Poor Quocks!" cried Obadiah. "He can't bear to be beaten! I don't like to be hard upon any man alive, but I can't help being a little hard upon him: he's so ignorant of history."

"But you don't mean to say," observed Pokey, "you can't mean to say, that you've beaten him this morning!"

"Beaten him! What did he run away for? I'd beat half a million of men like him before breakfast! Why, I'll bet you what you like, that, if you were to offer him five hundred pounds, he couldn't tell you who Peter the Great's mother was! What's the use of a man like that! I don't want to boast, but he's no more fit to be put in juxtaposition with me, than Bobby Peel is fit to be put in juxtaposition with Julius Cæsar. There's nothing in him! In all that relates to boney fide argument, he's what I should call a mere non compos;' and he knows just as much about fructifying logic as Harry the Eighth knew about this pint pot. The mind of a man must be properly amalgamated to be in a juxtaposition to stand against one who has studied things as I have. Study's the point, my boys! no getting on without study. Study will beat the world hollow; and Quocks has got no study in him."

"Well," said Pokey, "*I* must go to work. I've got a pair of buckskins to finish to-day."

"Business *must* be attended to," observed Obadiah; who, notwithstanding the loss of Pokey, continued to work his amalgamated fructifying boney fide juxtaposition until he was left quite alone.

Sylvester, meanwhile, deeply reflected, not only upon the events of the preceding night, but upon the whole of the equally mysterious circumstances which had occurred to him since he left the house of Mr. Scholefield. The event, however, upon which he dwelt chiefly, was that which formed the ground of Sir Charles Julian's action; and when he viewed the nature of the evidence against him, in connection with the idea of his being a somnambulist, it appeared to him to be perfectly clear that to nothing but somnambulism could it be ascribed

But how was the fact of his being a somnambulist to be proved? That was the primary question. The readiest and most effectual way of proving it appeared to be that of communicating the idea to some one by whom he might be watched; but his anxiety to conceal it from his aunt, whose mind he well knew would be for ever after filled with apprehension, induced him eventually to decide on endeavouring to prove it himself.

He therefore set to work and conceived various schemes, the operation of which were in his view calculated to prove the thing beyond all doubt, and having decided at length upon one which appeared to be the easiest and also the best, he, on retiring that night about ten, attached to one of his ankles a string which communicated with a bell which he ingeniously hung, so that it would of necessity ring in the event of his getting out of bed, and at the same time prevent him from leaving the room.

Having artfully adjusted this machinery to his entire satisfaction he went to sleep, and as his thoughts soon afterwards reverted to the "ghost," which he then felt an extremely strong desire to see, he with great deliberation removed the string from his ankle, rose, dressed himself, and left the house.

For some time he walked leisurely up and down the road in the full expectation of seeing this spectre, but as in this he was, as a matter of course, disappointed, he, perceiving a light at the Crumpet and Crown, and hearing voices within, at length went to the door.

That night Mrs. Legge, who had been having some more private brandy-and-water, *would* have the door bolted, and Sylvester in consequence could not get in. He therefore knocked, and immediately heard such a hissing as that which might proceed from a dozen young serpents anxious to cry simultaneously "*Hush!*"

"There it is!" said Pokey.

"That's it!" exclaimed Obadiah.

"It's the same knock," observed Quocks.

"Exactly!" cried Legge. "Now, then, what's to be done? Shall I open the door?"

"I'll have no ghost in this house to-night, if I know it," said Mrs. Legge pointedly; "not if I know it."

"Go to bed, my dear," observed Legge; "go to bed."

"I shan't go to bed! you are a rogue to me, Legge, you know you are."

"Hark!" cried Legge, who had been so used to these affectionate observations that they really passed by him as the "idle wind." "Did you hear?"

"What?" exclaimed Pokey.

"A groan. *Shall* I open the door? Will you back me?"

"*I* will," replied Quocks, "at all events."

"Then the door shall be opened."

"Don't!" cried Pokey. "Don't! pray don't!"

Legge rose; but Mrs. Legge on the instant threw her arms round his neck, and cleverly burst into tears.

Legge couldn't stand this. He could, as well as any man in England, stand any given quantity of abuse, but all was over the very moment he saw a tear. Mrs. Legge knew this—of *course* she knew it—she hadn't lived all those years with him without finding *that* out—it wasn't at all likely.

"If you won't go," said Quocks, who also knew Legge's weakness in this respect, "*I* will."

"Don't! Quocks!—Mr. Quocks!—don't!" cried Pokey. "For God's sake, *don't* do nothing of the sort."

"Why not?" demanded Quocks. "Hark! hark!" he added, as Sylvester again knocked. "I *will* go, and that's all about it."

"You *shan't!*" exclaimed Mrs. Legge, seizing his arm.

"What do you mean, woman?"

"Look at me—Mr. Quocks—pray consider my children."

Quocks had children of his own. He, therefore, resumed his seat in silence.

"Well, I'm blowed if *I* won't go," cried Bobber.

"Mr. Bobber," said Mrs. Legge, "haven't you a sister depending upon you? If anything should happen to you what will become of *her?*"

Bobber poured out another glass of ale.

"Well, but this ought to be seen to," cried Pokey.

"You remember what that young gentleman said? I'll open the door myself."

"I believe," said Mrs. Legge, "that you have an aged father. *Do* you wish him to come to the workhouse? Beware!"

Pokey knocked the ashes out of his pipe, and refilled it.

"Don't you think that we'd better just ask who it is?" said Obadiah.

"*You* may open the *door*, if you like," said Mrs. Legge, who well knew that he dared do nothing of the sort.

"No," returned Obadiah, "not a bit of it! *I* shall not open the door. Why don't *you* open it? I've heard that ghosts won't touch *virtuous* women."

"What do you mean by that?" demanded Legge angrily.

"Oh! I meant no offence. I merely said that I had heard that virtuous women were safe."

"Since it's come to that," cried Mrs. Legge indignantly, "I'll open the door myself, if I die for it."

Obadiah now seized the poker, and Quocks spat in his hand, in order to grasp his stick firmly, while Pokey and Bobber turned up their cuffs and doubled their fists.

"*Who's* there?" demanded Mrs. Legge.

"'Tis I," replied Sylvester; "don't be alarmed."

The bolt was withdrawn, the latch was raised, and in walked Sylvester calmly.

The moment he entered, Pokey and Bobber resumed their seats, and as Obadiah relinquished the poker, Quocks dropped his stick between his legs and felt better.

"I've been looking for this ghost," observed Sylvester, "but I can see nothing of it. Have *you* seen it to-night?"

"Not to-night, sir," replied Legge. "No, I haven't heard of it to-night."

"I should like to see it very much indeed. Am I too late to have a little brandy-and-water?"

"Oh, dear me—no; not at all, sir."

"These gentlemen probably will join me? Suppose, Mr. Legge, we have glasses round?"

"If you please, sir," replied Legge, who really felt very much obliged to him; "warm, sir—or cold?"

"Suit the tastes of these gentlemen; *I'll* have it cold."

"But really, sir," observed Quocks, "we don't wish that."

"You're a good fellow, I believe," returned Sylvester. "It appears to me that you are all good fellows; and as such you'll not refuse to drink with me?"

"Certainly not, sir. We're very much obliged to you, only we don't like to impose on good nature, sir: that's all."

"If that be all, then, don't say another word about it."

Legge—who had a brilliant eye to business—produced five glasses of brandy-and-water, and Sylvester, on counting them, observed, "You, of course, never drink brandy-and-water yourself?"

"Much obliged to you," said Legge, who at once took the hint, but had no more idea of his guest being asleep than he had of his being the "spectre." Nay, it is questionable whether he would have believed it, if he had even been told.

"Well," said Sylvester, "I wonder whether this mysterious swell intends to visit us to-night."

"The swell, sir," observed Legge; "beg pardon: whom do you mean?"

"The ghost!"

"Oh," cried Legge, who raised a hearty laugh, in which the rest, as a matter of gratitude, joined. "The idea of calling a ghost a swell. Well, I *never* heard anything better in my life."

"It's a boney fide 'un, that is," observed Obadiah. "Julius Cæsar couldn't have made a better joke than that."

"Was Julius Cæsar *very* fond of joking?" inquired Sylvester.

"Fond of joking! What, don't you remember when he and Pompey there welted the Dutch, what a game they had with 'em? Why, there wasn't a more fructifying joker in the world; he was the very first original inventor of joking: Joe Miller stole the whole of his jokes from Julius Cæsar."

"Indeed! Well now, I wasn't aware of that."

"Oh, yes. Why didn't the Greeks deify him—isn't he the heathen god of joking?"

"Very likely. *I* thought it had been Momus."

"Momus! Momus was a fool to him. He couldn't hold the candle to Julius Cæsar."

"That's true," observed Sylvester, who was highly amused.

"He wasn't fit to tie Julius Cæsar's shoe-strings," continued Obadiah. "There isn't a man alive like him, with the exception of Harry Brougham, and he's a rattler. Put all the Bobby Peels you can find in a lump, and they won't come half up to Harry Brougham."

"Brougham's a great man," said Sylvester.

"A *great* man, sir! He's a cut above a great man; he's what *I* call a boney fide fructifier of freedom. Talk of the Tories. Your Tories can't be put in juxtaposition with him. Look at 'em. What are they? A plundering set of blood-sucking pensioners, screwing a matter of ninety millions a year out of the vitals of the people, and putting men in prison for speaking their mind, while their bishops are living on the fat of the land. Do you call this liberty?" he continued, rising with the view of giving more emphatic expression to his sentiments. "Do you call this fructifying freedom? If the people were not most amalgamated fools they'd hang, draw, and quarter the lot. Look at France—would they have it? Look at Spain—would they stand it? Look anywhere you like—I don't care where you look; take Europe, Asia, Africa, and America, and point out a people groaning under such a heap of national debt, if you can. Look at the currency—there's a currency! Look at the corn-laws—only *look* at 'em. Was there ever such a mighty mass of monstrous corruption—isn't it enough to make one's hair stand on end? If a man becomes poor he must go to the workhouse and live upon gruel and such like muck, while the very men who have made him poor are swimming in sherry, and port, and champagne. Do you call this justice? Is this carrying out the eternal principle of equal rights? I'm for all men in the world being equal—why shouldn't they be? A'n't the poor as good as the rich? Haven't they got souls and bodies as well as the rich have? Why should they be crushed? Why should they be ground down and trampled upon? I'm for an equitable adjustment. I'd have whatever money there is in the country equally divided among us all. It belongs to us all as a matter of right, and therefore we all ought to have it. One man should be just as rich as another. The whole system ought to be changed, and it can't be changed without a rattling revolution. A revolution we must have. That would bring the beggarly aristocracy to their senses. That would let your bishops and your parsons and all the rest of your muck know what's what. We must have a revolution; and mark my words, *when* we have one they'll know it. What, isn't it monstrous that we should work and slave to let a limited lot of locusts live in luxury? Isn't it disgraceful to our intellects as men that we should suffer a parcel of puppet-show paupers to plunder and propagate the people in this way? Down with them. That's my sentiments! Down with the lot. We'll have no king—no constitution—no aristocracy!—strangle them all!—no bishops—no parsons—no church—no nothing. Down with tyranny and up with freedom; fair, fructifying freedom; unlimited liberty is all we require. Britons *never* shall be slaves!"

"Bravo," cried Sylvester; "bravo, bravo! Why are you not in the House?"

"The House—the corrupt House of Commons! If I ever put a foot into such a House as that I should feel it a national disgrace. No; if it was honest—if it was pure—if it wasn't what it is—a notorious den of thieves, I'd say something to you, but as it's rank, rascally, rampant, and rotten, neither you nor any other man in Europe will ever catch me there."

"I hope you've been amused, sir," observed Legge, aloud.

"I have indeed," replied Sylvester, smiling.

"Amused, sir," exclaimed Obadiah, who started again to his feet. "Why, when William the Conqueror welted the French, he said to Boney, said he, 'Now I'll tell you what it is'"——

"Don't let's have any more speechifying," interrupted Quocks.

"What do you mean?" demanded Obadiah contemptuously.

"I'd rather myself hear a song," observed Sylvester; "perhaps you will give us a song instead?"

"A song. With all my heart," cried Obadiah; "I'm ready for anything in nature. If you want a song, I'm the boy to sing one."

"*You* can't sing," observed Pokey.

"Not sing, you fool. Why, I'm open to sing against any man in Europe, for anything a-side you like to name. Not sing! Why, if you come to that, I'll sing you a song of my own composing. Now then!"

"Stop!" said Sylvester, "you've nothing to drink. Mr. Legge, you'd better replenish these glasses."

Legge, who was always on the *qui vive*, did so, when Obadiah put down his pipe, and commenced. "Anybody else," said he, "may call it what he likes, but I, my boys, call it

OLD ENGLAND.

Old England, my Britons, would but for the Tories,
   Be merry and happy and perfectly free:
The flat flag of freedom—that emblem of glories—
   Would wave, but for them, o'er the land and the sea.
Her men are so brave, generous, joyous, and witty,
   It's seldom, indeed, you'll discover a rogue,
While the girls are so precious, plump, prattling, and pretty,
   It's wonderful bigamy's not more in vogue.
      Tol de rol, lol de rol, lol de rol, diddle lol,
      Tol de rol, diddle lol, looral-li-day.

When Peter the Great once came over to welt us,
   With Harry the Eighth, and old Boney to boot,
His most valiant soldiers, the moment they smelt us,
   Were struck with such terror—pooh!—they couldn't shoot.
Then hurrah for Old England! She has boney fide
   A standard of liberty, which when unfurled,
Will govern the ocean! And she's in a tidy
   Good juxtaposition to welt the whole world.
      Tol de rol, lol de rol, lol de rol, diddle lol,
      Tol de rol, diddle lol, looral-li-day."

"Bravo!" cried Sylvester, "bravo!"

"What do you think of that, my boys?" exclaimed Obadiah. "That's more than Bobby Peel could do, I'll bet a million."

"And is it really your own composition?" said Sylvester.

"My own, and nobody else's."

"I should like to have a copy of it."

"That you shall have, with all the pleasure in life, because I know you're a boney fide trump."

"And wont you let me have a copy?" said Pokey.

"Yes, my brave boy, you shall have a copy, too."

"And you'll give me a copy, of course?" said Quocks.

"Well, I don't mind, because it'll fructify your views."

"You'll give me one, too," cried Bobber, "wont you?"

"Well *you* shall have a copy."

"I *must* have one," said Legge.

"How many more of you?"

"It's such a very pretty song," said Mrs. Legge archly; "you'll not, of course, refuse to give *me* a copy of it?"

"Well, I'd better have three or four secretaries of state down here, just to assist me. But you shall have copies, I'll take care of that; and you know, if I say that I'll do a thing, I'll do it. There's no mistake at all about me. I'm John Bull, right up and down straight, and I don't care who knows it; that's another thing, my boys."

"Well, but how about the ghost?" suggested Sylvester; "I'm afraid we shall not see it to-night."

"The ghost, sir, may come if it likes," said Obadiah, "or keep away if it likes, and do what it likes. I'd extend the eternal principle of liberty, even to a ghost. But, gentlemen," he added, rising, "I've a toast to propose—a toast which I'm sure you'll all fructify in juxtaposition with as much boney fideness as I do. It is a toast, gentlemen, which reflects upon the country the highest national honour a man can feel—a toast which, setting aside all party questions, is, perhaps, the most exuberant manifestation of manhood it's possible for any nation in Europe to show. The mind may amalgamate, the senses may soar, the human heart which beats in the breast of a man may fructify, and fructify, and keep on continually fructifying, till fructification is lost in the utter annihilation of words; but the toast I'm about to propose to you, gentlemen, is one which beats all your philosophy hollow. Gentlemen, we have been honoured to-night with the presence of one who shines a lustre in the atmosphere of intellect, and beats metaphysics into fits. He has come amongst us, gentlemen, to illumine our rays, like the rainbow in the heavens, great, glorious, and grammatical. He is, gentlemen, one of that boney fide nobleness of nature in his bosom, which scorns an act of meanness in his nature, and makes his mind throb with hospitality. He has, gentlemen, been with us to-night like a star in the horizon which sheds its refreshment around;

and I, as I think that you'll have no difficulty in guessing the party to which I allude, I'll at once, without preface, propose the good health of that boney fide trump, there, by which we've been honoured."

Cheers, of course, followed this eloquent speech, which so convulsed Sylvester with laughter, that it nearly awoke him. At length, however, assuming a look of gravity, he rose and said—

"Gentlemen, I duly appreciate the extremely high compliment which has just been paid me by our eloquent friend, who is, moreover, a friend to the human race, including Buonaparte, Peter the Great, and Harry Brougham. I call it a *bonâ fide* compliment, associated as it has been with fructifying freedom; and I ought to feel proud of being thus in amalgamating juxtaposition with a statesman whose chief characteristics have been so conspicuously developed."

"That's the time o' day, my boys," exclaimed Obadiah, as Sylvester, with appropriate gravity, resumed his seat. "*They're* the words to fructify the bosom of a Briton and touch the ideas of the human heart! What do you think of that, my boy, *eh?*" he added, slapping Pokey on the back in a state of ecstacy. "What do you think of that for a boney fide speech?"

"It *is* a boney fide 'un, that," replied Pokey; "it's what I call splendacious!"

The glasses were again replenished, and Obadiah sang another song, at the conclusion of which Sylvester suddenly rose, exclaiming—

"The ghost—I must see the ghost!"

"Oh, stop a little longer, sir, do," said Obadiah.

"Yes, do, sir," cried Pokey; "and then we'll go together."

"It may be there now," resumed Sylvester, whose eyes became fixed. "I *must* go and see."

"Well, come back again for five minutes," cried Obadiah; "do come back again, if it's only merely just to say good night."

Sylvester, who had by this time reached the door, left the house, and walked deliberately home; and having undressed himself, got into bed, and adjusted the string round his ankle again.

CHAPTER XXXI.

THE VILLAGE FAIR.

In the morning Sylvester's very first object was to ascertain whether the string was all right, and on finding that it was, he felt, of course, perfectly sure that he had not been out of bed.

This evidence, however, was not alone sufficient to convince him that he was not a somnambulist. He had first to learn whether the "ghost" had reappeared. If it had, then the evidence of the string might be held to be conclusive; but if it had not—if nothing of a mysterious character had occurred—he felt that he should be still in a state of uncertainty, seeing that he might be in reality a somnambulist, and yet not walk every night.

He, therefore, rose and dressed hastily, and being extremely anxious to make the necessary inquiries, went to Judkins, who was then in the garden.

"Well, Judkins," said he, "have you heard any more about the ghost?"

"No, sir, I don't think he came at all last night; leastways, I haven't heard nothing about it, and I know, if he had, I should have heard afore this. I wonder what it wants a-coming poking about here, a-frightening people in this here manner. I expect there's some money hid somewhere, or else there's been a murder committed, one of the two. It wouldn't come here, you know, for nothing, sir, would it?"

"It must have some object, I should *think*."

"Them's the very words I said to Legge yesterday. Says I, 'You may take your oath it don't come here for nothing;' and he agreed with me. Depend upon it, sir, there's something dreadful on the mind of that ghost. I remember, sir, a ghost came here somewhere about five years ago—you may have heard tell of it, perhaps?—well, that played the devil's *own* tricks: took the horses out of the stable—flew all over the country—frightened people into fits, and kicked up Bob's delight! I expect the parson laid it at last, for we haven't seen nothing on it since."

"Was that about *five* years ago?" inquired Sylvester, who felt his suspicion confirmed.

"Let me see," replied Judkins, leaning thoughtfully on his spade. "Five years! To be sure—it's more than five years. I've had these here breeches above five years, and they was made because the others was found in the pickle-tub shrunk up to nothing, so as I couldn't pull 'em on. It was five year last fall, sir—that was the time. I remember now—they cost me fourteen-and-sixpence, and Pokey, down here, was the man which made 'em. That was a rum start, that was! Up to this blessed day I could never make out how they got into that precious tub. I thought, at first, that cook put 'em there to spit her spite, but I don't think, now, that she could have been so vicious. No; it must have been the ghost—leastways, I think so; if that didn't put 'em there, I don't know who did. Why, let me see," he added, "five years!—why, you was down here at the time; to be sure you was! Don't you remember, sir! Don't you remember coming up to me and asking me whether I wouldn't put your *trousers* on? Why, that was the very time, sir—don't you recollect?"

"I do remember something of the sort," replied Sylvester. "But," he added, being anxious to check these reminiscences, lest they should tend to inspire Judkins with suspicion, "how do the peaches get on?"

"Capital, sir; they'll be beauties this year, sir. Just look at 'em. Loaded, sir—look here. There can't be finer than them. I expect to beat the parson this year. I never see bigger beauties yet. Don't you remember when you was here five years ago, sir, the parson would have it that he catched you on the wall, sir, a tucking in his'n?"

"Oh, yes," said Sylvester, smiling, "I remember that well."

"That was a rum start, too," resumed Judkins. "How he *did* believe it was you, to be sure. He was satisfied afterwards, certainly he was; but Jones will have it it was you to this day; and he'll die in the belief, I expect, for you can't drive it out of him no how."

Mary at this moment entered the garden with a note, addressed "*To S. Sound, Esquire, Junior.*" Sylvester smiled as he opened this note and proceeded to read as follows:—

"Sir,—It gives me great pleasure to have the honour of presenting the song of my own composing as promised. My ideas were not perhaps fructifying much when I wrote it: but if placed in juxtaposition with some, it *may* not amalgamate amiss. It is boney fide my own, and as such

"I have the honour to be,
"Sir,
"With great respect,
"And high esteem,
"Your most obedient,
"And most humble
"Servant,
"Obadiah Drant."

"*P.S.* I shall be at the Crumpet to-night, about nine; and if you should be there, I should feel highly honoured to see you."

Here followed the song of "Old England," which Sylvester read as a matter of course, and then asked himself what it all meant. He couldn't understand it at all. "It gives me great pleasure to have the honour of presenting the song of my own composing, as *promised!*" What could the man mean by sending it, "as promised"? "I shall be at the Crumpet to-night about nine!" Did he expect him to go to the Crumpet to meet him?

"Judkins," said Sylvester, having endeavoured to solve this small mystery in vain. "Judkins, do you know a man named Obadiah Drant?"

"Know him, sir! I think I do, rather. He's a lunatic, sir—that's my belief—a political lunatic. He'd talk a horse's hind leg off, sir; and then wouldn't be quiet. He's always contin'ally at it! *Chatter*, chatter, chatter, chatter—*gabble*, gabble, gabble! He's a wonder, sir—a political wonder."

"Why a *political* wonder?"

"Cause, sir, he's always talking politics."

"But he's a poet as well, is he not?"

"I never see none of his poetry. If he does write poetry, he takes care to stuff lots of politics in it, I'll *warrant!*

"Then you think he's insane?"

"Why, sir, I couldn't, we'll say, prove him to be exactly *that*; but it's my belief a man in his proper senses would never go on at the rate *he* does. You should just hear him talk, sir; you'd *never* forget it. He has got a lot of jaw-cracking words at his fingers' ends, and he stuffs 'em in any how, and no how."

Sylvester was now summoned to breakfast, and on entering the parlour with the note in his hand, he said—

"Aunt! I have received a highly important communication this morning, from one of your neighbours."

"Indeed, my dear! Of what nature?"

"Here it is! perhaps you would like to look at it."

Aunt Eleanor, with an expression of anxiety, opened the note; and having read, exclaimed—

"What in earth could have induced him to send this to *you*?"

"I can't imagine," replied Sylvester. "But read the song."

She did so, and laughed most heartily.

"Tol de rol, lol de rol, lol de rol, liddle lol,
Tol de rol, diddle lol, looral-li-day!"

"What is the meaning of all that, my dear?"

"That's the chorus," said Sylvester.

"Oh! the chorus; I understand," she exclaimed, and merrily laughed again.

"I'll show this to Rouse, when he comes," said Sylvester.

"No, my dear; you must not do that."

"Why not? He'll be amused."

"Do you think so?"

"He's sure to be. Besides, he ought to know what a genius he has in his fold."

"I fear that this person is not in *his* fold. I do not believe he belongs to the flock. *I* never saw him at church in my life."

"Judkins believes him to be insane."

"It is possible; but I never before heard it even hinted. But he says here, my dear, that he presents the song 'as promised.' *Did* he ever promise to send a thing of the kind?"

"Certainly not."

"Then the inference is that he must be insane. But we shall hear what Mr. Rouse says about him."

They then sat down to breakfast, and while they were at it, Sylvester highly amused his aunt by occasionally chanting this celebrated chorus.

"We must have this song set to music," said he. "You can do it admirably. It's a capital song. There's plenty of scope for the development of musical genius; for example, those two happy lines—

> 'While the girls are so precious, plump, prattling, and pretty,
> It's wonderful bigamy's not more in vogue—'"

"Sylvester!" exclaimed Aunt Eleanor, "my dear."

"Oh! but they are excellent; and might be rendered very effective. I don't know exactly whether he means 'precious plump,' or 'plump and precious,' but that you'll see. And then what effect may be given to *these* lines—

> 'Will govern the ocean, and she's in a tidy
> Good juxtaposition to welt the whole world!'"

"Sylvester! How *can* you go on so? You will not let me have half a breakfast."

"Well, but look at the 'tidy good juxtaposition.' There's a chance for a musical composer!"

"But what does he mean by the word 'welt?'"

"To welt, is to beat—to conquer. It ought to have been, perhaps, 'to *towel* the world;' but 'welt' will do. And then, 'the *flat* flag of freedom!' there's another opportunity. You have but to mark the note *flat* over the word, and there you are. But the thing might be studded with musical effects: and I submit that, as he has presented us with the song, we ought, as a matter of *courtesy*, to present him with the music."

"We shall have Mr. Rouse here *before* we have finished breakfast. I *know* that we shall."

"You are right; here he is," said Sylvester, as the reverend gentleman passed through the gate, and Aunt Eleanor felt—as she always did feel when he first appeared—somewhat confused.

As soon as the first cordial meeting was over, Sylvester said, "I have received a letter this morning."

"Containing some good news, I hope," observed the reverend gentleman anxiously.

"Why it contains no *bad* news."

"I'm happy to hear it."

"Do you like poetry?"

"I'm very fond of poetry; the poetry of the Scriptures, especially; there's a great deal of poetry in the Scriptures, and that, too, of the most sublime character. David's lament, for example, in the first chapter of the Second Book of Samuel, is beautiful and touching in the extreme:—'The beauty of Israel is slain!' and again, 'Ye mountains of Gilboa, let there be no more dew; neither let there be rain upon you, nor fields of offerings: for there the shield of the mighty is vilely cast away, the shield of Saul, as though he had not been anointed with oil. From the blood of the slain, from the fat of the mighty, the bow of Jonathan turned not back, and the sword of Saul returned not empty. Saul and Jonathan were lovely and pleasant in their lives, and in their death they were not divided: they were swifter than eagles, they were stronger than lions.' And then the conclusion, 'How are the mighty fallen in the midst of the battle! O Jonathan, thou wast slain in thine high places. I am distressed for thee, my brother Jonathan: very pleasant hast thou been unto me; thy love to me was wonderful, passing the love of women. How are the mighty fallen, and the weapons of war perished?'"

The fervour and solemnity with which these beautiful passages were delivered, prompted Sylvester to put Obadiah's communication into his pocket.

"This," continued the reverend gentleman, "is but one example: the Scriptures are *studded* with gems equally sublime. But why did you ask if I were a lover of poetry?"

"Because I have a piece to show you; but it is of so different a character that I must defer it for a time."

"Why not show it to me now—without variety what were life? It is perhaps a laughable piece? Well, I can weep with David or laugh with Swift. What is the nature of it—let me see it now? But first—and this is perhaps of more importance—you said you had a letter; what was *that?*"

"That and the poetry are intimately connected—they

come from the same source. The letter, in fact, has reference to the poetry."

"Then why not let me see it at once?"

"Well, as you appear to be somewhat anxious about it, there it is: but read the poetry first."

The reverend gentleman adjusted his spectacles, and assuming the expression of a stern critic commenced.

"'Tol de rol'—what this?" said he, on arriving at the chorus. "'Tol,' eh? 'Tol de rol,' what? 'Tol de rol, lol de rol, lol de rol, diddle lol,'—why, what's the meaning of all this?"

Sylvester couldn't answer him. He was so convulsed with laughter that he went round and round the room, holding his sides, while Aunt Eleanor perspired with the utmost freedom as she twisted and tortured herself on the couch.

"Well," resumed the reverend gentleman, whose gravity was still imperturbable, "let's try again: we may perhaps make something of it by-and-by. It's some foreign language, I *presume!* 'Tol de rol —no—'looral-li-day!' I can make nothing of it. Well, we'll pass that for the present. Let's go on. Here we are again," he added, having got to the end of the second verse: "here's some more 'tol de rol.' I can't understand it;—what on earth are you laughing at?" he exclaimed, as Sylvester burst into a roar.

"'Tol de rol's' the chorus," cried Sylvester.

"The chorus? Oh, I see: 'Tol de rol, lol de lol'— *exactly.*"

Aunt Eleanor, being utterly unable to endure it, left the room.

"Well, and whose composition is this?" inquired the reverend gentleman.

"Read the note," said Sylvester, "read *that* now."

The reverend gentleman calmly proceeded to do so, but when he came to the name, he was filled at once with indignation and amazement.

"What!" he exclaimed, "is it possible that you are in communication with this man. Why, he's a heretic; he never comes to church, nor does he ever go to any other place of worship. It surely cannot be possible that you associate with such a man as this."

"*I* know nothing of the man," said Sylvester, whose convulsions were by this time subdued.

"But he here says that he sends this according to promise."

"And what he means by that I can't imagine. *I* never received a promise from him."

"Why, the impudent fellow! Stop a minute; here's a postscript—'I shall be at the Crumpet to-night about nine:' why he writes as if he expected you to meet him. Well, of all the effrontery I ever heard or read of: but *I'll* see about it—I'll see about this; I've long wished for an opportunity of speaking to this man, and this is one which I'll certainly embrace."

"But he's *insane*, I understand."

"Insane! Not he. No, no, no, *he's* not insane. I know him well—alas: too well I know him. But however he could have had the unblushing impudence to write to you I can't conceive. But *I'll* see him on the subject. Do not name this my intention to your aunt, or she'll probably persuade me to have nothing to do with him; but I really do feel myself bound to check this unexampled insolence, and at the same time—if possible—to reclaim him. You received it this morning?"

"Yes; just before breakfast."

"Very well—very well. I'll give him such a lecture. The Crumpet—tchoo! However, I'll see about it."

Aunt Eleanor now re-entered the room. She felt much better, although still in pain: her cheeks were rosy, and tears were in her eyes. She was, moreover, still very warm.

"Have you made out the chorus yet?" she inquired.

"We have certainly made it out," replied the reverend gentleman. "But did you ever in your life hear of such consummate impudence as that which prompted this man to send a thing of that kind here?"

"Oh, I daresay that he thinks it excessively clever. He is evidently proud of its being his own—and I've no doubt at all that it is."

"But the idea—the impudent idea—of his sending it to Sylvester: that's what I look at."

"He, perhaps, conceived that Sylvester was the only one here who could appreciate its beauty, and he's not a man who imagines that he was 'born to blush unseen.' We must forgive these little exhibitions of vanity. They are really too ridiculous to excite anger. The song has amused me amazingly: I have not had so hearty a laugh for a long time."

"There is," said the reverend gentleman, "in your character but *one* trait of which I have reason to complain, and which is this: that you invariably take a too charitable view of the moral delinquencies of those around you. If you cannot conceive any actual excuse, you are sure to find something in extenuation. You are too good to live in this world: that's the only fault I have to find with you. If you had the absolute *rule*, you would wrest the sword from the hand of justice and administer nothing but mercy."

"Cotherstone Grange is the place for compliments, after all," observed Sylvester.

"Nay, but it's the truth," resumed the reverend gentleman. "It is invariably the case. If she were to fill the office of chief magistrate—an office for which she is not by nature qualified—we *should* have all mercy and no justice. You perceive she endeavours to palliate the insolence of *this* man, even after he has had the effrontery to state that he'll be at 'the Crumpet' at nine, and to intimate clearly that he expects you to meet him."

"Are you quite sure," said Aunt Eleanor, as Sylvester left the room smiling—"quite sure that this poor unhappy man is not insane?"

"There you are again, my dear Eleanor! He is not insane. Besides, he's a bad man. He never comes to church; there's no religion in him."

"Is not that a *proof* of his insanity?"

This puzzled the reverend gentleman. He felt unable to get over it. He, therefore, smiled, and kissed Aunt Eleanor, and exclaimed—

"God bless you, my dear: you are a kind, good creature! We'll say no more about it."

This defeat, however, did not at all interfere with that which the reverend gentleman conceived to be his duty. He was still resolved to speak to Obadiah on the subject; and in pursuance of this resolution, he, on seeing him with Pokey in the course of the morning, rode up to him, with an appropriate expression of severity.

"Here comes Ted," said Obadiah, as the reverend gentleman approached. "I wonder what he's up to. There's something in the wind, safe. He's coming to talk to you."

"Or to you," observed Pokey.

"To me? He knows better: I should just like to catch him at it. *Wouldn't* I walk in!"

"Mr. Drant," said the reverend gentleman solemnly, as Pokey touched his hat, and passed on, "I am desirous of having a word with you."

"Very well, sir," returned Obadiah, who didn't at the moment feel exactly self-possessed. "What is it, sir?"

"Is this your handwriting?" demanded the reverend gentleman, producing the letter containing the song.

"Yes, sir; that's my hand," replied Obadiah.

"Then, sir, let me ask, how you dared to send a letter of this description to Mr. Sound, accompanied too by this low trashy song?"

"*I* can see nothing low and trashy about it."

"It *is* low and trashy; and if it were not, how dared you presume, sir, to send it to him?"

"I presumed, sir, to send it to him because he wished me to do so."

"What, sir—what?"

"Because he liked it so much, when he heard me sing it, that he asked me to let him have a copy."

"Is it possible that you can stand here, sir, and look me in the face, and unblushingly tell me such a falsehood as that?"

"It is not a falsehood. I sent it at his own request."

"*Have* you forgotten the fate of Ananias? Have you *no* care for your immortal soul? Why do you not come to church, sir?"

"That has got nothing to do with the song. Let's settle that point of the compass first. I say that he, *boney fidey*, asked me to let him have a copy of 'Old England!'"

"When, sir?"

"Why, last night."

"And where?"

"At the Crumpet."

"Are you mad?"

"Not a bit of it! I suppose I know whether he was there or not? My mind don't amalgamate to such an extent, neither, as not to know that!"

"Do you mean, then, solemnly to assert that *he*, Mr. Sound, was with you there last night?"

"To be sure I do! He *was* there last night, and stood brandy-and-water all round like a fructifying trump as he is!"

"Like a what?"

"Like a fructifying trump! a good *boney fide* fellow! He's worth a million of your proud upstart muck, which turn up their noses at honest men, because they don't belong to the pauper aristocracy, which sucks so many millions out of their vitals."

"I don't understand this language," said the reverend gentleman; "nor was I speaking of the aristocracy. I wished to know whether you meant to assert that Mr. Sound was in company with you last night?"

"Well, sir, he was; I do mean to assert it."

"And to that assertion you intend to adhere?"

"Of couse I do, because it's the truth."

"Have a care—have a care!" cried the reverend gentleman. "You may not live to repent. You know, sir, that he was *not* there."

"I know that he was."

"I do not believe it."

"I can't help that, sir; no man in Europe can help it. He *was* there, sir, whether you believe it or not. Why, he was there till past twelve."

"Monstrous!" exclaimed the reverend gentleman, who really felt appalled. "I tremble for you!—you are incorrigible!"

"Well," said Obadiah, "have it your own way, if you will. I know what I know, sir, and that's all about it. I wish you a very good morning."

The reverend gentleman was so much amazed that before he knew either what to say or how to act, Obadiah had got a considerable distance; and even when he had somewhat recovered his faculties, he continued to sit as motionless as Irresolution's statue. Eventually, however, he turned his horse's head, and rode on to the Common, with the view of reflecting upon all that had passed, and deciding on what was then best to be done; while Obadiah proceeded to the Crumpet and Crown, to tell the news to his friends, who at once crowded round him.

"Well," cried Pokey, "well, well—what did he want?"

"Want!" exclaimed Obadiah. "He wanted to do as good as swear me out of my Christian name."

"Well, but what was his object?" demanded Legge.

"Why, his object, my boy, was to make me believe that young Mr. Sound was not with us last night drinking brandy-and-water."

"What!" cried Legge angrily, "did you tell him that he was?"

"Of course I did; and stuck to it, too, like a Briton."

"What *right*," cried Legge, "had you to tell him that? Do you think that he wanted *them* to know where he was? Can *no* man come to enjoy himself for an hour without its being known all over the place, you chattering fool? Had he even come in here and drank his glass to himself, you would have had no right to name it, but as he behaved so handsomely, and as you with the rest partook—and freely too—of that which he ordered and paid for, you ought to be *ashamed* of yourself."

"Shame!—shame!" cried the rest. "Shame!—shame! It *is* shameful!"

"*Stop* a bit, my boys," said Obadiah; "*stop* a bit. I'll soon fructify your ideas on that point."

"Fructify!" cried Legge, who was very indignant. "It would serve you right if we fructified *your* ideas, and that through the horse-pond."

"So it would!—so it would!" cried all the rest. "It's shameful; that it is—shameful!"

"Now you're all about five-and-*twenty* minutes too fast," said Obadiah. "If you will but just listen, I'll clear it all up"——

"You'll never clear *that* up," exclaimed Legge, "*I* know."

"Now, just look you here. Me and Pokey was walking and talking together; well, who should come up but Teddy Rouse. 'Mr. Drant,' said he, 'I want to speak to you.' 'Very well,' says I; 'what's the row?' 'Is this your handwriting?' says he. 'Yes,' says I, 'it is.' 'Then, how dare you,' says he, 'to send this letter with such muck as that to Mr. Sound?'"

"What letter—what muck?" demanded Legge.

"Why, he asked me last night—didn't he?—to give him a copy of my song. Very well, then—I wrote it out and sent it this morning, and that with a very polite note. Well. 'How dare you send it to him?' says he. 'Because,' says I, 'he wished me to do so.' 'When?' says he. 'Last night,' says I. 'Where?' says he. 'At the Crumpet,' says I. 'It's false,' says he, 'he wasn't there.' 'I know better,' says I, 'I know he was, and stood brandy-and-water all round,' and so we went on; he saying it was false, and I saying it was true, until I became so disgusted that I left him."

"Disgusted!" cried Legge. "You're a fool. What did you want to *stick* to it for, when you found that he wouldn't believe it? You'd no right to say that Mr. Sound was here at all."

"Well, but how did the *parson* get hold of the letter?" said Quocks, "that's what *I* want to know."

"Oh, I see how it was," returned Legge. "This fool sent the letter to the cottage, and it fell into the hands of Mrs. Sound, who showed it to Rouse, as a matter of course; and a pretty mess the young man's got into, no doubt."

"Well, now," said Quocks, "I don't know, but I don't think there's anything *disgraceful* in the fact of a man coming here to enjoy himself for an hour, do you?"

"No, Quocks," said Legge, "there may be nothing disgraceful in the fact, but we must look at it with reference to his position. *You* would not like to frequent the beer-shop behind."

"No, I certainly should not."

"And if you *did*—although there might be nothing disgraceful in the fact—your friends would in all probability *think* that you should aim at something higher. That young man enjoyed himself here last night; if he hadn't, he wouldn't have stopped so long; but his friends—and more especially Mr. Rouse—doubtless think that it is not a proper place for him to come to. We must look at the position a man occupies."

"I see," said Quocks; "I see. Oh, I see!"

"But I don't see," cried Obadiah.

"*You* don't see," said Legge contemptuously. "You can see to make mischief. I wouldn't have had it known that that young man was here standing brandy-and-water—as you told Rouse—for five times the money he spent."

"Well, but Teddy didn't believe me."

"You say that you stuck to it."

"And so I did. But he thought it was false: and he thinks so still. Mr. Sound, no doubt, denied it. And—as it proved—he believed him and not me."

"If I were sure of that I'd deny it too," said Quocks.

"And so would I," cried Pokey.

"Well, but how can we manage it?" said Legge. "How is it to be done?"

This was the question: and while they were engaged in discussing it, the reverend gentleman—who, after due deliberation, had decided on calling upon Legge, with the view of ascertaining whether Obadiah's statement was, or was not false—rode up to the door.

"I've been told," said he, when Legge went out to speak to him, "that young Mr. Sound was here drinking last night."

"Who told you that, sir?" demanded Legge.

"Drant—Obadiah Drant."

"Obadiah Drant!" said Legge, with a contemptuous expression; "why you surely don't believe a word he says?"

"Well, I certainly did not believe that," returned the reverend gentleman; "and I told him at the time that I didn't believe it; and yet I thought it strange—very strange —that he should adhere to his assertion so firmly."

"Oh, he'll assert anything, sir, that man will. His word's not worth a rush. Had he spread a report that you were here drinking last night, sir, I shouldn't have been in the slightest degree astonished."

"Why, he must be a very bad man."

"He's not a bit too good, sir: depend upon that. But no one takes notice of anything that *he* says, and I'm quite sure that nothing that he *can* say is worth *your* attention."

"Well, he's a bad man—a very bad man. I am sorry to find that there's a man in *my* parish so bad. Good day, Mr. Legge."

"I wish you good day, sir."

"If you see that wretched man, tell him from me that I hold his conduct in abhorrence."

"I will, sir," replied Legge; "depend upon that."

The reverend gentleman then rode towards the cottage, and Legge returned to the room, in which he found Obadiah secured by Quocks, Bobber, and Pokey. The cause of this may be briefly explained. Obadiah had heard all that passed outside; and, conceiving himself to be an ill-used man, became so highly indignant, that he was about to rush out and spoil all, with a view to his own complete justification, when Quocks and Bobber seized him, and held him in a chair, while brave Pokey stopped up his mouth with a towel.

"Well!" he exclaimed, on being released, "you've done it. *Haven't* you? You amalgamated nicely! *Didn't* you? What! do you think that I'm going to stand this? Do you imagine that I'm going to be made the scapegoat of that young wretch in this here sort of manner?"

"Do you call this gratitude," cried Pokey, "after drinking his brandy-and-water?"

"As for you," said Obadiah, with a most ferocious aspect, "I've as great a mind to give you a regular *boney fide* good welting as I ever had in my life, mind you that. If you ever touch me again—if you ever dare to lay so much as a finger upon me, I'll *welt* you till you can't see out of your eyes."

"Well, but how is this?" said Legge. "Haven't I heard you say, five hundred times, that you cared no more for Teddy Rouse than you did for Bobby Peel?"

"Nor do I. Care for him! Why should I care? What's Teddy Rouse to me? Care for him, indeed!"

"Well, it appears that you *do* care for him, or you wouldn't be so angry at what I said."

"Do you think that I'm going to have my character taken away then"——

"Your what!" exclaimed Quocks—"your character. If you can find a man who can take away your character, pay him well: he'll deserve all you give him."

"Indeed! I owe *you* nothing: so you needn't call out so loud. But if any man in Europe lays the function to his soul that *I'll* stand-being made the greatest liar that ever walked, he's mistaken."

"Well, the thing's done now," said Legge.

"Yes, it *is* done, but *I'll* call on Ted."

"And being done, I think we'd better drop it."

"Drop it! Yes, it's all mighty fine to say drop it; but I won't let it drop. And *you*—you little wretch," he added, turning to Bobber, "for two pins I'd *tan* you!"

"Tan *me!*" cried Bobber, who was not at all afraid of him; "you talk like an old woman generally, but now you are talking like a child."

"Well, come," said Quocks, "it's all over now: let's drink and forget it."

Legge brought in some beer, and endeavoured to pacify the incensed one, but Obadiah threatened still to call upon "Ted." As, however, he seldom carried his threats into execution, Legge had not the slightest fear of his doing so in this case, well knowing that as "Ted" never gave him an order he was a man whom—above all other men alive—Obadiah abhorred.

Meanwhile the reverend gentleman was anxiously waiting an opportunity of explaining to Sylvester the result of his interview with Obadiah, whom he conceived to be utterly irreclaimable. It was evening, however, before an opportunity occurred; but when it did occur, the reverend gentleman embraced it, and said—

"Well, I've seen that wretched man!"

"What, the author of 'Old England?'"

"Yes; I've had a long talk with him."

"Have you? Well, what did he say?"

"Why he absolutely had the audacity to tell me that you were at the public-house with him last night, drinking brandy-and-water till past twelve o'clock."

"What!"

"It's a positive fact, that he declared that you were there, treating them all, as he said, 'like a trump?'"

"The animal! Why, I went to bed soon after ten."

"He moreover told me that his reason for sending that song to you this morning was, that you heard him sing it last night, and admired it so much, that you begged of him to send you a copy of it."

"Oh, the man must be mad. *I* never heard him sing! But, of course, you don't imagine for a moment that I *was* there?"

"I have ascertained beyond all doubt that you were not; for, in order to satisfy my mind upon that point, I called upon Legge"——

"And of course, he told you"——

"Oh, yes, at once; and like a sensible man, treated the whole matter with contempt. Why, he absolutely told me that he should not have felt astonished if this man had spread a report that *I* was there drinking brandy-and-water! Why you know this is a very awful state for a man's mind to be in."

"The man *must* be insane."

"He is wicked, sir—desperately wicked. Such conduct can be ascribed to wickedness alone. But I'll not give him up: I must not give him up. I must *not* suffer his soul to be lost."

"Why, let me see," said Sylvester thoughtfully, "*you* were here last night till nearly ten o'clock."

"It wanted twelve minutes to ten when I left."

"I was in bed and asleep in less than half an hour after that."

"Oh, the idea of you being there is perfectly ridiculous. But that man *must* be reclaimed. You see it's dreadful, when you come to reflect upon it—positively dreadful! I understand his word is not at any time to be taken: that it's not worth a rush: that he never speaks the truth, and that no one believes him. Why you know this continual commission of sin must, of necessity, have its effect. However, if he is to be reclaimed, I'll reclaim him."

Sylvester—notwithstanding the reverend gentleman had thus expressed his conviction that he was *not* the previous night at the Crumpet and Crown—reflected deeply upon all that he had heard in connection with the idea of his being a somnambulist, and the immediate result of that reflection was the confirmation of his suspicion.

"And yet," thought he, subsequently, "Legge must know whether I was there or not; and as he says that I was *not* there, I have a right to infer that the statement of this Drant is false. Besides, how is it possible that I could have been there? The string was round my ankle when I woke this morning, precisely as I tied it round last night, and, of course, the idea of my having been able to leave the room with that on, or even to get out of bed, is absurd. It is certainly strange that this report should have been circulated just at this time. But then the fact of its being strange affords no proof. When suspicions of any description have been engendered, the slightest occurrences tend to confirm them. I shall now be apt, doubtless, to attribute every circumstance that occurs to this imagined somnambulism, as readily as a non-professional man who, on reading a medical work, conceives that he has the disease described. I must, notwithstanding, be satisfied; and until I am satisfied, I'll not only tie the string to my ankle every night, but I'll lock my room door, and hide the key."

Had Sylvester referred to his purse—out of which he had paid for the brandy-and-water—it might have thrown a little more light upon the subject: but this didn't occur to him; he tried to believe that Obadiah's assertions were utterly false, and on retiring that night, he locked the door, placed the key in his writing desk, locked that, and then put it under his bed.

But this was of no *use* at all. In less than an hour after he had fallen asleep, he released his ankle, dressed himself, got the key out of the desk, opened the door, and left the house with the utmost deliberation; and yet, in the morning, when he awoke, he found his ankle secured, the key in his desk, and the desk itself in precisely the same place as that in which he had the previous night left it.

And thus he acted night after night—adjusting the string and hiding the key, which he found and hid again, without having, when awake, even the most remote idea of the fact —but beyond this nothing at all worth recording occurred till the following Tuesday.

On that day, Cotherstone Fair was held, and gaiety was in the ascendant. Legge had, as usual, erected a booth— in a paddock adjoining his house—for dancing; and while the girls of the village, with their pink and blue streamers, were laughing and clapping their hands for joy, and cracking nuts, and promenading, and glancing at their sweethearts, in all the pride of youth and rustic beauty, the men were drinking and joking, and smoking their pipes, and apparently somewhat more happy than princes.

Legge, moreover, had procured prolific germs of amusement; and these prolific germs were chemises, shawls, scarfs, and a couple of fine legs of mutton.

The chemises were to be run for—and so were the shawls and scarfs—but the mutton was to be climbed for, by those whose ambition might prompt them to go to the poll.

These delights were, however, reserved till the evening, for Legge knew something of human nature. He had kept that house nearly twenty years; he, therefore, cannot be supposed to have been unconscious of the way in which the house had kept him. No; the prizes were exhibited throughout the day. None could think of leaving until they had been won; and while all beheld them with fond anticipations, they panted for pleasure, and drank more beer.

Anxious to witness the amusement of the people, Sylvester himself walked through the village immediately after he had dined, and as Obadiah, from one of the windows of "The Crumpet" saw him—for the first time since the night of the brandy-and-water—he rushed out of the house, and having followed him for a time, touched his hat respectfully, and asked him how he was.

"Quite well," replied Sylvester, who had forgotten him, "quite."

"Come, sir, to see the pleasures of the poverty-stricken?" observed Obadiah, who was not a man to be easily shaken off.

"The people do not *appear* to be poverty-stricken," returned Sylvester. "All whom I have seen look contented and happy."

"Ah!" exclaimed Obadiah, "thoughtlessness. It's nothing but that, sir, and ignorance. If they knew their power, they wouldn't be as they are."

"Would the knowledge of their power, then, render them more happy?"

"I allude to their position, sir, that's what I allude to. I mean that they wouldn't be in such a position; they would take higher ground, sir."

"What ground do you imagine they would take?"

"What ground, sir ? Why, they'd stand up for their rights."

"Have they not their rights ?"

"How can the poor have their rights, sir ? How is it possible ? "

"I conceive it to be quite possible for the poor to have their rights as well as the rich."

"But if men had their rights, sir, they could not be poor."

"Indeed ! Why—why could they not ? "

"Because the rich would have to divide their riches with them."

"Oh ! Ah ! That's it ! I see !" cried Sylvester, who began to be rather amused. "Then all who have their rights must be equally rich ?"

"Of course, sir. It's one of the laws of nature."

"Well, now, do you know, I wasn't aware of that."

"Indeed ! Well, that's strange, too. But don't you see now that it must be ?"

"Well, but suppose a division were to take place to-day, and that you were to spend your share to-night, how would you stand to-morrow ? "

"Why, of course, if I had spent it, I couldn't have it."

"They you couldn't have your rights."

"Ay, but that's altogether a different *thing*. We weren't speaking of spending our shares."

"We were speaking of wealth being equally divided— a state of things which couldn't last an hour—and, as you advanced as a proposition, that men could not be poor who had their rights, I put a case which, I apprehend, proved that men might have their rights, and yet be poor."

"Yes, sir, but——"

"Do you admit that ?"

"But were there two Adams ?"

"Nay, keep to the point."

"I'm coming to it—fructifying right direct to the point."

"Fructifying !" thought Sylvester, who thought that he had heard that word ill-used before.

"The question is," continued Obadiah, "were there, or were there *not*, two Adams ? "

"We read but of one."

"Was there an Adam connected with the aristocracy,

and an Adam pledged to support the eternal principles of the people?"

"I have always understood that when Adam was created, there was neither an aristocracy *nor* a people."

"No; but I was only just going to say, if there was no aristocracy in those days, why should there be an aristocracy now—an aristocracy which lives upon the vitals of the people, and sucks a matter of two hundred millions a year from the sweat of the poor man's brow. Did Nature ever make an aristocracy?"

"Yes."

"Never in this world."

"The aristocracy of intellect is Nature's own."

"Ay, but that's altogether a different thing; we weren't speaking of the aristocracy of intellect—that's a spark from heaven's anvil, struck to enlighten the world; like a boney fide star which shoots to another and tells it all it knows. *We* were speaking of the aristocracy of wealth—the aristocracy of corruption—the aristocracy of plunder—the profligate, pandering, puppet-show, pudding-headed, pompous aristocracy—*did* Nature ever make that?"

"Do you speak of the aristocracy of England?"

"Of course."

"Then what, I ask, do *you* know of that aristocracy?"

"What do I know of them!—what! Are they not a parcel of plundering, pandering, arrogant"——

"Stop," said Sylvester. "Language of that description tells only with a mob—men of sense despise it. The vulgar have been taught to believe that arrogance forms one of the chief characteristics of the aristocracy. They have yet to learn that the nearer we approach the apex of civilised society, the nearer we approach the perfection of civilised simplicity. But you appear to have lost sight of the point from which we started, and to which I imagined you were about to return."

"What point was that?"

"Equality."

"Just so. Well, don't you think it monstrous that some should have so much, sir, while others have so little?"

"Why, that depends entirely upon circumstances."

"Well, but just look you here, sir; you see that man

there, sir, in the smock-frock—him that's got a pipe in his mouth, sir?"

"Yes—well?"

"Well, sir, what do you think he has a week?"

"Ten shillings, perhaps."

"Five, sir. No more than five."

"Is that a fact?"

"I know it well, sir. Perhaps you wouldn't mind if I called him?"

"Certainly *not*. I should like to speak to him."

"You won't find much intellect about him; he hasn't been fructified to any amalgamating extent. Dick!"

Dick stopped as if he had some remote idea of his having been called, and turning round with about as much velocity as a man who is heavily ironed would turn, he had some slight notion that some one stood there whose face he had somewhere seen before.

"Dick," cried Obadiah again, "here."

A *new* idea seemed to have entered Dick's brains, and that idea was that he knew Obadiah. He therefore took the pipe out of his mouth and approached: but when he saw Sylvester, he didn't know exactly whether he ought to take off his hat or not.

"Well, Dick, how goes it?" inquired Obadiah.

"Oh; doon knoo, sir, mooch aboot the seame."

"How are wages in this part of the country?" inquired Sylvester.

"Bad, sir," replied Dick. "Very bad, indeed."

"This is a friend of mine, Dick," said Obadiah; "and he seemed to be fructified when I told him that you hadn't ten shillings a week."

"Ten, sir! I've only foive! Hard loins that, sir: foive shillin' a week."

"Well, but what do you *do* with five shillings a week?"

"Why it arn't too much to spend, *is* it, sir?"

"No; but how do you manage to get rid of it?"

"Oh, I never have not the leastest trouble aboot that. I'll tell'ee, sir, hoo I manage. First, then—jist'ee keep count—I pays a shillin' a week for me lodgin's. Well, that's one shillin' isn't it? Well, then, I has a stone o' flour a week; that's two-and-threepence. How mooch is that together? Two-and-threepence an' a shillin: that's three-an-threepence. Well, twopence the bakin', an' penny the yeast — that's threepence — that's three-an'-sixpence. Three-an'-sixpence, well; then I have two poound of flet cheese, to eat wi' me bread, at threepence a poound, that's sixpence. Three-an'-sixpence an' sixpence moor is foor shillin'. Well! then I can't do without *half*-a-pint o' beer a day—that arn't too mooch is it?—well, a penny a half-pint, seven days in the week, that's sevenpence. Sevenpence an' foor shillin's, that's foor-an-sevenpence. I arn't mooch of a scholar, boot that's soon counted. Foor-an' sevenpence. Well, I moost have a shirt washed once a week, an' a han'kercher, an' a pair o' stockin's, that moost be mended—I never see sich devils to goo into holes—well, the washin' an' mendin' takes away the other fippence, and that's hoo I meake ends meet."

"Well, but how do you manage when your clothes are worn out?"

"I gets a trifle more in the harvest time, sir; that's how I manages that."

"I see. But have men in this part of the country, in general, no more than five shillings a week?"

"Oh! 'ees, sir; soom have ten, and soom twelve! Boot I'm a bit of a cripple, you see, sir; that's where it is; I can't work noo as I used to could."

Sylvester gave him half-a-crown, which so astonished Dick that he burst into tears.

"Can you wonder at the fires after that?" cried Obadiah, as Dick, with a heart full of gratitude, left them.

"But this is a peculiar case," observed Sylvester. "You hear that the wages average from ten to twelve shillings. This man is a cripple, and can't do much work."

"Well, but have we got no *lords* cripples? Place him in juxtaposition with a lord, and "——

"Juxtaposition!" echoed Sylvester. "Your name is "——

"Drant, sir; Obadiah Drant. You recollect me, sir, don't you!"

"It is to you, I believe, that I am indebted for a song."

"Exactly, sir; I did myself the honour of sending a copy of it as you requested."

"As I *requested!* I am not conscious of having made any such request."

"What! don't you remember, the other night, at the Crumpet, when you heard me sing that song"——

"*I* never heard you sing the song."

"Oh, yes, you did, sir! when you were there the other night—you recollect?"

"But I was not there the other night. I understand that you told Mr. Rouse that I was"——

"Well, I am sorry for that, sir. I wish I hadn't mentioned it now."

"But how came you to think of such a falsehood?"

"I'm sorry it was named; but, of course, you know it wasn't a falsehood."

"I know that it *was* a falsehood, and a most atrocious falsehood too."

"Well, but you know you *were* there."

"What! Are you a lunatic?"

"A lunatic? No!"

"I thought you were," returned Sylvester calmly. "As you are *not*, I wish to have no farther communication with you."

"Well, sir; but *what!*—do you *mean?*"

"I have *nothing* more to say," observed Sylvester, who waved his hand, and with a look of contempt left Obadiah astounded.

The sports proceeded; the mutton was gained; the chemises, the shawls, and the scarfs were won; and when night came on, the booth was illumined, and dancing commenced, and was kept up with spirit till twelve, when a cry of "the ghost!" was raised.

The men rushed instantly out of the booth, and the girls shrieked and fainted by dozens, while the "ghost" walked leisurely through the village, fearfully shunned by all.

No one approached it. All kept aloof. The stoutest hearts shrank back appalled, and the ghost had the road to itself.

The night was dark; not a star could be seen; and when the ghost reached the chestnut-trees, beneath which all was gloom, the multitude breathed; but lo! it turned and walked through the village again.

Horror filled each manly breast, and all was consternation. But the ghost seemed to treat the whole throng with contempt. It walked up and down just as long as it liked, and then vanished, they knew neither how nor where.

CHAPTER XXXII.

SYLVESTER IS RECALLED TO TOWN.

WHEN Sylvester had ascertained in the morning that the ghost had been seen in the village again, he felt greatly relieved, having found the string, on awaking, round his ankle as usual, the key in the desk, and the desk beneath the bed. He held it, then, to be abundantly clear that he couldn't be the "ghost," and was about to repudiate the idea of his being a somnambulist, when he received from his solicitor a letter requiring his presence in town. This had the effect of re-inspiring suspicion. He might be a somnambulist, and yet not the "ghost." It was possible—nay, when he reflected upon the serious accusation of Sir Charles—he could not but think it highly probable. But how was the thing to be proved? That was the question still. He had in vain tried to prove it himself; and, therefore, felt bound to communicate his suspicion to another. This he eventually resolved to do; but as he had to go to London immediately, he thought it best to conceal it, at least for the present, from his aunt and her reverend friend, and on his arrival in town to consult Tom Delolme.

He accordingly communicated only the contents of the letter then; and no sooner had his aunt and the reverend gentleman become perfectly conscious of his intention to leave them that morning, than the cottage became a theatre of excitement. Cook, Judkins, and Mary were instantly summoned. Judkins was directed to get the phaeton ready; cook received instructions to make up a large fire for the purpose of airing the shirts; and while Mary went with her mistress to ransack the drawers, the reverend gentleman, with an infinite profundity of expression, was cutting sandwiches, in a peculiarly scientific style.

By virtue of this admirable division of labour, the shirts, within the hour, were aired and packed up—the sandwiches were enveloped in sheets of Bath paper—and the phaeton appeared at the gate. There had been, however, no time to impress upon Sylvester the necessity for his sending them every information having reference to the trial, at which they both of course intended to be present. Aunt Eleanor, therefore, hastily slipped on her things, and entered the phaeton with her reverend friend, with the view not only of seeing Sylvester to the coach, but of enforcing this necessity by the way.

As they passed through the village, Obadiah and Pokey were, as usual with Legge, at the Crumpet and Crown, and the very moment Obadiah saw them, he exclaimed—

"There, there you are, my Britons! That's the dodge —that's it. I'll bet you what you like of it: up to something, safe. Don't you see the portmanter? Going to the coach, perhaps, to get rid of that boney fide young fibber."

"What do you mean by a young fibber?" demanded Legge.

"What do I mean? What! Didn't he have the howdacious impudence, while we were fructifying yesterday in the fair, to tell me plump to my very teeth, that he wasn't here at all the other night!"

"Did he, though!" said Pokey.

"Did he! Did he not? I'll back him against life to lie. There's nothing like him in all flesh. He beats Peter the Great hollow, and he could lie a little."

"Some one was with him, perhaps," observed Legge.

"Not a bit of it! Not so much as half a one. There we were alone, quietly fructifying about equal rights, when, says he, all at once, says he, 'Isn't your name Drant?' Says I, 'Drant is my name,' says I: 'Obadiah Drant.' 'You sent me a song,' says he, 'didn't you, this morning?' 'I did,' says I, 'according to promise.' 'According to promise,' says he; 'what promise?' 'What promise!' says I; 'what, don't you recollect that I promised to send it?' 'You promised *me* nothing of the sort,' says he. 'What!' says I; 'what, not the copy of the song you heard me sing?' 'I never heard you sing a song,' says he. 'What,' says I, 'not the other night at the Crumpet?' 'The Crumpet,' says he; 'I was never at the Crumpet but once in my life, and that was in the morning.' 'The morning,' says I; 'I don't speak about morning, I speak about night.' 'I never was there of a night in my life,' says he, I'm blessed if he didn't, plump. Well, this kind of thing doubled me up: so, looking at him fierce, says I, 'What! —do you mean that?' 'Mean it,' says he; 'of course I do. You told Mr. Rouse,' says he, 'that I was there, drinking brandy-and-water.' 'Well, I'm sorry for that,' says I; 'but you know that you was there.' 'I know that I was not,' says he; 'and however you came to think of such a falsehood, I can't imagine.' 'A falsehood,' says I. 'Yes, a falsehood,' says he. 'But you don't,' says I, 'mean to tell me that you wasn't that night at the Crumpet at all?' 'I mean to tell you that you *know* I was not there,' says he: no better and no worse. Well, this staggered me a little above a bit. 'But,' says I, 'do you really mean to mean what you say?' 'Of course,' says he, indignantly; 'I was *not* there, and you know it.' Upon which I was so boney fidely disgusted that I left him to his own fructifying reflections. Now what do you think of that—eh? What do you think of it?"

"Why, it certainly is strange," returned Legge, "that he should deny it to you, there being no one else present."

"Strange! It's stunning!"

"Well, but didn't he laugh at the time?" inquired Pokey.

"Laugh! He looked, for all the world, as if there wasn't a laugh in him. I never, in all my born days, witnessed anything like it. I'll back him against nature. I never saw a fellow tell a lie with so much liberty. *He's* the swell to swear a man out of his christian name. There's no hesitation about *him:* there's no such thing as faltering —no such thing as a blush about him while he's at it. He'll lie like a lunatic, that fellow will. And there we see the force of example. He got it all from Teddy Rouse. Ted taught him—safe. I never saw two fellows lie so much alike. But when you come to look at it, isn't it disgusting to see a man like Ted—a man of his cloth—a man professing so much religion, teaching lads like that to lie? But then what can we expect from such a clerical lot of locusts? What can we expect when we allow them to suck here a matter of five hundred millions a year from the vitals of the poverty-stricken people? I say it serves us right: and, moreover than that, we ought to be served out ten thousand times worse. It's amazing to me that the people don't see this. As true as I'm alive, it makes my head turn quite round, when I think of their boney fide blindness. Is it a mite likely, do you think, that I'd stand it if I was the people alone? Do you think that I'd let them get fat upon me? Suppose I was the people—that's the way to put it—suppose that I was the whole of the people, do you think that I'd be swindled by a lot of pensioned paupers in this way? No! not a bit of it. I'll tell you what I'd do. In the first place, I'd send for the king, and I'd say to him, 'Now then, I'll tell you what it is, old fellow: I'm not going to stand this sort of thing any longer, so I tell you. You must abdicate and cut it. I'm not going to allow you to rob me of fifty or sixty millions a year in this sort of way. You've been amalgamating at a rare rate lately, and you ought to have saved money. If you have, why so much the better for *you;* if you haven't, go and work for your living like an honest man. I want no king: what's the good of a king to me? What use are you— what do you do? I'm not going to support you in idleness any longer; so that's all about it.' I'd then send for the ministers, and I'd say to them, 'Gentlemen, it's all very fine, I daresay, but you have no more money from me. You've been feathering your nests to a fructifying extent, I've no doubt; but your *valuable* services are no longer required. I am the people; I can govern myself: at all events I've had enough of *you!* therefore pack up your traps and be off.' Then I'd send for the bishops, but I'd make mighty short work of them; and the same with the parsons: I'd turn them all adrift. And so for the pensioners, 'What!' I'd say, '*I* support a lot of paupers in the lazy lap of luxury? I wish you may get it. No! go to work, and earn an honest livelihood. If you can't do that, apply to the parish. I daresay, indeed, I'm going to let a lot of lazy locusts live on my vitals in this sort of way. Be off! and never let me set eyes on you again.' That would be the only way to work it. What should I want with a king and a lot of lords, what should I want with bishops, parsons, and pensioners? I wouldn't have them. I'd form a republic within myself, and I myself would govern myself. That's what I should do, if I were the whole people; and that's just the way the people ought to do now. They should set to work, and act as one man, and send all the amalgamating obligarchies bowling!"

"There's something in that," observed Pokey.

"Yes, there *is* something in it," said Legge, who immediately left the room, smiling.

"I believe you," pursued Obadiah, addressing Pokey alone; "and I'm glad that you agree with me. I find that I shall fructify your ideas a little yet. Look you here. The thing lies in a nutshell. Just place yourself now in the juxtaposition of the people. You are the people. Very well. Now, do *you* want a king? Do you want a lot of lords, a myriad of bishops, and about fifty millions of parsons? Do you want them?"

"No, I can't say I do."

"Do you want about a hundred thousand pensioned paupers picking your pocket of five-and-twenty millions a year to live in luxury, and keep their carriages, and drive slap over you, and think nothing of it if you don't get out of the way? Do you want *them?*"

"Certainly not."

"Very well, then. If you were the people, and *you* wouldn't want them, why should the people want them now?"

"That's feasible; certainly, that's feasible."

"Feasible! Doesn't it stand to reason?"

"I must say it does."

"The thing, you see, only wants a little fructification in a simplified manner for every soul on earth to understand it. I'd undertake to make it clear to the meanest capacity; but then you see *I* can't travel about the country to open the eyes of the universal people, and the consequence is, they're on that important subject sand-blind. They listen to parsons; what's the good of that? Is there a parson in all flesh who'll tell them what I've told you now? Not a bit of it. *They* know better. They know that if they were to fructify the ideas of the people in that way, it would open their eyes, and their object is to keep their eyes closed to all the abuses, and all the swindles, and all the corrupt dead robberies of those who live upon the sweat of the poor man's brow. Oh! it's shocking when you come to look at the ignorance of the people—*boney fidely* shocking! If Billy the Conqueror could rise from his grave and talk over the matter with Peter the Great, they'd be right down astonished to find what the people—the ignorant people—will bear."

"There's a good deal of ignorance about, I daresay," observed Pokey. "No doubt there's a good deal of ignorance."

"A good deal of ignorance! It's stunning! Why, look at the lot of locusts now preying upon our vitals! Only look at them, and see what they cost! Will any man tell me, that if all those disgusting sums of money which they swallow up were in the pockets of the people, they wouldn't be better off! Don't it stand to reason, that if one man has five hundred thousand a year, and five thousand men, as good as he is, have nothing, the five thousand men would have a hundred a year each, if that money were equally divided?"

"Yes; that's clear enough."

"Clear enough! I believe you. It *is* clear enough: and yet the *people* can't see this. *They* can't see how they are plundered and oppressed, and rode rough-shod over, and trodden under foot. Not a bit of it. Their ignorant ideas don't fructify in that way. Besides, do you think that if I were the people, I'd suffer myself to be ground to the earth by any such thing as a National Debt?"

"Certainly," said Pokey, "that ought to be paid off."

"Paid off! Do you know what you're talking about? Paid off! Send I may live! Why, do you know that if you take five hundred millions of miles of ground and cover it over with fifty-pound notes, you would not have enough, even then, to pay it off? I've seen it calculated: so there *can* be no mistake about that. Pave Europe with sovereigns and you wouldn't have enough. Pay it off! Sponge it! That's the only way to pay it off."

"What, and let them as has scraped a little money together suffer?"

"Don't your ideas fructify? Wouldn't it be better for them afterwards?"

"I don't see that."

"Not see it! As true as I'm alive, you're as blind as the rest. Don't you see that we should then have an equal division?"

"Would the money I've got in the Savings Bank be divided amongst them as hasn't got none?"

"All, I tell you, would be equally divided."

"Then I wont vote for that."

"What, not to have a share of the millions upon millions which the pauper aristocracy have got?"

"It won't do," said Pokey; "I shouldn't be sure of that."

"Not sure of it! What's to prevent it?"

"Many things might. I say many things *might*. And 'a bird in the hand is worth two in the bush.'"

"Pokey, Pokey, I'm sorry to find you're a *bony fide* ignoramus still."

"I don't care a button about what you say: I mean to look after my money."

"You mean to look after your money! Why, you've no more patriotism in you than the ghost. By the by, I mean to *look* after that swell to-night. I've made up my mind to that. *I* know who he is."

"What! do you?"

"*I* know the gentleman."

"What! isn't it a ghost, then, after all?"

"A ghost! Not a bit of it. No, it's a man."

"Indeed! Is it any one *I* know?"

"Oh yes! you know him very well."

"Who is he?"

"Why, I didn't intend to say until I caught him; but I don't mind telling you. It's Bob Potts."

"Bob Potts! Lor, is it, though? Bob Potts. Blow him, he's always up to something. But how do you know?"

"Oh, I know all about it; but don't say a word. If it should come to his ears that I know him, he'll of course keep at home: therefore, don't say a syllable to any living soul."

"Not a word. Trust to me. I'll not open my lips."

"*I'll* cook the green goose of Mr. Bob Potts. I only want to catch him; and when I do, he won't play the game of 'ghost' again in a hurry. He's been carrying it on long enough; and if I don't place him in juxtaposition to make him ashamed of himself all his life, I'll eat grass like a cow; therefore, mum!"

Pokey again promised to be silent on the subject; and when Obadiah had explained to him the delicate minutiæ of the scheme he had conceived, they parted on the most affectionate terms to meet again, with the view of ensnaring Bob Potts.

CHAPTER XXXIII.

THE PROOF.

IMMEDIATELY on his arrival in town, Sylvester called on his friend Tom Delolme, who received him as usual with great cordiality, aud was indeed happy to see him. The greeting, however, was brief: for Sylvester's anxiety to communicate the idea he had conceived, prompted him to open the subject at once.

"Tom," said he, "you know, I believe, something about somnambulism?"

"Sobdabbulisb?" replied Tom. "Yes; I kdow pretty well all that *is* kdowd about the batter!"

"Well, then, I wish to consult you on the subject; for I have a strong suspicion that *I'm* a somnambulist."

"Dodsedse!" returned Tom. "You a sobdabbulist!"

"I really supect that I am."

"Well! what idduced that suspiciod?"

"Why, Tom, let me go where I may, mystery follows me. Something of an extraordinary and unaccountable character is sure to occur, and that at night. If I go down to Cotherstone Grange a 'ghost' is certain to appear in the village: which 'ghost' never appears there when I am away. I slept here, you will remember, just before I left town. Your servant declared that he saw a 'ghost' then."

"I recollect. That 'ghost' broke by pier-glass. I see. But have you do other groudds for suspiciod?"

"There have been innumerable occurrences for which I have been utterly unable to account; but that which makes me more immediately anxious to ascertain whether I am in reality a somnambulist or not, is the approaching trial. Sir Charles, you know, declares that he saw me there, while his butler is fully prepared to swear it. Now, I am unconscious of having been there—perfectly unconscious; and if I was there, to what but somnambulism can it be ascribed?"

"I see: I see it all clearly. You have dever beed discovered id a state of sobdabbulisb?"

"Never."

"Did you ever od awakidg fide yourself id ady stradge place, or id ady place id which you'd do idea of beidg?"

"Never; I have always, on awaking, found myself in bed."

"Have you directed ady persod to watch you at all?"

"No one has had ever the slightest idea of my having entertained this suspicion. You are the only man to whom I have breathed a syllable on the subject. I have been for some time endeavouring to prove the fact myself. I've tied strings to my ankle, locked my room door, and hid the key."

"Ah, that's of do use. You'd be certaid while asleep to fidd add hide the key agaid; that is, assubing that you *are* a sobdabbulist. We bust see about this. If it be as you suspect, the proof will be highly ibportadt. We'll talk the batter over agaid by-add-by. Add dow go upstairs add have a wash. While you're gode I'll ascertaid what we have id the house to eat."

Sylvester went up accordingly, and, on his return, found the table spread with cold chickens, beef, ham, and tongue, to the whole of which he did ample justice, and then had some coffee with Tom.

The library was then resorted to, and all the books they could find having reference to somnambulism were consulted. This occupied the whole of the evening; and it was at length decided that Sylvester should sleep that night in Tom's room, while Tom sat up in the room adjoining.

The preliminaries having been thus arranged, Sylvester about twelve retired; and Tom took his seat at a table spread with books, cigars, and brandy-and-water.

In order that he might at once hear the slightest noise, Tom left the door of his room open, and, impressed with the importance of the proof desired, continued to listen with so much attention, that Sylvester could not have moved unheard.

From twelve till two o'clock all was still; but the clock had no sooner struck two, than Sylvester walked from one room to the other, and anxiously inquired if Tom had seen him.

"Do," replied Tom. "Do, I've deither seed dor heard you; all has beed still up to this tibe."

"Then hadn't you better go to bed?"

"Do, I shall dot go to bed *to-dight*. That I have bade up by bidd to. Go to sleep agaid; sobethidg bay occur yet."

"I should like to have *one* glass of brandy-and-water," said Sylvester, taking a seat at the table.

"Well, have it, by boy."

"And one cigar."

"Oh, you'd better dot sboke."

"I think I should enjoy it."

"Well," returned Tom, who had not the slightest notion of Sylvester being asleep at the time, "if that's the case, you'd better go add put od your clothes. You'll sood get cold if you sit without theb."

Sylvester assented to this, and left the room; and having dressed himself partially, returned, filled his glass, lit a cigar, and began to smoke it.

"It's a singular thing that this cannot be proved," observed Sylvester, calmly, "isn't it?"

"Why," replied Tom, "this is but the first attebpt. We cad't have proof always the bobedt we wish it. It bay be proved yet, add that sood. We bust dot be ibpatiedt. I've just beed readidg here ad extraordidary case, that of a bricklayer's labourer, whose fellow workbed kdew hib to sleep regularly four or five hours a day while at work, although the work was of so perilous a character. It appears that whed they first discovered this they were extrebely apprehedsive; but as the dovelty of the thidg wore away, their apprehedsiods were subdued. His ebploybedt, of course, codsisted id supplyidg the bricklayers with hods of brick add bortar, which he codveyed up ladders to the tops of houses while asleep, just as well add as safely as he did whed awake. He would attedd to all orders, edter idto codversatiod, add receive add deliver bessages while id this state. He could, boreover, whed awake, recogdise voices which he happed to have heard while asleep, if eved the persods who spoke were the bost perfect stradgers. His fellow workbed frequedtly tried hib, id order to set aside all idcredulity, add dever kdew hib id ady sidgle idstadce to fail. He could tell the hour as well as they could, add therefore kdew as well whed to leave off work; he would dridk with theb, pay his share whed he had buddy, and play at cards while id a state of sobdabbulisb; iddeed, do ordidary observer could tell by his acts that he was dot thed perfectly awake. The way id which this rebarkable case was bade public was this: he was id the habit of washidg hibself add chadidg his dress whed he left off work—this he'd do, whether he happeded to be awake or asleep—add wud evedidg, havidg chadged his clothes as usual, add tied his workidg-dress id a haddkerchief, he was accosted od his way hobe by a wobad, whob, after sobe little codversatiod, he perbitted to carry his buddle, of which she do sooder got possessiod, thad she rad up Hattod Garded, wedt dowd Saffrod Hill, got idto a house add escaped. Well, the codsequedt excitebedt awoke hib; add as he clearly recollected all that had occurred, he related the whole of the circubstadce to ad officer, who fadcied, frob the descriptiod, that he kdew the wobad well. She was therefore apprehedded, add although placed with a dubber of other wohed, the bad id ad idstadt recogdised her persod add voice; add, od searchidg her lodgidgs, the clothes were foudd. Dow, this is a bost extraordidary case. You see, this bad could recollect perfectly whed awake all that occurred while he slept. Gederally sobdabbulists do dot whed awake recollect what occurs duridg sleep; but, od the codtrary, that which they either hear or see while awake bakes ad ibpressiod, upon which, duridg sleep, they will act."

"That, if I am a somnambulist, is precisely the case with me," observed Sylvester, who, while smoking his cigar calmly, had listened with great attention. "I can recollect nothing when awake which occurs during sleep. If I could the mystery would soon be solved. I should like to have one game of chess," he added; "I have not had a game for a very long time. Will you have a game with me?"

"Do, dot dow," replied Tom: "I wadt you to go to bed agaid. It's of do use by sittidg up, if you sit up with be—that's quite clear."

"Well, then, do you go to bed. I don't like the idea of your sitting up alone."

"I shall dot go to bed dow, that's settled. Cobe, old boy, cobe; fidish your glass add be off."

"Well," said Sylvester, "I will do so. What's o'clock?"

"Dearly half-past two."

"Half-past two. Then five hours more will settle it."

"I wish it bay, with all by heart."

"I'll drink that as a toast," said Sylvester; "I wish it may, with all my heart." And having finished his glass, he left the room, and calmly went to bed again.

From this time, Tom heard nothing of him till eight o'clock, when he awoke, and cried, "Are you there still, Tom?"

"Yes," replied Tom, going into his room. "What sort of a dight have you had?"

"I slept excellently well. You heard nothing of me?"

"Dothidg. You appeared to sleep souddly edough."

"I'm sorry for it. It's very strange. In *one* sense I'm sorry for it."

"Well," said Tom; "do you bead to get up, or lie a little lodger?"

"Oh, I'll get up now. Eight hours' sound sleep is enough for any man."

"Well, do so, thed; but you haved't had *quite* eight hours."

"It's eight o'clock now, and I went to bed at twelve."

"Yes, but you were with be dearly half ad hour."

"With you! when?"

"Why, frob two till half-past. You, of course, recollect?"

"What, this morning, do you mean?"

"This bordidg."

"Impossible!"

"Dod't you rebebber it?"

"No! I'm unconscious of having even *turned* since I came to bed at twelve o'clock last night."

"Iddeed. You dod't recollect cobidg idto the other roob, add havidg a cigar, a glass of braddy-add-water, add wishidg to have a gabe of chess?"

"Are you serious?"

"Perfectly."

"Then I recollect nothing whatever about it."

"Stop a bidite. Sobethidg bay be bade of this dow. I related an extraordidary case of sobdabbulisb—a case which I'd just beed readidg; that of a bricklayer's labourer—do you recollect that?"

"No. I recollect nothing that may have occurred since I came to bed last night at twelve."

"Thed, by boy, it is perfectly clear that your suspiciod is well foudded: that you are a sobdabbulist iddeed. You wedt idto that roob about two o'clock, add idquired if I'd seed or heard adythidg of you, and whed I told you that I had dot, you sat dowd add wished to have sobe braddy-add-water, add a cigar. I advised you to put od your clothes, add you did so, add sboked a cigar, add dradk braddy-add-water, add listedd to the case of sobdabbulisb to which I've just alluded, add thed wished to have a gabe of chess, but, as I refused to play, add urged you to go to bed agaid, you did so, after havidg fidished your glass, add I heard do bore of you."

"But is it possible for me to have done all this, while you were unconscious of my being asleep?"

"You *appeared* to be awake—perfectly awake. The idea of your beidg asleep at the tibe dever occurred to be. Stop a bidite."

"Might you not have dreamt all this?"

"I dod't thidk that I closed by eyes, eved for a bobedt."

"But is it not possible?"

"Why, it is possible. Add it certaidly does appear to be albost ibpossible that, while you were doidg all this, I should dot have discovered that you were asleep."

"Might not the purpose for which you sat up, have induced you to dream on the subject?"

"If I *slept*, it bight; but I dod't believe I wedt to sleep at all. Add yet I *cad't*, od the other hadd, thidk that you could thus have deceived be. However, we'll talk the batter over agaid by-add-by. Get up, add let's have a good breakfast. I'll go add have a wash; you'll dot be lodg?"

"I'll be down in ten minutes."

Tom then left the room, and Sylvester rose and dressed himself, thoughtfully, and went down to breakfast, but although they went over the matter again, conviction was not the result.

Sylvester, notwithstanding, felt justified in naming the subject to his solicitor, who was pleased with the idea of being able to plead somnambulism, but then he wanted absolute proof. Tom's evidence, under the circumstances, he feared, would be insufficient; still he resolved to see him on the subject, and accordingly called in the course of the day.

"Mr. Delolme," said he, "Mr. Sound has just informed me of that affair which occurred last night, or, rather, this morning, while you were sitting up. He imagines, as you are aware, that he is a somnambulist, and if we can absolutely *prove* him to be one, we can put in an excellent plea to this action, which can now be defended only by a plain blunt negative. Now, can you conscientiously declare that he *is* a somnambulist?"

"Do," replied Tom; "I have my doubts still. If he be dot a sobdahbulist, it is iddeed stradge; if he be, add cabe idto the roob id which I was sittidg, dradk, sboked, and codversed—as I ibagided he did—without idspiridg be with a sidgle thought of his beidg asleep, it is equally stradge; but whether, id reality, he is a sobdabbulist or dot, I *cad't*, at presedt, uddertake to say. I will, however, discover the fact, if, iddeed, the discovery be possible; add I have, with that view, laid by plads for to-dight, of which plads I bead to keep hib id igdoradce. If, as I suspect, he be wud who id his sleep recollects all that passes while he is awake, he is certaid to frustrate every schebe that bay happed to be codceived with his kdowledge. He shall, therefore, kdow dothidg whatever about it. I'll retire to by owd roob, as usual, to-dight, add I hope that, id the bordidg, I shall have the proof required."

"I hope so too, for, at present, all we *can* do is to put in a flat denial, and I fear that, as Sir Charles is no ordinary man, and as we can find nothing whatever against the character of his butler—whose career we have traced from his infancy, upwards—a mere denial of the facts sworn to will have no effect. If we could but get this proof of Sound's somnambulism, we should be able, with confidence, to go into court; but the proof must be absolute to do any good; suspicion alone will be of no use at all."

"I perceive," observed Tom, "the ibportadce of the proof, add if it be possible, I'll have it. You'll dot see Sylvester *agaid* to-day, I suppose?"

"I don't expect to see him again. He is gone, I believe, to call upon Scholefield."

"Well, if you should see hib, dod't explaid to hib adythidg which has passed betweed us."

"Certainly not. I see your object too clearly. Will you call upon me in the morning, or shall I call upon you."

"Oh, I'll call upod you about ted."

The solicitor promised to be at home at that hour, and being satisfied that everything possible would be done, took his leave.

In the evening, Tom attached strings to the window and door of the room in which Sylvester was to sleep, and having left lengths conveniently available, sat down with Sylvester to have a game of chess. The game lasted till eleven, and they then had a glass of grog each, and a cigar, and as Sylvester did not imagine for one moment that Tom meant to sit up again *that* night, they retired to their respective rooms about twelve.

Tom then got hold of the strings—one through the window, and the other through the door, and as he held them in his hand, it was perfectly impossible for Sylvester to open either the door or the window of *his* room without Tom's knowledge. And there he sat, with the strings in his hand, a cigar in his mouth, and a glass of grog before him; and there he continued to sit until two, when the string attached to the door was drawn out of his hand slowly.

Tom was up in an instant, but paused; and then proceeded with the utmost caution. He distinctly heard footsteps ascending the stairs; and he followed the sound noiselessly. That they were the footsteps of Sylvester he had not the slightest doubt; he felt sure of it, and panted with impatience; but as the value of discretion in such cases was not unknown to him, he followed them cautiously still. A door opened—slowly; the door of the attic—and closed again as Tom ascended; and when he had reached it, he stood and listened; but heard no sound within. For what imagined purpose was Sylvester there? That room was perfectly empty. It surely *was* Sylvester. Tom began to doubt it. He opened the door, and found the room empty still. He looked round and marvelled. "*Who's* there?" he demanded. No answer was returned. He could hear no sound. He ceased to breathe, and might have heard the breathing of another: but there was no one breathing there. The window was open; but that was usual; still, being open, to the window he went, and on looking out, to his horror beheld Sylvester pacing the parapet!

His blood in an instant chilled. He was breathless with terror. With uplifted hands he looked at him, appalled!

He expected that every moment would be his last. And yet *what* could he do? What *could* be done?

Sylvester slowly approached, and—passed him; Tom would have clutched him *as* he passed, but he then felt utterly powerless.

Again he came, and as he approached, Tom nerved himself to grasp him, and just as he was about to pass, he seized his arm, when Sylvester, with a convulsive start, slipped instantly over the parapet.

Tom, however, still held him—firmly; and cried aloud, "Sylvester!—Sylvester!—God! give me strength!—'tis I!—Sylvester!—I! Now!—make one effort!—for God's sake be firm! Seize the coping—the coping!"

Sylvester did so, but the stone gave way, and fell with a crash beneath him.

"Again, again!" cried Tom; "again!—now then!—fear not!—don't be alarmed!—raise yourself up!—there!—now then!—now then!—there!—there!—Well done—well done—well done—well done!"

The moment he had succeeded in dragging Sylvester into the room, he exclaimed, "My boy! Thank God!" and fainted.

For some time Sylvester stood over him aghast. The shock appeared to have deprived him of all his faculties. He had some slight notion—some glimmering of an idea—of his having been in peril, but that idea was so fitful and confused, that nothing ever existed between it and vacancy.

All that he understood was that Tom was at his feet; every thought of assistance being necessary was absent. There he stood, and there he continued to stand, until James, who had heard his master fall, came trembling up with a light. Nor did he move even then. Neither the presence of James, nor the light, made the slightest impression upon him.

"Sir!" exclaimed James, who was half dead with fear, "sir, Mr. Sound, sir, what's the matter?"

Sylvester still stood motionless; and James approached his master and knelt by his side, and as he conceived that he had ceased to exist, he seized Sylvester's hand and cried, "Tell me—tell me—is my master dead?"

Sylvester started, and looked wildly round, and consciousness slightly returned; when he knelt by the side of his faithful friend, and took his hand and pressed it.

"Is he dead, sir?" reiterated James. "Is he, sir? Tell me—tell me?"

"God forbid!" replied Sylvester faintly. "No, he is not dead."

James in an instant rushed from the room, and soon reappeared with some water, and anxiously bathed his master's temples, while Sylvester knelt by his side.

"Some vinegar," said Sylvester; "or salts, if you have them."

James again flew from the room, and having found some vinegar hastily returned, and very soon had the satisfaction of seeing his master begin to revive.

"Sylvester," exclaimed Tom, on opening his eyes, "you are safe. I was wrong—very wrong; but you are safe."

Sylvester did not exactly understand this. He could not conceive how Tom could have been wrong. He did not, however, seek an explanation then; but did all in his power to restore him.

Consciousness having returned, Tom soon felt able to walk downstairs, which he did with the assistance of James, who conducted him into his chamber.

"Oh!" he exclaimed, as he sank into a chair, "Sylvester, what an escape you have had!"

"I am anxious," said Sylvester, "of course, to know how, but wait till you are more composed."

"Jib," said Tom, "give me sobe braddy."

James looked at the bottle which stood by his side, and inquired if that contained brandy.

"Yes," replied Tom, "that's braddy, Jib."

James thought this strange—remarkably strange. He had never seen brandy in that room before. There were, moreover, sundry pieces of cigars lying about. He couldn't understand it at all. In fine, the whole of the circumstances of which he had become cognisant, since the noise above interfered with his repose, appeared to him to be a parcel of complicated mysteries. He did, notwithstanding, pour out a glass of brandy, and having handed it to his master, poured out another, and having handed that to Sylvester, put the bottle down.

"Pour out a glass for yourself," said Tom. And James

did so, and drank it, and relished it much. "Add dow, added Tom, "go idto Mr. Soudd's roob, add bridg dowd his clothes."

Certainly James thought it extremely correct that Sylvester should have his clothes, seeing that he had then nothing on but his shirt, while the night was not a hot one, nor anything like it. He therefore went up for the clothes in question, and having succeeded in bringing them down, Sylvester slipped them on.

"Dow," said Tom, "take adother glass, Jib, add thed be off to bed."

James liked the former part of this order much; but he didn't at all like the latter. He felt himself entitled to something bearing the semblance of an explanation; conscious of being—as far as all these most extraordinary circumstances are concerned—in the dark. He therefore stood and sipped, and sipped—in a manner, for him, unusual—until he found that no sort of an explanation would be vouchsafed, when, feeling that that kind of treatment was not exactly handsome, he indignantly finished his glass and withdrew.

"Syl, by dear boy," said Tom, "give be your hadd. You're alive, by boy; but your life was dot worth a bobedt's purchase. I was a fool, I kdow—a codsubbate fool—but I acted od the ibpulse of the bobedt."

"But how," inquired Sylvester, "how were you a fool? You said just now that you were wrong—very wrong. How were you wrong? In what respect?"

"I'll explaid. But first let us have just a little bore braddy. If ady bad had told be that I should ever have acted id a case like this with such bodstrous iddiscretiod, I should have felt disposed to kick hib. I *ought* to have kdowd better. The bost igdoradt bad alive would scarcely have beed guilty of so badifest ad act of folly."

"Well, but in what did this folly consist?"

"I'll tell you. You see these stridgs?"

"Yes."

"Wud of theb cobbudicates with the sash of your bed-roob widdow, add the other with the haddle of the door. Resolved od ascertaididg, if possible, whether you were a sobdabbulist or not, I, idstead of goidg to bed, kept these stridgs id by hadd, out of which wud of theb, about **two** o'clock, was slowly drawd. I kdew id ad idstadt thed that you had opeded your door, add as I heard you goidg upstairs, I followed. You wedt idto the attic. I followed you there, add od lookidg roudd I could see dothidg of you. But I wedt to the widdow, add there I saw you walkidg upod the very verge of the parapet."

"Good God!" exclaimed Sylvester, "is it possible?"

"There you were, add if I'd dot beed a fool, all would have beed well doubtless; you would have cobe id agaid, I've do doubt, id perfect safety. But to be, your positiod appeared to be so perilous, that actidg, as I said before, od the ibpulse of the bobedt, I seized your arb, add I'd do sooder dode so thad you fell over the parapet, add there I held you. How I got you up agaid *I* cad't explain. It is sufficiedt for be that I did get you up, add that here you are dow alive before be."

"My escape, then, must have been miraculous!"

"It was. I wouldd't see you id the sabe positiod agaid if ady bad were to lay be dowd a billiod of buddy. I shudder whed I thidk of it. Let us for a little while talk about sobethidg else. Wud thing, however, is certaid: you are a sobdabbulist, Syl, add a very idveterate sobdabbulist too. I see dow, who it was that got be idto all those scrapes five or six years ago. You're ad old hadd at it. There was parapet busidess goidg od thed! Dod't you rebebber?"

"I do," replied Sylvester, "and innumerable other things, which have appeared to me to be mysterious, are now solved."

"Dod't you recollect by study? Dod't you rebebber what a gabe you used to have id it dight after dight? I see it all dow, add I shall tell the goverdor of it in triubph, for I feel codvidced that, to this day, he believes that the whole of by eardest declaratiods of iddocedce were false. You it was that caused the destructiod of that wobad I used to prize so highly: it was also you that sbashed by glass just before you left towd. This explaids all! Jib's character is viddicated, add you are codvicted. I shall bridg ad actiod agaidst you, old fellow, for dabages."

"Do so," said Sylvester, smiling, "and I'll plead 'somnambulism' to it. However," he added, seriously, "the proof is now clear. That Sir Charles and his servant saw me I can have no doubt. What effect the proof will have in the forthcoming trial of course remains to be seen."

"The effect will be to give you a verdict," said Tom. "There cad be do doubt about that."

"I don't know. I fear that they will require it to be proved that I was in a state of somnambulism then. But, independently of this affair, isn't the fact of my being a somnambulist awful to contemplate? I can never be safe!"

"Dod't let's have ady bore horrible reflectiods. We have had sufficiedt horror for wud dight, at least. I'll take care of you, by boy, for the tibe beidg. You shall be safe. You shall sleep with be. I'll fix you. You shall dot, however, kdow exactly how."

"I had better be chained to the bed every night."

"I'll get a pair of haddcuffs id the bordidg, add while you are here, put wud od your wrist add the other od by owd. *I'll* dot allow you to go prowlidg about at dight id this stupid state of bide. But we'll say do bore about it dow. Let's go to bed. You lie od that side, add I'll lie od this. If you get away frob *be*, let be kdow, add I'll believe it."

They then went to bed; and when Tom was quite sure that Sylvester was asleep, he tied the tails of their shirts together, and quietly went to sleep himself.

CHAPTER XXXIV.

THE LAST REQUEST.

THERE are men whom nothing can apparently astonish—who take everything so coolly—hear everything so calmly—see everything wonderful with such seeming apathy—that the most perfect insensibility appears to form one of their chief characteristics. On the heads of these men no phrenologist can find either the organ of marvellousness or that of veneration—activity being essential to the development of both. Nothing appears to be new to them; nothing seems to strike them as being extraordinary; nothing on earth can induce them to manifest wonder. It is true that this stoicism may be very admirable—doubtless, were it not merely apparent it would be an invaluable blessing—but the question is, do not these "stoics" feel and reflect more deeply than those men whose feelings and thoughts are on the surface ready for immediate expression?

This, however, is a question which need not be learnedly answered here. We can get on with this history very well without it. The object is simply to show that Mr. Wilks—Sylvester's solicitor—was one of those men, and that when Tom—who kept his appointment punctually at ten—had explained to him the substance of all that had occurred, he didn't appear to be in the slightest degree astonished. He viewed it all as a matter of business. He thought it would strengthen the defence. The perilous position, the miraculous escape, and the feelings of horror which Tom had inspired were all set aside. He wanted Tom's evidence; that was the point. He looked at the facts; they were the things. And would Tom swear to them?—that was the question.

"Of course," said he, "you have no objection to appear as a witness?"

"Dode whatever," replied Tom. "I *cad* have do objectiod."

"Well, then, we'll take the facts down."

"Dod't you thidk that the evidedce of by bad Jib will be of sobe service?"

"Can he prove anything?"

"Why Soudd, just before he left Loddod, broke by pier-glass, id a state of sobdabbulisb?"

"Did your servant see him do it?"

"He saw hib go idto the roob at dight, add I foudd it sbashed id the bordidg."

"He saw him go into the room, you say?"

"Yes: with dothidg od but his shirt. He boreover saw id his badd a pistol, of which he subsequedtly heard the report, add I foudd the ball id the wall id the bordidg, just where the pier-glass stood."

"That'll do," said Wilks. "That'll do. There's nothing like a little collateral evidence. When can I see your servant?"

"Oh, I'll sedd hib to you id the course of the bordidg."

"Thank you. Very good. Now, then, I'll take down your evidence."

The facts were then reduced to writing, and appeared to be alone a sufficient defence; and when Tom had again promised to send James on his return, he left the office, fully convinced that Sylvester *must* have a verdict.

While Tom was thus engaged with the solicitor, Sylvester wrote to his aunt, requesting her to come to town immediately; and informing her of the fact of his being a somnambulist.

This may appear to have been indiscreet, and indeed to a certain extent it was so, for when the information reached Cotherstone Grange, Aunt Eleanor nearly fainted.

Sylvester's object was simply to prepare her for the reception of that intelligence which he had to communicate, and at which he conceived she might otherwise be shocked; but no sooner did the bare fact of his being a somnambulist reach her, than her anxious thoughts reverted to her brother, and she felt wretched.

Her reverend friend was with her when the letter arrived, and on perceiving her emotion, his anxiety was intense.

"Dear Eleanor!" he exclaimed, "what is it? What—what can have occurred?"

Aunt Eleanor gave him the letter to read, and he read it—hastily, being apprehensive of meeting with something dreadful; but finding nothing to realise his lively apprehensions, he read it again with more care.

"A somnambulist," said he, at length, thoughtfully; "a somnambulist. A somnambulist is a person who walks in his sleep; a sleep walker; one who walks while asleep, and imagines he is awake. I have read many strange accounts of these somnambulists. But what, my dear Eleanor, induced your distress?"

"The fact of his being a somnambulist," she replied. "My poor brother was one. It was that which brought him to a premature grave."

"Well, that was very lamentable—very. But Sylvester is young! He is in fact quite a youth! and I hold it to be extremely fortunate that the thing has been found out so soon! He must be cured of this propensity. I have not the smallest doubt that a cure may be effected. I am not, it is true, conversant with that which is termed the physiology of somnambulism; but, doubtless, when we look at the wonderful progress which the science of medicine has made within the last century, means of effecting a cure have been found."

"But what perils—what dreadful dangers—are encountered by those who are thus afflicted!"

"True; and these it will now be our care to prevent. I submit, that instead of uselessly lamenting the fact, we ought to congratulate ourselves on the discovery. Understand, my dear Eleanor, I do not mean to say that the fact itself is one which ought not to be lamented; my object is merely to convey to you my impression that we ought to be thankful that the discovery has been made before anything of a very serious character occurred."

"I understand; and I *am* thankful—oh! most thankful."

"And now, if I do not mistake—I know it is presumptuous to form an opinion without having the necessary data—still, if I do not mistake, I can see distinctly the cause of his being accused of that offence of which we both firmly believe him to be innocent. Sir Charles was quite right—I cannot conceive the possibility of a person in his station declaring that to be true which he knew to be false—he was doubtless quite right: he *did* see Sylvester leaving the house as described; and Sylvester was, I will venture to say, in a state of somnambulism then."

"*Very* likely!" exclaimed Aunt Eleanor suddenly. "That's it! Yes; it must be so!"

"I think it abundantly clear that it *is* so. I moreover think that there can be no doubt that the judge and jury will see it. Really, my impression is, that just at this time nothing could have been more fortunate than this discovery. A man in a state of somnambulism cannot be said to be a responsible agent, and if he be not a responsible agent, he cannot, with justice, be punished. I here assume, my dear Eleanor, the case of a man who, while in a state of somnambulism, commits an offence which is ordinarily punishable by law—such an offence, for example, as a sacrilege. We could not, with justice, punish any individual for committing such an offence while in a state of somnambulism. Hence it is that I feel quite certain that, when the fact of Sylvester being seen to leave the residence of this gentleman is viewed in connection with the circumstance of his being a somnambulist, the jury will, without hesitation, return a verdict in his favour. But have you never seen, my dear Eleanor, anything indicative of the existence of this extraordinary—what shall I call it—during his residence here?"

"Why really—although I never noticed the slightest indication of anything of the kind—I am now disposed to view him as the author of all those little mysteries by which we have been so perplexed. About five years ago, you recollect, we were terribly pestered?"

"I see!" exclaimed the reverend gentleman. "He was down here at that time. I see it all, now. It *was* he whom I then caught at my peaches. Jones is right—quite right—he's perfectly right. I must apologise to Jones at a fitting opportunity, for, albeit he declares to this day that it was Sylvester, I have persisted in repudiating the idea as being monstrous. And then the ghost—why, let me see—the ghost! Why the ghost never appears here when Sylvester is absent. He is the ghost; he must be the ghost. The thing is all explained. When he is in town no ghost appears; it is always seen when he is here. Nothing can be clearer. Bless my life and soul, now I wonder this never occurred to me before. He *is* the ghost. There cannot be a doubt about it. And this reminds me that I have been unwittingly guilty of an act of injustice. You remember that that man, Obadiah Drant, declared the other day that Sylvester was drinking one night at the Crumpet and Crown? Sylvester denied it positively—solemnly, and I, in consequence, told Drant plainly, and in no measured terms, that it was false. I now, however, firmly believe it to be true; I believe that Sylvester, while in a state of somnambulism *was* there, I must apologise to that unhappy man; it is but just that I should do so. Why, my dear Eleanor, this is the key to all. This affords a ready and a rational explanation of everything that has occurred."

"But is it not strange that *we* should never have discovered it?"

"It is—very strange. That, however, which strikes me as being most strange, is the fact of his having deceived *me* that night when he entered the parlour. I really believed him to be a spirit; I did indeed. That, my dear Eleanor, is the strangest thing of all. But we must see him—we must see him without delay. When shall we go, my dear—when shall we go? Shall we start off at once?"

"Why, I don't see how we can go to-day. I have nothing prepared."

"There is a coach, my dear, at twelve. Can you not, by the exercise of your ingenuity, manage to get ready by that time? I would not press the point, but I really feel so anxious to see him."

"So do I. But—well, I *will* get ready; we *will* go to-day. The coach starts from the inn at twelve?"

"Yes, and if we start from here at the same time we shall meet it."

"Then let it be so. You will have to go home; by the time you return, I'll be ready."

The reverend gentleman then left the cottage; prepared for the journey; returned at eleven; sat down to lunch; ate heartily; and at twelve o'clock they started.

As they left the village the carriages of Mr. Howard and the lady whose assumed name was Greville met at the door of the inn. It will doubtless be remembered that they, with Henriette, were introduced in the fifth chapter of this history. It will be also recollected that they had been in the habit of meeting at that place periodically; that Mr. Howard would never see Mrs. Greville; and that Henriette—who was allowed to remain in the room one hour—had been kept in perfect ignorance as to who she really was.

Henriette had a thousand times entreated her father to explain this mystery; a thousand times had she begged of him to tell her why they met there, and why Mrs. Greville—whom he felt she loved dearly—should be always so deeply affected when they met. His answer invariably was—

"She knew you in infancy; you remind her of her own dear child. I would not wound her feelings by neglecting to take you there on these occasions for the world. I promised long ago that she should see you twice a year."

Nor could Henriette obtain an explanation from Mrs. Greville.

"Why," she inquired on one occasion, "why does not my dear father see you?"

"He will not see me," replied Mrs. Greville. "I remind him of your mamma."

"You knew her, then?"

"Oh, yes; well."

"You have been married?"

"I have."

"You have had children?"

"One—one dear—dear girl."

"Your husband—is he dead?"

"Alas—to me."

"Your daughter, too?"

"To me—to me; yes, both are dead to me! But do not urge me, pray do not. You'll break my heart. I cannot bear it. Promise me—do promise me—that you'll never revert to this subject again."

Henriette, seeing her distress, did promise, and from that hour the subject in her presence was never named.

On this occasion, however, as the carriages met, Howard and Mrs. Greville caught each other's glance, and while his altered appearance so shocked her, that she was almost unable to alight, he suddenly sank back in his carriage and wept.

Having been with some difficulty assisted into the room

which she usually occupied, she sank into a chair and sobbed aloud, and when Henriette—who had marvelled at her father's sudden emotion—had joined her, she fell upon her neck and kissed and blessed her more passionately than ever.

"My *dear* Mrs. Greville," said Henriette, "what *can* be the meaning of this? I left my father weeping, and now"——

"You left him *weeping?* Oh, *did* he weep when he saw me?"

"I know not that he saw you, but he wept."

"Thank Heaven! I am not then despised."

"Despised! Surely you never imagined that you were?"

"I *have* thought so, my dearest love—I have thought so! But he is not well. He cannot be well!"

"He is as well as usual! or was when we left home this morning."

"Then what a change has been effected! Oh, my love, there *was* a time—but that time's past. Dear Henriette— you know not how I *love* you!"

"You love me. You *love* me, and yet you keep me in ignorance of that which I have been for years panting to know. Why are you now thus afflicted? Why did my dear father weep? If you love me, let me know all. I said *If!* —Forgive me. I feel, I know you love me fondly, but pray, pray keep me in ignorance no longer."

"My dear, dear girl," said Mrs. Greville, who continued to weep bitterly, "indeed you must not urge me. My lips on this subject are sealed. That seal must not by me be broken."

A pause ensued: during which Mrs. Greville sat gazing at Henriette through her tears, which she would have concealed but *could* not.

"Henriette," she said at length, having struggled with her feelings until she appeared to have almost subdued them. "Henriette, will you do me a favour?"

"My dear Mrs. Greville," replied Henriette, "why ask me? You know not what pleasure it will give me to do anything for you, of which I am capable."

"I believe your dear father is still in the carriage."

"He is."

"Will you go to him, my dear girl, and tell him that I

am anxious—most anxious—to see him for a few short moments?"

"It will give me great happiness to do so."

"Dear Henriette, tell him—pray tell him—that if he will but grant me this one request, I pledge my honour—ay, my honour—that it shall be my last."

Henriette kissed her, and flew from the room, and when the door of the carriage had been opened, she said, "Dear father, mamma—I feel, I *know* that it is mamma"——

"Henriette!" said Howard sternly, as he alighted.

He said no more, but handed her into the carriage, followed her, gave the word "Home!" and they were off.

CHAPTER XXXV.

THE TRIAL.

From the evening Aunt Eleanor and her friend arrived in town till the day of the trial, nothing occurred to Sylvester worth recording. He invariably slept with Tom, who had procured a pair of manacles—with a thin chain attached—with which he every night secured him to himself, and although he very frequently rose in his sleep, the chain instantly checked and awoke them both.

"Dot a bit of it, old fellow," Tom used to exclaim. "You dod't do adythidg at all of the sort. You wadt to go prowlidg about as usual, do you? Cobe alodg id agaid: cobe—cobe alodg."

When Aunt Eleanor heard of this arrangement, she felt perfectly satisfied of Sylvester's safety; and so did the reverend gentleman, whose whole time was occupied in the conception of ideas, calculated in his view to strengthen the defence. He was to be a witness—a most important witness —and when Mr. Wilks, the solicitor, had taken down his evidence, he called with the view of improving it, two or three times every day upon Mr. Wilks, until he found—and it really appeared to him to be the strangest thing in nature —that Mr. Wilks was never at home when he called. He was continually out. Nothing could be like it. Go when he might, Mr. Wilks was from home. He would occasionally wait an hour or two in the outer office—either reading the paper or conversing with one of the clerks—for there *was* one very nice young man in that office; all the rest, in the reverend gentleman's judgment, behaved with too much levity, for they were always laughing, they laughed whenever he entered, and continued to laugh all the time he remained—but it mattered not how many hours he waited, Mr. Wilks never returned while he was there.

This extraordinary fact engendered in his mind a strong suspicion that Mr. Wilks neglected his business; and he began to lament that some *other* solicitor had not been engaged in the case; but as the doctor and Mr. Scholefield —who at once perceived the cause of Mr. Wilks's extraordinary absence on those occasions—set his mind at rest on *that* point, he regularly conveyed his ideas twice a day to Mr. Wilks on a sheet of foolscap paper, which he invariably filled, and which Mr. Wilks invariably put under the table.

The morning of the day at length arrived: the day on which the trial was appointed to take place: and the reverend gentleman rose at four, and took a constitutional walk round Hyde Park. As he felt very fidgety he walked very fast, but Time seemed to fly much more slowly than usual. He had to be at Tom's at eight o'clock, but before six he felt quite knocked up. Two hours remained. How was he to pass those two hours? A thought struck him. He would go down to Westminster Hall. He would look at the building, and ascertain whether he thought it likely that justice would be administered that day. He accordingly wended his way towards the Hall, and as he met sundry females, whom he imagined impure, he walked in the middle of the road, conceiving that expostulation would be useless.

On reaching Palace Yard, he stood, and looked, and contemplated deeply, and wildly conjectured, and then went over the whole of his evidence, which of course, he thought perfectly conclusive.

"Cab, your honour?" said a man, who approached him.

"No, my good man," replied the reverend gentleman. "I was merely looking at Westminster Hall. There is a trial coming on to-day in which I am interested."

"Indeed!" cried the cabman; "what trial is it?"

"It is a *crim. con.* trial, 'Julian *versus* Sound,' but my friend, who is the defendant in the action, is a somnambulist."

"Beg pardon, sir; a how much?"

"A somnambulist. A person who walks in his sleep."

"Oh! one of them there svells—I see."

"He is innocent of the crime of which he is accused; quite innocent."

"No doubt."

"But then the plantiff in this case will not believe it."

"That's alvays the case, sir; they never vill."

"It is lamentable that it should be so!"

"Werry! but they alvays knows better than anybody else."

"They always appear to *believe* they know better."

"That's jist precisely my meaning."

"But then you know it's obstinacy: nothing but obstinacy!"

"Nothing; I've alvays found them svells the most obstropulusest going."

"If men would in all cases listen to reason"——

"That's the pint. Reason's the ticket!"

"But you see they will not. However, '*suus cuique mos!*'"

"Werry good."

"Hollo, Bob! what's the row?" inquired one of the cabman's friends.

"Why, Dick," said Bob, winking very significantly, "this here gentleman here is hinterested in a haction."

"Does his mother know he's out?" inquired Dick, with very great indiscretion.

"My mother," replied the reverend gentleman, "of whom you could have had no knowledge, has been dead twenty years."

Bob again winked at Dick, who withdrew.

"He's a wulgar man, that, sir," observed Bob, "werry."

"I must say that I don't think him very refined."

"But then vot can you expect? He's had no eddication."

"Then he's much to be pitied."

"Werry true. There you've just hit my sentiments.

Werry true, indeed. A cold morning, sir," added Bob. "Heverythink's werry dull. I hope you'll allow me to drink your honour's health?"

"Here's a shilling," said the reverend gentleman, "which, as you're a civil man, you may apply to that purpose."

"Beg pardon, sir: I hope you von't think me too intruding, but as I knows you're a gentleman as feels for distress, I'd be werry much obleeged to you if you'd be so kind as to lend me jist another eighteenpence. I ain't had a fare tonight, sir, reely. I shall be sure to see you agin, sir; and then I'll pay your honour."

"Well, my good man, I don't know you at all; but if, as you say, you *are* distressed, here is one-and-sixpence more: take it home to your wife and family."

"Thank you, sir: I'm werry much obleeged to you," said Bob, who winked at Dick in the distance, "werry."

And having delivered himself to this effect, he at once rejoined his "wulgar" friend, who burst into a loud roar of laughter.

The reverend gentleman didn't understand this: he conceived it to be imputable to the man's vulgarity, and left Palace Yard, and wandered about until half-past seven, when, feeling exceedingly fatigued, he knocked at Tom's door and was admitted.

At eight o'clock precisely, Aunt Eleanor, the doctor, Mr. Scholefield, the reverend gentleman, Sylvester, and Tom, sat down to breakfast, but there was not one of them who had the slightest appetite. Their anxiety caused them all to feel nervous. They *couldn't* eat. They drank tea and coffee, it is true; but nothing substantial could any one of them touch.

As nine o'clock was the time at which they were instructed to be at the court, they, at a quarter to nine, entered the carriages of the doctor and Mr. Scholefield, which were waiting at the door, and proceeded at once to the Hall.

This was the reverend gentleman's first appearance in a court of justice, and when he saw five or six rows of barristers as he entered, he really felt awed! He however said nothing; even *their* appearance seemed to have rendered him speechless; but when the Lord Chief Justice took his seat, he felt that it would be perfectly impossible for him to give any evidence at all.

Well, that being then the first case on the list, "Julian *versus* Sound" was called. Mr. Charles Phillpots appeared with Mr. Clark for the plaintiff, and Mr. Slashinger with Mr. O'Phail for the defendant.

The legal preliminaries having been arranged, Mr. Clark opened the pleadings, from which he wished his lordship and the jury to understand, that in this case Sir Charles Julian, Bart., was the plaintiff; that Sylvester Sound was the defendant; that the declaration charged the defendant with having assaulted Matilda Maria, the wife of the plaintiff, &c. &c.; and that the damages were laid at five thousand pounds.

Mr. Phillpots then rose, and spoke as follows: "My lord and gentlemen of the jury,—This is one of those cases which, to the honour of the mighty and moral empire in which we live—considering its importance, its population, and its wealth—are comparatively rare. I need not explain to you, gentlemen of the jury, that it is with the most profound anxiety that I approach this subject, for that anxiety will be appreciated when I state that I have confided in my hands the dearest interests of a fellow-creature, who has been wantonly—cruelly—vilely reduced from a state of supreme—of ecstatic happiness, to the deepest and most inconceivable misery. Oh, how I wish that I could place my unhappy—my heartbroken client before you, that his haggard brow, his sorrowing features, his wasted form, and his hollow eye, might manifest the horrible pangs he has endured! Oh, that I could bring him before you now, that you might see what havoc—what agonising havoc—his sufferings have caused! You would then behold a picture of appalling misery, which no words at my command can even feebly portray. I hope most fervently that you may never know how poor—how weak are the utmost exertions of an advocate, when placed under such afflicting circumstances as these! I hope that you may never experience the heart-rending pangs, the agonising sufferings of a man placed—basely placed—in the position of my unhappy client. Gentlemen, the plaintiff is the scion of an honourable family—a family whose antiquity stands unsurpassed, and upon whose escutcheon calumny never dared to breathe. In the affectionate bosom of that family he passed the early portion of his life: but becoming enamoured of her whose honour the defendant has thus vilely tarnished, he married, and for years enjoyed the most supreme felicity on earth. She was amiable, beautiful, and highly accomplished. She possessed every virtue that could adorn her sex. She was all his heart could wish. His soul adored her. In her his every earthly hope was centered. And thus years of bliss rolled on, till the defendant basely drew her into his accursed meshes, compassing the destruction of an amiable woman—crushing the spirits of an honourable man—and blasting his happiness for ever. Gentlemen, up to this period the plaintiff had not the most distant idea of his wife's infidelity. He believed her to be faithful—he believed her to be virtuous—he believed her to be pure—and I cherish a strong conviction that he was justified in believing her to be faithful, and virtuous, and pure: nor was it until he absolutely saw, to his astonishment and horror, the defendant leave the house at night, after having been seen in her chamber, that he entertained the slightest suspicion of his having been for ever dishonoured and disgraced. Gentlemen, I shall bring before you evidence of the most incontrovertible character to prove that the defendant was actually seen to come from Lady Julian's chamber, while the lady herself occupied it. I shall moreover prove to you, beyond all doubt, that the butler in the service of the plaintiff absolutely let the defendant out of the house! And what is the defendant? He is a medical man. He is a member of the Royal College of Surgeons. Now, if there be one man more than another in whose honour and integrity we feel ourselves justified in confiding, that man is a medical adviser. At all times, in all seasons, and under all conceivable circumstances, a medical adviser has free and unfettered access to our homes. Relying upon his honour, we place our wives and daughters freely under his care, and although the defendant was not the medical adviser of Lady Julian—although it cannot be said that he violated any confidence directly reposed in him by the plaintiff—if once the case of a medical man, guilty of so infamous a practice as that of which the defendant has been guilty, be suffered to pass without being strongly marked, farewell confidence, farewell security, farewell virtue, farewell peace. Gentlemen, the fact of the defendant being a medical man greatly aggravates his infamy, for, up to this time, it has been scarcely conceivable that so base, so heartless a reptile could be found connected with that ancient and honourable profession. We have hitherto looked for friends there, not for vipers: we have looked for integrity, not for abomination. I admit this unhappy lady's fall. I admit her utter worthlessness, but, not being skilled in that atrocious, that execrable species of necromancy, of which the defendant is so perfect a master, I cannot pretend to tell you by what witchcraft—by what hellcraft—he succeeded in destroying the soul of such a woman, by prompting her thus to disgrace and dishonour so fond, so affectionate, so doting a husband. And now, having thus briefly drawn the faint outline of this most abominable case, I have to direct your attention, gentlemen, to the only question open for your consideration—for the pleas of the defendant are not worth a rush—namely, what damages you ought to give the plaintiff.

> 'Had it pleased Heaven
> To try him with affliction; had it rained
> All kinds of sores and shames on his bare head,
> Steeped him in poverty to the very lips,
> Given to captivity him and his hopes,
> He would have found in some part of his soul
> A drop of patience:
> But there, where he had garner'd up his heart,
> Where either he must live or bear no life,
> The fountain, from the which his current runs
> Or else dries up: to be discarded thence!'

Turn your complexion there, gentlemen, and say what damages you ought to give him. Deeply do I lament that an injured husband has no other remedy; deeply do I regret that the legislature of this great nation has not made the outrage a criminal offence. He who steals your purse, steals trash; yet he forfeits his liberty—it may be his life; but he who basely plunders you of the dearest treasure of your heart of hearts, escapes, if rich, with comparative impunity. But the law is so, and your award can be merely that of money. And how are you to calculate the damages? There is but one rule—'Do as you would be done by.' Many of you are basking in the light of wedded love—blessed with a home to which you turn as to a haven from the storms of life, surrounded by joys, and sipping bliss from the lips of her whom you dearly love. What would you take to have this vision dissipated? What would you take to lose her? What you would take in such a case, give!—award that which you would feel yourself justified in receiving. The damages are laid at five thousand pounds. Would you think that sum too much for you to receive? Do I insult you by the question? No; not I. It is the law that interrogates you. 'Do as you would be done by.' If you think that that sum would be too much for *you*, give my client what *you* would think enough. Place yourselves individually in his position, and say what you—feeling the earthquake of your happiness beneath you, and looking round for one last prop to cling to, and seeing the visions you had cherished, the bliss you had enjoyed, the hopes you had idolised, with every household deity dearest and most divine, shivered to atoms round the hearth where they were worshipped—say what you would consider a sufficient compensation. Gentlemen, I now leave the case of my unhappy client—deprived as he has been by the vile, insidious arts of the defendant, of the society of her who formed the lovely centre of this happy circle—with the most entire confidence, in your hands. Your verdict must be for the plaintiff, of course. The only point for you to consider is, that which has reference to compensation. What you think would compensate you in such a case, award him. 'Do as you would be done by!'"

This address, of course, produced an extraordinary sensation. The great majority of those who were in court thought that the verdict *must* be for the whole five thousand; that Sir Charles deserved it, and that he, therefore, ought to have it.

James Thompson, the butler, was then called and sworn.

"Your name is James Thompson, I believe," said Mr. Phillpots.

"It is," replied the butler.

"You hold the situation of butler in Sir Charles's establishment?"

"I do."

"And have held it for the last seven years?"

"I have."

"Do you remember the night of the 5th of last month?"

"I do."

"State to the court what then occurred."

"About three that morning, on going upstairs, I saw Mr. Sound coming slowly from the ante-room, which leads to Lady Julian's chamber, and conceiving that he had called professionally, I returned, opened the door, and let him out."

"You know the defendant well?"

"Quite well."

"You know the defendant quite well. Now, just pay attention to the question I'm about to ask. Is it *possible* for you to have been mistaken?"

"No; that is quite impossible."

"Quite impossible. Did you let him in?"

"No."

"Who let him in?"

"Can't say."

"Did either of the other servants let him in?"

"They all declare that they did not."

"Is there any window through which he might have entered?"

"There is no window he could have got in at."

"Then the presumption is, that Lady Julian let him in herself?"

"I don't know; but I think that if she had let him in, she would also have let him out."

"I don't ask you what you *think!* You didn't let him in, nor did either of the other servants let him in. The presumption, therefore, is that she let him in herself. But you are quite sure that it was Mr. Sound, the defendant, whom you saw coming slowly from the ante-room, and whom you let out of the house?"

"I am quite sure."

"That you swear to?"

"I do."

"Solemnly?"

"Most solemnly."

Mr. Slashinger then rose to cross-examine this witness.

"You know Mr. Sound, the defendant in this action, quite well?"

"I do."

"You have known him for some years?"

"I have."

"As the assistant of Scholefield, the medical adviser of Lady Julian, he used to come frequently to the house?"

"Very frequently."

"Both with Mr. Scholefield, and alone?"

"Very frequently alone."

"Now, Mr. Thompson, I am going to put to you a most important question, and your well-known honesty and integrity prompts me to believe that you will answer it in a candid and straightforward manner. Did you ever, at any time, see anything in the conduct of Lady Julian, to induce you to believe that she was not strictly virtuous?"

"Never, sir! never!" replied Thompson, with emotion. "Nor do I believe that she is not virtuous now."

"You do not! What, not after the eloquent speech of my learned friend?"

"That has not shaken my belief: nor do I think that if Sir Charles had been here, he would have allowed him to go on so. So much about the money."

"I repeat," said Mr. Phillpots, rising indignantly, "I tell you again that we don't ask you what you think. Answer the questions that are put to you, sir."

"I do to the best of my ability."

"Then," resumed Mr. Slashinger, "you still believe Lady Julian to be virtuous?"

"I do."

"Sir Charles was not at home, I believe, when you saw Mr. Sound on that occasion?"

"He was not."

"You have no idea how he got in?"

"I have not the slightest."

"Were you in the house the whole of the morning in question?"

"Except for a few moments, when I went to speak to the butler at the house adjoining."

"Did you leave the door open—or partially open—when you went to speak to the butler?"

"I did."

"Might not Mr. Sound have walked in while you were absent?"

"He certainly *might* have done so."

"He might have done so. And you believe, notwithstanding you saw Mr. Sound coming slowly from the ante-room, that Lady Julian is virtuous still?"

"I do. I don't believe she knew that he was there."

"How did he look when you let him out? At all confused?"

"No; calm and serious."

"Did he make any observation?"

"None."

"Then he walked straight out, and took no notice?"

"He did."

"Very well."

"And now," said Mr. Phillpots, who looked very fierce, "*I* am about to put a question, which, from 'your well-known honesty and integrity,' to use the flowing language of my learned friend, I expect you, in a candid and straightforward manner, to answer. When did you see the defendant's attorney last?"

"I never did see him to my knowledge."

"But you have seen his clerk, haven't you?"

"Not to my knowledge."

"Is it not indiscreet," said Mr. Clark, in a whisper, "to throw a doubt upon any portion of the evidence of our own witness?"

Mr. Phillpots winked at Mr. Clark, and then resumed.

"It was about three o'clock when you saw the defendant coming from the ante-room leading to Lady Julian's chamber?"

"About three."

"And you couldn't by any possibility have mistaken any one else for the defendant?"

"I could not. The thing is impossible."

"Impossible. Very well. That will do."

This was the case for the plaintiff; and, after a pause, Mr. Slashinger rose, and said—

"My lord, and gentlemen of the jury,—My learned friend, with his usual tact, having but one single fact to adduce, has brought forward a multitude of figures. Knowing the actual weakness of his case, he has endeavoured to strengthen it with flights of fancy: feeling that the solitary point for you to consider was of itself insufficient, his object has been to carry away your judgment by a flaming flood of forensic eloquence. That object, however, has not been accomplished. If it had been, it would have been my duty to bring you back to the point from which you started. But as I feel that I have now to address intelligent men—men who will not suffer their judgment to be carried away so easily—my task is comparatively light. Gentlemen, what are the facts of the case?—nay, rather let me say what is the fact?—there being but one at present for your consideration. The fact, gentlemen, is, that the witness Thompson swears that he saw the defendant at the time in question, walking—slowly walking—from the ante-room which leads to Lady Julian's chamber. Now, gentlemen, I am not about to impugn Thompson's evidence. He gave it in a very proper manner, and I take it for granted that he believes that which he stated to be true. He may be correct. The defendant may have been there: he may have walked from the ante-room slowly: he may have been let out by Thompson: he may have been seen to pass the gate by Sir Charles. I don't know that he was not—nor does the defendant!—but if he *were* there, he was there while in a state of somnambulism! [This announcement created an extraordinary sensation. Even the reverend gentleman, whom the speech of Mr. Phillpots had perfectly bewildered, rubbed his hands, and smiled.] Gentlemen," continued the learned counsel, "unhappily my client is a confirmed somnambulist. I shall prove that to your entire satisfaction anon. At present I feel it to be my duty to account for his presence—for I assume that he was present—at the house of Sir Charles Julian on the occasion in question. Gentlemen, somnambulists generally, when asleep, remember everything which occurs to them while awake, but they remember nothing when awake which happens while they are asleep. I beg of you to bear this in mind. The defendant, Mr.

Sound, lived for the period of five years with Mr. Scholefield, Lady Julian's medical attendant. During that period, as the witness has told us, he was frequently—very frequently—at the house of Sir Charles. Now, gentlemen, may I not venture to say, that on the morning in question, he dreamt that Lady Julian required his professional attendance, and that, acting on that dream, he rose and went to the house? You have heard Thompson state that he left the door open when he went to speak to the butler at the house adjoining: you have also heard him state that the defendant might have entered the house during his absence. Now, is it too much to assume, knowing him to be a confirmed somnambulist, that the defendant did enter the house at that time, and with no other view than that of attending to Lady Julian professionally? I do submit, gentlemen, that when I have proved, as I shall prove beyond all question, that my client *is* a somnambulist, the case will be, in your judgment, perfectly clear. As to Lady Julian, I believe her to be still strictly virtuous, still pure: and in that belief I am joined, as you have heard, by the witness Thompson, who has had the most ample opportunities of observing her character and conduct. Gentlemen, my firm impression is, that this proceeding on the part of Sir Charles Julian ought to cause him to blush. He married Lady Julian in all the pride of youth and beauty, he himself being rather advanced in years; and although I will not say that it is natural for an old man to be jealous of a young and lovely wife, I *may* say that it is too often the case, and that the slightest circumstance is sufficient to create suspicion. I have, however, no desire to dwell upon this point. He saw the defendant coming from the house: his suspicion was aroused, and he brought this action: for damages!—for compensation for the loss of her whom, on these slight grounds, he turned out of his house, and who never was unfaithful to him. I do not envy the feelings of that man: I do not envy the feelings of any man who, on such slender grounds, casts 'his soul's idol' off—his soul's idol—psha!—it is sickening. But, gentlemen, he wants compensation!—he wants money! Yes: he wants you to award him an immense sum of money. Well, if you think him entitled to it, of course you'll award it. I would merely submit that such grovelling ideas do not in general co-exist with affection. *Money* is his suit! Well, let him have money, if you think that he has been injured—if you *can* believe Lady Julian to be impure. I shall not say one word in mitigation of damages—no damage has been sustained by Sir Charles. I will prove to you that the defendant is a somnambulist, and I have so much confidence in your judgment, that you will see that the object of Sir Charles Julian is money, that Lady Julian is still virtuous, still pure, that the defendant went to the house while under the influence of a dream, and that therefore he is entitled to your verdict."

The learned counsel then called Thomas Delolme, who promptly appeared in the box, and was sworn.

"Mr. Delolme," said Mr. Slashinger, "you are a medical man?"

"I ab," replied Tom.

"You have, I believe, an extensive practice?"

"Dot very *extedsive*. About a thousadd a year."

"About a thousand a year. You are intimately acquainted with Mr. Sound, the defendant in this action?"

"I ab."

"Is it your impression that he is a somnambulist?"

"It is."

"Tell the court how that impression was created."

"Id codsequedce of his havidg idforbed be the other day that he suspected that he was a sobdabbulist, I idduced hib to sleep at by house, add sat up id a roob adjoididg that id which he slept. About two o'clock he cabe idto the roob id which I was sittidg, add had a glass of braddy-add-water, add sboked a cigar, add codversed for sobe tibe, add thed wedt to bed agaid: but id the bordidg he recollected dothidg at all about it. Dot satisfied with this, I sat up the dext dight without his kdowledge, havidg previously attached a stridg to the sash of his bedroob widdow, add adother to the haddle of his door; add, at about the sabe tibe, that is to say, two o'clock, the stridg attached to the door was pulled out of my hadd; I wedt out, add heard footsteps ascedddidg the stairs. I therefore followed, add codtidued to follow udtil I had reached the attic, frob the widdow of which I saw Sylvester—that is to say, the defeddadt id this actiod—walkidg od the very verge of the parapet, with dothidg whatever od but his shirt. I was of course at the tibe appalled, add as he passed be, I iddiscreetly seized hib by the wrist, add the sudded shock caused hib to fall over the parapet. I held hib, however, still, add biraculously got hib up; add whed I had succeeded in doidg so, it appears that I faidted: but the fact of his beidg a sobdabbulist is sufficiedt to accoudt for bady extraordidary thidgs which occurred whed he lived id by father's house, about five years ago."

"Then you have not the slightest doubt of his being a somnambulist?"

"Dode whatever. His is the bost codfirbed case I ever bet with."

"Has he slept in your house ever since you made the discovery?"

"Yes, every dight; add with be."

"In the same bed?"

"Yes."

"And does he still walk in his sleep?"

"Do: he would do so, but I prevedt hib. Whed we go to bed I attach a sball haddcuff to his wrist, add adother to by owd. He therefore caddot rise without wakidg be."

"Which he does, I suppose, frequently?"

"Every dight."

"And that he is a somnambulist you solemnly swear?"

"I do."

"You have a practice," said Mr. Phillpots, who rose to cross-examine Tom, "which yields you a thousand a-year?"

"I have."

"Will you swear that?"

"Being dow od by oath, I codsider that everythidg I say I swear to."

"And you swear that your practice yields you a thousand a-year?"

"I do."

"You do. Well, you have known the defendant for some years, haven't you?"

"I have."

"And did it never occur to you that he was a somnambulist until the other night?"

"Dever."

"Isn't that somewhat strange?"

"Well, it certaidly bay appear to be so."

"I don't ask you what it may appear to be. I ask you whether it is, or not?"

"Well, perhaps it is stradge that I dever before discovered it."

"Perhaps."

"Yes, perhaps. He looks add talks whed he is asleep precisely the sabe as he does whed awake."

"Then, up to the time which you have named, you never *imagined* him to be a somnambulist?"

"Do, I certaidly dever did."

"Very well. That'll do."

Mr. Slashinger then called the Reverend Edward Rouse, and when the reverend gentleman had been sworn, he proceeded to examine him as follows—

"You are, I believe, a clergyman?"

"I thank God I am."

"You know the defendant?"

"I do. When first I knew him I fancied that I saw him on my garden-wall, helping himself to"——

"Exactly. We shall come to all that by-and-by. You reside at Cotherstone?"

"I do; and whenever he comes down there to visit his aunt, something extraordinary is sure to occur; sometimes a 'ghost' appears in the village—sometimes the horse is taken out of the stable at night—sometimes"——

"Exactly. And many other extraordinary things occur for which you have been utterly unable to account. Now, do these things ever occur when the defendant is absent?"

"Never. That's the point, as I said the other day"——

"Nothing of the kind ever happens at Cotherstone when he is in town?"

"Nothing. We are as quiet as possible when he is away; but the fact of his being a somnambulist affords a key—if I may use the expression—to all which we have heretofore regarded as inexplicable mysteries."

Mr. Phillpots then rose to cross-examine the reverend gentleman.

"You know the defendant?" said he; "you know him well? Now, will you take upon yourself, as a clergyman of the Church of England, to swear that he is a somnambulist?"

"Why, what else can he be?"

"No matter what else he can be; will you swear that he is a somnambulist?"

"Why, when we look at"——

"We don't want to look, sir, at anything but you. My question is plain. Will you swear that he is a somnambulist?"

"Well, perhaps I am not justified strictly in swearing it, but"——

"Of course not; there, that'll do; go down."

"But, my lord," said the reverend gentleman, addressing the bench.

"Mr. Rouse," interposed Mr. Slashinger, "you have given your evidence very clearly. You have not the slightest doubt of his being a somnambulist, but you do not feel justified in swearing that he is one, seeing that you have never exactly discovered him in a state of somnambulism."

"Exactly—that's what I mean—exactly."

"Very good."

The reverend gentleman then left the box, but he was not by any means satisfied.

This being the case for the defendant, Mr. Charles Phillpots rose to reply.

"In all my experience, gentlemen," said he, "I never met with anything more absurd than this defence. It *is* the most ridiculous on record. Somnambulism! Let us but once admit this plea, and we may shut up every court of justice in the empire. A man may seduce your wife, and plead somnambulism; he may ruin your daughters, and plead somnambulism; he may pick your pocket, and plead somnambulism; he may knock you down, and plead somnambulism; he may even murder you, and plead somnambulism; nay, there's nothing which he *could* do, that he might not do, and put in the plea of somnambulism. Can my learned friend produce any witness to prove that his client was in a state of somnambulism when he left Lady Julian's chamber? No! Somnambulism, indeed! The idea is preposterous. Suppose that either of you gentlemen, on going home tonight were to find a man in your chamber, what would you think of his plea of somnambulism? Suppose that, on your way home, a fellow were to stop you and rob you of your watch, what would you think of *his* plea of somnambulism?

Suppose that I were to say that I thought you sufficiently foolish to entertain such an absurdity, what would you say to *my* plea of somnambulism? Somnambulism, forsooth! Why, there isn't a crime under heaven that might not be committed with absolute impunity, if once we admitted, in justification, the monstrous plea of somnambulism. Repudiate it, gentlemen, with scorn! Treat it with the contempt it so richly deserves. I am amazed that in this enlightened age—in the middle of the nineteenth century—and in a country boasting, and justly too, its high and refined state of civilisation—such an absurd, such a perfectly ridiculous plea as that of somnambulism should have been entered. Why, gentlemen, it must be imagined that you are idiots—if, indeed, it be imagined that you are capable of entertaining such a vile plea as this! Repudiate it, gentlemen, indignantly. Look to the plaintiff, whose heart's dearest treasure has been stolen from him by the insidious arts of this *somnambulist*, and give exemplary damages, convinced, as you must be, that he has been abused, and that his relief must be to loathe her."

His lordship then briefly summed up, and the jury, without retiring, returned a verdict for the PLAINTIFF—Damages, two thousand pounds.

CHAPTER XXXVI.

SYLVESTER'S NEW PROTECTOR.

It is extremely questionable whether a trial ever yet gave unmixed satisfaction to either of the parties concerned. In civil cases, especially, there is sure to be, in the judgment of either the plaintiff or the defendant—and almost invariably in the view of both—something left undone which ought to have been done, or something done which ought not to have been done. Sometimes the attorneys are censured, sometimes the counsel, sometimes the witnesses, sometimes the jury, and sometimes the judge; but, most certainly, a case in which they *all* escaped censure, is not to be found on record.

It will not, therefore, be held to be extraordinary, that neither the plaintiff nor the defendant in this action was satisfied with the result. Sylvester could not have been expected to be; but, as it may have been expected that Sir Charles would be satisfied, it will be quite correct to state here that he was not. In his view, his own counsel made him appear to be most sordid. Money was *not* his object. His object was to establish legally the assumed guilt of Lady Julian with a view to a divorce. He was, therefore, not satisfied at all with his own counsel: nor was he satisfied with the counsel for the defendant: the remarks of both, in his judgment, tended to place him in a ridiculous and contemptible light; and he consequently, after the trial, felt wretched.

Sylvester, however, had not the wretched feelings of Sir Charles. He saw, of course, the importance of the verdict; he feared that it might, in a professional sense, effect his ruin; still, being perfectly conscious of his innocence, and having the sympathy of all around him, it cannot—although he was dreadfully annoyed—it cannot be said that he felt wretched. Aunt Eleanor was far more deeply affected; and as to the reverend gentleman, he absolutely swelled with indignation! He was indignant with the attorney, indignant with the counsel, indignant with the jury, indignant with the judge. They were all, in his view, lost to every sense of justice. And yet he felt strongly that, if he had been allowed to give his evidence in his own way, the jury would not have *dared* to return a verdict for the plaintiff.

"What!" he exclaimed. "Is it—can it be—possible that in a country like this—a Christian country—a country in which the principles of Christianity are professed and entertained more extensively, perhaps, than in any other country upon earth—is it possible that twelve men—twelve Christian men—can deliberately take a solemn oath to give a verdict according to the evidence, and then, having heard that evidence adduced, return such a verdict as this! Why, it really is fearful to contemplate! Those men must be guilty of perjury; and perjury is one of the most dreadful crimes that a man can possibly lay upon his soul! I should much like to talk to those men—to explain to them the peril in which they have placed themselves, not only in this world, but in the world to come! If I do not mistake, a perjurer, even here, is liable to be punished with very great severity. Surely, they cannot be cognisant of this!—leaving entirely out of the question the awful fact of their rendering themselves amenable to a much greater punishment hereafter! They really ought to be seen and talked to, and lectured and expostulated with! the crime of which they have been guilty is in its nature dreadful!"

"I do not think," observed Mr. Delolme, "that we are justified in accusing them of having committed perjury."

"But, my dear sir, just look at the nature of the evidence! Did not Mr. Thomas swear positively that poor Sylvester was a somnambulist? And did not I swear as positively and as solemnly, that I had not the slightest doubt of the fact? Ought not that to have been sufficient? And were they not bound to return a verdict accordingly?"

"Certainly, they were bound to return a verdict according to the evidence, but not according to your evidence alone; they were bound to look at the evidence opposed to yours, and to weigh it with yours, and thus to decide."

"Then it follows that they treated my evidence and that of Mr. Thomas with contempt!"

"Not necessarily. They might have felt that you both swore to the best of your belief, and yet conceived that your evidence was insufficient to establish the fact of Sylvester being a somnambulist."

"I only wish that I had been one of the jury."

"If you had been, a very different verdict would doubtless have been returned; but we must remember that those gentlemen were perfect strangers to Sylvester. They knew nothing either of him, or of the circumstances, previously to their coming into court; and while they manifestly conceived your evidence and that of Tom to be insufficient, they were strongly impressed by the counsel with the danger of allowing such a plea as that of somnambulism to obtain."

"I am aware of its being a plea which might easily be in all cases urged; and I hold the necessity for proving it to be absolute; all I contend for is, that in this particular case, it *was* sufficiently proved! And then, that man, the counsel—that barrister—that Mr. Charles Phillpots—what right had he to apply such abominable epithets to a person of whom he knew nothing. He ought to be talked to severely! He ought to be told that the character of Sylvester is the reverse of that which he represented it to be. I have really no patience with a man who will thus traduce the character of another without grounds. I only wish that I had been Sylvester's counsel; I should have told that person, without the slightest hesitation, that the course he was pursuing was most unwarrantable! I should have told him so publicly—before the whole court. And then the judge, we really might as well have had no judge at all! he did not conduct himself at all like a judge! he gave no judgment whatever upon the matter! I only wish that I had been the judge! But is there no appeal from this verdict? Would not a well-drawn-up protest have a very great effect?"

"We might move for a new trial, certainly."

"Then let us have a new trial; by all means let us have a new trial. That will be the very thing."

"I fear that unless we have much stronger evidence to produce, a new trial—if we obtained it—would be worse than useless."

"But we have stronger evidence. My evidence might be stronger—much stronger—I am sure of it."

The doctor shook his head, and having observed that that point had better be left to the lawyers, retired.

How often men know what they ought to have said when the occasion for saying it is passed. How forcibly—how eloquent in public, reflection proves that they *might* have been. The reverend gentleman had much afterwit. He saw, on reflection, invariably—for reflection invariably came when he had spoken—that he had omitted to say much that he ought to have said, and that which he did say, he might have said better. He was very seldom called upon to make a speech in public—his sermons required no subsequent reflection—but whenever he did make a public speech, the whole of the next day was devoted to its improvement. He would repeat it privately again and again, and polish every point he found in it, and if—as was sometimes the case—*no* point could be found, he would make one, and then polish that. He did on one occasion try a speech which he had written and learned by rote, but as he broke the thread in the middle and couldn't find the piece that came off, he abandoned that system—which is at best but a deceit—and stuck to the extemporaneous. Still, as he never made a speech which he did not subsequently very much improve, he never saw a speech of his in type which gave him the slightest satisfaction. There was always something said which ought to have been omitted, or something omitted which ought to have been said; and as his speeches, when in type, were never, in his judgment, what they ought to have been, the fact, that his evidence, when in type, gave him no sort of pleasure, cannot create much surprise. He was, indeed, exceedingly dissatisfied with it. He really felt ashamed of its appearance in print, and hence, being conscious—perfectly conscious—of his ability to give better evidence than that, he strongly urged the expediency of having a new trial.

By the advice of Mr. Scholefield, however, the idea of moving for a new trial was abandoned, and the reverend gentleman no sooner became cognisant of this than he went to work and conceived a scheme, of which the object was to settle the matter at once. He had a little money in the funds: he had, in fact, four thousand pounds in the three-and-a-half per cents; he therefore resolved on selling out to the extent required, and taking the two thousand pounds himself to Sir Charles Julian, unknown to any other living soul.

In this scheme "costs" were not contemplated: the idea of costs never occurred to him: he fondly imagined that Sir Charles would take the two thousand pounds and give him a receipt in full, and that there, as far as Sylvester was concerned, the whole matter would end.

He accordingly went to a broker whom he knew near the Exchange, and the sale of two thousand pounds stock was effected; but as he wished to expostulate with Sir Charles when he had paid him, and felt that such an expostulation as that which he contemplated required some previous thought, he returned to the residence of Dr. Delolme, with the view of rehearsing the most important points.

On his return, however, he found Mr. Scholefield there, engaged in advising both Sylvester and his aunt to return at once to Cotherstone—to leave the whole management of the matter to him, and to feel assured that all would yet be well—which advice was no sooner communicated to the reverend gentleman than he intimated to Mr. Scholefield that he wished to speak with him in private, and they accordingly withdrew to another room.

"My dear sir," said he, "I know and appreciate your worth; I know that you are a dear friend of Sylvester, I have the highest opinion of your judgment, and therefore deem it prudent to follow your advice: but will you—pardon me—will you, for my own satisfaction, explain to me your reasons for believing that all will yet be well?"

"Certainly," replied Mr. Scholefield, "with pleasure. I have just left Sir Charles, who is not at all satisfied now. The verdict of the jury has failed to convince him of his wife's infidelity. I find that, on the contrary, he is open to the conviction of her innocence; and I know him so well, that I feel that I shall eventually be able to satisfy him that Sylvester is a somnambulist, and thereby to prove to him, beyond all doubt, that Lady Julian herself is still virtuous—still pure."

"Why," exclaimed the reverend gentleman, "that is exactly my idea; my view of the matter precisely! I will now impart to you a most profound secret—a secret which I did not intend to reveal, but which I know will be faithfully kept by you. I have been this morning into the City to sell out two thousand pounds stock. I have the money here," he added, producing his pocket-book, "and what I intended to do with it, was this: I intended to take it at once to Sir Charles, and, having paid him, to adduce such a body of evidence as could not, I apprehend, fail to convince him that he had been perfectly uninjured. I intended to say to him solemnly, 'Sir Charles'"——

"I see," interposed Mr. Scholefield, "I see; and, believe me, I highly appreciate your motive: but I hope that there will be no necessity for this."

"But don't you think that if I were to call and offer him the money"——

"Why, my dear sir, if even he felt inclined to demand it, he would not receive it himself?"

"He would not?"

"Oh, dear me, no; he'd refer you at once to his attorney, whom the two thousand pounds wouldn't satisfy, believe me."

"What, would he want more?"

"He would present you with a document called a bill of costs, which might in some slight degree astonish you."

"Well, but do you not think that if I were to call upon Sir Charles and offer him the money, and tell him that his attorney's bill, whatever it might be, would be paid when presented, it would afford me an excellent opportunity for explaining to him the whole of my views on the subject, and laying before him that body of evidence which, I should say, must of necessity convince him that Sylvester is innocent?"

"It is possible that it might afford you this opportunity: I very much doubt that it would; but if it did, in my opinion, the pursuit of such a course would be imprudent. The very fact of your offering him the money would incense him, and the chances are that the interview would be instantly at an end. He is not a common man: he is not a man to be taken by storm. 'Let us,' said he to me, this morning, 'let us, if possible, get at the truth—let us conduct this investigation calmly—let us proceed quietly and privately—it is not, of course, proper that the existence of any doubt on my mind should be known.' I tell you this in confidence, and I am sure that you will perceive that the adoption of the course which you propose, although laudable

—highly laudable—in itself, would be, under existing circumstances, imprudent."

"Well, then, what would you advise me to do?"

"I should advise you, in the first place, to re-fund the money; in the second, to return to Cotherstone with Sylvester and his aunt; and, in the third, to write out a statement of facts, which, as collateral evidence, I may place before Sir Charles."

"Very good: *very* good. This shall be done. But mind! you must promise that—unknown to any living creature—you will send to me, and to me alone, in the event of this money being required."

"I pledge you my honour that I will do so."

"Very good. We can keep it to ourselves, you know; if it should be required, we can keep it to ourselves. If she were to know it, she would insist upon repaying me; and I would not have *her* income limited for the world. Mr. Scholefield,' he added, pressing his hand warmly, "God *bless* you for the interest you have taken in this matter. You are a good man: a *good* man: you'll have your reward. Now I'll go and urge them to start to-morrow morning. I'll in every particular follow your advice: I'll return to the City and re-fund this money, and send the statement up as soon as possible."

Mr. Scholefield then left him with many warm expressions of esteem, and he at once returned to Sylvester and his aunt, with the view of urging them to leave on the following morning.

"You have heard," said he, "what Mr. Scholefield has said, and Mr. Scholefield is a most sincere friend. We haven't a friend more sincere—we haven't a friend more valuable than Mr. Scholefield: you will know how valuable a friend he is anon. Now his advice is, that we return to the Grange immediately. What say you? When shall we start? I have to send up to him in the course of a few days a most important communication, and in order that I may do so, it will be necessary for me to start to-morrow. What do you think? Shall we all go together in the morning?"

"I have no objection," said Sylvester. "Have you, aunt?"

"No, my love; I have none whatever."

"Well, then," resumed the reverend gentleman, "suppose we make up our minds to go?"

"I am quite willing," replied Aunt Eleanor.

"Then we'll go," said the reverend gentleman—"we'll go. I have much to tell you on the road; and much more to tell you both when we get home. I feel assured that all will be right. At present I must say no more. I have to go into the City on a little matter of business, but I shall very soon be back. Good-bye. God bless you both. Keep up your spirits. We shall very soon get over this—very soon —I'm sure of it. I'll be back—let me see—in an hour and a half."

Their departure in the morning having thus been decided upon, Sylvester and his aunt, whom the important communication of Mr. Scholefield had greatly relieved, went to make a few farewell calls, and returned to the doctor's to dinner. Mr. Scholefield joined them, and so did Tom—who was in the highest possible spirits—and everything passed off cheerfully. Even Mrs. Delolme was seen to smile, for she now for the first time thought it *possible* that Sylvester was innocent !— which was charitable—very !—and hence couldn't fail to be appreciated.

Having spent an agreeable evening, Tom, as usual, claimed his "prisoder;" and when he had promised to deliver him and his chains into the hands of the reverend gentleman in the morning, he retired, and took Sylvester home with him, and gave him a most *recherché* supper.

"And dow, by boy," said he, having explained to Sylvester that he was going with Scholefield to have an interview with Sir Charles, "how do you bead to badage batters whed you get hobe?"

"Manage matters?"

"Ay. How do you bead to secure yourself at dight?"

"Oh! I understand. Why, I scarcely know how I'm to manage down there."

"You dod't thidk of sleepidg with the reveredd swell, I suppose?"

"Not exactly."

"Do; I should say that he's ad out-add-out sdorer!"

"I don't know about that, but I thought of being secured every night to the bed-post."

"You had better have sobe wud id the room. What do you thidk of wud of the baids?"

"I'd better have them both!" returned Sylvester, smiling. "But I don't see the necessity for having any one at all."

"If you have dot you are perfectly sure to get away. Sobdabbulists are the bost idgedious fellows alive. If left by thebselves they cad dever be safe. You, for exabple, bight ibagide that you were id prisod, add if you at the sabe [tibe felt boudd to break out of it, I dod't thidk that you have ady roob id your cottage sufficiently strong to prevedt you."

"Well, then, I'd better have Judkins in the room."

"Who's Judkids?"

"The gardener."

"Have Judkids thed. But as do cobbod scrubbidg ever got a gardeder clead, I would suggest that you had better have hib boiled every dight."

"Oh! I don't intend to let him sleep with me. We can make up a bed by the side of mine."

"Add secure yourself to hib?"

"Exactly."

"You haved't chaid edough! That, however, cad sood be badaged. We cad get ad additiodal ledgth id the bordidg."

This point having been settled, they reverted to the fact of Sir Charles being "open to conviction;" and having discussed it till half-past twelve, they made up their minds to retire. But Tom had a very poor night of it. Between one and four his rest was constantly broken, for the supper and the wine of which Sylvester had partaken caused him to have a variety of dreams, which prompted him unconsciously several times to pull Tom nearly out of bed. He was, however, after four, suffered to sleep, which, as far as it went, was a blessing; but when he rose about half-past six, he didn't look fresh at all. He was, notwithstanding, in very fair spirits, and rallied his prisoner gaily, and then went with him to get a longer chain, which they had no sooner bought than they entered a cab, and proceeded at once to the doctor's.

On their arrival, they found the doctor and Mrs. Delolme, Aunt Eleanor, and the reverend gentleman at breakfast, and when Tom had formally delivered up his prisoner, they joined them, and made a very fair meal—considering!

At the suggestion of the reverend gentleman—who always appeared anxious to be at the office at least twenty minutes before the coach started—the ladies soon after this retired, and when they returned dressed—for Mrs. Delolme had most graciously insisted upon seeing Aunt Eleanor safely to the coach—the reverend gentleman and Tom entered the doctor's carriage with the ladies, while Sylvester mounted the box.

On their arrival at Charing Cross, it was found that they were just half an hour too soon, which the reverend gentleman pointedly submitted was better than being half an hour too late. The propriety and truth of this original observation were indisputable of course, and Tom had him out of the carriage in consequence, and walked with him and Sylvester up and down the Strand until the horses were in, when he and Aunt Eleanor entered the coach, and Sylvester, who did not like riding inside, took his favourite seat on the box.

"Well, adieu!" said Tom, taking the hand of Aunt Eleanor, and pressing it with somewhat unusual warmth. "Good bye!—*good* bye! I shall rud dowd to Cotherstode wud of these days, and whed I do cobe, if you *should* be sidgle, the codsequedces bust be a batch."

Aunt Eleanor smiled as she bade him adieu, and so did her reverend friend, who moreover declared that he should be happy to see him, and wished him to name the time; but before he could answer, the coachman called "All right!—chit, chît!" and they were off.

Now it is in reality a singular thing—Aunt Eleanor couldn't pretend to account for it—but the journey always *did* appear to her to be short when her reverend friend travelled with her. It is, moreover, strange—remarkably strange—that she never felt fatigued when he was with her. She really did think that she could travel a thousand miles with him, without feeling anything like so tired as she always had felt after travelling fifty miles without him. Now this is, of course, an extraordinary fact—a fact which is *worthy* of being placed upon record. Whenever she had travelled by herself, or with strangers, or even in company with any other friend, she had always felt tired after the first twenty miles; but with him!—there, she positively thought that she could travel with him every day for a week, without feeling in the slightest degree fatigued. As to the journey from London to Cotherstone, why, it appeared to be nothing. They started from Charing Cross, chatted all the way, arrived within a mile and a half of the Grange, and there they were. It was so in this instance. They had a most agreeable journey; and Sylvester rendered it still more agreeable by coming down to speak to them whenever they changed horses. It was, indeed, essentially a journey of pleasure. Aunt Eleanor never enjoyed herself more: they appeared to have been but a very short time on the road, when the reverend gentleman exclaimed, "Here we are!"

The coach stopped; and instantly Jones with the phaeton, and Judkins with the pony, stood before them; and as they had decided upon sending the luggage on, in less than ten minutes they were home.

Sylvester's first object now was to communicate to Judkins all that had reference to his bedroom plans, and, therefore, having partaken freely of the elegant little dinner prepared for them, he went out, and found him in the tool-house.

"Judkins," said he, "do you know what a somnambulist is?"

"A somnambulist, sir! I *think* it's a species of convolvulus; but there is such a mob of names now, that I don't exactly know."

"Then I'll tell you. A somnambulist, Judkins, is a sleep-walker—a person"——

"Oh, ay, yes, just so, exactly! *I* thought you meant something in *my* way! I see! A somnambulist! Oh yes, *I've* heered on 'em; *I* know what they are."

"Well, then," said Sylvester, "*I* am a somnambulist."

"Lor', you don't say so! *You* one!"

"Unhappily, I am."

"Lor, I shouldn't have thought it. As true as I'm alive, sir, I couldn't have believed it. Well, but—Lor' bless me, you don't mean to say that you get up o' nights and walk about, and all that?"

"Yes, Judkins, I have long been in the habit of doing *all* that."

"Why, then—why, look here—you can't be safe to be trusted. You ought to have somebody always to sit up with you."

"I have rendered that unnecessary. I'll explain to you how. Since I made the discovery I have slept with a gentleman, to whom I have been secured—that is to say, fastened by means of a small chain, reaching from his wrist to mine, so that "——

"Exactly!" interposed Judkins: "I see, sir! Capital; you couldn't get away from him no how, then?"

"No, that was impossible; and as this entirely supersedes the necessity for any one sitting up with me. I want you to sleep in my room for the present, in order that I may be still secure."

"Just so; I see, sir; a capital plan."

"You have, I presume, no objection?"

"Objection, sir! No, not the leasest in life. I *can* have no objection."

"Well, then, you can bring your bed and bedstead, and place it by the side of mine, and "——

"I'll manage that, sir."

"There's plenty of room, I believe?"

"Oceans! But how long, sir, have you been going on so?"

"I have reason to believe that I have been a somnambulist for years."

"Indeed!"

"You remember that, five years ago, a variety of pranks were played here?"

"To be sure I do."

"Those pranks, I have not the slightest doubt, were played by me. The horse was taken out of the stable, you know, frequently, and galloped round the country during the night, and brought home again in a state of exhaustion."

"Well, but you don't mean to say you did that?"

"I have no more doubt of it than I have of my own existence."

"Well, sir: but—send I may live—could you go to the stable, and mount the horse, and gallop like that, all the while you were asleep?"

"I have done very many more extraordinary things than that."

"I wonder you didn't pitch off and break your neck. I couldn't have believed it, if you hadn't told me; and I can't understand it, I can't brain it now."

"And then the ghost: why, I was the ghost!"

"You was! Oh, what a kick-up there's been about that ghost."

"What, since I left?"

"The other day, sir. You know Drant, sir—Obadiah Drant—the man you were speaking to me about, you know, sir? Well, as he always knows everything nobody else knows, he set it about that he knew who the ghost was. *He* knew: *he* knew the man: and, on being pressed to tell who it was, he said that he knew that Bob Potts was the ghost. Well, *this* very soon got to Bob Pott's ears, and as soon as it did, Bob Potts hunted him up, and said to him quietly, 'A gentleman wants just to see you on the common.' 'Who is it?' said Drant. 'Oh, you'll see,' said Bob; 'he wants to give you something; you'd better bring Mr. Pokey with you.' Well, innocent enough, he went, and took Pokey with him; and when he got there, in course he asked where the gentleman was? '*I* am the gentleman,' said Bob, 'as wants to see you: I am the gentleman as wants to give you something. I'm the ghost, ain't I? You know I'm the ghost? Now, you must give me a sound out-and-out throshing, or I shall give you one: so pull off your coat.' 'Just look you here,' said Drant, 'if you lay a finger upon me, I'll take the law on you.' 'Never mind the law,' said Bob: 'one on us must have a throshing, so strip.' 'I shan't bemean myself,' said Drant. 'Then take that,' said Bob, 'to begin with.' And he hit him a wonder just over the eyes. Well, this made Drant naturally wild, and as he then saw that he *must* fight, he pulled off his coat, and went at it. But Lor'! he couldn't stand against Bob a minute and a half. In less time than that, Bob kept his promise, and gave him such a throshing as he *never* had before. Drant then went off to a lawyer, and the lawyer recommended him as a friend not by no means to take out a warrant; no, but to bring what he calls a action: so Bob has been served with a little slip of paper, and it's going to be settled at the 'sizes. But nobody pities Obadiah; he's always a gabbling: he's always making mischief: he's always setting people together by the ears. But it is about the rummest start in life, though, that you should be the ghost after all! But didn't you never remember nothing about it in the morning?"

"Nothing; it all was to me a perfect blank."

"Well, that is stunning, sir. I call it stunning. However, you'll be safe enough here. *I ll* not let you go out, sir, I'll warrant. Another thing is, sir, you may depend upon me: for in course you wish me to keep it a secret?"

"I wish you to answer no impertinent questions; but as for secrecy, that is now impossible, seeing that the fact has been published in all the papers."

"Indeed, sir! Has it though, really?"

"I have lately been concerned in a trial, and as the report of it will be, of course, interesting to *you*, I'll lend you the paper to read."

"I'm obleedged to you, sir. I should like to read it above all things in the world."

"You need not go and talk about it all over the village, although the affair is quite sure to be known. There is, however, one thing which need not be known, and that is the plan which we are about to adopt here. Cook and Mary will know, of course, that you slept in my room, but even they need know nothing beyond that fact."

"They shall not know from me, sir; depend upon that. I'll not open my lips to a single soul."

"Very well. Then you had better go now and remove your bed. Do you want any assistance?"

"Not the leasest in life, sir. *I* shall be able to manage it alone. But Lor'!—the ideor! Who *could* have thought it! But the paper, sir, please; I hope you'll not forget the paper?"

"You shall have it the moment you have finished your job."

"Thank you, sir; I'll bring it here to read. Not a soul shall set eyes on it, I'll take care of that. But of all the stunning things as I ever heered tell on, that of a man riding full gallop over the country fit to break his blessed neck, fast asleep, bangs Moses! It's a mercy you wasn't killed dead upon the spot. However, there'll be no more of that while you're here; so I'll go at once and get the bed ready."

He did so; and being most anxious to look at the paper,

he resolved on being the very shortest possible time about it. He hadn't worked so hard for a considerable period; nor had he for many months perspired so freely as he did while taking down his bedstead.

"Judkins!" exclaimed cook, who heard him at work; "what on earth are you after? Are you going to knock the house down?"

"Good luck to you," returned Judkins, "bring us a drop of beer."

"But what *are* you about?"

"Bring the beer up, old girl, and I'll tell you."

Prompted by a natural feeling of curiosity, cook drew him some beer, and went up with it at once.

"Why, what in the name of goodness," she cried, "are you doing?"

"Taking down my bedstead, that's all."

"I'm sure there was no call for that; there's no bugs!"

"Bugs! No, there's no bugs, I believe."

"Then, what on earth do you want to take it down for?"

"Because Mr. Sylvester wished me to do so."

"What *for?*"

"Because he wants me to sleep in his room."

"In his room! Well, that *is* a fancy."

"Yes," replied Judkins, "it certainly is a fancy."

"A fancy! I never heard of such a thing in the whole course of my life. In his room! Why, what in the name of goodness does he want you to sleep in his room for?"

"You'll know by-and-by."

"Is he afraid to sleep in a room by himself?"

"Yes."

"Then he's been up to no good. Depend upon it, he's been up to no *good.*"

"*Don't* be quite so fast."

"Fast! Why, if it isn't that, what does he want you to sleep in his room for?"

"Don't heat yourself, and I'll tell you. He is what they call a somnambulist."

"I thought so!" exclaimed cook. "As true as I stand here, I thought so."

"You did. Do you know what a somnambulist is?"

"Do I know what it is! Why, you *don't* suppose I'm so ignorant as all that comes to, do you?"

"Well, come now, what *is* a somnambulist?"

"Why, a man that marries other men's wives, to be sure."

"Pooh! you mean a bigamist; that's what you mean."

"Well, it's all the same, isn't it."

"No, quite different. A somnambulist is a man that walks in his sleep."

"Why, to be sure it is. How stupid! I know now. But—what—why—you don't mean to say that Mr. Sylvester does it?"

"He has done it for years, and does it now: and that's the reason why I'm to sleep in his room."

"But my goodness *me* though!—why"——

"I haven't time to say nothing more about it now. Just lend us a hand here. I want this job done; I have to go to him directly it is."

Cook did lend a hand, albeit she was at the time filled with wonder; she rendered him every possible assistance, and indulged in the most startling exclamations of surprise; while Judkins, who took no apparent notice of these exclamations, was silently working away like a slave, in order to get at the paper.

In less than an hour the job was complete: and when Judkins had made himself tidy, he went out and flitted before the parlour window, that Sylvester might know that it was done. And this certainly was an admirable scheme as far as it went, but he had to flit about there for some time, in consequence of Sylvester having his back towards the window. This, however, Judkins no sooner perceived, than he got a hammer and a couple of nails, and by virtue of pretending to nail up a branch, effected the object proposed.

"Well, Judkins," said Sylvester, on going to the door, "have you finished your job?"

"Yes, sir."

"You found plenty of room, I suppose?"

"Oh, lots, sir. And the room looks better with two beds than one. It looks fuller."

"No doubt. I'll go up and have a look at it presently."

"Beg pardon, sir," observed Judkins; "but I think, sir, you said you'd be kind enough to lend me a paper."

"Oh yes; I'll get it for you."

"Thank you, sir; thank you."

"Now," said Sylvester, on bringing the paper out, "although you will find that the verdict is against me, you must not suppose that I am guilty of the offence."

"Not for the world, sir; I shouldn't even think of such a thing."

"Well, this is the case," said Sylvester, pointing it out to him.

"Thank you, sir; thank you. I shall be in the tool-house if I should be wanted."

"Very well."

Judkins then left him with his eyes eagerly fixed upon the paper; but he hadn't got half a dozen yards when he stopped, and turning round, said—"Beg pardon, sir; I'm not much of a scholar; will you be so kind as to tell me what *crim. con.* means?"

"Criminal conversation."

"And this here other word here, sir, *versus?*"

"Against."

"Thank you, sir; I like to understand all I read, sir; and now I shall be able to get along."

He then went to the tool-house and shut himself in, and then gave a look at the length of the report. It was a long one; certainly for him, a very long one; for Judkins was anything but a quick reader. He, notwithstanding this fact, settled himself down, and very soon became so deeply interested in the case, that he never gave the length another thought.

Having got through the speech of Mr. Phillpots, it became so dark that he could see to read no more. He therefore rushed round to the kitchen for a lantern with all the velocity at his command.

"Where on earth have you been?" exclaimed cook, as he entered.

"Busy, busy," said Judkins, as he lighted his candle.

"Are you going out again?"

"Yes, yes; don't bother me now."

"Well, but I want to speak to you."

"Can't stop—can't stop a second," he replied, and rushed from the kitchen as hastily as he had entered.

On his return to the tool-house, he adjusted his lantern, and then, with an expression of the most earnest anxiety, resumed.

He liked Thompson's evidence. He thought it very good —very good—very good indeed; but when he came to the speech of Mr. Slashinger it threw him into an absolute state of ecstacy.

"By Job!" he exclaimed, striking his hand upon the nail-box, "that's stunning—stunning! Now, then, let 'em get over *that* if they can."

He then proceeded; and as he read Tom's evidence—having reference to the parapet—his countenance assumed an expression of horror, and his breathing became thick and difficult. At length he exclaimed, with a start—"He's saved!" and wiped the perspiration off his brow with his sleeve, and then stared at the candle, and sat and thought of the dreadful position described.

"He's a fine fellow, though," he eventually added; "a very fine fellow, that Mr. Delolme. He's a good 'un, every inch of him. Well, now—let's see what come's next. Very good," he continued at intervals. "He couldn't get away no how so. A thousand a *year*—what an enormity of money. But he deserves every penny of it, *he* does; I wish he had ten times as much. Very good. Now, who's next? The Reverend Edward Rouse. What, our parson! Was *he* in it? Oh, don't I wish I'd been there? His garden wall; that was five years ago when he lost the peaches. Jones then was right after all. The ghost; yes, that's quite right. No more it never is seen except when he's here. What do you mean by that, stupid? Ain't it as clear as the nose on your face?"

This last observation referred to the cross-examination of the reverend gentleman by Mr. Phillpots, for whom Judkins had a most thorough contempt, and whom he held to be the most incredulous fool alive.

"You won't believe it now, I suppose?" he continued. "Did mortal flesh ever set eyes on such a donkey? I thought not. I *knew* you wouldn't believe it. I should like to have the kicking of you, you old *ass!*"

Judkins then read the reply of Mr. Phillpots; and as he

did so, his contempt for the man turned to indignation. He struck and kicked at appropriate intervals, with just as much energy as he felt that he *could* have done if Phillpots had been there before him; and thus he proceeded with a groaning accompaniment until he had reached the last line of the report, when he loudly exclaimed—"Two thousand pounds!" and let the paper fall.

The verdict seemed to have deprived him, for a time, of all his moral and physical faculties. There he sat perfectly bewildered, and there he continued to sit till the candle had burned to the socket. This roused him from his reverie; he rose from his seat and folded the paper, and returned to the kitchen, but with his intellects still confused.

"Why, what in the world have you been after?" cried cook, as he entered the kitchen with thought on his brow.

"Don't talk," replied Judkins; "don't talk—my head's full."

"But *here's* a time you've been. I thought you never *was* coming. What *have* you been about?"

"My head's full, I tell you. Don't bother—I'm stunned."

"Well, what on earth is the matter? I suppose there's no occasion to keep it *all* to yourself."

"If I could, I'd give a pound out of my own blessed pocket."

"Well, come, take some beer," said cook, passing the mug in the fond expectation of melting him thus. "You don't look at all the thing. What will you have for supper?"

"Two thousand pounds," muttered Judkins indignantly.

"What say?"

"Nothing; I was talking to myself."

"But I want you to talk to me. Wouldn't you like now something nice for supper?"

"No; nothing—nothing: I don't want nothing."

"Oh, but you shall have something," said cook, who went to the pantry, and soon returned with the remains of a couple of chickens and some ham. "Judkins," she added, having duly placed these delicacies before him, "I know you have something on your mind—what is it? You don't now ought to keep anything from me;

for, although we're not married, we very soon shall be, and your cares now is my cares, Judkins, just as much as they will be then."

"Old girl," replied Judkins, whom this appeal softened, and who had engaged to marry cook as soon as a very old man, who kept a public-house in a neighbouring village, died, "don't make yourself by no means oneasy about me. My cares is not on my own account, but on account of one who's been very ill used."

"What, Mr. Sylvester?"

"Yes."

"Has he been ill used?"

"Dreadful."

"The wretches. Who are they?"

"I know who they are, and so does he."

"Highway robbers, I suppose."

"A million times worse than highway robbers."

"Well, but did they hurt him much?"

"Not in person, but in pocket. They robbed him of two thousand pounds."

"Two thousand! You astonish me. Two thousand pounds! How came he to be so foolish as to carry so much money as that about with him?"

"Carry it about with him!"

"I always have said, and I always will say, that it's foolish of any man to do it. I do hope to goodness that you'll never do so."

"You don't understand. He wasn't robbed on the road, but in a court of law."

"Oh! in a court of law. That's a different thing altogether. But how was it? Tell me; do tell me."

"I can't do so to-night, old girl; but if you'll now let me have my thoughts to myself, I'll promise to tell you all about it in the morning."

"Well, I'm not at all curious—but I should dearly like to know. I only hope that while walking in his sleep, the poor young gentleman won't do none of us no mischief."

"Mischief! Leave that to me. I'll take care of that. What am I to sleep in his room for?"

"Well, I only hope he won't. But come, come—eat some supper. I saved it for you."

Judkins turned round, and although deep in thought, tried, and did eat a little, and just as he had finished, Mary came into the kitchen and said—

"Missus is in bed and the parson's gone, and Mr. Sylvester wants you, Judkins, in the parlour."

Judkins rose on the instant, and attended the summons; and, on entering the parlour, was greeted with a smile.

"Well, Judkins," said Sylvester; "ready for bed?"

"When you please, sir; I'm quite at your service."

"Well, then, mix yourself some brandy-and-water, and then we'll be off."

"Thank you, sir; perhaps you'll be so kind as to mix a little for me."

"Very well. Take a seat, Judkins."

Judkins bowed, and closed the door, and then seated himself upon the edge of the chair near it.

"Draw up to the table, man; don't sit out there."

Judkins did so; but didn't feel himself at all at home.

"Now, then," said Sylvester; "just try that."

"Thank you, sir. Your health, sir."

"Is it as you like it?"

"Quite, sir; capital; particular good, sir; very."

"Health to you, Judkins. I hope we shall both have a good night's rest."

"I hope so, too," returned Judkins, who then began to feel a little better. "Here's the paper, sir," he added; drawing it carefully from his breast. "I'm much obleeged to you, sir, very."

"Have you read it?"

"Right through, sir. It's stunning! I know it has stunned me wholly. Why, that man, sir—that Mr.—What's his name—Phillpots—must be a regelar nateral born fool. He ought to have seen how it was with half an eye!"

"He doubtless did see how it was."

"Then he ought to be ashamed of himself for sticking out so."

"These men are *paid*, you know, to take a certain side; and they feel themselves bound—be it right or wrong, just or unjust—to do the best they can for those who employ them."

"Well, it mayn't become me, sir, to speak in this way

before you, but I'd rather get my twenty pound a year in an honest way, than I'd get twenty thousands in a way like that there."

"So would I; so would I; and should feel myself a happier, because a more honourable man. It matters not to them whom they injure; it matters not to them what misery they may cause. If I were a wealthy villain, and required their assistance in oppressing the fatherless and the widow, or involving any honest man in ruin, hundreds of them would jump at the job."

"Then they ain't fit to live on a civilised scale, sir: and that's my sentiments. Poor as I am, sir, I'll never sell myself in that there way. I knowed before that some on 'em wasn't over-nice. There was that Jerry Smith which was sent out of the country last 'sizes; they employed one of these here counsel for him, and he knew that he was guilty—Jerry told him so himself before the trial—and yet how he tried to knock it into the heads of the jury that he was innocent! how he tried to get him off, to be sure!"

"Ay! To prey upon society again."

"But, lor', sir! What an escape you had on the top of the house there; I shuddered when I read it."

"Yes, it was a dangerous position for a man to be in."

"Dangerous, sir! It made my very blood run cold. But it shan't occur again, sir—leastways, not while you're here. I'll take care of that, sir, I'll *warrant!*"

"Well, then, finish your glass, and I'll show you how it is to be prevented."

Judkins did as he was desired, and wasn't long about it; and then followed Sylvester up to his chamber, and closed the door, and waited for further instructions, while Sylvester opened and searched a trunk.

"Now then," said Sylvester, having produced the chain with the handcuffs attached, "we'll turn in." And, as Judkins began to strip immediately, it was not long before he was safely in bed. Sylvester's movements were not quite so rapid; but he didn't linger long: he got into bed very soon after Judkins, and then at once drew his attention to the chain.

"Now," said he, "this chain, you perceive, is quite long enough to reach from me to you; and that round affair at the end is for your wrist, while this is for mine."

"Very good, sir," said Judkins; "but I can't get it on."

"No; it must be opened first. And that is what I wish to explain. These things will close by mere pressure; but they cannot be opened without a key. Yours is somewhat larger than mine; but the same key will open them both—thus. Now try it. There; it fits you, does it not?"

"Exact, sir."

"It is not too tight for you?"

"Oh! Not a bit."

"Very well. Now take this key and hide it somewhere. Don't let me know where it is."

"I'll take care of that, sir."

"And if I *should* attempt to get out of bed, all you will have to do is to wake me gently. And now, good night."

"I wish you good night, sir."

"Good night," repeated Sylvester; who put out the light, laid his head upon the pillow, and was very soon asleep.

Not so, however, Judkins. He began to reflect deeply. He had previously thought but little of the fact of sleeping in the same chamber, but then, in silence and in gloom, his apprehensions became prolific. Cook's expression of the hope that he might do them no mischief recurred to him, and he hoped so too; but, at the same time conceived it to be possible, quite possible, that he might. "Who knows?" thought he. "He may get up and cut my throat! And if he should, where's the remedy? I wonder whether he's obstropolus. I dare say he is. He can't, in course, know what he's about. If he does, I don't think he'd hurt a hair of my head; but if he don't, why there's no knowing what he may do. And yet Mr. Delolme slept with him—that appeared on the trial—and he never hurt *him*. But then he might have done! And yet, is it likely a gentleman like him would do me any mischief; and, as to cutting my throat, how is he to get the razor? He can't do it without pulling me out of bed, and I'm just about as strong as *him*, I fancy. But, then, how do I know he hasn't a knife in his pocket? He can reach that without waking me, and may do so, who knows? And yet I don't think he'd attempt to hurt me. But then, if he doesn't know what he's about, he doesn't. That's the point. At all events, I'll keep awake this blessed night if I live, to see what sort of games he is likely to be up to."

And he did keep awake. He kept awake an hour; and then most unconsciously dropped off to sleep. He had, however, been asleep scarcely ten minutes, when Sylvester awoke him; and having done so, said calmly—

"Judkins! Give me the key."

"The key, sir! Yes, sir," said Judkins, who had not even the most remote idea of his being asleep at the time. "Here it is, sir."

"That will do," observed Sylvester; who, on the instant freed himself, and then very quietly proceeded to dress. He was not, however, long about this: he very soon slipped on his things; and when he had done so, he left the room, and—conceiving that he was then going out for a morning walk—took his hat, and deliberately quitted the house.

Judkins heard him open the front door, and it certainly did strike him at the moment as being possible that Sylvester was in a state of somnambulism then. And yet he asked for the key in a calm, collected manner, and dressed himself, and went out as if he had been awake. In Judkins's judgment, he *must* have been. He tried to repudiate the *notion* of his being asleep. But then what could he want to open the front door for? That was the question; and this question no sooner suggested itself to Judkins than he slipped out of bed, and commenced dressing. The chain, however, somewhat retarded his progress, for the key of the handcuff was not to be found; but he soon got over that; he slipped on his small clothes, his jacket, and shoes, and went down, of course with the chain.

The front door was open—that was what he expected; but which way had Sylvester gone? He thought he'd just look round the premises first, and he did so, but Sylvester could not be found. He then became in reality alarmed, and, having just latched the door, that he might let himself in again, went at once into the road. But which way should he go? It was clearly of no use his running to the right, if Sylvester had gone to the left. He heard footsteps in the distance, and on the instant started off in that direction, but found that they were those of a labouring man.

"*Have* you met a gentleman?" cried Judkins, in haste.

"Whoy—ees," replied the man, with provoking deliberation; "ah seed un aboot hafe a moile off."

"Which way was he going?"

"Whoy, ah didn't ax, boot a seemed to be goin' to Holler Bell."

Away started Judkins on the Holworth road, as the man shouted out "He's goin' moortal faist;" but, albeit he ran with all possible speed, Sylvester could not be seen. Still Judkins kept on, panting painfully; and although he had occasionally a "stitch" in his side, he would not give up until he reached the Bell at Holworth, a mile and a half from the Grange. Here he stopped; and as the house was still open, he went in at once, and inquired of the landlord if a gentleman had been there.

"I don't know," replied the landlord. "You'll find two or three in the parlour; you'd better look in."

Judkins looked in, but Sylvester was *not* there; still, feeling completely exhausted, he called for a small glass of brandy-and-water, and sank upon a chair.

Every eye was upon him, of course, and more especially the eye of one man, who, as soon as the brandy-and-water had been brought, rose and said, "Ah, old fellow, how are you?"

"Pretty well," replied Judkins; "only I've been running. But really you have the advantage of *me*."

"Not at all," cried the stranger. "Come, give us your hand; you'll shake hands with me, won't you?"

"Oh, I've no objection," said Judkins, who gave him his hand—the only hand he had disengaged, the other having been thrust into his pocket with the chain.

"What!" exclaimed the stranger; "the *left* hand! Is that the way you treat an old friend?"

"You're no old friend of mine," said Judkins, who began to feel very much embarrassed.

"Oh yes, I am," returned the stranger. "Come, give us your right hand, man."

"I shan't do nothing of the sort. I don't know you."

"You don't. I'll tell you who I am, if you'll give me your hand."

"I don't want to know who you are."

"Come, give us your hand, man."

"What do you mean? Can't I come into the house without being interrupted?"

"Not into this house while I am here. I'm the constable of Holler, and always on the look out for fellows like you."

"I don't care if you are the constable of fifty Hollers. I've nothing to be either ashamed or afeard on."

"I daresay not; but it's no use, you know. I saw it—I *know* I saw it. *Will* you let me see your right hand?"

"No."

"But I *will* see it."

"Will you?" said Judkins, whose blood began to boil.

"Will I! Yes. Now, then!" he added, seizing the right arm of Judkins, who on the instant knocked him down, and would have escaped, but that the landlord, who was coming into the room at the time, stopped him.

"What's the meaning of all this?" inquired the landlord.

"He's my prisoner!" cried the constable, rising. "I'll run all risks; he's my prisoner."

"What for?" demanded the landlord.

"Why, look at his right hand! Just look at it!"

"What do you mean? You are always kicking up some row; what do you mean?"

"Only look at that man's right hand—that's all."

"Let me look at it?" said the landlord, addressing Judkins calmly. "You shall not be ill-treated here."

Judkins drew his hand from his pocket, and with it a portion of the chain, of course.

"There it is!" cried the constable, in triumph. "There you are! I knew I saw it! And here's the other ruffle. Why, you're an escaped convict—that's what you are."

"I'm nothing of the *sort!*" exclaimed Judkins indignantly.

"It's no use, you know. Not a bit of it. Don't put yourself in a passion. *Come* along."

"But where—where?" exclaimed Judkins, in a dreadful state of excitement.

"Oh, I'll find a lodging for you. *Now* then. Here, Johnson! here, Smith!—come and assist me, will you?"

Both Johnson and Smith at once went to his assistance; and in spite of the expostulations of Judkins—in spite of his strong declarations of innocence — in spite of his struggles, entreaties, and threats, they hurried him off to the cage.

CHAPTER XXXVII.

THE MYSTERY SOLVED.

When the ghost of Banquo appeared at the banquet, it terribly startled Macbeth; but neither Macbeth nor any other individual was ever more startled than Mary was when, on entering the parlour alone the next morning, she saw a man lying asleep on the couch.

Of course she didn't stop in the room long. On the contrary, she very soon rushed out of it; and although she neither screamed, nor fell, nor fainted, on reaching the kitchen she felt "fit to drop."

"Oh, cook!" she sighed, as she sank on a chair; "there's a man!—there's a man!"

"There's a *man!*—where's a man?" demanded cook.

"In the parlour."

"A man in the parlour! Why, what's he after there?"

"He's asleep—fast asleep. I know he's asleep; but the moment I saw him my heart was in my mouth."

"But what sort of a man does he look like?"

"I *don't* know, I couldn't stop to look; I only know he's a man."

"And asleep, you say? You're quite sure he's asleep?"

"Oh, quite."

"Then, I'll go and have a look at him. Come, come along."

"Oh, I dursn't."

"Fiddlesticks! You're not afraid of a man when he's

fast asleep, are you? Come along, *do!*—and don't be silly."

Mary reluctantly rose from her chair and followed cook softly and slowly; and when cook had reached the parlour door, she peeped, and beheld—the man!

"Why, it's only Mr. Sylvester, girl!" she exclaimed. "How stupid you are, to be sure."

"Mr. Sylvester!" said Mary, whose courage returned; and she looked in, and then found that he *was* the man.

"I wonder where Judkins is?" said cook, who had an idea that something was wrong. "He certainly ought to have been down by this time. Shall we go up and knock at the door?"

"If you like," replied Mary, who didn't at all understand cook's feelings, and therefore couldn't appreciate them; still she went up with her, and found the door open, and further, that Judkins was not in the room.

"Why, where on earth is he?" cried cook, who began to feel very much alarmed. "He's not in the garden!" she added, looking out. "No. Why, where in the world can he be?"

"In the tool-house, perhaps," suggested Mary, and cook at once ran down and went to the tool-house; but no, he was not there. She called to him—no! Why, what could be the meaning of all this! Had Sylvester murdered and buried him? She really thought this extremely possible, and shuddered, and ran back to Mary, and told her to go to her mistress immediately, and let her know that Sylvester was in the parlour, while Judkins could nowhere be found.

Mary accordingly went and told her mistress, who feeling quite certain that all was not right, slipped on her morning-gown hastily, and with great trepidation descended.

Sylvester was still on the couch, and she approached him, and sat by his side, and found that he was in a deep sleep.

"Sylvester, my love!" she cried. "Sylvester!—*Sylvester!* —my *dear!*"

Sylvester opened his eyes, and started. "Why," he exclaimed, looking round, "how is this? In the parlour!"

"How long," said Aunt Eleanor affectionately—"how long have you been sleeping here?"

"Oh! aunt, I'm sorry—very sorry for this. It's galling in the extreme." He added, angrily, "Judkins ought to have known better. It's monstrous, that a man like that is not to be trusted."

"Do not vex yourself, my love," said Aunt Eleanor; "pray do not vex yourself. Let us thank God that you are safe. Where is Judkins?"

"I know not, aunt: nor do I know how I came here. I know only this, that we went up to bed about ten; that I was well secured to him, and that here I am now."

"But is it not strange? He is nowhere to be found."

"It'll be no great loss if he never *be* found. I might have gone and broken my neck; what did *he* care? I thought him a different man."

"Nay, my dear, do not thus censure him yet. First ascertain the *cause* of his letting you free. I have always found him faithful and obedient."

"Why, I thought that I might have trusted my *life* in his hands; and yet, although I enjoined him not to suffer me to leave the room, here I am, while *he* is gone no one knows where, and no one cares."

"I hope, sir," observed cook, with tears in her eyes, "that you haven't been doing nothing with him: I *hope*, sir, you haven't been doing him no mischief!"

"Mischief!" cried Sylvester. "What do you mean?"

"No, cook: certainly not," said Aunt Eleanor. "He will, I have no doubt, return by-and-by, and when he *does* return, I shall expect him to give a good account of his conduct. Now go and get the breakfast ready. Mary, come with me. Do not be angry, my dear," she added, addressing Sylvester, and kissing him with the deepest affection. Let us thank Heaven that nothing dreadful has occurred."

She then went up to dress, and so did Sylvester, who found the key on the bed, but, of course, not the chain: and while he was indignantly shaving himself, cook was utterly lost in conjecture. What a number of dreadful deaths she conceived that Judkins *might* have died while she was getting the breakfast ready! What stabbing, drowning, poisoning, strangulation, and burying alive, rose before her vivid imagination then! She was wild!—quite wild! She put the eggs upon the gridiron instead of the ham, and the ham in the saucepan instead of the eggs, and felt strongly that the landlady of the "Cock and Constitution"—the house which Judkins had been after—she never should be. This thought alone was maddening; but when in addition to this she reflected upon the assumed dreadful fact, of a man like Judkins being thus cut off in his very prime, without having left anything *like* a will: it was *too* much: she couldn't endure it; and as she found she couldn't, she let the ham and eggs go on just as they pleased, sank into a chair, and wept.

And thus she remained until Mary came down, when she most unreservedly opened her heart. And Mary sympathised with her, and boiled her eggs for her, and cooked two slices of ham, and begged of her earnestly not to "take on" so, and then took the breakfast in.

"Has Judkins returned yet?" inquired Aunt Eleanor.

"No, ma'am; he's not come back yet."

"Dear me, it's very strange; I cannot at all account for it. Have you no *idea* where he is?"

"Not the leastest in life, ma'am, I'm sure."

"Well! we must of course have patience; but at present his conduct appears to be extraordinary. That will do, Mary; I'll ring when I want you."

Mary withdrew, and returned to cook, whose affliction was most intense: she sighed and sobbed vehemently, and would not be consoled. Her Judkins—oh! her Judkins—lived, she feared, in her memory only. His absence—his deeply mysterious absence—tugged at her heartstrings, and withered her hopes. Oh! that she knew where he was to be found!— she would have him—dead or alive she would have him! In vain did Mary appeal to her philosophy; in vain she preached patience, and talked about hope: cook suspected strongly that Judkins had been murdered, and felt at length that she knew it.

"Oh! what is this life?" she in agony exclaimed—"what is this life but a tub full of eels! The moment you think you have got the one you want, it slips through your fingers, and there you are!"

She got the cards, and Mary shuffled them, and gave them to cook to cut. The first she cut was the nine of spades.

"Trouble, trouble, trouble!" she cried, and proceeded to cut again. The next she cut was the *ace* of spades. "Death!" she exclaimed, and sank back in her chair.

The bell rang. Mary was summoned to the gate. The reverend gentleman was there. He seemed excited—dreadfully excited—and Mary had no sooner let him in, than she ran to tell cook that he was so.

Sylvester met him at the door, and the moment the reverend gentleman saw him, he grasped his hand, and with fervour exclaimed—

"I am happy to see you—most happy. I feared," he added, as he entered the room, "that some new calamity had befallen us, for Judkins"——

"Have you seen him?"

"He is now at my house, in the custody of a constable, with irons, not only on his hands but on his legs."

"Is it possible!" exclaimed Aunt Eleanor. "Why, what in the world has he being doing?"

"The constable will have it that he's an escaped convict."

"A what!" cried Sylvester, bursting into a loud roar of laughter, in which Aunt Eleanor could not help joining.

"He will have it," repeated the reverend gentleman gravely, "that he's an escaped convict; but I don't at present know the particulars, because the moment I ascertained that he had missed you in the night, I ran over to see if you were safe."

"Missed me, indeed!" exclaimed Sylvester. "I've no patience with the man!"

"But he may not be in fault after all, my dear," suggested Aunt Eleanor; "you had better go and see."

"Ay, come with me; come," said the reverend gentleman, "let's go and hear the particulars at once."

"I may not accompany you—may I?" inquired Aunt Eleanor.

"Yes," replied the reverend gentleman; "do by all means."

Aunt Eleanor ran for her bonnet and shawl, and they left the cottage together.

On reaching the parsonage-house—at the door of which stood the chaise-cart in which the "escaped convict" had been brought—they proceeded to the library, and there found Judkins feeling much degraded and looking very ill.

"Well, Judkins," said Sylvester sternly, "what have you been doing?"

"I an't been doing o' nothing, sir, but running after you."

"You ought not to have allowed me to leave you at all, sir."

"I can explain all that, sir—I know I can; if you will but satisfy this here person that I'm not what he takes me for."

"Why have you this man in custody?" demanded Sylvester of the constable.

"Why, sir, it's as this," replied the constable. "Last night, when I was at Holler Bell, the prisoner came running into the house to ask if some gentleman had been there, and when he came into the room where I was, to look round, I saw that he had a handcuff on, and therefore, as he was a stranger to the place, I felt it my duty, as a constable, to take him into custody."

"What time was that?"

"About half-past eleven."

"Could you not have returned with him at once, or sent to inquire about him?"

"That's what I wanted him to do," exclaimed Judkins.

"And that's what I daresay I should have done—although not bound to do so—if you hadn't been so violent. In the first place, he tried to conceal the handcuff—that looked suspicious; in the second place, when I asked him to shake hands with me, he wouldn't; in the third place, when I tried to raise his arm, he knocked me down; and in the fourth place, it required three powerful men to carry him off to the cage."

"Why were you so violent, Judkins?" said Sylvester. "Why did you not at once explain who you were?"

"I didn't suppose it to be necessary at first, and when I *would* have done so they wouldn't let me."

"There was, I daresay, unnecessary violence on both sides; but when you found that appearances were against you, you ought to have been calm."

"I couldn't, sir, after he'd called me a convict."

"He certainly was justified in supposing that you had escaped from custody."

"To be sure I was, sir," exclaimed the constable; "and, as such, it was my bounden duty to take him."

"I don't dispute that; but I think that you might have come with him to the Grange, instead of thrusting him into a place of confinement. He is our servant; and I have an affliction which renders it necessary for him to sleep in my room. I am, unfortunately, in the habit of walking in my sleep, and in order to prevent this, I am secured to him by these manacles. Last night it appears, I, by some means, managed to get away from him, and when he missed me"——

"I heard that you'd gone on to Holler," said Judkins.

"He heard that I had gone on towards Holworth—ran after me—rushed into the Bell to ascertain if I was there —and there you saw him. I presume that you are now quite satisfied?"

"Can you unlock them there handcuffs, sir?"

"Yes," replied Sylvester; "here is the key. You will find that that will unlock them both."

"Well," said the constable, having found this to be correct, "as I've had him in custody, I ought, by good rights, to take him before a magistrate."

"There cannot, surely, be the slightest necessity for that."

"I don't know, sir, whether I am justified in letting him go without."

"Nonsense," said the reverend gentleman, "nonsense; *I'll* be responsible for him, and that's sufficient."

"Well, sir, so long as *I'm* held harmless, sir, that's all I want. *I'm* satisfied myself."

"Very well then," said Sylvester, "take those things off."

The constable did so at once; and when Sylvester had privately placed in his hand a sovereign, he bowed and left the house.

"Now, Judkins," said Sylvester, "how came you to let me leave the room last night?"

"I'll tell you, sir; I'll tell you exact how it was. I hid the key up as you told me. Well, a little after eleven you woke me up, and said to me, 'Judkins, just give me the key.' You spoke just as you speak now, and I thought, in course, that you was awake. I didn't dream of your being asleep. Well, sir, you got up and dressed yourself, and went out of the room, and it wasn't until I heard you open the front door, that the idea struck me. I then became alarmed, and got up and whipped on my things, and went out, and as I heard, when I got in the road, that you or some gentleman had gone on to Holler, I ran fit to split myself right to Holler Bell, and there, in course, the constable saw me."

"I see how it is now exactly. You fancied, of course, that I was awake."

"I did indeed, sir. Oh, if I hadn't, I wouldn't have suffered you to have left the room for the world."

"Another time, Judkins, let me on no account have the key: give it to me under no pretence whatever."

"*I'll* take care of that, sir. *I've* had a lesson. You won't catch me doing it again, sir, I'll *warrant*."

"I hope not. Now run home and get some refreshment. What sort of place were you in?"

"Oh, horrid, sir. Worse than a pigstye, and *so* cold —*oh!*"

"Then you didn't sleep much?"

"Never got a *wink*, sir, all the blessed night."

"Then if you feel disposed to go to bed, do so. There, run away, and make yourself as comfortable as you can."

"Stop," said the reverend gentleman. "Drink that. It's brandy."

Judkins knew it. He didn't require to be told. He took the glass and emptied it, and then ran home to comfort cook.

The reverend gentleman now began to descant at full length on the conduct of the constable, and while he was thus occupied, a servant entered, and presented him with a card. He *looked* at it, and, after a pause, slightly started. "Mr. George Augustus Howard!" thought he; "why, that is the name of the gentleman whom Sylvester's father was supposed to have injured;—surely this is the same man!"

"Have you shown this gentleman into the parlour?" he inquired.

"No, sir," replied the servant; "he is in his carriage at the door."

"Ask him to walk in; I'll be with him immediately. You will excuse me for a short time," he added, addressing Aunt Eleanor.

"Oh, Sylvester and I will return now. We will only take a walk round the garden."

"Well," said the reverend gentleman, who felt somewhat tremulous, "I *expect* that I shall have, in the course of an hour, something of *importance* to communicate."

"Indeed! Well, we shall be happy to see you. Do not let us detain you now."

Sylvester and his aunt then went into the garden; and when the reverend gentleman had nerved himself sufficiently, he joined Mr. Howard in the parlour.

"Mr. Rouse, I believe I have the honour to address," observed Mr. Howard calmly.

"My name *is* Rouse," returned the reverend gentleman. "I beg that you will be seated."

"Sir," said Mr. Howard, "I ought to apologise for introducing myself thus; but I think that, when I have explained to you my object, you will pardon me. I saw in a paper last evening the report of a trial in which you were in some degree interested."

"Julian *versus* Sound?"

"The same."

"I was indeed, and am still interested *deeply*."

"And so am I—*so* deeply, that every hope I have of happiness in this life depends upon my conviction of the truth of that plea upon which the defence rested. You know Mr. Sound, of course?"

"Intimately. He was here just this moment. There he is with his aunt, now leaving the garden gate."

"Indeed!" exclaimed Mr. Howard, looking round eagerly: "I should much like to know and converse with him."

"Shall I call him back?"

"I thank you—I thank you: not now—not now. Did you know his father?"

"No; I never did. I saw him once, I believe; but only once."

"Do you know what his Christian name was?"

"Let me see; Dr. Sound—*Dr.*—dear me—Horatio! yes, that was it; I recollect now, it was Horatio."

"I was right in my conjecture, then; that was the man. And now I'll explain to you why I came here. You stated, I believe, in your evidence on the trial, that you had not the slightest doubt of the fact of Mr. Sound being a somnambulist?"

"I did so. Nor had I the slightest doubt on the subject: nor have I now. Nay, I had an additional proof of the fact this very morning."

"*Can* it, think you, be proved, sir, to *my* satisfaction?"

"Most certainly! I'll undertake to prove it to the satisfaction of any man alive."

"I will tell you why I am anxious to be satisfied. Some years since, this young man's father and I were bosom friends. We had known each other for many years, and fancied that we knew each other's hearts. We visited each other constantly, and continued thus to visit, until one fatal night, when he was absolutely found in my wife's chamber, sitting by the side of her bed!"

"Exactly—yes—well?" cried the reverend gentleman.

"Well, he being not only a friend, but the medical adviser of my wife, I, on hearing of the circumstance, thought but little of it; conceiving that of course he had been to attend her professionally; but when my wife denied strongly all knowledge of the circumstance, my suspicions were aroused; and these suspicions were confirmed by Sound himself in the morning, for he declared, most solemnly declared, that on that particular night he never entered the house at all! This I thought conclusive. Had not the fact been denied, the thing would have passed off, of course; but being thus induced to believe that they had conspired to deceive me, I felt most abundantly convinced of her guilt. I did not, however, proceed as Sir Charles Julian has proceeded. I had too much regard for my own feelings, and the feelings of those around me. I—as I then conceived, *justly*—cast her off with a sufficient allowance to secure to her all personal comforts; and there, sir—there was an end."

"Poor lady! And did she live long after that?"

"She is living—still."

"And does she still declare her innocence?"

"She does, most solemnly."

"Then, be sure that she is innocent. Oh! be sure of it."

"I would to God that I could be sure."

"You have seen her since?"

"But once—but once; and that was recently. My daughter sees her twice a year. *That* request I could not deny her. They meet here, in this very village."

"Why," exclaimed the reverend gentleman, "I have seen two carriages at the door of the inn frequently, and always on particular days; and now I come to look at it, yours is one of them! Bless my life and soul, how extraordinary that is! How *often* have I wondered why they met there?"

"They have met for that purpose; but my daughter, until a short time since, never knew that she had a mother living."

"I now," said the reverend gentleman, "understand and appreciate your anxiety to be satisfied on this important point; and that satisfaction, be assured, as far as Sylvester is concerned, I will give you."

"If I can be satisfied with reference to *him*, I shall be satisfied completely: for his father, just before his death, wrote to me, and stated that if he *were* there the night in question, he was there in a state of somnambulism; the idea of which I then utterly rejected, but feel disposed to entertain it now. If, therefore, I can be satisfied with reference to the son, I shall be satisfied with reference to the father. It is true I never heard of somnambulism being hereditary, but that will sufficiently satisfy me."

"Then that satisfaction you shall have. I pledge myself to satisfy you. I undertake to bring before you proofs which you yourself shall hold to be irrefragable. I am now preparing a statement of facts to be laid before Sir Charles— who, although he has a verdict, is not at all convinced of its justice—and a copy of that statement you shall have. I will bring before you witnesses here, to prove all that has occurred in this place: and I'll take you up to town and introduce you to Dr. Delolme and his son, whose evidence I am certain you will hold to be conclusive."

"Is the Mr. Delolme who appeared on the trial the son of Dr. Delolme?"

"Yes."

"I knew him well. He was one of the most intimate friends of Dr. Sound."

"He was so."

"Oh, I knew him perfectly well; but I have not seen him for many, many years. Since that unhappy affair, I have kept myself entirely aloof from the world."

"Then let us go to London together and see him, and Thomas, his son."

"I would go, sir, to the end of the world, to be satisfied."

"That is sufficient. You shall first have this statement—the truth of every word of which I undertake to prove—and then we'll go up to town together."

"I need not explain to you how highly I appreciate your kindness; but believe me"——

"Not a word on that subject. I am more deeply interested in the vindication of Dr. Sound's character than you imagine. Where can I communicate with you? Do you live a very great distance from this place?"

"Scarcely four miles off. Borton Hall is my residence."

"Borton Hall! How very strange that I should never have heard of your living there!"

"I have, as I before observed, kept myself completely secluded."

"Well, that accounts for it, of course. But yours must have been a weary life."

"It has been, indeed. But, then, what pleasure could society impart to me? It could but inflict additional pain. I have not, my dear sir, for years and years, spoken so freely to any man as I have now spoken to you: but I feel as if you had lifted a weight from my heart, and as I now begin to doubt, I now begin to hope. I feel already a different man; and hence you may be sure that my mind is prepared for conviction. Nay," he added, as tears chased each other down his cheeks, "so much lighter do I feel, that I am about to solicit your company to-day. Come and dine with me! It is a long, long time since I entertained a friend; but say that you will come?"

"My dear sir, I will."

"Could you bring Mr. Sound with you?"

"Certainly. I will do so. Nay, I shall be most happy

to do so. He need not know your object exactly. It would not be wise, perhaps, to tell that to him yet. You are a friend of mine; that will be sufficient. The subject of somnambulism can be easily introduced, and you will then hear his views on that subject explained."

"My dear friend, I feel extremely grateful to you; you know not how grateful I feel. However, I *may*, of course, expect you at four?"

"I will most assuredly be there."

Mr. Howard took his hand and pressed it warmly, and having received such additional assurances as could not fail to strengthen his hopes, returned to his carriage, and gave the word "home."

The reverend gentleman was now in a state of rapture. All, in his judgment, was perfectly clear. He had but to prove this to Howard's satisfaction—which he felt, of course, sure that he *could* do—and poor Mrs. Howard would be restored to her husband, who would, of course, in consequence, be once more happy—his own dear Eleanor would be delighted with the fact of her brother's character being vindicated—Sylvester's innocence would be proved to the world, and Lady Julian would return to Sir Charles, who would be in a state of felicity again. If there be a pure pleasure on earth, it is assuredly that of imparting pleasure to others, and the reverend gentleman—who imagined that he saw all this with the most perfect distinctness—experienced this pleasure in an eminent degree. Of what an immense amount of happiness did he then possess the germs. In his view, no man was ever placed in a more fortunate position. But he would not keep the knowledge of his position to himself. No; he'd go and begin to spread this happiness without delay. His Eleanor should be informed of all that had transpired; and as she was the first to be made happy, he went to the cottage at once.

"Sylvester," said he, as he entered, "I am going to dine with a friend to-day at four; will you go with me?"

"I shall be most happy to do so."

"We shall be by ourselves; everything quite quiet. I offer no apology at present to you," he added, turning to Aunt Eleanor, "for thus depriving you of his society. But come, let us take a little turn in the garden."

Aunt Eleanor, who inferred from this that he wished to

say something to her in private, smiled, and left her work, and went into the garden with him.

"Now," said he, "I told you that I thought—and it did at the time strike me—that I should have, in the course of the morning, something important to communicate."

"And have you?"

"I have, my dear Eleanor; I have."

He then led her into the arbour, and there, to her utter amazement, told her all that had occurred. At first, on hearing him mention the name of Howard, she nearly fainted; but recovering her self-possession, she subsequently listened with almost breathless anxiety. He remembered nearly every word that had passed, and every word that he remembered he communicated to her, embellished only with a description of the feelings inspired.

"And now," said he, at the conclusion of this intelligence, "ought we not to be most thankful? Out of evil cometh good. The very thing which we held to be a great calamity, may prove to be a blessing indeed. Thus we, in our blindness, complain; events occur, of the tendency of which we have no knowledge, no conception; and, because we are too short-sighted to see their tendency, we presumptuously pronounce them to be evils, and, instead of being grateful, complain. How wonderfully is everything ordered! And what poor, weak, dependent, helpless creatures we are? We are but instruments in the hands of Him who employs us to work out His great design. But come, dear Eleanor, why so sad?"

"I am not sad," she replied; "believe me. You have said that we ought to be thankful; I am, indeed, thankful; most thankful. But—should Mr. Howard, after all, not be satisfied"——

"That, my dear Eleanor, I hold to be impossible. Why, Sylvester, I have not the slightest doubt, will this very day satisfy him."

"But did I not understand you that Sylvester was to have no knowledge of his object?"

"Exactly! But, when I have introduced the subject, Sylvester will join in the conversation, of course."

"I perceive. Well, I hope to Heaven that you may be successful!"

"Be sure that we shall be. I feel certain of it. I never felt more certain of anything yet. And now let us go in again. Sylvester may suspect that there is something which we are anxious to conceal from him, and I wish him to go there free from all suspicion."

Then they returned to the parlour, in which Sylvester was reading, and, as they entered, the reverend gentleman said, "Well, my dear boy, now what time will you be ready?"

"Oh, at what time you please!" replied Sylvester. "How far have we to go?"

"About four miles; it can't be more than that."

"Then I suppose we ought to start about half-past three? Shall I drive you over in our machine, or will you go in yours?"

"Oh, we may as well go in mine."

"Very well. Then, in the meantime, aunt, you and I will go for a drive somewhere; shall we?"

"I should like it, my dear, much."

The reverend gentleman then left the cottage, and Sylvester went to look after the chaise, while Aunt Eleanor—to whom Borton Hall had become an object of the most intense interest—decided on getting Sylvester to drive round Borton, in order that she might just look at the Hall.

Accordingly, on getting into the chaise, she intimated to him the road she wished to go—of course without explaining her object—and they went that road and passed the Hall, of which she could get but the slightest glimpse, so perfectly was it surrounded by trees.

"How should you like to live there?" inquired Sylvester, perceiving the eyes of his aunt fixed upon it.

"I think not at all, my love;—should you?"

"I might if I wished to be buried alive. What place is that?" he inquired of a man who was passing at the time.

"Borton Hall, sir," replied the man.

"Who lives there?"

"Don't know, sir. Nobody knows. Nobody never did know."

"Nobody, I suppose, then particularly wants to know. Of course it's inhabited?"

"Sir?"

"*Some* one lives there, of course?"

"Oh yes, sir, two or three lives there, if they call that livin'. They're rollin' in riches too, if that's any good to 'em."

"Is the master of the house then a miser?"

"A miser, sir! no, sir; he's one of the most liberalist men as is—only he won't let nobody know him. He don't care what he gives away nor what he pays for what he has."

"Is he never to be seen?"

"Oh yes, sir—sometimes. *I've* seen him often, and he looks for all the world, sir, as if he'd been committing a million of murders."

"Well, he's an extraordinary fellow, certainly," said Sylvester, who threw the man sixpence, and then drove on.

That this colloquy, short as it was, deeply interested Aunt Eleanor, is a fact which may well be conceived. *She* knew the cause of Howard's seclusion and dejection; but, as Sylvester did *not*, he thought no more about the matter.

"*There*'s a lovely girl!" he exclaimed, as a carriage passed them about half a mile from the Hall. "Did you see her?"

"I took no particular notice, my dear; I was looking at the carriage."

"Oh, you should have seen her—one of the most beautiful creatures I ever beheld!"

"Young, my dear—very young?"

"She seemed to be very young. An older person—her mother, I imagine—was in the carriage with her."

This at once banished the thought she had conceived of its being Howard's daughter. She had *no* mother to ride by her side: of every comfort—of every joy which a mother could impart—she had been most unhappily deprived.

"I wonder," said Sylvester, "whom she can be. Do you know the carriage?"

"I thought as it passed that I'd seen it before. But it cannot be the one I imagined."

"I should much like to know who she is."

"Why, my love—why?"

"Oh, I don't know. Perhaps because she *is* the most charming girl I ever saw."

The subject then dropped, and as Sylvester's thoughts were fixed on her, while those of his aunt were engaged with Howard, they returned almost in silence to the Grange.

At ten minutes past three precisely—the usual twenty minutes before the appointed time—the reverend gentleman drove up to the gate; and having alighted, felt anxious to be off; but Sylvester, knowing this propensity of his, had him in and expostulated with him, and pointed out to him the monstrous absurdity of supposing that his horse couldn't do more than four miles an hour.

"Did you ever see a carriage," he inquired at length, "an olive carriage, picked out with white?"

"I have seen such a carriage," replied the reverend gentleman, colouring up on the instant; "I certainly have seen such a carriage!"

"And so have I; and of all the lovely creatures I ever beheld, she who was in that carriage this morning was incomparably the *most* lovely!"

"What!" exclaimed the reverend gentleman, who didn't on this point wish to be urged. "What!" he reiterated, pointing to a portrait for which Aunt Eleanor had sat twenty years before. "*Have* you ever seen that portrait?"

"Of course I have; and see it now."

"Did you ever see the *original?*"

Aunt Eleanor smiled, and playfully patted the cheek of the reverend gentleman and blushed, and said that she thought it was much too bad.

"Well, but do you know to whom that carriage belongs?" inquired Sylvester.

"Was this young lady alone?"

"No; her mother was with her."

"Then I don't know at all. But come; let's be off. We shall keep them waiting; I *know* we shall!"

"Oh, we have plenty of time. Shall *I* drive?"

"If you please. Yes, do."

"Very well. Is there any exhibition about ten miles off?"

"Not that I'm aware of. Why?"

"If there had been, we might as well have seen that first."

"But really we have no time to spare! we haven't, indeed."

"Well, then we'll be off."

They then took leave of Aunt Eleanor—who made them promise to be home by ten—and while she prayed for their success, they started.

On reaching the avenue which led to the Hall, Sylvester suddenly stopped and exclaimed—

"Why, we passed this wilderness this morning! Are you going in here?"

"Oh yes. Go on."

"Are you sure that you can find your way out again?"

"I have not the smallest fear of that."

"Oh! *Well*, then we'll explore! Are we going to dine with the proprietor of this den?"

"We shall dine with the gentleman who lives at the Hall."

"He's a natural curiosity, is he not?"

"A natural curiosity!"

"Yes; the man of whom I inquired this morning in the road said that *he* didn't know him, that nobody knew him, and that he never was known!"

"He certainly leads a life of seclusion, but you will find him a most perfect gentleman, notwithstanding."

They now reached the circular lawn before the house, and as they drove round two servants appeared at the door, and immediately afterwards Howard came forth, and proceeded to welcome them warmly.

This ceremony ended, he led them into a spacious and most elegantly furnished room, and at once introduced them to Henriette.

Sylvester recognised her in an instant. It was the sweet girl whom he had that morning seen. And there was the lady whom he had conceived to be her mother, but who was introduced to him as Miss Duprez.

Having been presented, Henriette retired to one of the windows—gracefully, but with a timidity which proved that she had not been much accustomed to society—and while Howard was conversing with the reverend gentleman, and glancing at Sylvester—who was an object of peculiar interest to *him*—Sylvester and Henriette were glancing at each other, for he was equally, although with far different feelings, an object of interest to her. And thus they were engaged until dinner was announced, when Howard gave Henriette to the reverend gentleman, and —as Miss Duprez had left the room—took Sylvester's arm himself.

Miss Duprez, however, joined them in the dining-room, and they sat down to a most delicious dinner—a dinner which the reverend gentleman highly enjoyed—but of which neither Sylvester nor Henriette—who was exceedingly tremulous the whole of the time—partook freely.

It will not appear amazing that Henriette—who had never before dined with strangers—should feel, on this occasion, nervous; but it is very questionable whether she would have felt half so nervous, had there been but one guest, and that guest had been the reverend gentleman. It will be extremely rational to believe that she would not: for her eyes and those of Sylvester constantly met—so constantly, indeed, that it really appeared as if they had not the power to keep them off.

Very soon after dinner the ladies withdrew, and then Sylvester felt more at ease, and, as Howard—who was highly pleased with him—paid him every attention, he joined in the conversation freely and gaily, until the subject of somnambulism was introduced, when he became at once thoughtful and silent.

Conceiving, however, that, being a friend of the reverend gentleman, Howard knew, of course, all about the recent trial, he eventually shook off all unpleasant thoughts, and, on being appealed to, entered into the subject fully. He related all those circumstances connected with the case which did not transpire on the trial—how Sir Charles had attacked him; how the duel was prevented; how the pier-glass was broken, and so on—and then described the scenes which he unconsciously produced while residing with Dr. Delolme.

This description not only amazed Howard, but amused him; and, as the reverend gentleman after this related, with his characteristic gravity, all that had occurred at the Grange—commencing with the peaches, and ending with the fact of poor Judkins being caged as an escaped convict—he appeared for a time to have forgotten all his cares.

"But," said he, at length, addressing Sylvester, "you seem to have passed over five years! What occurred while you were living with Mr. Scholefield?"

"Nothing that ever came to my knowledge; and that I have often thought of as being most strange."

"It is strange, certainly. Now, had you any supper last night?"

"Oh yes; I always take supper: it is, in fact, the meal I most enjoy."

"What are the habits of Mr. Scholefield? Is he a free liver?"

"Quite the reverse. He is a particularly abstemious man."

"And were you abstemious while you were living with him?"

"I was: I lived very nearly as *he* lived."

"And never ate suppers?"

"Why!" exclaimed Sylvester, as the thought on the instant struck him; "how strange that that never occurred to *me!* That must have been the cause!"

"A friend once wrote to me," said Howard, with emotion, and the reverend friend knew whom he meant, "stating that he *had* been a somnambulist, and that abstemious living had, in his case, effected a cure!"

"And will do so in my case, I have not the slightest doubt of it!"

"I should strongly recommend you to *try* it."

"Try it, sir! What would I *not* do to cure myself of this awfully perilous practice! Nothing of the kind ever occurred, to my knowledge, while I lived with Mr. Scholefield: I am, therefore, bound to believe that nothing ever did occur, and that, as I lived while there abstemiously, the fact is ascribable solely to that. I thank you for the suggestion. I feel grateful to you beyond all expression. I shall adopt it, most assuredly, at once."

"And I hope, most sincerely," added Howard, "that it will prove to be in your case effectual."

They then rejoined the ladies, and had coffee; and Sylvester chatted with Henriette—whom he found to be a highly intellectual, as well as a most lovely girl—while the reverend gentleman and Howard were conversing most earnestly in private. The result of this conversation was, that they resolved on posting to town on the morrow, and, soon after this resolution had been fixed, the guests took leave of Howard and Henriette, and left the Hall—the reverend gentleman with *such* news for Eleanor, and Sylvester with feelings of gratitude and love!

CHAPTER XXXVIII.

THE RECONCILIATION.

In the morning, about half-past five o'clock, Sylvester—who not only went to bed the previous night supperless, but, in order to counteract the effects of the wine, had taken a cooling draught—awoke; and feeling anxious to get up, for his stomach, being empty, was very rebellious, he at length pulled the chain, and awoke his protector.

Judkins, in an instant, sat upright in bed, and looked at him very mysteriously, and then shook his head with peculiar significance, and then said, "No; it *won't* do; not a bit of it; nothing at all of the sort; I won't have it. You want to cut away again, don't you?"

"I want to get up," replied Sylvester.

"Then I'd rayther you'd remain where you are, for I don't want to get into any more cages."

"I'm not now asleep!"

"No, I dessay you're not; no doubt you're wide awake in a state of somnambulisation!"

"No, indeed, I am not : look at me."

"That's of no use! I can't tell by looking. What do you want to get up for, here, a little arter five?"

"In the first place, I feel very hungry; and in the next, as I can't sleep, I may as well get up as not."

"But don't you recollect you told *me* not to let you get up before the usual time, on no account whatsomdever? Now, this here's a very onrational time, you know, for *you* to get up, so you'd better lay down ag'in, and make your life happy."

"Nonsense," cried Sylvester, who couldn't avoid laughing; "I tell you distinctly that I'm now quite awake. Where's the key?"

"Well, but *are* you awake now? Upon your soul, are you awake?"

"I am."

"Well, I don't know; you know, sir, whether you are or not: I'll defy all flesh to tell that: you look as if you was, and if you will have the key, why, you must have the key, and I'll go with you wheresomdever you please, but may I be burnt if you gets away from me, or even so much as quits my sight."

"It's all right, Judkins. Come, the key."

Judkins gave him the key, and, not being satisfied, got up at once, and dressed himself, and stood by the door, and watched him closely, until he was ready to leave the room, when he took his arm and shook him well, and bawled in his ear, "I say, *sir!* Mr. Sylves*ter!* are you *awake?*"

"*Yes!*" replied Sylvester, who, although convulsed with laughter, bawled in the ear of Judkins as loudly as Judkins had bawled in his. "Yes! I *am!*"

Judkins was now pretty nearly convinced: still he followed him, and kept his eye upon him, and would not allow him to go out of his sight, until Aunt Eleanor came down to breakfast, when he saw him safely into the parlour, and felt that he had thus done his duty.

"Well, my dear," exclaimed Aunt Eleanor, who was in high spirits that morning, "what sort of a night have you had?"

"I slept well," replied Sylvester, "till half-past five, when I felt so desperately hungry, that I was really compelled to get up."

"Then you did not, before that time, disturb Judkins?"

"I don't believe that, until I awoke, I even moved."

"Thank Heaven. *That* is the remedy, my love!"

"I feel sure of it."

"You need not, during the *day*, be particularly abstemious. All I apprehend you have to do is, to abstain from eating suppers. But you, of course, know how to act now, much better than I can tell you."

They then reverted to the Howards, and, while Sylvester was giving a glowing description of the beautiful Henriette, the reverend gentleman passed through the gate, and Sylvester rose to meet him.

"Well," he exclaimed, as he entered the parlour, "how are you both this morning? I presume, of course, that nothing has occurred."

"Nothing," returned Sylvester.

"Then my friend is right?"

"I believe him to be quite right."

"That's a blessing. Well, you know I have to be with him at eleven."

"And I go with you, of course?"

"Oh, dear me, no; I'll not trouble you. I'll take Jones, you know. He can bring the phaeton back."

"But, of course, having dined there, I must make a call, as a matter of mere etiquette."

"Oh, well, if that's it: ah, I didn't think of that. Then we'll both go together—we'll both go together. Now, just let me see. I have to send to my friend, Mr. Dixon, to beg of him to officiate for me to-morrow."

"Are you sure that he is not engaged?"

"A good thought—a very good thought, that. He may be."

"Shall I ride over now, and ascertain? I shall not be gone more than an hour."

"Well, now; really—now that's very kind of you. If you *would*, I should, indeed, esteem it a favour."

"Oh, I'll go at once!" returned Sylvester, who immediately had the horse saddled, and was off, much to the gratification of the reverend gentleman, not only because he should know whether his friend, Mr. Dixon, was or was not engaged, but because it enabled him to have an hour's private conversation with his Eleanor before he started.

Of this hour, he, of course, made the most, and, when Sylvester returned with the information that Mr. Dixon would officiate for him with pleasure, he sent for his phaeton, and, having reiterated "Good-bye! God bless you!"

at least twenty times, they left the cottage and drove to the Hall.

On their arrival, Howard received them with the utmost cordiality, and they sat down to lunch. Henriette—who, in Sylvester's view, looked even more lovely than she did the previous evening—presided, and at half-past eleven, Howard—having taken leave of Henriette most affectionately—entered the carriage with his friend, and they were off.

Sylvester now scarcely knew what to do. Love prompted him to linger, but propriety urged him to leave. While, however, the influences of love and propriety were struggling for the mastery, Miss Duprez gracefully expressed her belief that he had not seen the garden.

He could have blessed her—and so could Henriette—who endeavoured to conceal the tears which the departure of her father had occasioned—and when Sylvester had acknowledged the politeness of Miss Duprez, he elegantly drew the arm of Henriette in his, while her governess opened the garden gate.

This was indeed delightful. But Sylvester was not eloquent at all; nor was Henriette eloquent. Miss Duprez ran about gaily, and gathered an infinite variety of flowers, and went into the arbour, and made a bouquet; but Sylvester and Henriette were almost silent, although in a state of rapture.

"Now," said Miss Duprez archly, having completed her task, "this is for you to take home; and after all the pains that I have taken, I really must beg of you not to spoil it."

Sylvester smiled, and received the bouquet; and turning to Henriette, said, "This is kind; but will you not add *one* flower?"

The face and neck of Henriette were, in an instant, crimson!—but as Miss Duprez ran to the arbour again—she added one flower—one little flower—it was the Forget-me-not.

That Sylvester prized this above all the rest, is a fact which need not be explained. She again took his arm, and he pressed her hand; and when Miss Duprez had led them to the gate at which they had entered, he warmly and gracefully bade them adieu, and, with feelings of ecstasy, left them.

Nothing now worth recording occurred until nine the following morning. It is true that Sylvester had in the night attempted to get out of bed; but as he did not expect to be by any means *immediately* cured, this neither distressed nor amazed him. But there was, at the hour named, *one* man near him struck—absolutely struck—with amazement, and that man was Obadiah Drant.

He had gone as usual to the Crumpet and Crown to have the first look at the Sunday paper, and when his eye rested on the case of *Crim. Con.*, and he found that Sylvester was the defendant, he *called* out to Legge—

"Hallo! *Here* you are!—*here's* a go! Send I may live! *Look* here!"

"What is it?" inquired Legge. "Anything fresh?"

"Fresh! I fancy it is fresh. You recollect that young scamp that wanted to fructify me into the belief that he wasn't here at all that night, don't you?"

"What, young Mr. Sound! What of him?"

"I wish I may die if he ain't been *crim-conning* it."

"What?"

"*Crim-conning* it with one of the aristocracy. Didn't I always *say* they were a foul lascivious lot! There isn't one virtuous woman amongst them."

"Psha!" exclaimed Legge.

"Well, but doesn't this prove it?"

"Let me have a look at it."

"Shall I read it to you?"

"Yes, if you'll read right on, and let us have none of your comments."

Obadiah undertook to do this; and having readjusted his spectacles, commenced, and read the opening speech with peculiar gusto.

"What do you think of *that*, my boy?—what do you think of that?" he exclaimed.

"Go on," said Legge; "go on."

"Well, but what do you think of it? *That's* a tidy juxtaposition to be placed in."

"Go on—*go* on, or give me the paper."

Obadiah proceeded; and when he had got through Slashinger's speech, Legge, rubbing his hands, inquired what *he* thought of it.

"*We* shall see, my boy—we shall see!" replied Obadiah. "I don't care for that."

"Have you seen what the verdict is?"

"No."

"Then I'll bet you what you like he gets off."

"Done! I'll bet you he don't."

"A glass of grog."

"Done!"

Obadiah resumed.

"Hallo!" he exclaimed. "What—Ted!"

"What, our parson?"

"The Reverend Edward Rouse! Parsons are sure to put *their* noses in. Nothing can go along now without a parson. Now, then, what's *he* got to say about the matter? The ghost," he added, on reading the evidence; "what—is that a fact?"

"What do you think of your glass of grog now?" cried Legge.

"Why, I think I've lost it," replied Obadiah; "but stop a bit, mind you—it ain't over yet."

He then read the reply, and exclaimed triumphantly—

"What do you think, now, of *your* glass of grog?"

"What's the verdict," cried Legge; "what's the verdict?"

"The verdict is for the plaintiff, my Briton. Damages, two thousand pounds! What do you think of that? Two thousand pounds, my boy! Eh!—what do you think of that?"

"Why, I think," replied Legge, "that every man on that jury ought to have two thousand lashes."

"Not a bit of it. What, don't you see?'

"Yes, *I* see all about it. But give me the paper; I'll read it myself."

Panting to spread this "glorious" news, Obadiah at once went to call upon Pokey, for this was an extensive foundation indeed for him to build upon. Nothing but a "rattling revolution" could have given him greater scope.

"Here's your works!" he exclaimed, as he entered. "You know young Sound, don't you?"

"Young Sound," said Pokey; "oh yes—what of him?"

"Do you know what he's been up to?"

"No—what?"

"What! Why, he's been up to crim-conicalisation!"

"Crim how much?"

"Crim-conicalisation! He's been seducing one of the wives of the aristocracy."

"You don't say so?"

"Oh, it's in the papers. There it is, in black and white! You'll see it at the Crumpet. Damages, two thousand pounds, my boy; what do you think of that? But she's as bad as him; nay, she's twenty times worse. Haven't I always told you what they were? Haven't I always said that the pauper aristocracy were steeped to the very eyes in amalgamating vice? Look at 'em. What are they?—why, there isn't a woman amongst 'em fit to be trusted, nor has there been since the time of Peter the Great; and yet these are the wretches—I call 'em *wretches*—who wring a hundred millions a year out of the vitals of the poverty-stricken people. Isn't it monstrous — isn't it disgusting for any civilised mind to amalgamate upon? Why, before I'd stand it, if I was John Bull, I'd kick 'em all over to Botany Bay. I wouldn't have it!"

"Well, but who is this woman?—who is she?"

"Why, a lady of title to be sure!—a *Lady* Julian—*Lady* Matilda Maria Julian. Why, her very name shows what she is! And do you *think* that I'd support my *Lady* this, and my *Lady* that, and my *Lady* the t'other, to kick up such boney fide pranks as these. I'd amalgamate 'em all! —I wouldn't have 'em. I'd place 'em in the juxtaposition of the French, when Boney went to Bunker's Hill. I'd place 'em horse de combat, and make 'em fight their way through the world for a living—that's how I'd serve 'em. *I* wouldn't have the locusts! If paupers are paupers, they ought to be treated as paupers."

"But is she a pauper?"

"A pauper! Don't I tell you she's a lady of title! and ain't they all paupers? I say it's a most disgusting shame that these titled drones—these imps of the universe—should be allowed to plunder the people in this way."

"Well, but two thousand pounds—I say—that'll be a bit of a *pull*, won't it?"

"Oh, they must sell off, you know; safe to be a sale; they can't pay two thousand down without. There'll be an execution in the house, I expect, to-morrow. But when you come to look at it, isn't it disgusting that such a lot of wretches are suffered to breathe!"

"Who gets this money—this two thousand pounds?"

"Why, the husband, of course! Don't your ideas fructify? Can't you perceive that it's all a planned thing? 'I want money,' says he to her, 'and you know this young fellow. Get him to come some night to the house, and I shall gain two thousand pounds.' Don't you see? Ain't it as plain as the nose on your face? This is your *aristocracy*—your *pauper* aristocracy! If I'd *my* will, I'd hang the lot! bishops and parsons and all. They're all alike! and, mark my words, nothing but a flaming revolution will ever do justice to the eternal principles of the people!"

He then left Pokey and called upon Bobber, and told the news to all whom he met; and then called upon Snorkins, and then upon Quocks, and thus he went round with this "glorious" news—building as he went, and coining new words to express his contempt for the "pauper aristocracy"—and as this gave him unspeakable pleasure, he spent a "glorious" day indeed!

That day Howard dined with Dr. Delolme, and met Scholefield and Tom—with whom he had an interview in the morning—and when the doctor had explained to him a variety of circumstances which tended to prove that not only Sylvester, but Dr. Sound himself, was a somnambulist, he became so perfectly satisfied of the fact, that in the full conviction of the innocence of his wife, he resolved on returning to Borton on the morrow.

The reverend gentleman was of course delighted! He had hoped that Howard, before he left town, would have an interview, through Scholefield, with Sir Charles; but, under existing circumstances, he would not have hinted a wish to detain him for the world.

They remained at the doctor's till eleven, and then returned to the hotel; and as they left town as early as six the next morning, they arrived at the Hall before twelve.

On the road, the chief question discussed was, how Mrs.

Howard should be informed of the fact of her being believed to be guiltless; and it was at length decided that the reverend gentleman should go and have an interview with her, with power to act precisely as circumstances might prompt.

He accordingly—having partaken of some refreshment—entered the carriage, and proceeded to the residence of Mrs. Howard, which was nearly nine miles from the Hall, while Howard himself, to the amazement as well as the delight of Henriette, explained to her all that had occurred.

On his arrival, the reverend gentleman inquired for "Mrs. Greville;" and having sent in his card, was shown into the parlour, in which a portrait of Howard hung conspicuously. This struck him as he entered; but his thoughts soon reverted to the task he had undertaken, and just as he had seated himself near the window, a tall commanding figure firmly entered the room.

"Mrs. Howard," said the reverend gentleman, "I believe I have the pleasure of addressing?"

"Mrs. Howard!" she echoed, with a look of surprise. "My name," she added, in deep tones of sadness, "my name is Greville, sir—Greville, now."

"My dear lady, pardon me," said the reverend gentleman; "I addressed you as Mrs. Howard. I did so, because I now come as a mediator."

"A mediator!" she exclaimed. "A mediator! From whom?"

"From one whose affection for you is unbounded, and from whose heart of hearts you have never been estranged."

"Why, what am I to understand by this?"

"My dear, dear madam, I am cognisant of the whole of the circumstances connected with your unhappy case. Your husband did believe you to be faithless."

"He did!" she exclaimed; "he did. But," she added, clasping her hands fervently, "I am—before God, I here declare that I am—innocent!"

"I believe it, I believe it; I firmly believe it."

"You said that he—my husband—*did* believe that I was faithless. Of course he believes it still?"

"No—no!"

" He does *not !* "

" He does not."

" Thank Heaven ! " she cried. " Thank Heaven ! Oh ! most fervently do I thank Heaven for that ! A mediator ! " she added thoughtfully, " a mediator ! Tell me—pray tell me at once what you mean."

" My dear madam, your husband now believes you to be guiltless. Your innocence has been severely tested and proved."

" Proved ! How proved ? "

" It has been, through my humble instrumentality, proved that Dr. Sound was a somnambulist ! And now I am come to communicate to you the fact of there being open arms and warm hearts to receive you at Borton Hall."

" Sir," said Mrs. Howard, who appeared to be bewildered, while her woman's pride was struggling to gain the ascendancy—" I thank you. I appreciate your kindness—believe me, I appreciate it highly ; but Borton Hall is no place for me."

" My dear madam. Now, you will distress me. If you assume this tone, you will very much distress me."

" Look ! " she exclaimed, as she bitterly wept, " look at the indignities that have been heaped upon me ! Oh ! it was cruel—cruel ! "

" I said that I came as a mediator. I also came to offer my advice. You saw the carriage in which I came ? "

" I have not yet seen it."

" Look : it is there. It was yours, I believe ? "

" It was."

" And is still. Now, my advice is that you enter that carriage, and go at once with me to the Hall."

" Sir, I cannot do it."

" Not to be restored to him, whom I well know you love fondly, and who will receive you with open arms ? You made a request, I believe, some time since—a request which you said should be your last."

" Yes, and he cruelly, contemptuously spurned me."

" He feels that it was, on his part, cruel ; but he then imagined that that pledge had been violated "——

" It never was violated by me."

"He believes, he knows, that it never was. But you then, I believe, wished to see him."

"I did."

"And do you not wish to see him now?"

She made no reply: her heart was too full. She covered her face, and wept aloud.

"My dear madam," he resumed, "be comforted. I know that you have had to endure much: I know that your sufferings have been great"——

"They have indeed."

"I know it: but now that you have a bright prospect of happiness"——

"No: I shall never be happy again."

"Now, my dear madam;—really you must not say so."

"If even I were to return, I should always be the victim of some foul suspicion."

"You wrong him: *indeed* you wrong him. It is true that he for a long time entertained suspicion; but look with me—look, my dear madam—at the extraordinary circumstances under which that suspicion was created."

"Nothing could justify it—nothing."

"Suppose that you had been Howard, and that he had been you, would not *you* have felt justified under such circumstances"——

"If I had—even if I had—I should never have treated *him* so cruelly."

"This answer I ascribe to that amiable characteristic of your sex, which prompts you always—with or without justice—to sympathise and to forgive. But come—now let me—pray let me prevail upon you to accompany me to the Hall."

"I cannot, sir—I cannot go."

"You cannot go to make *him* happy, who has long been a stranger to happiness: you cannot go to fill the heart of Henriette with joy?"

"My poor child!" she exclaimed convulsively, as a fresh flood of tears gushed forth. "My poor child!—stay, sir!" she added, as the reverend gentleman rose and turned to the window, with the view of concealing the tears which sprang into *his* eyes. "Stay, sir: one moment."

Howard, and Henriette, had the happiness of being introduced by Sylvester to his aunt.

Aunt Eleanor was also much pleased with the introduction; for although they had been the cause of her brother's premature death, she felt that they had been most innocently the cause, and that, therefore, they were blameless.

Knowing, of course, that they would call, she had prepared for them a luncheon, and soon won the hearts of Mrs. Howard and Henriette by her elegant and amiable manners.

"My dear madam," said Howard, as he led her to the window, "I shall deprive you of Sylvester's society for a time, but be assured that as circumstances have rendered him fatherless, I will, while I live, be *like* a father to him. We need not revert to those circumstances now, but I hope that when we return, our friendship will be cemented, and that we shall live thenceforward in unity and peace."

Aunt Eleanor responded to the expression of this hope, and as the ladies were by this time ready, they affectionately bade her adieu, and were conducted by the reverend gentleman to the carriage.

"We may not return for a week," said Howard, "but Sylvester will write to you to-morrow." And having taken leave of the reverend gentleman, he entered the carriage, and they were off.

On the road Howard perfectly well understood the affectionate feelings which existed between Sylvester and Henriette; but as he believed him to be worthy of her, and knew her to be worthy of him, he did not attempt to check the development of those feelings, but, on the contrary, felt justified in promoting their cultivation.

Having arrived at the fourth stage they stopped and dined, and nothing could exceed in intensity the happiness of both Henriette and Mrs. Howard; for while the former had commenced a new state of existence, the latter had returned to that state in which, formerly, her guileless heart had known nothing but joy.

They were happy, indeed!—most happy; they wept, they were so happy. And Howard wept too; nay, tears sprang into Sylvester's eyes—their happiness was so contagious.

Having dined, they went on, and reached town about six, and had coffee, and went to the Opera with Tom; and in the morning, Scholefield introduced Howard to Sir Charles, and had a long and most interesting interview with him.

Sir Charles had previously felt convinced of the fact of Lady Julian being innocent; for Scholefield had related to him the whole of the circumstances connected with the case of Mrs. Howard, and therefore, when Howard himself had stated that a reconciliation had been effected, Sir Charles felt so perfectly satisfied, that he exclaimed, "This young man is innocent, I see! Both he and Lady Julian are innocent! The damages shall not, of course, be enforced. I'm entitled to no 'damages.' I've received no damage. I have not—I feel that I have not—been injured. They made it out that I wanted the two thousand pounds. I'll not have the two thousand pounds. But if that young man should ever want two thousand, let him come to me, and he shall have it!"

This was the result of the interview; and before Howard reached his hotel, Sir Charles was with General Lloyd.

The general, on receiving his card, felt quite inclined to treat him with contempt; but, on reflection, he thought it would be better to see him, and therefore sent word down that he'd be with him anon.

"Well," said he haughtily, as he entered the room, "what do you want *here*, Sir Charles Julian?"

"What do I want here!" exclaimed Sir Charles, not anticipating *such* a reception. "If we can speak to each other *calmly*, let us do so: if not, our interview is at an end."

"Calmly! *What* do you want here?"

"I *scorn*," replied Sir Charles, with indignation—"I scorn to answer any question put in that tone."

"What *tone*, Sir Charles Julian—what tone should I assume to him who has *blasted* the reputation of my child, and who has affixed a stain of *infamy* upon her, like a fool —like a fool—like a *villain* and a fool? She is innocent!

I care nothing for your verdicts! Five thousand verdicts will not be sufficient to make me believe that she is anything but pure!"

"General Lloyd," said Sir Charles, "while you pursue this irrational course, I cannot talk with you."

"While I pursue this *irrational* course! What course would you have me pursue, Sir Charles, since you deem that of warmly defending my child—believing her to be innocent—irrational?"

"I do not deem *that* to be irrational. *I* will defend her as warmly as you *can*."

"You defend her! *You*, who have basely cast her out of the pale of society, and branded her a wanton!—*you* defend her! If she had no stronger defence than yours, the weakness of her position would be pitiable indeed. But she has a more potent defender than her *husband*. She has a father, who will defend her while he has life and breath; she has, moreover, the strength which conscious innocence imparts, and that surpasses all. *Have* your trials—sue for your divorce—she is innocent—innocent still!"

"I believe that she is! I now firmly believe it!"

"You do?"

"I do, most firmly."

"And how has that belief been inspired?"

"By the knowledge of the fact that that young man is, in reality, a somnambulist. I have proved it. I have proved it beyond all doubt. I am therefore satisfied."

The general rang the bell, and desired the servant to request "Lady Julian" to come down, and not another word was spoken until she appeared.

As she entered, Sir Charles was the first to address her—

"Matilda," said he, "I am here to inform you that I have happily become quite convinced of your innocence."

"Sir Charles Julian!" she exclaimed, with an expression of scorn, "whether you have or have not become convinced, is a matter to me of the most perfect indifference. You have injured me irreparably—you have brought yourself into profound contempt—and now all you have to do is to sue for a divorce, and the sooner you obtain it the better."

"Matilda," resumed Sir Charles calmly, "I did not expect this from you."

"What *did* you expect, Sir Charles Julian? Did you expect that, like a guilty thing, I should tremble, or be silent, or sink before him who has thus vilely cast upon my character a stain of infamy?"

"I expected that you would at least have been calm; for although I have now no desire to urge it, still the event justified suspicion."

"It did not justify—it could not justify—your conduct in publicly *branding* me with so much precipitation."

"Look you, Sir Charles," interposed the general, who had been thoughtfully pacing the room; "you believe her to be innocent?"

"I do—most firmly."

"Very well. You are convinced of it?"

"I am."

"Very well. Then how do you propose to remove the stigma?"

"Why, in the first place, I am anxious for Matilda to return."

"Return!" she exclaimed. "What, to live again with *you!* Never!—never!"

"Very well," said the general; "that's settled. Now you can leave the room."

"I should feel myself degraded"——

"Very well; that'll do. Leave the rest to me."

She then cast a withering glance at Sir Charles, and withdrew with an air of disdain.

"Now, then," resumed the general, "how is this stain to be removed?"

"Why, the fact of our living together again would have the effect of removing it."

"No—no such thing. It would be said that, like an infatuated old fool, although conscious of her guilt, you took her back and forgave her. No, that'll not do. The stain cannot thus be removed."

"What, then, would you suggest?"

"I would suggest to you, Sir Charles, the necessity for acting, as you are bound to act, as a man of honour."

"I am quite prepared to do so. But how do you conceive that I am *bound* to act?"

"You are bound to declare, both in public and in private, your settled conviction of her innocence."

"In private I have already done so; but how am I to do it in public?"

"Through the medium of the papers. Consult your attorney. *He* will be able to get your conviction, and the facts which induced it, made known to the world. Let this be done, Sir Charles; let this be done."

"If it be possible, it *shall* be done."

"Very well. When it *is* done, we'll see what can be done next; but until it be done, and that *effectually*, she shall never, with my consent, return."

Resolved on doing all in his power to counteract the effects of the report of the trial, by making her innocence known to the world, Sir Charles then left the house.

* * * * * * * *

Little now remains to be told; for here the history of Sylvester, *as* a somnambulist, ends. The means adopted with the view of preventing a recurrence of somnambulism —those of taking much exercise and living abstemiously— proved to be in his case effectual; and when this had been proved—there being no obstacle whatever in the way, and as they loved each other passionately—he and Henriette were united.

And so were the reverend gentleman and his Eleanor! —ay, and so were Judkins and cook. Lady Julian, moreover, was eventually prevailed upon to leave the general's house and return to Sir Charles; and while Howard himself recovered his former health and spirits, Mrs. Howard was happy in the possession of the affection of all around her. She indeed formed the centre of a most delightful circle; and if even Sylvester had not been cured effectually, he would after marriage have been quite safe; for Henriette by day and night ever kept strict watch over her beloved husband.

THE END.

www.ingramcontent.com/pod-product-compliance
Lightning Source LLC
Chambersburg PA
CBHW051201300426
44116CB00006B/401